In The Shadows of The Flames

Baltimore's 1968 April Riots

Praise for *In the Shadows of the Flames*.

"Mr. Ross's account of the 1968 Baltimore fires triggered by the assassination of Dr. Martin Luther King Jr. is a valuable addition to the city's history during the racially confrontational governorship of Spiro T. Agnew." Jules Witcover, author, *White Knight: The Rise of Spiro Agnew*

"Anne Arundel career and volunteer firefighters held their own while battling the April fires side-by-side with the career veterans of Baltimore City. *In the Shadows...* a stirring and interesting narrative about the April riots captures this and much more." Division Chief Raymond W. Smith, Retired, Anne Arundel County Fire Department

"Ross' book *In the Shadows...* adeptly depicts the role of first responders during the (1968 April riots). Ross' meticulous research shines a light on the firefighters who worked tirelessly, and at times under great duress, to stem the fires that erupted throughout the city during this bleak chapter in Baltimore's History." Thomas L. Hollowak, Co-editor, *Baltimore '68: Riots and Rebirth in an American City*

"Ross' *In the Shadows...* provides us with a deeper understanding of larger developments through the city firefighters who were on the front lines. His story provides the reader with insider perspective and links of changes in the station houses to broader patterns, which contributes greatly to this deeper understanding of one of the most traumatic and consequential episodes in twentieth-century Baltimore." Tracy Matthew Melton, author, *Hanging Henry Gambrill, The Violent Career of Baltimore's Plug Uglies 1854 -1860*.

"*In the Shadows...* an account of the rioting endured by the city of Baltimore in days following the assassination of Dr. Martin Luther King Jr., is written with the clear eye of the professional emergency responder, the historians thorough and conscientious respect for detail, and the emphatic heart of a storyteller. Insight fills every page." Brent Lewis, author of *A History of the Kent Island Volunteer Fire Department*

Other books by Joseph B. Ross, Jr.
Arundel Burning: The Maryland Oyster Roast Fire of 1956

In The Shadows of The Flames

Baltimore's 1968 April Riots

Joseph B. Ross Jr.

The Roz-Burns Publishing Company
Linthicum, Maryland
2013

In the Shadows of the Flames

Manufactured in the United States of America.

ISBN-978-0-9886607-0-0
ISBN- 978-0-9886607-1-7
ISBN - 978-0-9886607-2-4

Library of Congress Control Number: 2013900562

Available wherever fine books are sold.

Roz-Burns Publishing Co.
P.O. Box 312 Linthicum, Maryland 21090
Arundelburning.com

To the memory of my parents
Joseph B. Ross (Rozmarynowski)
and
Iris (Peggy) Clark-Ross

"Firefighters are the ones who pick up the pieces when violence rips at the decency of our society."

Assistant Chief Michael Kernan, Retired
Baltimore City Fire Department
From his book, *First Due: Baltimore*

Riot
A tumultous disturbance of the public peace by three or more persons assembled together and acting with common intent.

Merriam-Webster Dictionary

Contents

Preface and Acknowledgements

One of the most memorable tragic national events occurred when I was 13 years old. I will never forget that cloudy, cool and dreary Friday afternoon as long as I live. It was approximately 2 p.m. on November 22, 1963 and I was sitting at my desk in a classroom with about 35 other kids on the third floor of the Andover Junior-Senior High School in Linthicum, Maryland. Mrs. William's eight-grade math class was the last class of the day and we were all looking forward to going home for the weekend. Just minutes after the class started we were informed by the school's principal, Mr. Leroy Carter, through the school PA system, that President John Kennedy had been assassinated in Dallas, Texas.

For many of the approximately 78 million baby-boomers, November 22, 1963 will always be vividly remembered as a defining moment in their lives; an earth-shattering day that changed us forever.

A life-defining event for our mothers and fathers had been the Japanese navy's surprise attack on the U.S. naval and army facilities at Pearl Harbor 22 years earlier in 1941. Like Pearl Harbor, there was a before and after in the Kennedy assassination. Before the assassination we were innocent—this was not supposed to happen to us. Presidents were not assassinated while riding in motorcades surrounded by white-helmeted policemen on motorcycles and dozens of secret service agents wearing dark suits and riding alongside in cars. But it did happen; we saw the colored photos in *Life* magazine and the Zapruder home movie. The after would never be the same—could it ever happen again? Now we were not sure. After that day and for the first time we were finally aware that we were living while history was being made.

From that day forward, to make conversation or small talk many baby boomers would ask one another, "Where were you when Kennedy was shot?" It was a question that would be asked again and again as we, mostly teenagers, met others for the first time or made new friends.

Asking the question, "Where were you when Kennedy was shot?" was a "rite of passage." Most responses would be the same; I was in class; I was home sick; I was home babysitting a younger sibling while watching "As the World Turns," and CBS news anchor Walter Cronkite interrupted with a special report about the tragedy.

For most of us, there was nothing that occurred up to that point in our lives that had so much impact, that received so much media coverage, and that evoked such emotion. For many of us it was the worst thing that had ever happened. However, that would all change in April 1968.

On Thursday evening, April 4, 1968, a buddy and I were visiting two girls from high school at one of the girl's houses in the community of Ferndale, not far from the school. It was our senior year and we were supposed to be working on a major homework project for our Mrs. Susan Reynold's English class. After about an hour of research and note-taking, someone turned on the radio and the topic of conversation switched from English Literature to high school drama and other gossip.

It was then that we heard the news that Dr. Martin Luther King was shot in Memphis, Tennessee. It was bad news, but we continued with our light-hearted conversation and tried to finish the English project.

About 20 minutes later another special report was broadcast that Dr. King had died at the hospital. Now this was really serious. My buddy and I were volunteer firefighters and we had fought some serious fires throughout northern Anne Arundel County during the previous year. We were very aware of the race riots that had occurred in Newark, in Detroit, and in Cambridge, Maryland, during the summer of 1967. We both believed that riots would start in Baltimore that night, but they didn't.

At school the next day most of the conversation centered on the assassination and the anticipated riots in the cities. The African-Americans that attended the school, many of whom I knew from playing sports, seemed different—distant and no doubt shocked and bewildered. The assassination news made me feel uncomfortable around them. Maybe it was a result of sadness, shame, or possibly fear of the unknown—I'm not really sure. I don't believe I ever made eye contact with any of them let alone talk with them—this was their John Kennedy Assassination—they were left alone.

By the time school let out for the day, we knew that riots had broken out in Washington, D.C., just 40 miles to the south. And as I did every day, I hitched a ride with someone who dropped me off at the Linthicum fire station, which was less than a mile away from the school.

At 17 years old, I had been an active member of the Community Fire Company, Linthicum-Shipley (Company #32), for approximately one year. During this time I had gained valuable hands-on experience as a nozzleman on structure fires, had torn out ceilings and walls in search of hidden fires in dwellings and commercial buildings, and had responded to what seemed like countless vehicle, brush and dump fires throughout north and west Anne Arundel County. I had never fought a fire in a city during a riot. My anticipation escalated.

On Friday evening, April 5, all of the Linthicum fire company members were notified to report to the fire station. That night the 25 fire companies that made up the Anne Arundel County fire service prepared to send firefighting apparatus to Prince George's County to fill empty stations that had been vacated when fire companies sent engines and ladder trucks to fight the fires in Washington, D.C. We were also anticipating riots in Baltimore City; however we didn't turn a wheel.

Saturday, April 6 was much the same. There had been some minor disturbances in Baltimore, but they were isolated and dealt with quickly. As the riots in Washington, D.C. were winding down and Baltimore was quiet, there was no mandate to report to the fire station. I decided to attend the local teen center dance at the high school. At approximately 8:45 p.m., someone ran through the doors of the school's cafeteria entrance and announced excitedly, "Baltimore is burning!"

The teen center had a policy that you could not leave before 11 p.m. unless you signed out. I informed Mr. Whiting, school guidance counselor and the center's chaperone that riots had broken out in Baltimore and as a volunteer firefighter; I had to report to the fire station ASAP. He told me to go and I ran all the way to the fire station.

Completely exhausted after my approximate one-mile run, I walked up the fire station ramp from Camp Meade Road as the station's overhead doors opened. Company #32 had been requested, along with another seven Anne Arundel County fire companies to transfer engines to the Baltimore City stations.

The older, senior firefighters were taking all of the hand tools and hose fittings and couplings mounted on the exterior of Engine #321 and securing them in the engine's compartments and in the cab. I walked over to my turnout locker and picked up my boots, laid my heavy bunker coat over my shoulder, picked up my aluminum helmet with my free hand and walked over to the engine. I asked one of the officers what position he wanted me to take. He replied, "How old are you, Ross?" I said, "Seventeen sir." He said that I was not old enough to go up to the city with the riots going on. At the Linthicum department it was required that firefighters going into the city under riot-conditions had to be at least 21.

I spent the rest of the weekend at the fire station responding to local brush, debris, and small structure fires, while the biggest firefighting event since the Great Baltimore Fire of 1904 was in full swing about eight miles away.

Baltimore was burning and every morning before school I rushed to the fire station's kitchen on the second floor to listen to all of the "war stories" from the men who had responded to the city fires the night before. Many of those stories are retold in this work.

The week following the end of the riots, Anne Arundel County Schools were closed for a Spring vacation. I worked part-time for three Anne Arundel County Fire Department firefighters who had formed a construction company as a side business. We installed above-ground swimming pools and replacement windows in houses. Most of our work that week was in west Baltimore, not far from west Baltimore's Fulton Avenue and Franklin Street area. The air was still filled with a strong smell of burnt wood. National Guardsmen and their vehicles could still be seen at major intersections. Piles of burned debris were still in the street in front of burned-out mom-and-pop grocery stores and liquor stores. It looked like a war zone.

The following September the Catonsville Community College started a new curriculum entitled "Fire Protection Technology." It was a two-year program that would result in an Associate of Arts degree. Firefighters could now take college-level classes in firefighting tactics, hydraulics, fire sprinkler systems, building construction, personnel management, fire prevention codes and investigation techniques, as well as traditional classes such as English, Math and Science.

I enrolled at the Catonsville Community College and found myself the youngest in a class of mostly middle aged Baltimore metropolitan firefighters and officers—many of them chiefs.

I was very fortunate to be surrounded by a cadre of classmates that were on their way to becoming known as some of the best in the area's firefighting profession. Most of the time I sat next to Division Chief Raymond Smith of the Anne Arundel County Fire Department Training Division, Lieutenant Bobby Pryor of the Baltimore County Fire Department, Captain Lester Helfrich of the Baltimore City Fire Department Training Division, and Firefighter Herman Williams, who was also assigned to the city's training academy and would progress through the ranks and ultimately become Baltimore's first African-American fire chief.

I intently listened to all of the firefighting veterans' war stories discussed before class, after class, and during class breaks. Sometimes the veterans discussed the fires that they experienced during the April riots. There were a couple of occasions when the veterans let me tag along to the taverns on Catonsville's Frederick Avenue. With the beer flowing, the stories were always more detailed and more colorful. If my mom or dad knew where I was they would have killed me.

I strongly believe, as I did when I wrote my first book, *Arundel Burning*, published in 2008, that these firefighting experiences, as well as researched related subject material, need to be available for the public to read and learn from. *In the Shadows of the Flames* reveals society's good and bad judgments—good intentions vs. bad intentions—through the eyes of a firefighter.

People need to know what happened during the riots, why it happened, and why history's tragedies should not be repeated. People should know about and appreciate the tough decisions made and the bold actions and risk-taking performed by firefighters and police officers in the shadows of the flames —what happened behind the scenes.

When there is injustice, tragedy or social upheaval, many types of people emerge. There are the evil who take advantage of the defenseless to unleash their repressed anger, to make up for feelings of inferiority, or for personal gain. There are evil and good followers who really don't care one way or the other, but tend to follow the crowd they are most familiar with. Then there are the good, the people who step up to control, repair and improve upon the turmoil. They are the ones that stand out head and shoulders above everyone else. Whether they are salaried firefighters, police officers, soldiers, or government officials, community volunteers, or just private citizens, they step up among the controversy to do what they believe is right. They are role models for us and for our children. Many of them assisted me in writing this book.

I express my heartfelt gratitude to the following retired firefighters and officers for their help, advice, encouragement, and more importantly their eyewitness accounts:

Baltimore City Fire Department retirees: Firefighter and currently Fire Department Chaplin Reverend Lloyd Marcus, Firefighter Jerry Alfinito, Lieutenants Robert Mueller, Charles Urban and Walter Lemmon, Captain Frederick Riedel, Battalion Chief Charles "Bud" Chaney, Shift Commander Lester Helfrich, and Assistant Chief Michael Kernan. In addition to Chief Kernan's personal observations, he was very instrumental in the editing, and provided needed fire department technical information that has undoubtedly enhanced this work. Anne Arundel County Fire Department retirees: Firefighters Tom German, Melvin Morrison, Doug Shanks, Forrest "Bunky" Wharran, John Miller and John Michael Hoy, Lieutenant Kenneth Klasmeier, Captain Ron Bierman, Division Chiefs Raymond Smith and Harry Zlotowski, Deputy Chief Burton Phelps, and Chief of Department Paul Haigley.

Also I would like to thank Captain John Berryman, retired, Baltimore County Fire Department; Henry "Butch" Lawall, retired, Baltimore-Washington International Airport Fire Department; Charlie Doegen, retired, Chief of the Brooklyn Volunteer Fire Department; Sonny Harvey and Charles J. Wright former members of the Community Fire Company, Linthicum-Shipley, retired Baltimore Police Col. Joseph Cooke, and Henry Shoffer, owner of Shoffer's Furniture.

Washington, D.C., Department of Fire and Rescue Chief of Department Dennis Rubin, retired; Battalion Chief Darl "Micky" McBride, retired, and District Chief Michael Clemens of the Montgomery County Fire and Rescue Services were all very helpful in providing information about the Washington, D.C. riots which are also briefly covered in this work.

I spent an entire rainy March 2011 afternoon in the law office of former Baltimore Mayor Thomas D'Alesandro III. He and I went through the entire manuscript. He generously provided me with so much information that my hand hurt from taking notes. I can't thank Tommy enough.

I would also like to thank Mr. Bill McCartin of the Maryland Fire Museum in Lutherville, who provided me with a tour and explanation of the museum's re-creation of the Baltimore City fire alarm "pull" box system and dispatch center status board, refurbished to as it existed in 1968.

Baltimore *Sun*'s Fred Rasmussen, who writes the paper's weekly "Back Story Section," always took time to assist me no matter how busy he was. I am grateful to Fred for all of his advice and support. Annette M. Ryburn assisted me by fixing broken sentences and mistakes in tense. Thanks Annette.

The final design, layout and editing was performed by Blackchip Solution's Staci Dennis and Heather Joy Fairchild—I cannot thank them enough—the three of us make one awesome team!

I would also like to thank design consultant Richard Warr for his assistance and advice in the book's layout and design as well as Fairfax County Fire Department, Captain Clayton Thompson, retired, who was very supportive and assisted in the review of the manuscript.

History writers cannot escape spending many hours conducting research in libraries. Librarians are indispensable.

I would like to thank Laura Cleary, Coordinator, Maryland Room, Marylandia and Rare Books/National Trust Library, University of Maryland. As in my previous work, Laura was instrumental in assisting me in navigating through the numerous volumes of *Baltimore News-American* micro-film and old photographs now owned and generously provided for this book by Jay D. Smith, Office of Counsel, of the Hearst Corporation. At the Maryland Room at Baltimore's Enoch Pratt Free Library, Jeff Korman and his staff kept me supplied with what seemed like a never ending collection of news clippings and official reports about the riots. Paul McCartin of the *Sun* spent an entire morning with me going throughout the *Sun*'s extensive photo archives.

I would also like to thank University of Baltimore's Jessica I. Elfenbein, Elizabeth Nix, Thomas Hollowak and their staffs who put together the seminar '68 Riots and Rebirth. I attended all three days of the enriching seminar and captured valuable information that was very important to this work. The '68 Riots and Rebirth website was also a valuable source of material and timelines and provided direction to other sources.

Sunni Khalid of Baltimore Radio Station WYPR provided me with the entire CD collection of '68: *The Fire Last Time*. A recorded narration of the 1968 riots was broadcast on WYPR during April 2008. I can't thank Sunni enough.

Denise K. Masimore was very helpful in providing me information on the Maryland State Police (MSP) contributions in response to the riots, and on former MSP Superintendent Robert J. Lally.

Many others have provided support, information or contributed to his work: Baltimore City Fire Chief James Clack and Assistant Chief Donald Heinbuch, Anne Arundel County Fire Department Battalion Chief John McNally and his wife Carol McNally, and Lieutenant Robert Mueller.

I want to especially thank my friend David Marcus who first revealed to me years ago that his father Lloyd was a Baltimore City firefighter and provided me with his contact information. Also, thanks to Captain Steve Wurzberger of the Howard County Department of Fire and Rescue Services who provided me with a number of contacts.

As in Arundel Burning, I would like to thank Deputy Chief Michael Defina Jr. of Reagan National Airport, Metropolitan

Washington Airports Authority Fire and Rescue Department along with our colleague Joseph MacDonald for providing photos from their extensive collections of fire apparatus and fire stations.

I would also like to thank Civil War writer, historian, and friend, Dan Toomey for his assistance and guidance.

There are also a number of people who contributed to this work, but did not want to be acknowledged. I am grateful for your assistance, you know who you are.

Finally and most of all I cannot express enough heartfelt gratitude to my wife Kathy for all of her understanding and support and to my sons, Joe, Chad, Andy and Ryan for all of their support and assistance.

Author's Note: It would have been splendid to include a photo of every engine and ladder truck that responded to Baltimore City's April 1968 riots. But space, along with cost, made that impossible. However, I have provided photos for most of the apparatus mentioned in the book. The majority of the photos provided of the engines and ladder trucks are post 1968 (1980s - 90s). The reader will notice the protective plexi-glass, fiberglass and wooden enclosures installed over the tailboards of the engines and the tiller seats of the tractor-drawn ladder trucks. As you review the photo please keep in mind these modifications were not there in 1968. They were a result of the riots. Same goes for the photos of most of the fire stations. They too have been modified since April 1968.

Most fire station photos show over-head-doors protecting apparatus bay openings. In April 1968, with the exception of a couple of the stations built in the 1960s, the doors were large wooden side hinged doors that needed to be manually opened and closed.

Maps are also provided to help the reader follow the number and location of fires. The fire symbols indicated are approximate in location and numbers. Not all fires were recorded. A fire symbol probably had more than one fire at or near the same location.

Introduction

They said it couldn't happen here, not in "Charm City." An article appearing in the March 1968 issue of *Readers Digest* revealed that since the police department had expanded and improved its involvement in community relations with the city's large African-American population, the rioting experienced in other American cities only nine months earlier during the turbulent summer of 1967 would not occur in Baltimore, Maryland.

A few weeks later, though, an event occurred that changed everything. On the evening of April 4, 1968, Reverend Doctor Martin Luther King Jr., Director of the Southern Christian Leadership Conference and the apostle of non-violence in the American civil rights movement, was gunned down. An assassin's bullet struck him in the lower jaw as he walked out of his room on a stairway landing balcony at the Lorraine Motel in Memphis, Tennessee. He died within an hour at the city's Saint Joseph's hospital at the age of 39.

Upon first hearing the news of the assassination, Baltimore's population of 400,000 African-Americans, shocked and angry; remained calm, even as deadly and catastrophic riots broke out in other cities throughout the nation. Only 40 miles south of Baltimore, Washington, D.C. was in flames as would be some 100 cities from coast to coast within the next few days. Baltimore held out for approximately 48 hours and then the dam burst, unleashing on a Saturday evening what would be the most deadly and destructive four days of rioting in the city's 239-year history.

Baltimore was just another casualty in a long list of U.S. cities that witnessed turmoil during the 1960s beginning with the deadly riots that erupted in the Watts section of Los Angeles in 1965. According to the Kerner Report, a commission appointed by President Lyndon Johnson following the 1967 summer riots to study causes and to prevent further devastation, found that the majority of the riots were perpetuated by despair, frustration, economic deprivation and social injustices suffered by blacks living in the ghetto.

As a result of the 1967 summer riots in Detroit and Newark, Baltimore's civil defense plans were evaluated and revised. Leaders of the fire department and law enforcement agencies anticipated and prepared for possible hostilities. When the riots did break out, the authorities at that time met tough and overwhelming challenges that couldn't even be imagined during the planning stages. As this work will reveal, the rank and file rose to the occasion by improvising tactics, accomplishing more with less resources and focusing on their strengths in the city's dangerous streets to minimize the destruction and violence.

During the week of March 19, 1968, fire officials from throughout the nation were attending the four-day 40th annual Fire Department Instructor's Conference in Memphis, Tennessee. Fire chiefs and fire training instructors met, attended thought-provoking seminars, and discussed the latest innovations in fire fighting operations, technology and training methodology.

During this time period the city of Memphis was in crisis. Approximately 1,300 black sanitation union workers walked off their jobs on February 11. Fire officials attending the conference witnessed firsthand the unsanitary and filthy conditions created by the strike. Even more shocking was the sight of shotguns in the cabs of the Memphis City fire engines and ladder trucks. Fire officials at the conference sensed the tension at the sight of guns and the smelly despicable garbage that was piled high and throughout the streets of this historic southern city.

After the instructor's conference, Fire Service officials traveled back home to their departments and described to others the deplorable unsanitary conditions resulting from the strike. They discussed the shotguns that Memphis fire fighters were carrying on their fire engines in order to defend themselves in the event of a full-scale riot in the city. Gun-toting firefighters were unheard of. Maryland's conference attendees wondered if they should carry guns on Baltimore's metropolitan-area fire engines.

Originally Dr. King was scheduled to speak at a conference in Baltimore in late March of 1968. A visit to Baltimore may have broken the chain of deadly events that laid just beyond the horizon. King canceled the Baltimore visit in order to travel to Memphis to support the Poor People's Campaign.

The Poor People's Campaign, a civil rights organization formed to address the nation's poverty and housing issues, was supporting the striking sanitation workers, and while visiting with this group King was assassinated.

In the Shadows of the Flames is a story of the perseverance and struggle that endured as police, fire fighters, soldiers, government officials and conscientious citizens confronted the violent and angry mobs. They fought to put an end to the disobedience and vandalism that swarmed through the inner city streets like some biblical pestilence leaving a path of destruction and plight in its wake.

This work sheds light on numerous heart pounding and unparalleled events occurring during the riots as it attempts to reveal the actions, responses and thoughts of the people involved. The story reveals their experience and tenacity especially those serving in the firefighting and law enforcement organizations.

During the long, dangerous, and unpredictable days of the riots, public safety professionals defended themselves from hurled rocks and bottles as well as from gunfire as they fought hundreds of structure fires and attempted to control rioters. Despite the turmoil and uncertainty, these tough-minded men and women, black and white, put their lives on the line.

Did the riots in Baltimore City, brought on (as in other cities) by despair, frustration, economic deprivation and social injustice, bring about any positive change? In the Shadows of the Flames will explore that issue, as well as the dismal events leading up to the riots and the social setbacks and scars left in its wake.

As riots broke-out throughout the country, people were killed, injured, displaced and the nation's major cities went up and flames. This work will explain how all of this turmoil was addressed and handled in Baltimore.

1

"The Great Migration"

Baltimore, Maryland, founded in 1729, is a true American city. It has a diverse population that has historical roots in many different countries throughout the world.[1] The city has earned, in its own right, disparate nicknames such as "mobtown" and "charmed city." It is a historical entity dating back to colonial days with an abundance of culture, business, industry, and transportation assets such as shipping and rail. Baltimore is renowned for its fine educational and medical institutions.[2] The city was named after Lord Baltimore, Cecilius Calvert. Calvert, a member of the Irish House of Lords, was the founding proprietor of Maryland, one of the original 13 British colonies.

Baltimore is located along the tidal portion of the Patapsco River which flows east into the Chesapeake Bay a gateway to international trade. The port, graced by its natural inland harbor, is closer to the country's Midwest than any other major port located along the east coast.

Near the end of the 18th century, Baltimore, a rising thriving seaport, became the logical pathway to markets in the country's expanding Ohio Valley and points further west. After the Battle of Baltimore in 1814, when heroic Maryland guardsmen, along with a very stubborn Federal force assigned to Fort McHenry, halted the British advance into the state, the town became a major seaport and working class city. By 1850, Baltimore was the second largest city in the U.S. It also became a hub for ground and rail transportation.[3]

Baltimore, an ethnic "melting pot," was built by men and women of English and Scot-Irish decent along with African-Americans, slaves at the time.[4] Later the city would be home to the descendants of Germans, Irish, Italians, Poles, Greeks and free African-Americans, all mostly arriving in the latter part of the 19th century and the beginning of the 20th. "In the last few decades of the 20th century, immigrants from Asia, Latin America and the Caribbean brought a new diversity to the city."[5]

Baltimore City has had a distinctive history of riots and civil disorders. President Street, on the eastside, is today the location of some of the city's most modern and charming hotels, museums, and high-end shops. This cobblestone street which bustled with activity near the waterfront area in the early 19th century would set the stage for the opening act of the city's first and deadliest riot. This tragic event would result in the first fatalities of the American Civil War.

During the 1850s, the Philadelphia, Wilmington and Baltimore (PW&B) Railroad built a passenger station on the west side of President Street named the President Street Station. The station, which would eventually be taken over by the Pennsylvania Railroad later, also served as a stop on the "Underground Railroad" used by southern slaves fleeing north.

The station was only a half-a-mile west of the city's Fells Point section where the African-American abolitionist, editor, orator and writer Frederick Douglas was taught the alphabet as a youngster. At the time Douglas was a slave who loaded and unloaded ship cargo on the docks of Fells Point. The education of slaves was illegal prior to 1863 and when Baltimore businessman and slave owner Hugh Auld found out that his wife Sophia was secretly tutoring Douglas, all lessons ceased.[6]

On April 19, 1861, a thirty-one car train transporting the 700 soldiers from the 6th Massachusetts Regiment arrived at the President Street Station. Since the station was the furthest stop south for the PW&B rail line, the train cars needed to be uncoupled and pulled by horses.

The cars were brought one at a time over rails installed in the streets of the inner harbor until the troops arrived at the Baltimore and Ohio Railroad's Camden station approximately one mile west. At the Camden station the cars would be re-coupled to a locomotive and the 6th Massachusetts Regiment would continue the remaining leg of the trip 40 miles to Washington D.C. to await further assignment.[7]

Baltimore in 1861 was a pro-southern city, as many inhabitants were sympathetic to the seceding Confederate states. The new Confederate army had just attacked the U.S. military installation at Fort Sumter, which protected Charleston's harbor in South Carolina, seven days earlier. The surrender of the fort to southern forces bolstered Marylanders in their support of the southern states. Only the day before, at Baltimore's Bolton Hill railroad station, the 25th Pennsylvania volunteers just in from Harrisburg had been harassed by an angry hooting, yelling, and rock-throwing crowd.

As a team of horses pulled the train cars containing the blue uniformed 6th Massachusetts, over the street rails approximately one to two companies per car, angry crowds were gathering along Pratt Street, a main through-fare which served many of the city's docks and piers to the south. Near the intersection of Howard Street, a malicious group of southern sympathizers commandeered a wagon full of sand and gravel from a near-by road repair crew and dumped its contents creating an obstruction on the tracks. Others scavenged all kinds of debris including heavy steel anchors from the docks which groups of three to five people dragged on to the tracks.[7]

The crowd's anti-north actions halted the movement of the horse-pulled cars. Not to be discouraged, the remaining troops formed into their companies outside of the cars and marched from President Street Station through the ever increasingly hostile Pratt Street crowd. As tempers boiled over, soldiers were pelted with rocks, bottles and other debris just as the Pennsylvania soldiers had been. It wasn't long before shots rang out. One soldier was killed and many injured by the flying projectiles as well as bullets.[9]

The blue-uniformed units regrouped and "fired a volley into the crowd, killing or wounding a number of citizens." Baltimore City Police officers formed behind the troops and with pistols drawn protected the soldiers from further bloodshed until they safely arrived at the Camden Station.

In this street skirmish, four soldiers were killed and 36 wounded. Twelve civilians were killed and a number wounded. The incident would forever be remembered in Baltimore as the Pratt Street Riot.[10]

As the Civil War continued, a battle which would significantly contribute to the abolishment of slavery occurred 80 miles west of Baltimore. On September 17, 1862, Union forces under Major General George B. McClellan launched attacks against General Robert E. Lee's first Confederate invasion of the north. McClellan was able to successfully stop the invading Confederates at a little town along Antietam Creek near the western Maryland town of Sharpsburg.[11]

Forever known to northerners as the Battle of Antietam and to the southerners as the Battle of Sharpsburg, it would be the bloodiest single-day battle in American history, resulting in approximately 23,000 casualties. Although not a clear victory for either side, it would be significant in not only abolishing slavery, but also in spurring the movement of African-Americans towards the northern cities.[12]

U.S. President Abraham Lincoln used the positive press from the battle's military success to issue the Emancipation Proclamation abolishing slavery and freeing the African-American slaves. The executive order that went into effect on January 1, 1863, proclaimed the freedom of 3.1 million of the nation's 4 million slaves.

The decree immediately freed 50,000 slaves and more were freed as the Union army advanced into the Confederate States of the south. Unfortunately the proclamation did not cover the 800,000 slaves in the slave-holding border states of Missouri, Kentucky, West Virginia, Maryland or Delaware which were Union States. Most of these slaves were freed by separate state or federal action.[13]

After winning re-election Lincoln pressed Congress to pass the U.S. Constitution's 13th Amendment banning slavery in all U.S. states and territories. Approximately 12 months later the required number of state legislatures ratified the amendment and all slaves were liberated. At the time of the proclamation's historical signing, less than 8 percent of the African-American population lived in the northeast and the mid-west. The remaining 92 percent still lived in the country's south.[14]

Although the Emancipation Proclamation freed the slaves, African-Americans were not free from the cruelty stemming from prejudice and racism. This cruel behavior was especially prevalent among the defeated Confederacy's southern whites who had not only lost a bloody four-year war but also suffered from the total destruction of their infrastructure and wide spread poverty.

As a result, thousands of African-Americans would leave the south to make better lives for themselves and their families. Unlike the thousands of Italians, Poles, Germans and Irish-Scots who disembarked from large ocean going vessels and crowded into northeast port cities, the blacks migrated north in a piece-meal fashion. They migrated north to cities such as New York, Philadelphia, Baltimore, Minneapolis, Detroit, Chicago, Milwaukee, Saint Louis and Cleveland. Migration was the only way to escape failed sharecropping, worsening economic conditions and lynch mobs. The north promised better wages, better homes, and political rights.[15]

Although the north held greater promise for blacks than the south, this trickling migration to the north that continued for the next 50 years resulted in a number of new problems—poverty, unemployment, racism, inferior education, poor housing, frustration and despair. By 1900, approximately 90 percent of all blacks lived in the south, however that was all about to change.[16]

THE GREATEST MOVEMENT of African-Americans to the northern cities would occur during the years of the American involvement in World War I (1917-1919). This movement was known as the "Great Migration."[17] This mass movement was encouraged by the black's desire to share in the new social and economic opportunities available in the North. Approximately 500,000 blacks made the long journey to the northeastern industrial cities during this period.

Many white workers had been drafted or had joined the military to fight the Germans in France, creating various vacancies in factories that were working frantically to meet the increasing need for war materials. Many blacks were available to fill these vacancies and northern industries sent recruiters to the South to find workers. As the need continued for factories to meet general production, and war demands increased, many black workers were hired. In addition, the boll weevil, a devastating beetle insect, was destroying cotton crops during the years between 1910 and 1940 sending even more unemployed blacks north to work in the factories.[18]

The mass movement was also encouraged by numerous evolving African-American newspapers such as Chicago's *Defender* and *The Crisis*. *The Crisis*, now heavily in circulation among the black population, encouraged southern blacks to move north to escape segregation. The papers claimed that jobs would pay higher wages at the factories and the ship-yards.[19]

The *Afro-American* newspaper whose mission was to educate and empower African-Americans and promote civil rights is today one of the oldest remaining family-owned newspapers in the U.S. The popular and widely read newspaper was founded in Baltimore during 1892 by a former slave, John H. Murphy Sr.[20]

After World War I, Baltimore was still dealing with the effects of segregation, as were many cities throughout the nation. In hospitals, black patients were segregated from white patients if they were admitted at all. The University of Baltimore was not integrated until 1935 resulting in black students not graduating from the school until the 1940s.[21]

Blacks who lived in the area and wanted to attend law school and could afford to do so attended Howard University in Washington, D.C. Baltimore resident, Thurgood Marshall, the first African-American appointed to the Supreme Court, attended Howard University law school and graduated in 1933.[22]

As black men and their families moved north and found employment they rented apartments, purchased homes, or moved in with relatives and friends. As a result many northeastern and midwestern cities had thriving and growing black communities by the mid 1920s. However, by the end of the great migration the African-American still struggled with the problems of segregation, compounded by racism.[23]

Because of segregation, African-Americans were often forced to live in specific neighborhoods within cities.

In Baltimore, it was not uncommon to see "For Sale" signs in the front lawns of city houses or "For Sale" newspaper advertisements that stated, "No Colored."[24]

Another discriminatory process involved Redlining, whereby banks and real estate companies created city maps with zones designating areas of urban blight and poverty. Many lenders refused to invest in these areas which were frequently African-American neighborhoods. Inner city blacks were deprived of mortgages and business loans which may have assisted in rehabilitating these neighborhoods.[25]

As World War II erupted in 1939, and men and women were needed in the factories, rail-yards and shipyards for the war effort, a second "great migration" occurred that would last through the 1960s. In addition to the thousands of jobs that opened up in the northern cities due to defense production, the population boom that started in the late 1940s would create a need for expanding service-related industries to shelter, feed, clothe, and educate the country's new "baby boomers."[26]

In 1940, Baltimore's population was just 150,000 shy of a million at 859,100. There were 165,843 African-Americans living in the city. By 1970 the city's population increased to a record high of 905,787, with 420,210, almost half, black residents.[27]

Unfortunately and mainly after World War II, in some of what were now a number of African-American enclaves in the city, the poorer communities experienced poverty, decay and crime. In the white communities surrounding and in close proximity to these poorer areas, fear would set in and white families would move to other parts of the city or the suburbs where they felt less threatened.

This movement, known as "White Flight," would contribute to the spread of urban decay. As whites moved out, their homes were purchased by landlords who would convert the structures into apartments. Elegant buildings incorporating characteristic flat roof lines with classical cornices and white marble trim in the form of flat lintels or sills, were now crowded with renters. Unfortunately because many "absentee" landlords were unresponsive to the complaints of the tenants, the buildings along with their utilities deteriorated.[28]

White Flight was also encouraged indirectly by the federal government. During this period, many "federal subsidized home mortgages made it easier for families to buy new homes in the suburbs, but not to rent apartments in the city."[29] So blacks who were not welcome in the majority of the suburbs in nearby Anne Arundel, Baltimore, Harford and Howard counties were forced to stay in the city, many in the large three-story brick row homes turned into crowded apartments.

For the white inhabitants who stayed, many practices were put in place to preserve the racial imbalance in the neighborhoods.[30,31] For instance, a number of blacks who were financially able to live in these white neighborhoods were restricted or discouraged from doing so due to trumped-up mortgage costs, the refusal of banks to make loans, and more importantly the realization that their families would be harshly treated by the whites.

When blacks could qualify for mortgages they were typically restricted to buying in certain areas. *The Sun* wrote in 1943, "Blacks had nowhere to live but the Negro archipelagoes. These included historic black communities in south Baltimore, such as the Sharp-Leadenhall area near Baltimore and Ohio (B&O) Railroad's Camden train yards, east Baltimore, just beyond Oldtown and west Baltimore along Pennsylvania and Druid Hill Avenues—the hub of Baltimore's African-American life."[32]

Many blacks moved to the Upton, Bolton Hill and Harlem Park areas in west Baltimore from the Sharp-Leadenhall community when their housing was torn down to make way for the B&O Railroad's expansion of Camden station and freight yards in the latter part of the 19th century.[33]

Unfair practices that discouraged the African American from seeking a better life were not unique to Baltimore, but throughout all the U.S. cities. One practice that was common nationwide was the construction of limited access highways in a manner which would completely cut off the black's access to services, jobs and further isolating the black community from the mainstream.

Other unethical and underhanded practices to keep African-Americans "in their place" were instituted. Banks, insurance companies, and businesses began denying or increasing the cost of services. Blacks were refused access to jobs, quality health care "or even access to supermarkets in certain, often racially determined areas."[34]

Data collected on home prices suggest that in the mid-twentieth century, segregation was a product of collective actions taken by non-blacks to exclude blacks from outside neighborhoods."[35] Unfortunately, the exclusion of blacks was not only practiced in the neighborhoods, but also in the work place. "During the height of World War II, managers at Bethlehem Steel in Sparrows Point tried to hire 15 black riveters. Thousands of white employees walked out."[36]

In Baltimore, other conditions were put in place to curb and slow integration. The city's council districts or wards were split in the city's predominately black communities so the African-American vote was very ineffective in city elections.[37] In the city that journalist began referring to as "Apartheid Baltimore," it was common practice to prohibit blacks from moving into blocks of homes where fifty percent of the owned homes were white. "One of the hidden agendas of slum clearance was the prevention of black encroachment into white neighborhoods," which brought about many Federally subsidized housing projects such as McCulloh Homes and Cherry Hill.[38]

DURING BALTIMORE'S HOT and humid summers one of the few integrated beaches in the area blacks could take their families to was the Sandy Point State Park, 30 miles to the east near Maryland's Chesapeake Bay Bridge. The other was city owned Fort Smallwood Park located in Anne Arundel County on the Patapsco River. All of the closer private and community beaches in Anne Arundel County along the Magothy and Severn Rivers and Baltimore County's Middle River area were closed to African-Americans. (Many of these beaches remained segregated up to and through the late 1970s.)

In the spring Baltimore's white school children attended class field trips to amusement parks such as the whites-only Gywnn Oak Park in west Baltimore with its fun filled rides, while the black children were bused to the little "no frills" Enchanted Forest park 14 miles west near Howard County's Ellicott City.[39,40]

By 1950 African-Americans comprised 11 percent of the US population.[41] Adverse conditions brought about by segregation and prejudice were improving for blacks, but at a snail's pace. A leap forward for African-Americans occurred on May 17, 1954, when the U.S. Supreme Court overturned earlier rulings and declared that state laws that established separate public schools for black and white students denied black children an equal education.[42]

This landmark decision, Brown vs. Board of Education of Topeka, Kansas, ruled that racial segregation was a violation of the Equal Protection clause of the 14th Amendment of the U.S. Constitution. The victory paved the way for integration and the civil rights movement.[43]

In Baltimore there was a great need to integrate the city schools. Equally urgent was the need to address the aging structures which created a safety concern. "In the early 1920's a special commission had recommended demolition of nearly 60 dilapidated schools. Three decades later more than half were still in use as colored [black] schools."[44]

By the late 1960s nationwide, 43 percent of African-Americans remained in the south, 40 percent lived in the northeast, 7 percent made the west their home, mostly in California and 10 percent were scattered throughout other areas of the United States. Of these, 80 percent lived in the cities. The concentration of African-American populations supported the creation of numerous black-owned businesses such as insurance firms, funeral homes, hair salons and barbershops.[45]

During this period, African-Americans organized in great numbers to rally for their civil rights and improve their mediocre living conditions. Nightly television news broadcasts frequently showed marches and large demonstrations throughout the nation mainly in the segregated south.[46]

The most famous march "for jobs and freedom" occurred in Washington, D.C. on August 28, 1963. On the steps of the Lincoln Memorial in front of tens of thousands of people, Doctor Martin Luther King delivered his famous "I have a dream" speech. The speech along with his timeless effort in accelerating the civil rights movement would land him "Man of the Year" by *Time Magazine* in 1963 and 1964. King would also be the youngest person ever awarded the Nobel Peace Prize.[47]

Unfortunately for African-Americans living in the cities, especially in the ghettos, there were still the issues of unemployment, racism, inferior education, poor housing, frustration and despair.[48] All of these conditions would lead to the upcoming social upheaval.

2

"Long Hot Summers"

The 1960s would see civil disorder, riots and destruction, like no other time period in U.S. history. In large massive riots, in devastating church and school bombings or in smaller isolated incidents such as cross burnings, fire seemed to be the weapon of choice to intimidate, destroy, injure and even worse, kill.

In 1960s Baltimore, as well as in other U.S. cities, the subject of world history was probably not on the minds of poor, frustrated, and angry African-Americans living in the inner city ghettos. Nor was it on the minds of the angry white supremacy hot heads that lived mostly in the nation's south. However, world history was to heavily influence the tactics used by both parties in the upcoming violence.

Approximately 5,120 miles east of Baltimore, on the other side of the Atlantic Ocean in Eastern Europe lays Russia. During the 1950's Soviet Union Russian capital of Moscow, a leading Soviet politician and diplomat, Yacheslav Molotov, served under the murderous reign of soviet dictator Joseph Stalin. Stalin governed treacherously over Russia from the 1920s until his death in March 1953.[1]

As Soviet secretary, Molotov contributed to historic decision-making. He would participate in numerous high level meetings and discussions with world leaders during Stalin's and later Nikita Khrushchev's reigns, but regardless of what he accomplished, his name would "become famously synonymous and linked forever" with the destructive homemade fire bomb known as the "Molotov Cocktail."

"A Molotov cocktail is a poor man's weapon. It consists of a glass bottle filled with a flammable liquid such as alcohol, turpentine or gasoline. A fuel soaked cloth wick is stuffed down the neck of the bottle. When the saboteur selects a target, the wick is lit with an ignition source and thrown very forcefully" at the object.[2]

Saboteurs, rioters, hateful criminals and arsonist throw the concoction with the flaming wick, mashing it against its target and causing the fuel to be exposed and ignited readily. "Sometimes thickening agents are added to the fuel such as tar, sugar, motor oil, dish soap even egg whites to assist the flammable liquid in sticking to the target such as a tank, other vehicle or a door to a structure."[3]

The Molotov Cocktail was first used as a weapon against tanks during the Spanish Civil War (July 1936 to April 1939) and the Finnish would adopt and use the concept months later when the Soviets attacked their country in November 1939. The Finnish soldiers threw the flaming bombs successfully against the invading Soviet tanks.

Years later in 1956, Secretary Molotov was the Soviet foreign officer when the Soviets invaded Hungary. The name "Molotov cocktail" really stuck as angry Hungarians threw the homemade bombs at Soviet tanks rolling into Budapest as the world watched the turmoil, devastation and killing on television—the first time an incident of this magnitude was ever broadcasted. Little did the Europeans (nor anyone else) know that this inexpensive device would be the weapon of choice during America's civil disorders only eight years later.[4]

In 1963 serious disorders involving both whites and blacks broke out in Birmingham, Savannah, Cambridge (Maryland), Chicago and Philadelphia. The most violent encounters took place in Birmingham, Alabama, where police used dogs, fire hoses and cattle prods against protest marchers. In many of these incidents even children were injured by the authorities.[5]

Chicago would see a multitude of riots and disturbances during the 1960s. On five consecutive nights in July 1963, Chicago's South Side erupted into violence. The disturbance started when a black family moved into an all white apartment complex. Whites protested and threw rocks at the apartment building and at blacks who were demonstrating there. Numerous fights broke out between blacks and whites resulting in some of the city's worst racial violence ever.[6]

In the hot 1966 summer, city dwellers opened fire hydrants in the ghetto areas to bring relief from the July heat. City officials worried that there would not be sufficient water pressure to fight fires, shut the hydrants off infuriating the African-Americans who lived there. Tensions mounted.

During the same time period, a black woman was killed when she was hit by a Chicago fire truck as a result of a traffic accident. Since all fire stations in Chicago were staffed by whites only at the time, the accidental killing along with the shutting down of open fire hydrants, played a major role in perpetuating civil disorders that lasted for four nights on the city's South Side.[7]

The rock, brick and bottle throwing crowds involving hundreds of angry blacks damaged and looted businesses throughout a 140 square block area. Two would die, many were injured and hundreds would be arrested, before 1,000 police officers and 1,500 Illinois National Guardsmen were brought in to end the hostilities.

On March 23, 1964, blacks in Jacksonville, Florida, used Molotov cocktails to set fires in the city.[8] The disturbance was a result of an altercation between a black man and a white sailor, involving shots fired, in a black nightclub district of the city.

Before the two hour melee was under control a black female bystander was killed by gun fire from a passing car. A black sailor and a white sailor were both wounded by gunfire, and a white man was tied to a tree and slashed with razor blades.

At least 10 Molotov cocktails exploded in hotels and bars resulting in approximately $2,000 in damage. Eight to ten adults were arrested along with 15 juveniles.[9] A few months later in July during the civil disorders in the Bedford Stuyvesant section of Brooklyn and in Harlem in New York City, Molotov cocktails were used for setting many of the fires.

The 1965 Watts riot was the worst in the U.S since the Detroit riot of 1943, and the first major riot to capture national attention.[10] The population of the Watts section of Los Angeles was 98 percent African-American. The riot started out as a routine traffic stop on August 11, 1965, when white police officers pulled over a young black man for a traffic offense. When questioned, the driver, who was drunk and abusive, resisted arrest and a scuffle broke out.

To those living in black neighborhoods at the time, the overwhelming white and male Los Angeles Police force resembled an occupying army that was quick to beat or shoot anyone regardless of guilt. As police violently restrained the man, a large crowd gathered and began throwing rocks and bottles. When more police arrived at the scene, the crowd size increased. As additional violence ensued, the scene took on the look of a bloody uprising.

In Washington, D.C., President Lyndon Johnson was stunned when he was alerted to the turmoil. It was only five days earlier that he signed the "Voting Rights Act" into law. The Voting Rights Act was considered by Johnson's aides as his "dream legislation" to support the nation's black civil rights progress.[11]

Regarding the landmark legislation and the turmoil in Watts, Johnson said to White House aide Joseph Califano, "[This] triumph for freedom is as huge as any victory that has been ever won on a battlefield. "How is it [the riot] possible after everything we have accomplished?"[12] According to Califano, President Johnson refused to believe what was happening and would not acknowledge the cable messages pouring in from Los Angeles describing the situation.

The President also refused to take calls from generals who were requesting government planes to fly the California National Guard into the Los Angeles metropolitan area. Califano tried to reach Johnson numerous times since decisions were greatly needed. However, Johnson would not respond, resulting in a severe delay in the response of the National Guard whose presence would have most likely reduced the injuries, death and destruction.[13]

Although black leaders including preachers, teachers and businessmen tried to restore order in Watts, the riots continued. On the second day they called together a meeting of all the community leaders to put an end to the crisis however it failed.

By midnight Saturday (the fourth day) there were over 13,900 national guardsmen on the ground and within 24 hours the riots subsided. The Watts riot resulted in 34 people killed, 1,032 injured, 3,952 arrested, 1,000 buildings either damaged or destroyed and 40 million dollars in property damage. The violence exploded through 150 city blocks and for five days people looted and burned.[14]

The riots were devastating not only to the white business owners but to the city's black inhabitants as well. People couldn't buy a loaf of bread, a quart of milk or needed medicine in their neighborhoods after the riots. Without these neighborhood stores the city dwellers couldn't get their checks cashed, they couldn't obtain store credit to purchase needed groceries and pay later. In some cases people from the neighborhood, who were employed by the stores, lost their jobs. Many neighborhoods never recovered.

While hundreds watched white-owned businesses go up in flames, the rioter's battle cry; "Burn Baby Burn" was born. The battle cry would be repeated thousands of times by rioters coast to coast as over 400 major and minor riots were recorded in the U.S. between 1964 and 1969. The Watts riot was the precursor to more than 100 major riots that stretched out for three long hot summers. And like the riots in Watts, the majority of disorders were usually ignited by a minor incident fueled by antagonism between the African-American population and the police.[15]

BALTIMORE WAS VERY FORTUNATE not to experience the racial violence that was occurring in some of the U.S. cities in the early 1960s. However, there were disturbing indicators surfacing that were symptomatic of the frustration experienced by the city's African-Americans.

On "All nation's day," July 4th 1963, Baltimore's blacks and white civil rights supporters decided to put an end to the discriminating polices at the near-by Gwynn Oak Amusement Park. The 64 acre privately owned and popular amusement park was located about a quarter of a mile off of Liberty Heights Avenue at the corner of Gwynn Oak and Gwynndale Avenues.

The park was situated on land currently owned by Baltimore County. The Gwynns Falls Creek, that runs throughout West Baltimore and empties into the western branch of the Patapsco River, swerves through it. The park featured three roller coasters, a trolley and carousel, among other amusements and the Dixie Ballroom.

On July 4th, Baltimore's Congress of Racial Equality (CORE) sponsored a demonstration. The black and mostly white demonstrators, including Protestant, Catholic and Jewish clergymen took part in the event. The demonstrators arrived in buses, tried to enter the park and were stopped by the parks security.[16]

As the park authorities read the demonstrators the "Trespass Order," the marchers remained silent, but did not leave the premises. Baltimore County's Police Chief Robert J. Lally moved his officers into the "stately acting" crowd of marchers and placed them under arrest. As demonstrators were loaded into paddy wagons and later buses, more demonstrators moved in. Many sat down on the ground and refused to budge. Police officers hauled them off "bodily."[17]

To make matters worse, a white crowd formed inside the park and there were catcalls and shouts of "dump them into the bay, black n_____, white n_____, castrate them, and send them to the zoo." Fortunately Lally's officers maintained a firm control on both sides and prevented any actual violence from breaking out. Two hundred and eighty-three demonstrators were arrested and carried off to jail. Twenty-six of them were clergymen.[18] Gwynn Oak Park was the site of many racial protests until it was integrated later in 1963. Nine years later in June 1972, Hurricane Agnes would dump 10" inches of rain throughout the Maryland—Pennsylvania region causing major flooding of Gwynns Falls. The flood severely damaged the popular park closing it for good the same year.[19]

In 1966, Baltimore's branch of the National States Rights Party, a white extremist organization that advocated deporting African-Americans and other minorities, encouraged racial hatred at a series of rallies. In July after a large rally at Patterson Park, bands of white youths were incited into chasing and beating blacks in the neighborhood. A court order was obtained to bring an end to the rallies.[20]

During this period it was reported nationally that students and youths were the principal participants in at least six of the 13 spring and early summer racial disorders,[21] as two young black men, representing the civil rights movement's radical faction emerged on the scene. Their names would eventually become synonymous with black rioting in the streets. They were Stokely Carmichael and H. Rap Brown.

Stokely Carmichael, born June 29, 1941 in Port of Spain Trinidad and Tobago, moved to New York City when he was two years old and later attended Bronx High School. He entered Howard University in 1960 where he became involved with the civil rights movement's Student Nonviolent Coordinating Committee or SNCC. The SNCC was very active in sit-ins, freedom rides and in supporting the 1963 protest march on Washington. The committee was formed in response to discrimination practices that were occurring throughout the country, mainly to an incident in Greensboro, NC.

In Greensboro, African-American college students from the North Carolina A&T University refused to leave a Woolworth's store lunch counter when they were refused service. This protest sparked a wave of sit-ins throughout the South. The Greensboro incident was instrumental in the coming together of this new activist arm of the National Association for the Advancement for Colored People (NAACP).[22]

In 1966, Carmichael became chairman of the SNCC. Later he would endure a number of arrests in various cities for making speeches about "Black Power," "Black Pride" and socio-economic independence.

After personally experiencing the police officers harsh treatment of non-violent protest marchers in the South, Carmichael would come to believe that more aggressive tactics needed to be applied. He did not agree with Martin Luther King's assertion that blacks needed to be integrated into "existing institutions of the middle class mainstream." Unlike moderate civil rights leaders such as King, Carmichael advocated that "blacks first need to unite in solidarity and become self-reliant."[23]

In 1967, when the SNCC membership became displeased with his growing celebrity, Carmichael stepped down as chairman and was replaced by H. Rap Brown.

Hubert Gerold Brown was born in Baton Rouge, Louisiana, on October 4, 1943. An activist with the civil rights movement he would prove to be a pivotal figure in the upcoming storm. Brown would become notorious for statements such as, "Violence is as American as cherry pie" and "If America don't come around, we're gonna burn it down." [24]

The most deadly summer of race riots yet took place in 1967. Reports of the devastating riots now aired on the nightly television news and appeared in headlines on the front pages of America's newspapers along with reports on Cold War tensions with the Soviet Union, hostilities in the Middle East and the Vietnam War.

On June 11 in Tampa, Florida, three businesses burned during a riot. It started when a 19 year old black robbery suspect was shot in the back as he ran from police. Several days of rioting followed. Even though 20 percent of the city's population was African-American and there were no blacks in the city's fire department, there was no confrontation between the rioters and the firefighters standing in the streets trying to extinguish the fires.[25]

The next day in Cincinnati, Ohio, disorders lasted two days (June 12 - 13). Fires were set and buildings burned. However, unlike firefighters in Tampa Bay, responding fire fighters arriving at the Cincinnati fires were met with a barrage of bottles and rocks. Fire damage was heavy as a number of structural fires were set with Molotov cocktails. H. Rap Brown would arrive four days after the riot started, but fortunately for law enforcement and firefighters, his appearance in the city despite his twenty demands had no galvanizing effect.[26]

In 1967 the population of Atlanta, Georgia's largest city, was 44 percent black. Twenty-eight percent of the city's police department was African-American and 55 percent the city's municipal employees were black. Due to the typical racial tensions radiating from the city's black communities, Stokely Carmichael visited the city on June 17. A meeting was held by Carmichael where he purportedly delivered conflicting messages to a group: "play it cool" and to "take to the streets." And take to the streets they did.[27]

After four nights of rock throwing violence in the Dixie Hills' section of the city, three persons were shot, one fatally. Several were arrested after they broke out a number of windows in businesses located in a shopping center. Once additional police officers and an armored car were brought in to break up the crowds, the violence subsided.[28] After authorities arrested Carmichael, the local black community leaders demanded that Carmichael get out of town. Later, H. Rap Brown visited the city to organize a "demon" strategy; however his tactics and plans were met with no response from the community.[29]

Throughout June there would also be riots in the cities of Boston and Buffalo. On July 12, Newark, New Jersey, would experience a riot that would last five days. At the time, the crime rate of Newark, with a population of fifty-two percent African-American, was the highest in the nation. The police force was one of the largest of any major city.

The city's public safety personnel were under attack. The police station was hit by Molotov Cocktails and when fire fighters responded to an automobile set on fire they were pelted with rocks. Fortunately in both incidents there were no injuries and little damage occurred.

Many businesses in Newark displayed "Soul Brother" signs to keep rioters from looting or burning their stores; however, when the National Guardsman arrived, some soldiers actually shot into stores displaying the signs. During the riot one firefighter was killed.[30] In near-by Plainfield, New Jersey, a Molotov cocktail, thrown into a fire engine whose crew included an African-American firefighter, burned a white firefighter.[31] And in Jersey City a young black youngster threw a Molotov cocktail into a cab, killing a black passenger.[32] (Martin Luther King would visit Newark and tour the damaged city in March 1968, eight days before he was slain in Memphis.)[33]

During the 1950s in Detroit, Michigan, the city's African-American population swelled "as the whites fled to the suburbs [and] low income black families flooded the area."[34] Regarding civil riots, they said "It couldn't happen here." But it did! On July 22, 1967, a blaze started by the throwing of a Molotov cocktail and fanned by 20-25 mile per hour winds burned down an entire Detroit city block. Mostly stores owned by whites were targeted.[35]

During the course of the riots firefighters were so pummeled by the barrage of bottles and stones that they withdrew from their operations approximately 283 times. In an attempt to subdue the crowds in one violent section, officials decided to send in an engine staffed by all African-American firefighters under the supervision of a black captain. The idea failed, as they too were also pelted with bottles and bricks."[36]

At one point on Sunday afternoon, the Detroit Tiger's left fielder and slugger, Willie Horton, drove his car into middle of the struggle straight from a game at Tiger Stadium. Horton, who grew up in the riot torn area, stood on top of a car in his white Tiger uniform pleading with the rioters to stop, but the angry crowd continued on.[37]

During the firefighting, in other sections of the city, blacks were actually protecting the fire fighters and pitched in to help. Some actually organized rifle squads to protect their firefighters. Justice would prevail in one incident when the fire burned down the house of the arsonist. Still fire damage was heavy as 683 structures were destroyed or damaged.[38]

In July there would also be riots in Birmingham, Chicago, Rochester, Milwaukee, Minneapolis, New Britain (Connecticut) and Cambridge, Maryland. In Maryland with most African-Americans living in the major urban centers of Baltimore and Washington, it is somewhat puzzling that the state's first racial riot would occur not in those big cities, but in the small eastern shore working class town of Cambridge.

Only 85 miles, an hour-and-a-half drive from Baltimore, Cambridge, located along the Choptank River on the eastern shore of the Chesapeake Bay, became a place "where small time troubles intersected with national policies."[39]

IN JULY, 1967, Cambridge, a depressed working town which included a harbor, a canning factory and a few light manufacturing businesses was hurled into the hot summer's national civil rights chaos. And, this would not be the first time violence broke out in this small blue collar municipality of 13,000—a troubled municipality where troops would need to be sent in by Maryland's governor to bring about law and order.[40]

In 1960, one-third of Cambridge's residents were African-American. The police department employed three black officers who were restricted to patrolling the African-American area of the town and who were not permitted to arrest whites. Restaurants, churches, the movie theater and the local hospital were segregated. Racial tensions were so severe that an imaginary dividing line was imposed along one of the streets to separate the white community from the black.[41]

The dividing line was Race Street, which runs in a north-south direction near the mid-section of the city. The street could not have had a more appropriate name as it was never crossed by whites or blacks. It served as an imaginary wall between the two segregated communities. Today many black residents remember not being allowed to use the public swimming pool, skating rink or other public facilities on the white side of the street while growing up in Cambridge.

By 1962 the town had fallen on bad times. Under Federal poverty guidelines, Maryland's Dorchester County, where Cambridge is the county seat, was in the same income category as West Virginia and Tennessee's Appalachia (a very poor region in the Appalachian Mountains).[42]

Cambridge's major manufacturer had closed its Cambridge plants and many had lost their jobs. "Two of the remaining factories, both defense contractors, had a tacit [silent] agreement with their white workers on the city council: the companies will not hire African-Americans in return for the workers rejecting any attempt at unionization.[43]

The tension that existed in Cambridge was only a small footprint of the larger racial attitudes that seemed to permeate throughout Maryland's eastern shore at the time. Although the Supreme Court's ruling in Brown vs. Board of Education was in effect, Maryland's Dorchester County maintained separate schools for blacks and whites. Black children received used text books along with inferior accommodations and treatment.

Due to these inequalities, African-Americans in Cambridge held sit-ins, rallies and church meetings, agitating for their civil rights throughout the early 1960s. The Student Non-violent Coordination Committee (SNCC) a group set up under the NAACP sent activists, such as the Freedom Riders into the town. The Freedom Riders were made up of black and white protesters and were typically sent to integrate buses crossing state lines.[44]

Another incident occurred which resulted in a large protest demonstration on U.S. Route 50, a four lane highway which runs straight through Cambridge. This demonstration was the result of the treatment of an African diplomat. The diplomat, while visiting the United States, complained that he could not stop along the highway between Cambridge and Baltimore to eat or use the restroom facilities since all the restaurants were segregated.[45]

Unfortunately, not all protests were peaceful. It was not uncommon for fights to break out in the town's streets between jeering whites and angry blacks or for weapons to be displayed. Several businesses were fire-bombed and in some incidents shots rang out.[46,47] During these unpredictable times, Cambridge was not a very pleasant town to live in.

There were two riots in the town in 1963. The first, in May, resulted from the arrest of black civil rights activist, Gloria Richardson, who was protesting segregation at the town's "Dizzyland" Restaurant. Approximately 62 people were arrested in the demonstrations that occurred after her arrest.[48]

On June 10 and 11, 1963, the protest/demonstration resumed; however this time it turned violent. "There were shootings by blacks and whites, brick throwing and fires started by Molotov cocktails." Twenty people were arrested and Governor J. Millard Tawes ordered in the Maryland National Guard. It was the first time the guard was sent to Cambridge to keep the peace.[49]

Four years later, in midsummer 1967, H. Rap Brown was invited to Cambridge by Gloria Richardson. After the 1963 civil disorders, Richardson had become the town's chief activist and was now well established on the National level. She was substantially in tune with the current civil rights issues and formed strong bonds with National level organizations. She eventually had the good fortune of meeting with Robert F. Kennedy in 1965 to discuss equal rights issues and other related concerns.[50]

The 1967 Cambridge Riot started as a low level disturbance on the evening of July 24, there was no looting. Only one arson incident occurred—at the dilapidated Pine Street elementary school, attended by blacks, where several fires had been set even before Brown came to town.

H. Rap Brown arrived and delivered a speech on top of a car on Pine Street which was the main thoroughfare in Cambridge's all black 2nd Ward. After the speech Brown walked with a girl toward Race Street and the crowd followed. On Race Street, the town's racial divide, a police officer fired a shot gun, wounding Brown. Gunshots were then exchanged between police and some 2nd Ward residents. The school was torched about two hours later. Residents believe the fires were a response to the shooting of Brown.[51]

The out of control fire spread from the school and eventually burned a two-square block area that included several black businesses. Seventeen buildings were either destroyed or damaged by the fires.[52] Many residents believed the fire spread was the result of the Cambridge Fire Department failing to respond to the school fire. The fire chief refused to send his men into the African-American section of town claiming his men feared being shot by snipers.

Repeating 1963, Maryland National Guardsman again poured into the little eastern shore municipality. The guardsmen intervention, patrols and encampment would last through the remainder of the summer.

In August of 1967, thousands of white families traveled through Cambridge on their way for a week's vacation in Maryland's "Summer Mecca," Ocean City on the Atlantic Ocean. As families in cars and station wagons packed with kids, deflated rubber rafts, umbrellas, folding beach chairs and other supplies drove along U.S. 50 enroute to a week's stay at the beach, it was not unusual to see Army olive green drab National Guard (deuce and a half) Trucks parked along the median strip. Helmet clad soldiers could be seen directing traffic or in small groups sitting, standing around, talking, smoking cigarettes and drinking coffee.

Because of the 1967 summer riots—considered the worst period of rioting in American history, President Lyndon Johnson established the National Advisory Commission on Civil Disorders. Also known as the Kerner Commission as its chair was Governor Otto Kerner Jr. of Illinois; the commission was made up of mayors, senators, congressmen, fire and police chiefs and members of government agencies and private industry.

The commission's mission was to determine the cause of the riots and what could be done to prevent future rioting. The commission visited the devastated remains of the summer urban violence, talked with citizens, fire and law enforcement officials and crafted a very comprehensive report released in March 1968.[53]

Elected officials as well as fire and law enforcement personnel responsible for the protection of major cities needed to seriously heed the report's findings. They needed to consider if their emergency plans for handling civil disorders addressed all possible scenarios now that large numbers of African-Americans were living in their cities—two thirds lived in the northern states and one third lived in the nation's 12 largest cities.[54]

The report stated that "Segregation and poverty have created in the racial ghetto a destructive environment totally unknown to most Americans. It's a brutal fact that for millions of Negroes now living, and perhaps for some unborn, the ghetto is all they are ever going to know."[55]

The report discussed patterns of disorder. "Disorder did not typically erupt without pre-existing causes, or as a result of a single triggering or precipitating incident. Instead it developed out of an increasing disturbed social atmosphere in which typically a series of tension heightened incidents over a period of weeks or months becomes linked in the minds of many in the Negro [African-American] community with a shared network of underlying grievances."[56]

Continuing, the report stated, "As for the rioters—those ominous looters and arsonists whose eruption into violence precipitated this study, they tended curiously, to be somewhat more educated than the "brother's who remained uninvolved."

Fortunately numerous black counter-rioters walked the street urging rioters to cool it. The typical counter-rioter resembled in many respects the majority of the African-Americans, who neither rioted nor took action against rioters. They didn't want to get involved one way or the other.[57]

Why did the riots happen? The record before the commission revealed that the causes of the 1967 racial riots were "imbedded in a massive tangle of issues and circumstances." The riots occurred due to social, economic, political, and psychological issues which arose out of the historical pattern of Black-White relations in America.[58] The Kerner Commission report determined that the "disorders" were a result of five factors: crowded ghetto living conditions, youth on the street, hostility towards police, delay in appropriate police response and a persistence of rumor and inadequate information.[59]

Throughout the report's 426 pages, it emphasized and repeatedly reminded the reader "of the basic evil precedent and perpetuating philosophy, which everybody already knew, was that our nation is moving toward two societies, one Black, one White both separate and unequal."[60] The commission would also discover that the average black rioter ranged in age from a teenager to young adult. Most were male and lifelong residents of the city, and typically high school dropouts, unemployed or employed in menial jobs. They were proud, but hostile to whites and to middle class African-Americans. The rioters were also highly distrustful of the political system and political leaders.

Some officials believed that the disorders were organized by black militants. However the commission would report that the rioters had no list of priorities and that most of the disobedience and violence seemed more random than not. Unfortunately, the rioting and looting only served to fuel the flames of the anti-civil rights backlash among the whites.[61]

In Baltimore, the Catholic Church was very instrumental in attempts to provide some kind of anti-dote to this backlash. Priest talked to the local white organizations and reminded them not to turn their backs on the African-Americans. Baltimore Catholic Archdiocese leader Cardinal Sheehan would stand out as a strong advocate in promoting civil rights and adequate housing.[62]

It was said that President Johnson stated privately, "The negro is still nowhere. He knows it. And that's why he is out on the streets. Hell I'd be there too."[63]

3

"A Ticking Time Bomb"

The national optimism toward civil rights in the early '60s was fading by 1968.[1] Instead of going two steps forward, civil rights for African-Americans was going one step forward and then one step backward. Funding that might have been directed to poverty programs in the cities was being sent to Southeast Asia to support the Vietnam War. During a recent protest at South Carolina State College three black demonstrators were killed.

To the dismay of the nation's African-Americans, President Lyndon B. Johnson, an advocate for civil rights legislation, announced that he would not be running for a second term. Jack White of Time Magazine wrote, "A pervasive anxiety prevailed" as Vietnam along with racial discrimination further divided the country. The war and racial discrimination was in addition to the recent summer rioting, looting and destructive fires in numerous U.S. cities.[2]

By and large, the rioters were young blacks, natives of the ghetto, not the south, and hostile to the middle class blacks who accommodated themselves to the dominating whites. The rioters were mistrustful of white politicians, hated the police, were proud of their race and were acutely conscious of the discrimination they suffered. The hostility, mistrust, and hate, mixed with pride and suffering, had created a "time-bomb ticking in the heart of the richest nation in the history of the world."[3]

In Baltimore, however, it was believed that the future of the city's African-Americans was improving. They were for the first time in years getting decent paying jobs. Blacks found employment in Bethlehem Steel's plants and shipyards.[4] The city was also hiring blacks to drive the street cars and buses and to work as firefighters and police officers. There were black doctors, dentists and business owners. In 1955, Reads Drug Stores, the largest local chain in the city, opened its lunch counters on a city wide basis "to seated Negroes."[5]

Although a white "backlash" ensued, as mobs protested the integration of the city's public schools, the hiring of African-Americans for municipal positions, and the movement of African-Americans into communities, that for years had been traditionally white, continued.

As blacks continued to climb the steep ladder of racial desegregation, they still experienced an occasional missing rung or at times had a rung pulled out from under them. A good example of this, was "Block Busting." A tool real estate agents used to enhance segregation.

In fear of an African-American family moving next to them, whites panicked, sold their properties at rock bottom prices and moved out. The realtors would resell the property at higher prices to blacks. The house sales would be only advertised in the Afro-American papers, so whites who wanted to upgrade, and could afford the purchase, were not made aware of the sale.[6] Because of "Block Busting" tactics, urban communities where blocks of brick homes were once filled with mostly white families now became mostly black.

Unfortunately many of the old Jim Crow laws were still in existence throughout the city. These state and local laws mandated racial segregation in public facilities—schools, transportation, restrooms, hotels and restaurants.[7]

At the stylish designed multi-level grand stores, shops and restaurants that lined both sides of Baltimore's downtown Howard Street, blacks were still treated badly. Whites were always waited on first. African-Americans could not try on new clothes or hats. They could not dine in the department store restaurants or use the bathrooms. And where they could eat, blacks were designated a special area away from the main lunch counters and drinking areas. Because of this harsh treatment, the prevalent feeling among African-Americans was that they were invisible.[8]

"Although Jim Crow laws, many [of] which restricted where blacks lived, had been struck down by the courts, Baltimore remained a Southern city in culture as well as geography."[9] Thurgood Marshall, a Baltimore native and the first African-American to serve as a judge on the Supreme Court, once stated, "The only thing different between the South and Baltimore was the trolley cars. They weren't segregated. Everything else was segregated." Baltimore was still a very segregated city.[10]

Although Baltimore City did not experience the turmoil and destruction as other U.S. cities during the racial rioting of the mid 1960s, it could not boast of having a sterile record of non-violence. As a matter of fact, "White" 19th century Baltimore prior to 1860 was called "mobtown." Riots and disorderly conduct were part of everyday life on this bustling city's cobblestone streets, in places and among organizations that one would least expect; mainly the volunteer fire departments.[11]

IN THE EARLY 19th century North American cities rapidly expanded. Buildings, held together by wood framing and protected by wood-shingle roofs, brick shells or clapboard siding were jammed together along narrow city streets.[12]

Throughout these communities open flame provided heat and light, and buildings were equipped with stoves, fireplaces, and chimneys. At night, lanterns and candles were used extensively. To fuel these fires, residents and business owners stored flammable liquids such as camphene and ethereal oil, sometimes haphazardly. Fire was always a threat and subsequently volunteer fire companies were organized and flourished.[13]

In Baltimore, from 1810 to 1856, approximately 19 volunteer fire companies were established and in 1836 formed the Baltimore United Fire Department to provide fire protection to a city that frequently experienced destructive fires which burned sheds, shops, residences, and warehouses.[14] (From 1851 to 1854 the city averaged approximately 260 fires a year—many set intentionally)

The Baltimore United Fire Department was established to oversee the operation of the fire companies and resolve disputes, "often violent among them."[15] The companies worked out of fire stations located throughout the city where company members bunked and kept their equipment. Fire companies were supported by funding from the city government, insurance companies and private contributions from neighborhood residents and businesses. Two of the departments established fire insurance companies to help pay the bills.[16] Most of the fire companies were equipped with hand-drawn manual pumping engines with leather hose attached to reels. Others were still organized as bucket brigades.[17]

A volunteer firefighter was a "wonderous sight to behold—resplended in high hat, gaudy cape, huge belt, and buckle with his insignia engraved thereon. Fully equipped he proudly bore horn and axe, leathern bucket and linen bag (to protect salvage from looters)."[18]

The fire scene, on the other hand, was not a "wonderous sight." It was chaotic characterized by lawlessness as thieves flourished and fights broke out. As fires were fought, property that had been salvaged and placed in the street was dragged away. As nearby residents left their homes to watch the fire or assist with firefighting, their homes were robbed. Spectators had their pockets picked.[19]

Unfortunately, the fire companies became very competitive—fights frequently broke out between rival companies to determine who would receive the fire insurance money for putting out the fire. Antics included hiding or covering the adversary's water supply. The most powerful department was the New Market Company located on Eutaw Street. It was said that company members "had beaten, maimed and murdered for a decade." Company members numbered 300.[20]

Local politicians protected the volunteer companies. Polictical leaders, many serving as department officials, built strong ties with the companies and recruited members for "political muscle." It was not uncommon to find politicians in bars buying drinks for the volunteer members, as well as, finding them employment.[21]

Throughout the 1840s usually on Sunday evenings, a report or cry of "fire" would be shouted and as one volunteer organization's crew would respond, members of the rival company would ambush them, throwing bricks torn from the streets or debris from the alleys. Pistols would be fired and engines captured or damaged.[22]

In October 1858, as powerful heavy-horse drawn steam engines were making their way into the city's fire houses, replacing the old outdated manual pumpers, the competitive strife between departments reached its peak. Around midnight on October 8 a fight broke out between the "Rip Rap Club" department and the "New Market" company at Lexington Market. The shooting of pistols was heard throughout the area as some great battle was descending again upon the city. Many wounded and dead were carried away. The fight led to the "Rip Rap Club" raiding the New Market's fire station, located at Eutaw and Lexington Streets, where the station was ransacked by the rival gang.[23]

As a result of this turmoil and disgrace, the fed up and embarrassed elected city officials laid the groundwork for the new fully paid Baltimore City Fire Department which went into service on February 15, 1859. The new department consisted of seven engines and two ladder companies which were staffed through selecting "the best men obtainable from the volunteers." The first chief engineer (fire chief) was Charles T. Holloway, from the volunteer Pioneer Hook and Ladder Company.[24]

During the period between the start of the fire department and the late 1870s, the department was not actually "fully" paid. Each station had a full-time foreman, an engineer to operate the steam pumper and an assistant engineer who typically drove the accompanying hose wagon. There was also a "hostler" who cared and administered to the needs of the horses and drove the pumper. All others were paid call men—paid when they were on duty at night (to sleep at the station) or when they reported to fires. When a fire occurred in the city, the station's tower bells would peal and call men responded to the station or to the fire.[25]

In July of 1859, the Fire and Police Telegraph Bureau opened its new fire alarm office at 225 Holiday Street. At the time the fire alarm office was an independent entity of the city government. The city's new fire alarm "pull station" system, constructed and outfitted by the famous Gamewell & Phillips Company, provided iron painted red fire boxes mounted chest high on iron posts along the sidewalks of some of the city's busy intersections. These were also located near buildings that were considered to contain high occupant loads, or had hazardous storage or manufacturing processes.[26]

Once the lever on the box was activated or "pulled," it would send out an electrical telegraph signal through overhead or buried electrical wires. The signal would reveal the alarm box by a series of bell rings corresponding with the number of the box. For example, for Box 414, there would be "four" short rings of the bell, a pause, and "one" short ring, a pause then "four" more rings. The system would also punch holes on a "joker" ticker tape in the same sequence.

Each fire station throughout the city had a "joker" tape processor on a desk in the watch office and gongs installed on the walls. The firefighters maintaining the watch office, usually located near the front of the building, would hear the bells, read the tape and look up the number on the run cards which would have a corresponding street location of the box. Companies assigned to the box number would respond. Over time, most firefighters had the box numbers and street locations committed to memory and knew automatically when or when not to respond as they heard the gongs ring out.

The fire alarm boxes were also equipped with a key to transmit additional alarms to request more apparatus and equipment. Chiefs were issued a key to actually open a door on the box to access the transmission key.

By July 1873, responding to structural fires throughout the city, the Baltimore City Fire Department could boast of 10 engines and three ladder trucks. On July 25, the department would fight it biggest fire yet when the Joseph Thomas Mill, on Clay Street between Park Avenue and Howard Street, caught fire. A prelude to the Great Baltimore Fire of 1904, this fire 31 ycars earlier; would get out of control and damage or destroy over 100 buildings in the busy downtown merchant district bordered by Mulberry, Lexington, Park Avenue and Howard Street.[27]

In January 1904, 25 horse drawn engines and 11 ladder trucks protected the city from fire. These units were housed in one and two bay two-story brick fire stations strategically located throughout the city.

The city's worst fire occurred on February 7, 1904. The out of control fire, fanned by brisk, icy winds with 30 mile-per-hour gusts, forever known as the "Great Baltimore Fire," burned for two days. When it was all over and the smoke cleared, "140 acres of the central business district had been consumed. The fire destroyed 1,526 buildings causing over $100 million in damage. Miraculously, only one man is known to have perished in the conflagration."[28] However, there were 60 people injured and three persons, as well as, one firefighter each from Philadelphia and New York who would all later die from illnesses brought about from extreme exposure to the harsh weather.[29]

There was one major event that occurred during this fire that never happened before. For the first time ever, outside firefighting assistance was requested and sent into Baltimore. Help was requested from throughout Maryland and neighboring states. Firefighting assistance came from Washington, D.C., Philadelphia, Wilmington, Harrisburg and Atlantic City. New York City sent 10 engines on railroad flat cars.[30]

Requesting outside assistance to battle the city's fires would not occur again for 64 years. And for the first time since the Railroad Strike of 1877, the Maryland National Guard was activated to prevent looting. Two thousand soldiers and sailors were sent into the city.

As a result of the catastrophic fire, the department would diligently embark on a plan to build a modern fire department by expanding its fire fighting arsenal to 40 engine companies (including two fire boats) and 19 ladder truck companies by 1914. The new fire department would also have the benefit of a special high pressure water system to boost its master fire streams during multi-alarm building and ship fires.[31]

Starting in 1919, with the annexation of Baltimore and Anne Arundel County fire stations along with its modernization plan, the city would expand to a total of 58 engine companies (including 4 fire boats) and 26 ladder companies by 1935.

The department began to respond to emergency medical incidents in 1927, with five ambulances expanding to 12 units by 1957. This number of fire suppression forces and medical units stayed constant well into the 1970s, before companies were slashed with the budget axe starting in 1979.[32]

Baltimore's ninth chief, since the creation of the department in 1859, was August Emrich. Emrich would serve the department for 50 years, retiring at the age of 70. On April 2, 1912, the 50 year old Emrich took the reigns as fire chief. He would lead the department for 20 years and was responsible for many progressive programs—especially overseeing the transition of horse drawn apparatus to motorized units in 1919. Baltimore was one of the first fire departments in the nation to achieve a fully motorized fire response organization.[33]

Another progressive program under Emrich's reign, which would be a major factor in controlling fires in the city during April of 1968, was creating and ordering the formation of a second line firefighting apparatus fleet in July of 1926. As engines and ladder trucks were replaced by newer units, they were not traded-in, sold or discarded at the local junkyard. Chief Emrich would send the units to the fire department shop to be refurbished if necessary. They were then fully equipped, reassigned and housed in the fire stations, where space permitted, as back-up units.

The Baltimore City Fire Department shop was probably the most underrated division in the fire department. The employees didn't receive the recognition that the firefighters experienced working the city's dangerous fires. They didn't receive the occasional "pat on the back" that the dispatchers were rewarded working the phones and radios, while dispatching and communicating with units on the street from the fire alarm office. However the fire department shop would perform miracles on the city's damaged and aged apparatus and equipment saving the city costly repairs.

Assigned to the fire department shop were blacksmiths, mechanics, carpenters and painters who together could build fire engines from the ground up. In the 1940s the city would purchase Mack truck chassis with enclosed cabs. The shop mechanics would cut off the roofs of the cabs to increase visibility for the driver and officer riding in the front seat. They also built the hose beds, installed the pumps, water tanks and metal baskets, named the "Baltimore Basket," that hung over a portion of the hose bed to carry buckets, tools, salvage covers and rope. The shop workers were truly an invisible asset that contributed to the fire department's performance and success.[34]

Thanks to the fire department shop and Chief Emrich's second line apparatus program, the majority of fire companies in the city would have a back-up if the first line unit was placed out of service for repairs. The new, progressive program would also create an entire second department in times of crisis as units could be staffed by off-duty shifts and just about double the city's fire suppression capabilities. With the second line program in place the department could quickly transition from 58 engines and 26 ladder companies to 83 engines and 30 ladder trucks.

The tremendous response by the firefighters and their apparatus to quickly prevent the April 1968 riot fires from escalating to a second "great Baltimore fire" was by no means an accident. It was a shear combination of the dedication to planning and training by future chiefs, Howard Travers, Michael H. Lotz and John J. Killen who modeled themselves after Emrich. This dedication to planning and training, coupled with the experience garnered by the tough minded hard-working rank and file that honed their tactics and skills to work the everyday fires, is what would bring about the future success.

Unfortunately, the department would experience a major loss of experienced firefighters when six were killed and more than 15 injured when a major fire occurred at the Tru-Fit Clothing Company, located at 507-509 East Baltimore Street on February 15, 1955. A fire that started in the basement of the 80-foot long three story clothing store, worked its way through the upper floors. After more than an hour the fire reached six alarms.[35]

After thousands of gallons of water were applied to the brick walled-structure, the fire was knocked down and firefighters entered to complete the extinguishment. As firefighters entered and started working in the one-story addition to the rear of the building, its roof collapsed, with no warning whatsoever; pulling the walls down on top of numerous firefighters. Eight firefighters were able to dig themselves out; one was found later in the rubble and rescued. It would take a total of nine hours to remove all of the bodies.[36]

IN 1953, THE MOST SIGNIFICANT CHANGE occurred in the department since motorized apparatus replaced the old fire horses. The department hired its first African-American. The Baltimore Urban League, fighting at every step tooth and nail, was successful in putting blacks on the police force and as drivers and operators on transit buses and street cars. The league had been battling the city for 20 years to put black firefighters on the city's fire engines and ladder trucks. Since 1947, 14 different black men had applied and successfully tested for the position, however the Board of Fire Commissioners failed to approve their admission to the "all white" department. The NAACP threatened to sue the fire board.[37]

Herman Williams, who would become the first African-American chief of the Baltimore City Fire Department, stated in his book *Firefighter*, "The firefighters union opposed Blacks on the grounds of segregation. Firefighters lived together in the station houses, and the union's all-White membership wouldn't tolerate sharing living space with Blacks."[38]

However, times were changing as the number of blacks living in the city had now risen to approximately 266,000 and thousands could vote. Baltimore's mayor at the time, Tommy D'Alesandro Jr., was no stranger to Baltimore politics, and better than anybody understood the significance and power of the vote. In 1953, D'Alesandro Jr. could brag of having 27 years experience as an elected official. Starting in 1926, he had served in the Maryland House of Delegates, on Baltimore's city council, and as a member in the U.S. Congress. He served as Baltimore city mayor since 1947. The handsome Italian-American politician was nobody's dummy and wanted to court the black vote for his 1951 re-election.[39]

D'Alesandro Jr. was going to make civil rights one of his campaign issues and, if necessary, he would sack the entire fire board if need be.[40] Due to D'Alesandro Jr's. savvy efforts the board reconsidered its position and opened up the hiring process to Baltimore's African-Americans.[41]

In February 1954, Williams was hired and assigned to Engine Company #35, which shared quarters with Truck Company #21. Both were located in the two-story, two bay brick and wood fire station on the corner of 5th Street and Pontiac Avenue in Brooklyn. Williams was in the third mixed class of blacks and whites which consisted of 20 white and 10 black firefighter training recruits.

In those days recruits would train in the rear of Engine Company #36 located on Edmonson Avenue. In the yard behind the station there was a five-story concrete and brick training tower for laddering and a one-story maintenance and storage building that contained training equipment. The maintenance building was used for "life net training." A firefighter-recruit would jump off its roof into the canvas life nets held by five or six other recruits. The large circle shaped life nets would be carried on the ladder trucks until the mid 1970s. The station's second floor bunkroom doubled as the recruit's classroom.

The men would train daily Monday through Friday. On Saturdays the recruits would spend time in the stations they would be assigned to after the one month's training was completed.[42]

The new African-American recruits would quickly find out that being black in a fire department that had been white since its inception 100 years previously, would be no picnic. Besides dealing with the dangers that all firefighters were subject to when the apparatus rolled out of the station, blacks would also have to learn to endure a very tense atmosphere in the fire station.

Blacks would be subject to racial jokes, catcalls and slurs. At times their protective gear would be tampered with. Dangerous objects, such as broken glass were shoved down their boots and placed in their turnout coat pockets. "Reserved" signs attached on walls over the beds indicated where the black firefighters were to sleep. The same signs would be placed over sinks in the bathrooms and over the toilets.[43]

African-Americans could not eat meals with the white firefighters. They were required to keep their own plates, cups, pots, pans and silverware separate from the white crew members' cookware. If a black was found using anything that wasn't his, it would be tossed into the trash. Blacks could not contribute to the "food fund," set up to purchase condiments and staples such as salt, pepper and spices for the station's kitchen cupboard. The fund was also used to pay for the newspaper and to purchase the television set. Blacks could watch TV but could not change the channel. They could read the paper when the white firefighters were finished with it. They were required to "know their place."[44]

White firefighters would not talk with black firefighters. The officers would only talk with the blacks when they wanted something done. In a station with 10 firefighters and officers assigned per shift, as in the Brooklyn station, the silent treatment could make for a long shift if you were the only African-American.

Blacks would be assigned leave days, but no one would tell them they were off until they showed up for work. At that time they would be told to go back home. When they wanted or needed a particular day off, especially for vacations, it would be denied. Williams remembers the battalion chief tearing up a leave request right in front of him and saying "denied."[45] It would be years and a long court battle before African-Americans would be able to join the firefighter's union and receive the protection they so badly needed.

On fire calls the job seemed to improve somewhat since to work as a "team," firefighters needed to communicate with one another, especially when operating hose lines or raising ladders. At times, Williams remembers, when he was ordered into houses owned by whites, the owners would shout racial slurs and demand the officer in charge to keep Williams outside. Sometimes the officers honored the requests and at times, depending on the seriousness of the situation, they were ignored.[46]

Surprisingly discrimination across city fire stations was situational. After almost two years assigned to Engine Company #35, Williams was reassigned to Engine Company #57 located on Pennington Avenue in Curtis Bay. He would be the first black firefighter ever to be assigned to the station. At first the crew tried to maintain a segregated dinner table, however the tenacious Williams ignored it. The practice was shortly dropped and Williams began to share in the cooking and ate meals with the rest of the shift.[47]

There were no "RESERVED" signs at Engine #57. Williams could belong to the food fund. He shared a bed in the bunkroom like everybody else. In his book, Williams stated, "Captain Martin Klensmith would not tolerate any discrimination in any form….some of the guys were dyed-in-the-wool racists, but there would be no fights set up to get me kicked out of the fire department, like at Company #35."[48] By 1956 there were 179 Black firefighters in the department.[49]

Another black firefighter who entered the department in 1956 was Lloyd E. Marcus. Marcus, who grew up in Baltimore, left Carver High School at 17 and joined the Merchant Marine in 1945. He married his wife, Rodell, when he left the service in the early 1950s and worked in a slaughterhouse and as a general laborer at Bethlehem Steel in Sparrows Point.

Marcus had always wanted to be a police officer, so he applied, took the test and was interviewed by department officials. As a back-up measure though, he also applied and went through a similar hiring process with the fire department. [50]

Although he felt he performed very well during the interview, Marcus never heard from the police department, so when the acceptance letter from the fire department arrived at his residence, he took the job. Years later, he would find out that Rodell and his aunt, who the couple lived with, picked up and destroyed the letter from the police department when it arrived at the house. Rodell and the aunt believed that being a police officer was too dangerous a profession for Marcus.[51]

Marcus, hired in May 1956, was sent to the old training school located at Company #36 with a basic training class made up of nine black and 50 white recruits. Fellow classmate, James Thomas would later become the first African-American promoted to the position of lieutenant in the history of the department.[52]

Upon graduating from fire school, Marcus was assigned to one of the oldest fire houses in the city, Engine Company #6, located at the corner of Gay and Ensor Streets in Baltimore's Oldtown. The station that seems to resemble a church more than a fire station, with a tall bell steeple over the main front bay door, was and to this day, remains a historical city landmark.[53]

At Engine Company #6, Marcus would be subject to all of the same racial remarks and discriminating behavior as Williams had experienced at the Brooklyn station. It can be assumed that other black firefighters working in fire stations throughout the city experienced similar treatment. Blacks who complained to the officers about their harsh treatment were labeled as "trouble makers."

Rather than fretting and agonizing over the silent treatment he experienced between fire calls, Marcus would go up to the station's second floor spare office designated the sewing room. The room contained, in addition to the sewing machine, a chair and a desk. There Marcus would read the bible and pour his thoughts and energy into his homework from the Baltimore Bible College. Eventually, Marcus would complete the program, receive his Bachelor of Theology degree and enter the ministry, his second career.[54]

Marcus's father ran a tailor shop in Baltimore's Oldtown and while Marcus was growing up, his father taught him the skills of sewing and the operation of the associated delicate machinery. When he wasn't responding to fire calls, cleaning, performing maintenance on the engine or attending to his ministry studies, Marcus started the meticulous task of performing light repairs and alterations to the station firefighters' dress uniforms, heavy protective canvas bunker fire coats and pants.

Before long word got out amongst the battalion regarding his sewing talents, and Marcus became the department's unofficial tailor. Now he didn't have to scrub the floors, polish the long brass pole and huge wall gongs or clean the engine or the bathroom; he would occupy the second floor spare room during most of his shift. He repaired firefighting gear and fabricated the canvas hose covers protecting the hundreds of feet of hose carried in the beds behind the cabs of the city's engines. Marcus also made and repaired the canvas covers that were placed over the open cabs on the engines and ladder trucks during inclement and severe cold weather.[55]

There was an incident one morning in the station's kitchen between Marcus and one of the white firefighters, a big white wise guy Irishmen, a bully, and a dyed-in-the-wool racist. Marcus, hurriedly used a spoon belonging to the white firefighters to put sugar in his coffee cup. Watching Marcus from the kitchen door, the bully started screaming at him for not using his own spoon.

Marcus tried to explain that he was in a hurry and he wasn't using it to "feed himself;" he had used it just to drop in the sugar. The bullying continued on. Finally, at the height of the heated dialog that followed, Marcus said, "That's enough!" "I have had it with this garbage!" and put his fists up! However, before the fists flew and both of them (most likely Marcus) lost their jobs, another firefighter intervened and was able to break up the heated conflict before it turned into a fight.[56]

In the late 1950s, and before the much improved self-contained cylinder equipped breathing apparatus would become available for the nation's fire service in the early 60s, firefighters used, "All-Service" canister filter masks to enter burning and smoke-filled buildings.

The "All-Service" masks were carryovers from World War II and the Korean War and were also used in the mining industry. They were light and easy to strap on and covered the entire face. Other than that, they were extremely dangerous! The mask-filters, small tin canisters carried on the side of the waist and secured by a shoulder strap, could filter out the by-products of smoke as long as the atmosphere contained at least 19 percent oxygen—a level that is rarely reached during an interior structure fire making interior firefighting all the more dangerous.[57]

Sometimes the dangerous job of firefighting brings out the best in men as Marcus would find out months later. On February 6, 1960 at around 11:15 p.m., a hot and smoky fire broke out in a four-story business at 304 East Lombard Street. The first and second floors of the building contained the New Commerce Restaurant and the fire started in the ceiling between the two floors. The crew of Engine #6, including Marcus, entered a second-story window of the restaurant's dining room, by use of an extension ladder from the street, and started working on the fire. Wearing the "All-Service" masks, in addition to their firefighting protective gear, Marcus, the Irishman and another firefighter worked the hose line throughout second floor dining room trying to cut off the fire.[58, 59]

After making little headway with the hose line and as conditions worsened, the firefighters withdrew to the ladder and climbed back out onto the street. When the crew members were safely outside of the building, they realized that Marcus had not escaped with them. Marcus lay unconscious on the second floor overcome by the carbon monoxide laden smoke. The two firefighters re-climbed the ladder, searched the floor and found Marcus. They dragged him back to the window and carried him down the ladder to the fresh air that immediately revived him. The fire would quickly escalate to three alarms and the white racist bully who wanted to fight Marcus over a spoonful of sugar saved the black firefighters life. Years later, the two of them would become good friends.[60]

On Saturday, January 29, 1966 at approximately 4 p.m., a light snow started to blanket the Baltimore-Washington area progressing to a heavy snow around midnight. The snow continued through Sunday and ended on the morning of Monday, January 31. City and county schools were closed for days. The 20-inch snowfall accompanied by howling winds became known as the "Blizzard of '66."

On Monday, in a city blanketed with snow, Marcus and his crew were working the night shift at Engine Company #6. Around 9:38 p.m., Box Alarm 3 was sounded for a fire at the Bee-Hive Restaurant at 214 East Lexington Street. The fire, started in the basement and worked its way through the buildings three stories, and up through to the roof. Three alarms of apparatus pushed through the snow-covered streets to assist.[61]

The crew of Engine Company #6 was working on the second floor maneuvering a hose line, when some kind of explosion occurred forcing the crew to make a hasty retreat out of a second-floor window onto a ladder.[62]

As Lieutenant Robert Bayne made his way out of the now burning room he slipped and fell trying to grab onto the ladder. He was going to fall head first out of the window and away from the ladder when Marcus grabbed Bayne's foot and saved him from the 14 foot (or so) fall. Marcus continued to hold on until Bayne repositioned himself on the ladder. Member firefighters now climbed the ladder from the street to assist Bayne as he crawled down the ladder headfirst. With flames now rolling through the upper portion of the window, Marcus stretched out on the ladder headfirst and held on to Bayne.

Seeing the predicament that Marcus and the lieutenant were in, Deputy Chief Joseph P. Piechocki ordered a flowing hose line directed to the window to knock down the fire and protect Marcus. Eventually, Bayne made his way down, with Marcus hot on his heels. Both escaped without injury. Marcus would receive the "Jack E. Dyke Award" for Fireman of the Year 1966 for assisting Bayne at great personal risk.[63]

In 1958, Herman Williams, was also recognized for bravery and received a departmental medal. A motorized crane was traveling east on Pennington Avenue at a high rate of speed and flipped over off the little bridge crossing Cabin Branch that feeds into near-by Curtis Creek. When Engine #57 crewmembers arrived on location they could see that the passenger cab of the vehicle was in 10 feet of water about 25 feet from the bridge. The driver in the cab was trapped, pinned by a collapsed steering wheel. A co-worker was trying valiantly to keep the driver's head above the rising tide.

Williams and Firefighter Andy Kovoski, took off their shoes and dove into the murky water with their clothes on and swam out to the wrecked vehicle. The cab door was open, but something was keeping the victim's foot from being released. Williams dived down into the water and without being able to see anything, felt his way around "the foot pedals, gear levers and steering column" until he located the victim's leg and foot.

Williams experienced a number of unsuccessful attempts to untangle the foot. After each attempt, he came up out of the water for air and heard the yells and screams of the victim. Finally, he was able to free the nearly drowned driver. By then the large 1950 "Mack" well-equipped Rescue #1 truck, from the downtown Paca Street Station pulled up and a number of firefighters along with Williams and Kovoski removed the victim safely to land with rope lines and a rescue basket. After it was all over, Williams suddenly realized something. He turned to Kovoski and said, "Andy, how in the hell did I do that out here? I can't swim." [64]

IN APRIL OF 1968, THE BALTIMORE FIRE DEPARTMENT'S 1,800 firefighters in 67 stations were commanded by 60 year old John J. Killen. A veteran firefighter and officer for 30 years prior to becoming chief, Killen looked every bit the part. Although widely respected and extremely intelligent the firefighting veteran was also known for having the "foulest" mouth in the department. Veteran firefighters from that time state, "That Killen cussed worse than a sailor." Not many could believe that Killen spent his early years studying in the Catholic seminary.[65] Firefighter Jerry Alfinito, who was on the job from 1959 to 1980 and spent many of those years under Killen's reign, said, "Chief Killen managed with a firm hand, but the guys seemed to like him."[66]

As Baltimore's fire chief for the previous 9 years and 11 months, the seasoned Killen was responsible for modernizing the department. During his tenure he increased the department's ability to fight ship fires and to fight building fires along the busy world-renowned harbor by adding three new fire boats for a total of four in the marine force.

Killen managed the city's fire stations, strategically placed throughout the city, which housed 53 first line engines and 29 ladder trucks. Considering that the National Fire Protection Association (NFPA), the nation's fire service standard making organization, recommended that an engine and ladder truck should be able to remain in front line service for 20 years; the city's fleet of fire apparatus was in good shape.[67] The average age of the engines was 14 years and the ladder trucks was 8 years.[68]

In 1960, Killen also oversaw the renovation of the fire alarm office located on the second floor of Fire Department Headquarters at 410 East Lexington Street near city hall, outfitting the center with the latest electronic communications and signaling devices. He championed the renovation of the apparatus repair shop on the north side of Key Highway near Webster Street in August of 1962 and the High Pressure Pumping Station on South Street in 1966. All renovations would prove to be significant in the coming firestorm.[69]

4

Law Enforcement

A Needed Reorganization

The Baltimore City Police Department was established by the Maryland Legislature on March 16, 1853, six years before the fire department was organized.

In 1857, the Baltimore City Police Department consisted of a chief, a deputy chief, eight captains, eight lieutenants, five detectives, 24 sergeants and 393 patrolmen. To provide 24-hour coverage on the city's streets, the patrolmen worked two shifts. Shift one began at 6 a.m. and continued until 6 p.m. Shift two ran from 6 p.m. to 6 a.m. Since the department was assigned the additional responsibility of keeping Baltimore's streets safe at night through efficient lighting, the department also employed four superintendents as well as, 42 lamplighters.[1] In 1861 at the outbreak of the Civil War, the police department was taken over by the Federal government and was managed by the U.S. military until 1862.[2] The Federal government took this precautionary action due to the large population of southern sympathizers living in the city and as the result of the President Street Riots.

During the 1880s, in addition to the police headquarters building on East Fayette Street near the Fallsway, Baltimore had erected four station houses throughout the city to supervise the field operations duties of the patrolmen.[3] By 1912 the city's force had expanded to 1,052 officers deployed to eight police stations throughout the city. As the department continued to grow with the city, it made progress in enhancing its ability to perform law enforcement. In 1896, the Bertillon system was adopted and implemented by the department, making it easier to identify criminals. Widely practiced by the British and a number of American cities, the Bertillon system used measurement of head and body parts, along with individual markings such as tattoos, scars and personality characteristics, to assist officers and the public in the apprehension of criminals. As new technological advances became available Baltimore strived to modernize. The department installed radio communications equipment in patrol cars in 1933 and established a new police laboratory in 1950.[4]

The Baltimore City Police Department was made up primarily of Irish-Americans. The department did not hire African-Americans until 1937 when Violet Hill Whyte became the department's first black officer. A year later, three more blacks were hired and assigned to plain clothes. It wasn't until 1943 that black officers were allowed to wear uniforms. By 1950 there were 50 African-Americans in the department.[5]

It was apparent that the Baltimore Police Department had a non-existent relationship with the city's African-American community. At times, black citizens were subject to greater use of force and abuse than would be employed on white civilians. It was not uncommon for blacks playing "craps" in the back alleys off of North Avenue, to hear the distinct sound of an officer's night stick striking the ground. As if a coded signal was delivered, the players would stand up from their knelling position and walk away leaving their money on the ground. The white police officer would pick up the money and continue on his patrol of the streets. The black gamblers would get backdown and resume the rolling of the dice.[6] Blacks would not only expect, but would tolerate the paying of "ground rent" to the corrupt police officers. What blacks wouldn't tolerate was the intervention of black officers. On East Baltimore's North Milton Avenue, Patrolman Henry Smith Jr. was killed in 1962 for breaking up a "dice" game. Smith was the first African-American Baltimore police officer to die in the line of duty.[7]

If you were black and living in the city prior to the 1970s there were two instances that could bring about trouble from the police. If you talked back to a white police officer, you were pulled into an alley, roughed up and possibly beaten.

The second, and worst offense, was if you ran from a white police officer; you were surely to be beaten if not fired upon.[8] These injustices only added to the bitterness that ran generations deep among the African-Americans living in the city's tough ghetto. They could only believe that they had no hope and nothing would ever change.[9]

Black police officers were often harassed by their white co-workers and were typically subject to racial slurs and insults during roll calls at shift changes. On the streets, the white officers would seldom talk to them. And if that wasn't bad enough, black officers were also harassed by African-Americans who lived in the communities where they patrolled. Black police officers were not permitted to patrol white neighborhoods. They were prohibited from riding in the patrol cars and were limited in how far up the career ladder they could progress. A black officer lived with a dismal expectation that his entire career would consist of foot patrols in black neighborhoods or as an undercover in narcotics investigations.[10]

David Simon wrote in his award winning book, *Homicide — A Year on the Killing Streets*: "Even the most prominent members of the Black community were made to endure slights and insults, and well before the 1960s, the contempt felt for the [police] department was close to universal."[11]

By late 1965, with pressure from community, as well as, civil rights groups and fearing a "Watts" like racial riot in Baltimore, city administrators hired the International Association of Chiefs of Police (IACP) organization to perform a comprehensive study and evaluation of the city's police department.

The association sent 49-year-old retired Marine colonel and law enforcement consultant Donald Pomerleau to Baltimore to perform the evaluation. The report's goal was to identify problems and develop solutions that would improve the department and prevent racial rioting.[12]

At the time Pomerleau was working with police in Nashville, Tennessee in reorganizing their department. He also provided consulting services to the Jacksonville, Florida and Dallas, Texas law enforcement agencies and worked as the public safety director officer for Miami, Florida and Kingsport, Tennessee.[13]

After the seven-week study, the IACP report strongly indicated that the department was severely troubled. In addition to noting discrimination against black police officers, the report acknowledged that black citizens were subject to excessive force by police, and worse that black citizens often faced retaliation from other community members for interacting with the police.[14]

After his investigation Pomerleau reported that the Baltimore Police Department was among the nation's most antiquated and corrupt police forces. The report made it perfectly clear that the city police department had perpetuated a very poor relationship with the large African-American community in addition to discriminating in its hiring and promotion of black officers.[15]

City and state authorities were very impressed with the study and more so with Pomerleau. In February 1966, the police commission wisely and successfully convinced the then chief of police to retire and assigned General George M. Gelston — Adjutant General of the Maryland National Guard and veteran of the Cambridge riots, as acting police chief. As Gelston temporarily took on the reigns of the city's top law enforcement office, the commission embarked on a nationwide search for a new police chief.[16]

Gelston immediately started to implement some of the recommendations cited in Pomerleau's report. Gelston's first appointment was a police community aide, who could start the process of improving relations between the police and Baltimore's black communities. Gelston chose William A. Harris, a black major in Maryland's National Guard who had worked very closely with Gelston during the Cambridge, Maryland riots only two years before. A police department reorganization plan was formulated based on Pomerleau's study and it would go into effect on July 7, 1966.[17]

During Gelston's short interim period as police chief an unfortunate racial situation occurred at the Tommy Tucker Store, located at 1707 Pennsylvania Avenue. The Tommy Tucker Store, a five and dime type variety store, one of five in the Baltimore area, paid blacks only 75 cents to $1.05 per hour in wages-considered a very low wage at the time.[18]

Congress of Racial Equality (CORE) members representing the Maryland Freedom Union, complained to the store's manager about the meager wages and after talks stalled, decided to picket the store on July 10, 1966. The black protesters after picketing for hours in the 96-degree heat started to block customer access to the front door. Police were brought in and a small disturbance ensued as protestors struggled with police officers. Two protestors actually laid themselves under the wheels of the police paddy wagon. The incident resulted in the police arresting seven demonstrators; two others were hurt and transported to the hospital.[19]

Gelston immediately involved himself in the negotiations with union leaders and the store's owner. Once he was able to bring the sides together he handed off the talks to the newly created Police Community Relations Division and local ministers who eventually reached an agreement with the owners.[20]

The police commissioner's search would result in a short list of qualified candidates. In addition to Pomerleau and Gelston, the list included a police chief from Cincinnati, a former superintendent of the Pennsylvania State Police and the local training division chief of the Maryland State Police. Gelston was offered the job, but declined wanting to return to Maryland's National Guard. The police commission, without Geltson (who honorably excluded himself) conducted the interviews and in the end unanimously chose Pomerleau.[21]

As the Baltimore City Police Department is an instrumentality of the state, the commissioner is appointed by the governor. Honoring the commission's wishes, Governor J. Millard Tawes appointed Pomerleau to a six-year term to take on the awesome challenge of policing the city of Baltimore. The governor gave Pomerleau a clear mandate to clean up the department at a salary of $52,000 a year.[22]

Although Pomerleau was a large, well-tailored man, who spoke with authority, he was surprisingly flexible and was willing to experiment and to risk failure.[23] In an interview with Baltimore *Sun* writer Floyd Miller, two years after becoming police chief, Pomerleau said, "We have not solved all our problems...far from it. But we're working at them as hard as we can, and I think the people know that. This gives them hope and patience."[23]

Pomerleau played a huge part in lifting the restrictions on African-Americans in the department. Prior to the new chief being hired, there was very little responsibility placed on black officers, so they were limited to foot patrols and meager specialty assignments. Pomerleau would changed all of that and set the wheels in motion to fully integrate the police department.[24] One of his first actions after coming on board was to set up a course in "Negro History," which all city police officers were required to attend.

David Simon would write, "Pomerleau's arrival marked the end of the Baltimore department's Paleozoic era. Almost overnight, the command staff began stressing community relations, crime prevention and modern law enforcement technology. A series of city wide tactical units was created and multi-channel radios replaced the call boxes still used by most patrolman."[25]

Chief Donald Pomerleau was very popular among the nation's police chiefs and was requested to speak at the National Police Executives Conference in Memphis, Tennessee, June 12 through 14, 1967 on "Community Tensions"[26] According to Pomerleau, the Congress of Racial Equality at the national level, declared Baltimore City the "Target City" for Social Revolution."[27] It would be Pomerleau's challenge to see that the "Social Revolution" was carried out peacefully.

In 1967, Chief Pomerleau administered the city's police department with a $46.8 million budget. The department consisted of 4,162 employees in which 3,290 were sworn officers assigned to nine districts and a central HQ.[28] The community relations division, a Pomerleau initiative, was still led by the African-American National Guard Major William Harris (Gelston's pick who entered the program laterally). Harris, a Morgan State College graduate, brought a world of experience in race relations. The outstanding program required each of the nine police districts to have an integrated community relations council to maintain peace and harmony within the city.[29]

Pomerleau expanded the division with additional personnel and told them to" penetrate the negro community, not with gun and nightstick, but with service."[30] Harris would say that "I want the children to become familiar with the [police] uniform;

to learn that we are not monsters but men—Black men, just like their daddies."[31] In the ghettos of most major cities a black police officer was a special target of abuse. He was called Uncle Tom and worse. But in Baltimore, thanks to the success of the community relations division, the African-American officer seemed to be held in respect, sometimes even regarded with affection.[32]

According to retired police colonel Joseph Francis Cooke, who was a sergeant at the time assigned to Cherry Hill in Baltimore's Southern District, Pomerleau was an excellent choice for police chief. Cooke stated that Pomerleau was very successful in cutting all the old time political connections and restraints which sometimes paralyzed innovation and advancement. Under Pomerleau's leadership the department started to move toward becoming a top-notched modern organization.[33]

Under Pomerleau's watch, officers became more accountable for their actions which resulted in a much needed professional police force patrolling the streets of Baltimore.[34] Pomerleau stressed higher education and sent officers to schools and various seminars so they would become better educated and trained. At the time 60 percent of police officers had less than a high school education.[35]

Pomerleau spent at least 80 percent of his work time on the streets of the city talking and working with black civic groups and community leaders.[36] An editorial in the *Afro-American*, published on February 17, 1968, entitled, "Get Tough Police," liked the stance taken by Pomerleau.[37]

The editorial criticized the police commissioner in East Saint Louis who ordered his officers "to shoot anyone seen throwing a fire bomb before questioning." The paper also criticized the Miami Chief of Police for his get tough policy, which went overboard when two of his officers hung a young black youth from his heels from a highway bridge to teach him a lesson for talking back to them.[38]

The editorial also stated that Pomerleau told a gathering of official leaders in Baltimore, "Whether we like it or not the time has arrived when symptoms of crime as well as the immediate criminal act need to be dealt with," the paper went on to say that "but he [Pomerleau] would never issue an" unprofessional, panic, or crash type program as witnessed in Saint Louis and Miami." The *Afro-American* stated that Pomerleau was "wise and effective."[39]

Pomerleau was not in favor of using the police in quelling riots and anarchy. His beliefs were based on the fact that "police officers cannot be a big brother to all the people one day and a force prepared and expected to do battle with when coping with racial and other community disorders the next."[40] In early March 1968, Pomerleau stated, "the department has no aspirations to stockpile weapons or to acquire tanks. It's not the function of the police department to extinguish full-scale riots comparable to those that have taken place in Newark, Detroit and Watts."[41]

However, Pomerleau knew that he still needed a specialized unit to dispatch for the purpose of suppressing and reducing spontaneous disorders before they could expand into major incidents. So he tasked the police department to develop what was identified as a "Phase Five" program designed to pyramid emergency forces to handle civil disorders.[42]

Pomerleau believed that the Phase Five program would be a "fast striking, hard hitting, well-trained and equipped task force capable of subduing dissident forces to uphold law and order." As his lieutenants moved to create and train personnel to build this new specialized force, Pomerleau would continue to believe that civil disorders/riots should be handled by the National Guard.[43]

By April of 1968, Commissioner Donald Pomerleau would have two years of experience under his belt in managing the police department in the nation's seventh largest city with a population now nearing 900,000. The department consisted of 3,055 sworn police officers, the sixth largest police department in the nation. Of that number, 266 patrolman (approximately 8 percent) were African-American.[44]

MARYLAND'S ARMY NATIONAL GUARD has a long and distinguished history that goes back to 1634. Prior to the 1870s, the Maryland National Guard was known as the Militia. In the early years of America's Revolutionary War, it was the Maryland Militia that held back the British advance during New York's Battle of Long Island which allowed the majority of the Continental Army to withdraw putting off a complete British victory that could have easily ended America's revolt. During the battle of Cowpens in South Carolina, it was the Maryland Militia that repeatedly launched bayonet charges against a larger British Army turning the tempo of the battle and resulting in an American victory.[45]

In the Battle of North Point in 1814, when the British attacked the City of Baltimore, it was Maryland's Militia that held the line against the British for hours to allow Baltimore valuable time to build up its defenses. During the Civil War, Maryland's Militia would fight on both sides and would serve with distinction by defending the strategic Culp's Hill for the Union during the 1863 Battle of Gettysburg.[46]

The guard was called out to mitigate the Great Railroad Strike of 1877. Troops were sent out to Cumberland and Baltimore's Camden Railroad yards to break up the strike gang's disruption of the state's rail service. At Camden yards, the site of the City's second worst riot, a mob attacked the Guard troopers and the soldiers fired upon the crowd killing 10 and wounding 25. Before long more than 50,000 angry supporters of the strike besieged the guard who later had to be rescued by Federal troops who arrived hours later.[47]

In addition to providing law enforcement during the Great Baltimore Fire in 1904, the Guard would serve with distinction in both World Wars. In World War I the unit served with the 29th Infantry Division and participated in the Meuse-Argonne actions in France near the town of Verdun in the fall of 1918. The guard also provided troops to the first segregated company, an all African-American unit, which served in the 372nd Infantry Regiment assigned to the 93rd Division.[48]

During World War II, the Guard, again assigned to the 29th Infantry Division fought in the bloody landings during D-Day at Omaha Beach in Normandy, France, and fought through the hedgerow country until the allied breakout many months later. The 29th Infantry would suffer more than 20,111 battle casualties in its 11-month deployment from D-Day to the end of the war.[49]

In 1950, the 231st regiment of the Maryland Guard served in Korea as a transportation truck battalion. It was instrumental in keeping supplies flowing on the Pusan Peninsula during the early days of the conflict. Originally a segregated African-American unit, the 231st was integrated into the regular Guard during Korea only to be segregated again when it returned to the states.[50] During the Cold War in the 1960s, the Guard was assigned to NIKE missile battery sites that surrounded the Baltimore-Washington area to defend against a possible Soviet attack.[51]

In 1968 the 7,000 man Maryland National Guard was commanded by General George M. Gelston — Adjutant General of the State of Maryland. The general was a career military man with a civilian approach to problem solving. He believed that when urban hostilities broke out, Guard's forces will assure full responsibility in the problem area.[52]

The chain-smoking Gelston with his trademark military crewcut served in active duty during World War II from 1942 to 1945 and during the occupation of Germany until 1948, at which he accepted a full-time assignment to the Maryland National Guard. The general also attended the Army Command and General Staff College in 1960 and the Army War College in 1964.[53]

General Gelston was a veteran in dealing with civil disorders gaining considerable experience in deployment and field operations as commander of the Maryland National Guard forces sent to Cambridge in 1963 and 1967.[54] Starting in February 1966 until June of that year, Gelston was assigned as acting police commissioner for the City of Baltimore. The assignment provided him with insight and crucial experience in dealing with the African-American communities, their leaders, and the reorganization of the police department.

Gelston believed that it would be "a terrible thing to have to use any kind of weapon against Americans."[55] He believed in a less lethal force. He stated, "tear gas is the most effective and humane weapons available for riots."[56] As Baltimore's interim police commissioner, Geltston drew praise from black civic and civil rights groups for his handling of racial situations.

The general did not believe there would be any major civil unrest in the city, due to the city's efforts over the years to resolve the frustrations of Baltimore's African-American population.

Gelston strongly believed there were more jobs and better education now available for the African-American community, which addressed the "prime immediate solutions to racial unrest." The general also suggested that "good communication" between the city administrators and the black community would greatly assist in avoiding "racial trouble."[57] During the Cambridge Riots, in the summer of 1967, General Gelston was in charge of the 700 strong National Guard force sent into town. "He issued his men 12 rounds of ammunition each, told them to fire if fired upon, but also displayed admirable diplomatic skills in dealing firmly with the white troublemakers as with the angry blacks."[58]

On June 1, 1966, General Gelston relinquished his police duties to the newly appointed Chief Donald Pomerleau and resumed his duties as adjutant general of Maryland. Approximately one month later, a significant incident that would serve as a precursor to the riots of April 1968 and enhance the Baltimore fire and police service's emergency coordination and communications capabilities was a major fire that occurred at Baltimore's Maryland Penitentiary on July 8, 1966.

THE SUMMER OF 1966 WAS ONE OF THE HOTTEST Baltimore summers on record and inmates in the city's packed prison were tense. The antiquated 154-year-old Maryland state correctional facility, located at Madison and Forrest streets, was originally built to house 950 inmates but now held 1,461.[59]

The huge multi-story Norman-styled stone structure with gray colored walls kept the city's worst inmates separated from Baltimore's somewhat peaceful society. At approximately 11:30 a.m., about 1,000 prisoners arrived in the prison mess hall expecting to sit down for the afternoon meal. Un-expectedly the prisoners emerged armed with stones and clubs and violence erupted. In the mess hall groups of inmates attacked other groups along with prison guards. As groups of prisoners scattered, a number of fires were set throughout four buildings. The largest fire was set in the three-story tag and print shop.[60]

As a plume of heavy black smoke rose over east Baltimore's blue summer sky and bright orange flames appeared in the building's upper stories, eight alarms of fire department apparatus consisting of 250 firefighters were sent out along with 300 city police officers in riot gear, some with gas masks and 25 K-9 dogs.

The fire was smartly fought from a defensive posture as ladder pipes and deluge gun operations were set up safely away from the violence and heavy streams of water were applied to suppress the fire. It was an opportunity for police and fire departments to hone their coordination skills and communication abilities. The fire was under-control by 2:30 in the afternoon and the cost in damage was high.[61] It was the most destructive rioting incident in a Maryland correctional facility in 30 years.[62]

By 1968 the 92-square mile Baltimore City benefited from the protection of a progressive and modern fire department built and expanded on the lessons learned from the great fire 64 years before. With a tested and polished police administrator, a progressive law enforcement philosophy and new technology, the city police department was moving forward in its attempts to maintain peace in the city. Combined, the Baltimore City Police Department, the Maryland State Police and the Maryland National Guard were trained and on alert for the outbreak of violence on the streets of Baltimore.

Due to major improvements within the police department and improved police relations with the city's growing African-American community, city officials and authorities believed everything was well at hand. Supporting that belief was a distinguished record in civil rights achievement that had been slow but progressing in a positive direction since the mid 1960s. Baltimore's civil rights achievements were a key reason the NAACP (National Association for the Advancement of Colored People) selected the city for its national headquarters.[63] Even in Maryland politics representation was improving for blacks. During the last session of the Maryland Legislature, the House of Delegates had more African-American representation than ever before. There was even more black representation in the city's council districts. In early 1968 blacks were now being appointed to leadership positions in newly elected Mayor Tommy D'Alessandro III's city government.[64]

Most believed that the charmed city with a population of just under one million, with 43 percent of that African-American, would be spared the devastation, death and injury that occurred in the previous summer's wave of civil disorder and violence. That belief unfortunately would become the "great myth."[65]

THERE WAS ONE PROMINENT MARYLAND POLITICIAN who would quickly step up to the plate in April of 1968. His actions would not only have a major impact on maintaining law and order in Baltimore City, but would also thrust him into a larger stage and national spotlight in a very short period of time. His name was Spiro Theodore Agnew.

Born in Baltimore in 1918, "Ted" Agnew was the son of a Greek immigrant father and a mother from Virginia,[66, 67] who owned a Baltimore lunchroom. Growing up in the Arlington section of West Baltimore, Agnew attended Forest Park High School, near Liberty Heights Avenue. After graduation in 1938, he attended Johns Hopkins University, majoring in chemistry. During World War II he was drafted into the army, served as a company commander of the 10th Armor Division and won the Bronze Star in the Europe campaign.[68]

After the war Agnew worked as a grocer and insurance salesmen while attending law school at night. He received his law degree from the University of Baltimore and passed the Maryland Bar in 1949. Agnew moved to the Loch Raven section of Baltimore County in the early 1950s. In 1962, the 44-year-old zoning, labor union and personal injury attorney ran for county executive in Baltimore County and won.[69]

Agnew saw himself as proponent of civil rights and a strong opponent of disobedience. He was conservative in his views of law enforcement, moderate on civil rights issues and a Rockefeller Republican. Agnew was also instrumental in desegregating the Gwynn Oak Amusement Park. He was a "man of great personal pride who put great stock in personal loyalty."[70]

In 1966, the married father of four, campaigned and won the governorship for the State of Maryland, beating out the democratic challenger and ultraconservative segregationist,

George P. Mahoney.[71] According to Agnew biographer, Jules Witcover in *White Knight*, "More out of fear of Mahoney than love of Agnew, moderates and liberals of both parties had flocked to the side of the Republican alternative Agnew."[72] Agnew was the fifth republican governor in 180 years and "would prove to be an eminently competent and an imaginative chief executive." He would sign the first statewide open-housing law below the Mason-Dixon Line.[73]

Agnew was characterized as expressionless, humorless, and cautious, yet straightforward and unaffected at the same time. President Richard Nixon would later remark, "Agnew—there is a quiet confidence about him."[74] At press conferences in Annapolis, it was widely known that Agnew would usually not speak until he had absolute silence.[75]

Agnew was among the new breed of suburban politicians. A liberal republican, he was never "fully attentively attuned" to the "brutal reality of Baltimore's gritty ghettos." Agnew also believed that permissive attitudes in the black communities contributed heavily to urban problems. Within the first year of his freshman administration he ordered the National Guard to Cambridge when the riots broke out in July 1967.[76]

The 6'2", 192-pound heavy-set Agnew had little tolerance for disobedience. He took "disobedience personally as disrespectful rhetoric—Evil men not evil conditions and fight force with force...[He] had blamed the SNCC chairman H. Rap Brown for inciting the Cambridge violence with speeches and rhetoric that Agnew equated to a call to arms."[77] Although Agnew was supported by blacks for the office of governor, a race that he decisively won, his initial appeal to the African-American community would severely change during the riots.

5

"An Untimely Loss"

On Thursday morning, April 4, 1968, the headlines in the city's newspapers reported the latest news from war- torn Vietnam, "Khe Sanh Relief — Just One Mile Away." A relief force of 20,000 U.S. Marines would join the already 6,000 defending the forward base surrounded and taking a pounding by the North Vietnamese army. This would be the first breakthrough in relief in 11 weeks for the marines pinned down in a siege that started three months earlier during the Vietnam War's Tet offensive.[1]

The papers also reported on the rising crime on Baltimore's streets. Since April 2 a springtime crime wave had sprung upon the city. Six victims lay in hospitals recovering from stab wounds. People were stabbed and robbed in the 1800 block of Cherry Hill Road, the 1000 block of East Monument Street, and the 300 block of Kenwood Avenue. In the 600 block of Dolphin Street a teen was shot in the chest as a result of an argument over splitting stolen money. Windows were shattered in the 1700 block of Pennsylvania Avenue, as teens broke in and looted Pop Kelly's Men's Shop. The Baltimore police department needed to step up its patrols.[2]

Thursday's weather wasn't much better than the news reports thought Baltimore City Police Patrolman William D. Vane as he finished up his shift and drove home from police headquarters downtown where he was assigned to the K-9 Corps. The early morning air was a chilly 40 degrees and the morning sky was overcast.

While driving down Madison Street in East Baltimore, Vane could smell wood burning. Within a minute he quickly pulled his car over and stopped as smoke billowed from the second floor of a row-house in the 2200 block. Vane ran to the house as a pregnant 35-year-old Anne Schroeder started to drop one of her children out of a smoky second floor apartment window.[3]

Vane managed to catch the 3-year-old girl before she hit the hard ground. As he looked up, the desperate, yet brave, mother told him to wait. A few seconds later she appeared through the smoke, leaned out the window and dropped a 4-year-old girl who Vane caught. Vane assisted two more girls 6-and 10-years old from the upper story window.[4]

As her anxious children watched from below, Anne Schroeder crawled out feet first. She hung onto the window sill with her hands, stretched and dropped into Vane's waiting arms. The courageous patrolman would later say, "I kept wondering how many kids she had as the woman kept [leaving the window sill] going back in to find another one and each kid got bigger."[5]

Schroeder's 9-year-old son, Paul, managed to escape through the apartment's front door and contact the fire department which arrived once Mom, Marsha, Lois, Edith and Elizabeth were safely out of the burning building.[6] Unfortunately, as bad as it was for the Schroeder family, their misfortune would not be the worst thing that happened on this day.

Throughout the week demonstrations were being held at the predominately African-American Bowie State College in Bowie, Maryland. The 16 red brick educational buildings, which made up Bowie's campus, are located about 20 miles west of Annapolis. In 1968, Maryland still ran separate college systems for black and white students.[7]

The students were protesting the poor conditions at the college. The school's buildings were old and three quarters of them were infested with termites. The heating plant was inadequate and there was faulty wiring, crumbling paint and deteriorating plaster in the dormitories, classrooms and faculty offices. As a result of approximately 50 student and faculty complaints, students had begun boycotting classes.[8]

Although Governor Agnew increased expenditures to address the college's problems, he was greatly opposed to the student disobedience. When students occupied the Administration Building to protest the run down condition of the campus, he sent in the Maryland State Police to take back the building. Agnew would not negotiate.[9]

On Thursday, April 4, the students planned an afternoon demonstration at the State House in Annapolis. If enough students turned out, maybe the governor would talk with them. When Agnew failed to show up, the students engaged in a sit-in on the state capital building's steps. At 5 p.m. when the State House officially closed for the day and the students refused to leave, the State Police moved in an arrested 225 of the demonstrators.[10]

The demonstrators were arrested peacefully. At 7 p.m., Governor Agnew held a press conference to announce that he was ordering the college to be temporarily shutdown. As the governor spoke to reporters, 75 state troopers arrived at the school, entered classrooms where students were currently attending classes and ordered everyone off the campus. The students had five minutes to leave the school grounds.[11] Approximately one hour before the Bowie State students were ordered off the campus, and as the state house demonstrators were being booked at the Anne Arundel County Detention Center in Annapolis, a devastating event occurred that would send the nation into unprecedented fury.[12]

As a light rain fell over the Baltimore and Annapolis metropolitan areas, special reports were now appearing on television and being broadcast on the radio announcing the dreadful news that Dr. Martin Luther King Jr. had been shot in Memphis, Tennessee.

The reverend was gunned down at approximately 6:01 p.m. as he walked out of his room onto a stairway leading balcony in front of Room 306 at the Lorraine Motel in Memphis. With Ministers Ralph David Abernathy and Jessie Jackson by his side, King was rushed to Saint Joseph's hospital, where within the hour he would die. Dr. King was just 39 years old.[13]

Upon hearing the news of the assassination of their beloved leader, Baltimore's African-Americans headed out into the wet streets as a now partial visible sun set on a city of uncertainty. The Baltimoreans were stunned, sad and angry all at the same time. Although the groups, now hanging at street corners, churches and neighborhood gathering places, were calm, one could sense the tension in the air. Little Melvin Williams, the city's local pool hustler, stated that "there is going to be hell to pay."[14]

There seemed to be more people in the streets than at any time before. Pro football hall of fame running back, Lenny Moore of the Baltimore Colts said, "You could feel the tension, you knew something was going to happen, but you didn't know when or where."[15]

AT CATHEDRAL AND MADISON STREET, in the Alcazar Hotel's popular restaurant, a large banquet party was in full swing. The restaurant's "Fiesta Room," was the site of some of the city's most grand and glamorous cabarets, cocktail parties and dinners. These events were typically attended by Baltimore's well-to-do and the movers and shakers of the city of 970,000. Around the ballroom's dance floor aligned with white ceramic vases of boxwood, people in their best dress mingled, conversed and drank unaware of the tragic news reports on the radio and television.[16]

As the youthful looking Mayor Tommy D'Alesandro III sat down at a large table set for ten and adorned with white and gold colored cloths on which sat small vases of yellow flowers, other politicians and businessmen joined him. Once seated, they were served their choice of terrapin or chicken ala king with biscuits and sides.[17]

Across from D'Alesandro sat Louis Azrael, editorial columnist for the *News American* and the two of them shared in the typical table conversation, listened to speeches and enjoyed the food. Halfway through the festivities it was announced that Dr. King had been assassinated. As the tone of the dinner quickly changed from festive to a mixed atmosphere of shock, sadness, and uncertainty, Azrael leaned across the table toward D'Alesandro and said, "Well Tommy, you're really going to have trouble now."[18]

But the popular *News American* columnist didn't say anything that the mayor hadn't already figure out on his own. Within a half hour D'Alesandro was back in his second floor office at city hall meeting with his entire group of department heads. Due to the significance of Dr. King's death, D'Alesandro had immediately called all of them in to discuss the possibility of trouble and to develop a contingency plan. The first thing he did was have Police Commissioner Donald Pomerleau send out undercover cops throughout the ghetto neighborhoods in an attempt to take the pulse of this new situation.[19]

Baltimore's Cherry Hill community is isolated and perched on high elevation just northwest of Brooklyn, south of the Hanover Street Bridge and east of near-by Westport. The area would be the site of the first signs of the upcoming storm.

Before the community's construction in 1945, Cherry Hill was the location of an amusement park for African-Americans, which burned down in 1922.[20] The garden-style city and planned community for the city's blacks consisted of neat rows of brick townhouses and apartments. The community was a source of pride for the African-Americans who lived there.

However, this isolation of 20,000 residences was by no means an accident. The complex was mandated by federal government public housing legislation for African-American war factory workers and their families. Cherry Hill Homes, its official title, a mix of private and public housing, was funded by $8 million of federal public housing money. At the time it was considered one of the largest public housing projects east of Chicago.[21]

Although its lack of commercial establishments was inconvenient requiring residents to travel and shop in the downtown black enclaves of the city, this inconvenience would prove to be an advantage over the next few days.

At approximately 10:38 p.m., only three hours and 33 minutes after King's death, Baltimore City Fire Engine Companies, #58, #35, #26, Ladder Trucks #21 and #6 and Battalion Chief #6 responded to the 600 block of Cherry Hill Road for a structure fire reported at the shopping center.[22]

When firefighters arrived they found a door and its frame on fire in the rear of the Cherry Hill Supply & Variety Company. While a hose line was being placed into service to extinguish the fire, a second doorway burst into flames five doors down at the S&S Pharmacy and other fire fighters were re-assigned to fight that fire.[23]

Later firefighters would find that the rear door to the A&P (Atlantic and Pacific) grocery store was soaked with gasoline. A gas can, gasoline soaked matches and newspapers were all found lying on the ground nearby. The shopping center contained 10 stores that served the Cherry Hill population of 38,000 African-American residents. Minor incidents signaling unrest, such as fire engines being pelted with rocks as they entered the community, had occurred in the neighborhood in the past, but this was the first malicious act since the assassination.[24]

Still not believing that a major wave of violence would break out in the city, but to be on the safe side, Chief Donald Pomerleau set up an emergency command post on the fifth floor of Baltimore City Police Headquarters located at East Fayette Street. At around 11 p.m. Lieutenant Colonel George Davidson of the Maryland State Police and Mayor D'Alesandro joined him there. Per Governor Agnew, General Gelston, who was attending a meeting in Atlanta, Georgia, was contacted and ordered immediately back to Maryland's Silver Spring Maryland National Guard Armory command post.[25]

After midnight, the city's fire engines would roll out of their stations again. At approximately 12:38 a.m. in northwest Baltimore, two fire bombs were thrown through a window at Hoffman's Bar and Liquor Store, 4451 Park Heights Avenue, a block north of Cold Spring Lane. The bombs landed on a pool table and an ADT Burglar Alarm sounded. When Engine #46, from the 5116 Reisterstown Road station, arrived at the structure, crew members found that the owner, 53-year-old Howard Hoffman, notified by ADT, had arrived and extinguished the fire with a fire extinguisher.[26]

As violence started to break out in major cities across the country, Baltimore experienced less than half a dozen fires. The Monumental City could sleep tonight.

ON THE MORNING OF FRIDAY, APRIL 5TH, the city streets were still damp from the light overnight showers. Baltimore residents awoke to what seemed like a terrifying nightmare. Reality would eventually sink in as the city's 970,000 inhabitants realized that the King assignation was not just a bad dream. Residents felt an uncomfortable numbness as most were still in shock. From his second floor office at city hall, Mayor D'Alesandro III ordered all city flags flown at half-mast. [27]

D'Alesandro had said a little less than a month before, "Baltimore is programmed for services, not war in the streets."[28] However, realizing he needed to stay in town and prepare for the worst, D'Alesandro quickly postponed a meeting that he was to attend in Washington, D.C. to seek restoration of $100 million for anti-poverty funds. The new mayor, whose election platform promised to "restore public confidence in city government," and who worked diligently some 14 hours a day, seven days a week, with only three months of office under his belt as mayor, started preparations to address anticipated trouble.[29]

It wasn't long before there were indications of unrest appearing in city schools. At Coppin State College, located on North Avenue, and at Northwestern High School on Park Heights Avenue, students refused to follow the regular academic routine and just roamed the halls.[30]

D'Alesandro immediately called for the second planning meeting in less than 12 hours, which was held in the city solicitor's office of George L. Russell.[31] The smart and sophisticated Russell was the first African-American ever appointed to the position.[32] Russell was also the first black to ever be appointed to Baltimore's Supreme Court Bench after serving as a city magistrate for a few years. He would serve as the civic center commissioner from 1959 to 1963.[33]

Also attending the meeting was the newly appointed, first African-American fire board commissioner, 43-year old Reverend Marion Curtis Bascom. At the time the fire commission consisted of a president who earned $5,500 per year and two board members, one who was named Bascom, who received $3,000 per year.[34]

Bascom grew up in Pensacola, Florida, and in 1949 he began what would become nearly a "half-century" tenure with the Douglas Memorial Church in Baltimore. A veteran of numerous civil rights protests and demonstrations, including the 1963 protest at Gwynn Oak Park, he was very active in Baltimore politics.[35]

Fire Commissioner Bascom would become instrumental in de-segregating the Baltimore City fire stations, removing the Jim Crow "Reserved" signs over bathroom toilets, sinks and beds. The reverend was also successful in removing the red tape that prevented qualified blacks from receiving promotions to pump operator and lieutenant.[36]

When told of the assassination of Dr. King, Bascom could only express, "The shock that everybody feels over the untimely loss of America's best friend."[37]

Sometime around noon, D'Alesandro was driven to Annapolis where he met Governor Agnew at the State House. They discussed their mutual concerns and plans. D'Alesandro shared his thoughts with the governor who was also his friend. "Ted," he said, "The city is calm and my gut feeling is it is too calm." D'Alesandro also told Agnew, "If we can just hold out until Church Services on Sunday."[38]

D'Alesandro had a wonderful rapport with the city's black Ministerial Alliance. He would later say, "There were a number of young black ministers who were bright and articulate. They served as ambassadors of hope and stability for the younger blacks." D'Alesandro had a strong belief that if the African-American community leadership could get the majority of young blacks into church, the ministers would be able to persuade them to mourn their slain leader by staying off of the streets and not participating in the violence that was occurring in other cities.[39]

Little Tommy, as D'Alesandro III was referred to, was the oldest of seven. He was born a "Democrat" and launched into Baltimore City politics at an early age. According to *Evening Sun* reporter, Alan Lupo, "he [Tommy] was always in the shadow of his father in the [smoked filled] backrooms of the politicians learning the game." The father of the handsome "skinny boy" with the thick patch of black hair was former Baltimore Mayor Thomas J. D'Alesandro Jr. It was said of D'Alesandro Jr. that "city ward politics was his bread and butter." Thomas D'Alesandro Jr. enjoyed a very successful political career as he was a Maryland State Delegate, a two term U.S. Congressman and mayor of Baltimore for three consecutive terms from 1947 until 1959.[40]

D'Alesandro Jr. was very supportive of the fire department. On September 14, 1956, a new city fireboat was named the "Mayor Thomas D'Alesandro Jr." The modern vessel was assigned as Engine #49 located at a pier and with attached living quarters at the foot of Benhill Avenue on Curtis Creek. With a pumping capability of 12,000 gallon per minute, the 104' craft, the "nation's most modern and speediest fireboat," was noted for its maneuverability and operating efficiency.[41]

The D'Alesandros lived on Albemarle Street, in Baltimore's Third Ward in Little Italy. Little Italy is located just east of the city's harbor and west of historic Fells Point. It is populated by thousands of Italian-Americans whose parents and grandparents settled in this section of the city as immigrants in the latter part of the 19th and early part of the 20th Centuries. It boasts as one of the finest restaurant districts in Baltimore. Over the years Little Italy became a popular, active and tight-knit family neighborhood with one of the lowest crime rates in the city, a fact that the D'Alesandros, as well as the residents, takes great pride in.[42]

In Little Italy "the neighborhood bond was the old world background, the language they [the residents] spoke, the church they attended and the fact that people married within their own group." It would be heresy for an Italian to marry a Polish girl from East Baltimore and visa versa." During the early period of the 20th Century, people with strong ethnic backgrounds stayed close to their own kind. In this part of town, families sat and gathered around the white marble steps in front of their brick row homes and talked with other Italian families. In nice weather, especially when the Orioles were playing ball on the weekends, the "sidewalks were always filled with people sometimes spilling into the street."[43]

Little Italy's contribution to fire protection in the city occurred during the Great Baltimore Fire in 1904. As the wind driven fire threatened Little Italy, residents stood on rooftops extinguishing spot fires started by flying brands from the cold dry forceful wind. Other residents went to nearby Saint Leo's Catholic Church. At the neighborhood church the group prayed for a miracle from Saint Anthony.[44]

The miracle was executed by firefighters from Baltimore city as well as cities as far away as New York, along with an accompanying wind shift. Some 37 engines with steam powered pumps were lined up along the Jones Falls where crew members drafted needed water from the falls through large hard rubber tubes up into their pumps.[45]

The combined companies of firefighters put up a fight that the city has not seen since as hundreds of hose streams were directed at the fire and Little Italy along with the rest of east Baltimore was saved. The tight-knit neighborhood sponsored a Saint Anthony's day fete along with a parade every year from there on to honor the great saint who was believed to have saved the Italian community from the devastating conflagration.[46] Tommy D'Alesandro III has participated in the parade every year since he was old enough to walk.[47]

After graduating from University of Maryland Law School and a brief three-year career in the Army, D'Alesandro was appointed to the city's board of election supervisors in 1957. With his father's contacts and tutelage, Little Tommy was able to take full advantage of a very unusual political succession that very seldom, if ever, occurred.[48]

As destiny would have it, Joseph Harold Grady who became mayor of Baltimore in 1959, was nominated by Maryland Governor Millard Tawes and accepted an appointment to serve as judge on Baltimore's Supremc Court and resigned as mayor in 1962. City regulations specified that in the event of a mayoral resignation, the city council president, (who was then Phillip Goodman), would automatically succeed Grady and complete his term until the next election.[49]

Goodman's move to mayor left the city council president's position vacant and the city regulations specified that in the event of a vacancy, the replacement could not come from the council. It had to be filled by someone outside of the council. Goodman nominated D'Alesandro III as his replacement and it was decided by a vote of 12 to eight that "Little Tommy" would fill the council president vacancy. During his appointment D'Alesandro performed so well, that when his term ended in 1962; he was not only elected to the city council, but was elected again as its president by the council members.[50]

Although "his father's reputation made it easier for him," D'Alesandro established his own identity. His friendly, spirited and positive personality often supported with comments like "you're mah boy" and "give me a shot," assisted him in presiding over some of the toughest council sessions dealing with civil rights, poverty programs and budget issues. His abilities as an accomplished storyteller and humorist attracted others who aspired to be within his sphere of influence.[51]

As president of the council, D'Alesandro was "mature, calm, ready to moderate and call for compromise, searching always for the peaceful solution." In 1967, D'Alesandro ran for mayor on the platform of enlightened leadership with a full-time attention to the programs of government. He also emphasized taking a tough stand for civil rights which strengthened his vote getting power in the growing African-American community. D'Alesandro was persevering, not overbearing and was regarded as a winner at compromise. He won the election by a landslide wining at all of the city's 555 polling places.[52]

D'Alesandro was instrumental in improving Baltimore's emergency services departments. In 1967, as council president, he approved a $2 million program that would enhance the fire and police pension system, reducing employees' contribution from 11 percent to six percent of their salaries.[53]

Tommy's father always advised him to "keep the men in blue close to you."[54] In January of 1967, Police Chief Donald Pomerleau requested a multi-million dollar package for a three-year-program to enhance law enforcement. The package included 350 radio-equipped marked patrol cars (to be on the street by March), 100 portable radios so all patrolman would be able to communicate with headquarters and patrol vehicles, and increased training. The $10 million package also included $5 million for increased salaries. The enhancement would raise the new police officers starting salary of $5,604 to $6,780 which would move up to $8,640 after five years. Heeding his father's advice, D'Alesandro approved the chief's request.[55]

Although D'Alesandro loved the fire department, he didn't always vote in its favor. In 1966, when the city's fire board wanted $3 million to eliminate eight old fire stations and replace them with modern structures, D'Alesandro balked, stating, "We don't have the money." Although he understood the request, he wanted to replace the dilapidated school buildings before the fire stations.[56] In May of 1967, when the city wanted to slash salaries, D'Alesandro approved the request with the stipulation that cuts would not occur until 1968 and they would not apply to police officers, firefighters and teachers.[57]

Unlike his father, a conservative, who was "pretty much tethered to Third Ward politics," Little Tommy, "a political disciple," became the bridge between the new and old eras.[58] He strived for cooperation between the city and its surrounding growing counties. His vision was to form a greater working bond with state and federal government. D'Alesandro's goals, in addition to promoting civil rights, were to eliminate the slums of Baltimore, and the only way he could accomplish that was with the money from Federal programs.[59]

In the wake of the Kerner Commission report released in March, D'Alesandro used the report's recommendations to improve the city's civil rights issues. He took great pains to develop programs that would "soothe the sore spots identified in the report" as factors contributing to urban riots.[60] Unfortunately, his programs involved long range plans that depended upon the "good faith" of the city administration, and would not have any immediate measurable effect on the high unemployment rates in the African-American community, the slum housing, or the poor conditions experienced in the inner city's dilapidated schools.[61]

D'Alesandro stated, "We have good dialogue with all segments of the community. Negro leaders have indicated that they are willing to move along without violence." D'Alesandro strongly believed that racism on the part of the white population was responsible for much of the problem between blacks and whites.[62] The new mayor's long range plans called for creating a "job bank" to provide permanent employment, as well as, summer jobs for people in the hard-core unemployment category. Since approximately 17 percent of people over age 16 were unemployed, D'Alesandro requested that local industry provide up to 5,000 jobs by June 1, 1968, and hoped to have at least 1,000 people employed at that time. D'Alesandro directed his city planners to determine whether decent low-cost housing for low income families could be built on vacant city lots.[63]

In order to address the dilapidated schools problem, D'Alesandro planned to spend $120 million during the next four years to build new schools. To assist police in improving community relations, he planned to open new community centers in the Cherry Hill, Pennsylvania Avenue and Greenmount Avenue areas. D'Alesandro pledged to address job discrimination by issuing executive orders for city purchasing agents to only buy products from companies that did not discriminate. Many other programs were established to terminate discrimination in business and housing markets.[64]

On Friday, April 5, the still handsome 39-year old mayor with "hair graying at the sides and a tough beard that darkens as the day grows old" had a lot on his mind. In addition to the concerns he had for his wife and children who lived in the Mount Washington section of the city, D'Alesandro realized that he was ultimately responsible for the safety and welfare of 970,000 city inhabitants and the city employees of the fire, police and public works departments. This was a full plate for the Italian-American who had stood at Baltimore's War Memorial Plaza to be sworn in as Baltimore's 42nd mayor in front of an unprecedented gathering of over 3,000 faithful supporters and VIPs. The ceremony took place on a mild and sunny December day, to the day, only four months before.[65,66]

ON FRIDAY MORNING there was a flurry of activity at the two-story dark-red brick fire station located on 3130 North Avenue in the Walbrook section of the city. The 56-year-old station, which had opened in May of 1912, was the home of Engine #20, Truck #18, Ambulance #8 and Battalion Chief #7. The firefighters assigned to the engine, a 17-year-old open-cab Ward La France, were checking out the hose, tools, appliances, and air masks, and testing the unit's engine and pump. The station's captain was reading the headlines of Baltimore's *News American* Paper, "Mayor Urges Calm—City Joins in Mourning."[67]

"It figures, Little Tommy would give everyone off in the city but us and the cops," stated the captain. But seriously, most of the firefighters didn't want to be off today. Although many of them, especially the black members assigned to the shift, were saddened by the assassination, they were somewhat filled with a mix of excitement and anxiety. It was already reported that nearby Washington was experiencing riots and fires as were a dozen other cities. If there was going to be any action in the wake of the tragedy, the firefighters didn't want to miss anything, especially 23-year-old Doug Shanks.

Shanks loved the fire department. Originally residents of west Baltimore, Doug's family moved from Baltimore to Linthicum, in Anne Arundel County south of the city near Friendship International Airport in 1956. As a teenager, Shanks became interested in firefighting and joined the Linthicum department as a volunteer. After graduating from the first senior class of Andover High School, in Linthicum in 1963, Shanks was hired as an airport firefighter at nearby Friendship (now BWI Thurgood Marshall) in 1966. At the time, Baltimore City owned the airport and as a city employee it was just a matter of transferring into the city fire department when vacancies occurred. The process was a fast track into the fire department which Shanks, among others had already followed.[68]

Assigned to Truck #18 right out of the fire academy in 1966 at a handsome salary of $7,824 a year, Shanks, was checking out an air mask and steel-encased air bottle with accompanying valves and harness, mounted to the tractor-drawn aerial ladder truck. The good-looking dark short-haired Doug was thinking about the possible fires and turmoil that the day could bring.

Truck #18, a 6-year-old Peter Pirsch-built tractor-drawn 100' aerial-equipped ladder truck was an awesome sight. As Baltimore City fire apparatus were concerned, the white with red trim painted vehicle was still considered a "newer" piece of apparatus, and Shanks was proud to be assigned to it. Since the trailer section of the unit is abnormally long, there is a seat and steering wheel located at the back of the trailer known as the "Tiller-men's" position. The steering wheel turns the rear trailer wheels to assist the unit in making tight turns in the city's narrow streets. The feature also helps the tractor driver, called the Emergency Vehicle Driver or EVD, maneuver the vehicle to spot the unit in the most advantageous position to use the ladder in a fire fighting operation.

Engine #20's first-due response area was a prime and sought after assignment for a young firefighter who desired to see a lot of action. The response area mostly residential, was filled with countless inner city row homes, small businesses, mom and pop groceries, and liquor and drug stores. Many homes, especially in the ghetto enclaves, were vacant. Throughout the city there were thousands of vacant dwellings. There was at least one working fire daily in which the engine firefighters would actually put supply hose in the street coupled to a fire hydrant, charge attack hose lines and enter a smoke filled structure.

As water under pressure filled the large supply hose attached to the fire hydrant, the men would pull the smaller attack hoselines from the engine. Equipped with heavy canvas bunker coats, aluminum helmets, gloves and ¾ rubber boots that would only protect them from getting wet up to their crotches, and with air masks and steel air bottles strapped to their backs, the firefighters entered the structures and put out the fires.

The engine firefighters were focused on maneuvering and operating hose lines with nozzle pressures of 100 pounds per square inch (psi). The truck company firefighters would search throughout the structure for victims, ladder the exterior of the building and ventilate the hot smoke from the structure by breaking out the glass in windows and/or cutting holes in the roof. Shanks would be tillering Truck #18 today, whose first due response area was much larger than Engine #20's. Many stations throughout the North Avenue corridor and West Baltimore only had one engine, so ladder trucks typically covered larger areas to provide the much needed support.

All structure responses required at least three engines, a ladder truck and a battalion chief. Unfortunately, in this segment of the city, pockets of residential areas were deteriorating with urban blight. There were many incidents of arson fires in vacant buildings. Firefighters also responded to auto fires, piles of debris fires and trash fires, and false alarms (In 1967 there was a reported average of 500 false alarms per month and since 1964, one firefighter had been killed and 19 injured responding to false alarms). This variety and frequency of fire calls kept the inner city companies extremely busy.[69,70]

APPROXIMATELY 40 MILES SOUTHWEST of Baltimore, Washington, D.C. was experiencing riots and fires on an unprecedented scale. The problems had started the night before soon after the news of Dr. King's assassination was broadcast over the television channels and radio waves. On 14th Street north of the White House at the entrance to the Southern Christian Leadership Conference (SCLC) office, small crowds of blacks began to gather. The gathering would be later described as one with a "hostile anti-white tone."[71]

Located at the office was 26-year-old civil rights activist Stokely Carmichael. Carmichael with the "startling handsome face" and green fatigue jacket, was shocked, angry and yet somewhat cautious. He knew he needed to take action, but was not really sure in what direction he should move.[72]

For the present, Carmichael, the leader, actually calmed the gathering of angry and mournful blacks and started to visit the local stores and shops near U and 14th streets to request that management close their stores in honor of the slain civil rights leader. The first store he visited was the "Peoples Drug Store" at 14th and U streets. As more crowds gathered along 14th Street, additional stores were asked, and in some cases ordered, to shut down business operations.[73]

At approximately 10 p.m., someone threw a rock through the store window of the Peoples Drug Store and like a dam bursting from the built-up pressure of a raging river, all hell broke loose. Although other SCLC workers tried to stand in the way of violence, their bold effort was futile.[74]

Large display windows were smashed up and down 14th Street as crowds broke into the stores and started looting. The previous mourning and hostility seemed to be forgotten in the now-carnival-like excitement produced by the out-of-control violence and looting.[75]

As D.C. Metro police arrived, they flailed night sticks at the law-breakers forcing them into small isolated groups where violators could be arrested or in many cases chased away. As a light rain started to fall in the area, the violence continued, and a number of incendiary fires broke out in the businesses fronting both sides of 14th Street.[76]

Around 11:30 p.m., the mild rain changed into a downpour, which actually assisted the D.C. firefighters who were trying to deal with the fires and the angry mobs. About an hour later, D.C. Fire Chief, Henry Galotta arrived at the department's headquarters and implemented the fire department's emergency response plan. Galotta ordered off-duty shifts back to work and doubled the staffing at the fire stations The fires would continue to burn for the next four hours.[77]

Down the street at the White House, President Johnson was in shock, as were many of the country's elected leaders. Although truly saddened by King's death, Johnson could not understand why blacks would turn to violence. Civil Rights legislation that he proposed was being enacted and the ink on the Kerner Commission Report was still wet. The president was numb as he searched for answers. As President Johnston, read the reports describing the violence in a number of cities and as he watched the devastation on television, he paced back and forth in the Oval Office. At midnight his aides drew his attention to the glow in the sky less than a mile away. As Johnston looked into the sky from the White House windows, one of his aides stated that the fires were out of control. Joseph Califano, Special Assistant to the President, "handed the president a report saying that militant African-American leader Stokley Carmichael was planning a march on Georgetown, home to many of the media elite LBJ [President Johnson] so distained. 'Goddamn!' the president caustically joked, 'I've waited 35 years for this day.'"[78]

On Friday morning the sun rose over partly cloudy skies in the nation's capital. Across the country there were 19 dead as a result of urban violence with Chicago being the hardest-hit city with 20 buildings burned to the ground. Presidential advisor Cyrus Vance requested 2,000 troops of the 82nd Airborne from Fort Bragg, North Carolina, who arrived at Andrews Air Force Base and were quickly sent to Washington, D.C.[79]

D.C.'s African-American Mayor Walter E. Washington, along with his aides, believed that school attendance was the key to a peaceful Friday. If the city's "150,000 pupils could be kept in classes," DC Metro Police felt they would have a chance to maintain law and order. It didn't work; principals and teachers wanted the schools closed in honor of Dr. King. Many students stayed home and of the small numbers who actually attended school that morning, the majority left. [80]

Stokely Carmichael now changed his tune as he spoke to a large number of college students at the nearby Howard University. He urged black students to take to the streets in retaliation for the assassination. He also demanded that Maryland's Governor Agnew have charges dropped against H. Rap Brown. Carmichael said, "If Agnew doesn't drop charges against Brown we will take our troops back into Maryland and turn the state upside down!" In Richmond, Virginia, H. Rap Brown was awaiting a hearing on extradition to Cambridge, Maryland, on charges of inciting a riot the previous summer.[81]

Agnew's response to King's killing and the accompanying urban violence was what anyone would expect. He said, "Words at a time like this are inadequate to express the overwhelming horror of this senseless act." However, "There is no excuse, no possible justification for this kind of violence. I condemn this action and deplore the people who resort to violence, any violence."[82]

Unfortunately the students and many other young blacks heeded Carmichael's "battle cry" and headed to the streets. By late afternoon on Friday, Washington, D.C. was in turmoil. Billows of smoke poured into the sky. Five hundred fires had been set and 200 were still burning.[83] Twenty to 30 new fires were being set per hour as "thousands of rioters continued to loot and burn at will in a mad carnival spirit."[84]

Fires burned only 10 blocks from the White House and the D.C. Fire Department was now being assisted by approximately 100 fire engines from Maryland's Montgomery and Prince George's counties as well as units from across the Potomac in Virginia. [85] Washington D.C. received the biggest outpouring of assistance since the Baltimore City Fire Department had sent 20 engines to a rash of arson lumber yard fires in the district in 1927.[86]

A small-scale riot in the city in August 1967 was actually a dress rehearsal for this major operation. As a result of the summer riots, the D.C. Fire and Metro Police departments had conducted intensive planning which produced "Plan F—Total Mobilization and Sustained Emergency Operations."[87]

In the 1960s, the D.C. Fire Department ran a "two piece" engine company fire response operation for structure fires. Each company consisted of two engine or pumper trucks. One, a single engine was loaded with extra hose and was designated the "wagon." The wagon was staffed with the responding officer and firefighters while a second engine the "pumper" was staffed with a pump/operator driver and always followed the wagon out of the fire house door. Upon arriving on the scene, the wagon would lay one or two hose lines from a hydrant to the fire. The pumper would tie or hook into the hydrant supplying the hoselines at the fireground. If necessary the wagon could lay hose back and forth from the fire and the hydrant all day or until it ran out of hose in order to meet the water supply needs of the firefighters fighting the fire.[88]

Plan F called for the department to reorganize the 32—two piece engine companies into 64 single engines enabling the department to respond to more fires. The 17 truck companies' use and response was typical to that of any other city department's and there was also reserve apparatus on hand. With the emergency reorganization of wagons and pumpers and the arrival of personnel from the off duty shifts, the department could now put 80 engines and 22 ladder trucks on the street.[89]

These plans were worth their weight in gold since at the height of activities on Friday afternoon there were over 200 fires burning simultaneously. More importantly firefighters made over 120 civilian rescues.

D.C. Metro police performed an outstanding job protecting the men fighting the blazes, and firefighters experienced very little interference from the rioters. Unfortunately for the business owners, the looters in many situations ran rampant as the police watched the backs of their brothers in the fire department. There were only nine incidents where firefighters were actually pelted with rocks and bottles. There were hundreds of firefighter injuries from the fires and from airborne projectiles, however only 24 firefighters needed to be hospitalized.[90]

D.C. Mayor Washington imposed a curfew for the second night in a row lowering the starting time to 5:30 p.m. The curfew included a ban on firearm and liquor sales. Trouble areas extended from Anacostia to within blocks of the White House.[91]

On the Prince Georges County side (Southeast) of Washington, D.C., county police officers were ordered to shoot any looters or rioters that stepped out of the city into the county. Meanwhile, the Commanding General of the Military District of Washington contacted the Maryland National Guard and requested a liaison officer be sent to the District's Operational Center in the event TASK FORCE TANGO was implemented.[92]

TASK FORCE TANGO was the code word for sending a reserve of Maryland National Guardsman to Washington, D.C. if necessary. The Task Force would consist of the lst Battalion of 115th Infantry and the 121st Engineering battalion. At 4 p.m. officers were sent to each of the Maryland National Guard headquarter stations and one enlisted man to each armory throughout the state. At 6 p.m. the TASK FORCE TANGO units were sent to nearby Washington D.C. armories in Silver Spring and Greenbelt, Maryland for drills.

The D.C. riots produced the largest series of fires since the British invaded and burned the capitol in 1814. During the three days of rioting in Washington D.C., there were a total of 1,100 fires with an estimated loss of $13.3 million. There were also 350 people injured and more than 800 arrested.

FORTY MILES TO THE NORTH IN BALTIMORE, special police details continued to patrol the Cherry Hill section of the city due to the arson attempts at the shopping center late Thursday night. OPERATION PLAN OSCAR, Baltimore's civil disturbance plan was implemented and the Operations Center activated at the Fifth Regiment Armory.

In addition Gen. Gelston ordered up the 29th Military Police Company of the Maryland National Guard to assemble at the

Pikesville Armory. Later in the evening the police company was sent to the Fifth Regiment Armory in the city to provide Task Force Security. Otherwise, compared to the rioting and burning in Washington, D.C., Baltimore was calm as the city slept peacefully for the second night.

6

Oldtown
"The Situation is Well in Hand"
Saturday, April 6, 1968

On Saturday, April 6, Baltimoreans woke to a sunny, but chilly morning. The temperature was in the 50s. The Baltimore *Sun*'s headlines reported, "19 Dead in Widespread Rioting-Sniping, Looting Erupts in D.C." Washington, D.C. was described as a "debris-strewn battlefield," while Baltimore to the north was reported as calm. The papers also stated that according to Major-General George M. Gelston, the Maryland National Guard had been ordered to a state of readiness by Governor Agnew Friday night.[1]

Sometime after midnight, fire engines and police cruisers raced to the 600 block of Pennsylvania Avenue as an attempt was made to set fire to the Penn Lumber Company. Fortunately, when the units arrived on location, they could only find a small smoldering fire. They discovered that a 22-year-old man, a former representative of the Congress of Racial Equality (CORE), a civil rights organization whose goal was to address the needs of the oppressed, had thrown a Molotov cocktail into the lumber yard. The Molotov cocktail burst into flames upon hitting a wall, but the fire only smoldered and did not spread. The subject was found, arrested and charged with attempted arson.[2]

By mid-morning young African-Americans were passing out leaflets to businesses along North and Greenmount Avenues. The leaflets stated, "THE BLACK COMMUNITY IS IN MOURNING OF THE TRAGIC LOSS OF A BROTHER,

MARTIN LUTHER KING. SHOW YOU[R] RESPECT BY CLOSING YOUR STORE AT NOON TODAY AND REMAINING CLOSED TILL MONDAY." Upon reading the leaflets and receiving bomb threats by telephone, many store owners closed their businesses.[3]

In Annapolis, Governor Agnew arrived in his office early and signed a General Assembly Emergency Act, giving him the power to impose martial law, clear the streets of traffic, prohibit sales of gasoline and alcohol, close public assemblies and taverns, and occupy or evacuate any building. With this new power, the governor declared a state of emergency and issued a curfew from 11 p.m. Saturday to 6 a.m. Sunday. As a precautionary move, the Governor ordered 6,000 Maryland National Guardsman to standby for possible deployment into the city.[4]

As Baltimore television stations broadcast an appeal for calm from Mayor Tommy D'Alesandro III, Police Chief Donald Pomerleau at police headquarters downtown reminded his officers that in the event of hostilities police officers were to use restraint. They were not to fire on escaping looters or suspected arsonists unless in self-defense.[5]

At noon, 300 mourners met on Pennsylvania Avenue for a memorial service for Dr. King. The crowd began dispersing around 2 p.m. Police reported that there were no signs of trouble.[6]

Around 4 p.m., Fire Lieutenant Robert Mueller reported for his shift at Engine Company #6's quarters located at the corner of Gay and Ensor streets in the city's "Oldtown" section. The 42-year-old, with 10 years under his belt as an officer, was regularly assigned to Engine #32, located less than a mile southwest on Gay Street near Baltimore's famous red-light district known as "The Block." But since Engine #32 was located in a double house, a single fire station that housed two companies and that included a number of company officers, Mueller was routinely detailed to Engine #6 any time its regularly assigned lieutenant took off.[7]

Mueller had been interested in being a firefighter since he was a student at the Westport Elementary School. The four-story brick school building, located on a high hill, overlooked the fire station of Engine #58 located on Annapolis Road. Anytime young Mueller saw, from his seat, the station's apparatus doors open, he immediately sprang across the room to the windows to watch Engine #58 respond to a fire. Over time, Robert's parents accumulated a drawerful of notes from the teachers requesting that he discontinue the practice since it was very disrupting to the class.

As many young men did during the early years of World War II, Mueller left high school to fight for his country. In 1943, he joined the Coast Guard and was assigned to a vessel protecting the merchant ship convoys running from Texas to Africa. Toward the end of the war, he was assigned to a Coast Guard rescue operations unit in the North Atlantic.[8]

By 1947, Mueller was hired by Baltimore City as a firefighter and assigned to Fire Boat #49 stationed at the foot of Benhill Avenue in Curtis Bay. Within a year, he would be re-assigned to Engine #38 at Baltimore Street and Fremont Avenue where he would over time respond to some of the city's worst fires.

Mueller helped fight the 12-alarm ship and pier fire at Hawkins Point along the Patapsco River involving the George Washington military transport ship that caught fire in early January 1951. The 25,000 ton ship, used to transport German prisoners back to the States during World War II, and 1,000 feet of a wooden pier were destroyed as 40-mile-per-hour winds fanned flames, tying up over 500 firefighters with 70 pieces of apparatus and four fire boats for hours. Eight workers were injured and the fire loss was estimated at $15 million.[9]

One of the most dangerous fires Mueller worked was at a storage building located at Fallsway and Monument streets. As Mueller fought the fire on the building's loading dock on a hoseline with other firefighters, the dock's roof caved in. The firefighters escaped by jumping off the dock at the last minute before tons of burning debris would bury them.

The most tragic incident Mueller remembered occurred at the Tru-Fit Clothing Store fire on Baltimore Street. On that night, he was the driver-operator on Engine #38 working off of a hydrant with the brand-new open-cab Ward La France pumper. He can still remember hearing the shouting and screams as a back wall buckled out, collapsing floors and sending the roof down on working firefighters. Six firefighters were killed and 15 injured.

Mueller stood in the overhead door opening on the Ensor Street side of the 115-year-old Engine Company #6 fire station and watched passing cars and a couple of people walking up and down the street. The Engine #6 fire station, one of the city's original volunteer fire stations, had a huge marble multi-level bell and clock tower modeled after one built by the Florentine artist, "Grotto," in Florence, Italy, in the 14th century. Mueller than took a stroll around the station. From his location in the front of the building on Gay Street, he could see the market north of his location about a block away and a number of shops up and down on both sides of Gay Street. The shopping crowd seemed typical for a Saturday afternoon.[10]

Around 5 p.m., back inside the station, Mueller relieved the day shift officer and at the watch desk, located in a corner at the front of the station, the two exchanged information. They discussed recent reports involving disorderly conduct that could negatively impact firefighting operations later that night. In addition, the two officers talked about the condition of the engine and tools, the location of closed streets and fire hydrants out of service, and the assigned firefighters who would be working that night's shift.[11]

Approximately five minutes later, as the day shift officer left for home, Mueller heard the sounds of car horns blaring from the Gay Street side of the station. He left the watch office and walked outside to get a better view. He noticed a line of cars driving off of the Orleans Street Viaduct ramp onto Gay Street. The honking horns, blaring radios, and hollers and shouts of people reminded Mueller of the city's charged atmosphere after the Baltimore Colts had won the sudden-death NFL championship against the New York Giants almost 10 years earlier.

Mueller knew very well that it wasn't football season and opening day for baseball was scheduled for the coming Tuesday. The cars were full of excited African-Americans. As Mueller observed the caravan making its way up Gay Street he noticed a couple of cars with New Jersey license plates. The loud "soul music" playing on the radio was typical for Oldtown, but the

air of palpable excitement, and the cars with out-of-state-
tags and blaring horns didn't sit right with Mueller and made
him uneasy.[12]

Already aware and on guard because of the devastating
riots in nearby Washington, D.C., Mueller called fire alarm
communications to have Battalion Chief #2 contact him as
soon as possible. When Chief Burt Bedford called the station,
Mueller reported the heightened civil activity. Bedford, who
was calling from Engine #9's fire station located on East Oliver
Street blocks north of Engine #6, stated that he would be
right over.

Immediately after hanging up the phone, Mueller and his
Engine #6 firefighters heard a roar and a crash which sounded
like an explosion. The entire crew ran over to the Gay Street
side of the station and three blocks to the north they could
see orange and red flames blowing from the broken-out main
showroom window of one of the stores. Mueller picked up the
direct phone line to fire alarm communications a second time
to report the situation and then the crew boarded Engine #6 and
headed up Gay Street to the fire.[13]

In any historical military battle, there is always an early
significant incident that stands out and constitutes the "first shot
fired." To draw an analogy between the Baltimore riots and a
battle, the "first shot fired" occurred when the huge display
window at the Sun Cleaners "exploded," shattering glass across
the sidewalk and onto the cars parked on the opposite side of
the street. It is not known what caused the explosion, but this is
what the firefighters from Engine #6 heard before they observed
the flames blowing out of one of the stores.[14]

At approximately 6:15 p.m., Engine #6, an American
La France built pumper with an enclosed cab, painted white
with red trim, made its way through congested Gay Street.
The astonished firefighters who knew very well the Oldtown
geography, the people, the building construction, the fire hazards
and the firefighting challenges were for the first time ever
responding in uncharted waters. A reckless sea of excitement
and abandonment prevailed as mobs of people heckled and
shouted catcalls and profanity at the firefighters. Men, women
and children exited stores with armfuls of cigarette cartons,

lamps, small televisions and radios. Some cars were backed up to stores loading up on looted goods.[15]

The downtown central police communications office was now receiving numerous calls from the eastside of town. There were reports of store windows being smashed and disturbances in the 400 block of North Gay Street. Engine #6's crew spotted the closest fire hydrant. The engine stopped and a crew member stepped off the back tailboard step, grabbed the hose and hydrant fitting appliance with attached wrench and wrapped the hose around the cast-iron hydrant mounted on the sidewalk. Hooking up to a fire hydrant is a one-person task; Mueller, concerned about the hostile and out-of-control crowd congregating in the area, assigned another firefighter to assist.[16]

As a youth in an orange shirt ran down Gay Street carrying a small color television under his arms, followed by a women carrying a pair of matching lamps, other engines and ladder trucks responded with Engine #6, as fire alarm dispatch acknowledged their status, which could now be heard over the engine's radio speaker.[17] When the hydrant firefighters waved the engine to move up the street toward the fire, Mueller heard more radio traffic as dispatch acknowledged engines on the west side of town that were responding to a fire bombing at a vacant dwelling at 1002 West Baltimore Street near the Hollins Market area.[18]

While the larger supply hose slid out of the large hose-bed in the back of Engine #6 and fell into the street, Mueller's driver-operator maneuvered the engine up Gay Street. Police could be seen struggling to disperse a disorderly and angry crowd of approximately 200 as they broke store windows throughout the 400 and 500 blocks.[19,20] Now up and down Oldtown's Gay Street "ghetto" corridor police radios chattered that "all [police] officers assigned to the Central District are ordered to their post." [21]

The Sun Cleaners located near the burning store was filled with looters. Young teenagers and a few adults ran out of the front doors with bundles of clothes on hangers covered in plastic wrap. Some of these bundles were thrown in cars, some were lifted on the looters' shoulders and carried home, and many were just left on the sidewalk or in the street as more lucrative opportunities arose.

With the uncharged supply hose lying in the street, Mueller pointed out a good location to the driver-operator that would place the engine in close proximately to the fire and also allow the ladder truck access to the front of the building. Just as importantly, Mueller's location would spare the engine in the event of a building collapse.[22]

As the driver-operator positioned the engine along the 700 block of Gay Street, Mueller sized up the situation. He could now make out the metal red sign with white lettering hanging over the sidewalk, partially obscured by the heavy brown-colored smoke: "IDEAL FURNITURE DEPARTMENT STORE/ NORGE APPLIANCES/ EASY TERMS"[23]

Mueller saw that there was a tremendous amount of fire, but that the main body was located in the front portion of the one-story brick building. He picked up the engine's radio microphone and reported the fire's location and status to fire alarm communications. His peripheral vision picked up the Battalion Chief #2 vehicle swinging around the corner on the north side of his location. Seeing his battalion chief on location brought Mueller some comfort as Chief Burt Bedford called for a second alarm to bring in additional firefighters and apparatus.

Now out of the engine's cab and standing on the debris-littered sidewalk, Mueller pulled up his turnout coat collar, pulled down his helmet ear flaps and pulled gloves over his hands. The firefighters were already in position in front of the building. They called out to Engine #6's driver-operator, "Charge the line!" Mueller decided to look for a way into the store to cut the fire off and quickly communicated his idea to Chief Bedford who was now standing in Gay Street next to Engine #6. Bedford was directing other units via Engine #6's radio while simultaneously putting on his helmet and heavy white protective turnout coat.[24]

A "swish" was heard as the attack hose line exhausted itself of air and coiled like a snake as the water and pressure gushed through it. Mueller became more assured as he saw the powerful spray of water backed by 100 pounds of pressure hit the flames and heard the pops and sounds the water made as the hose stream hit hot glass and water turned to steam. The heavy cotton double-layered hose supply line in the street was now getting hard as it filled with the needed water from the opened fire hydrant. The initial engine company set-up was complete. Mueller now focused his attention on fire attack with his crew while Chief Bedford managed the overall scene.

When Mueller's regular Engine #32 crew of four firefighters arrived on location, crew members pulled the 200 feet of large pre-connected 2½-inch fire hose off the back hose bed of Engine #6. Mueller knew the capabilities of the crew members very well and joined them as they entered the fire-and smoke-filled building to cut off the fire.[25]

The hostile crowds were now growing larger along Gay Street as Mueller and Engine #32's crew moved the hose line through the store. In order to bring about a successful outcome to this incident, Mueller knew the importance of getting the charged hose-line between the fire and the unburned portion of the building. Not having taken the extra minute necessary to don their protective self-contained breathing apparatus, the firefighters were now coughing from the wretched smoke as they crawled along the floor next to a wall.

The store's sale items—sofas, overstuffed chairs, tables, carpet—were blazing along with the combustible ceiling tile as thick brown smoke rolled off the ceiling and down onto the firefighters. The Engine #32 crew members could hardly see, but they could hear the truck company firefighters now on the roof operating the carbon-tip blade gasoline-powered circular saws to make ventilation openings. Mueller and crew members knew that in a few minutes these openings would exhaust the hot smoke and dangerous gases and visibility would improve. Finally the Engine #32 crew members opened up the nozzle and worked the powerful fog stream on the fire—they were doing what they did best.[26]

Battalion Chief Bedford directed fire crews from other arriving companies to enter the adjacent businesses to check for fire extension. One business, the "Launderama," a self-service laundry, was also burning. As engine and ladder trucks attempted to access the fireground, the intersection at Gay and Monument Streets looked like one huge combination flea market and yard sale as hundreds stole, destroyed, celebrated and laughed in the faces of city police who at the moment were powerless to do anything.[27]

As more police officers arrived, they started working in teams of three to move out the rioters. Some policemen were now wearing protective riot gear and were pelted with stones and bottles as they exerted a tremendous effort to seal off the wrecked and debris-strewn corridor between the 400 and 700 blocks of Gay Street. They decided that the best tactic to apply to move out the rioters was to slowly drive into the unruly out-of-control crowd with their patrol cars.[28]

While police and firefighters struggled with threatening and arrogant rioters, flames were leaping out of the broken display window at the nearby Lewis Furniture Store. Within 10 minutes this building would also require two alarms of firefighting equipment to bring the fire under control.[29]

In the street, all anyone could hear was the sound of sirens, fire engine air horns, breaking glass, and radio traffic chatter on the fire and police radios as other nearby areas fell into chaos. At 6:38 p.m., Police Chief Pomerleau ordered Phase Four of the mobilization plan put into effect and the National Guard was called in for deployment four minutes later. Another call went out at 6:44 p.m. for all off-duty police personnel to report to their respective districts and divisions.[30] Canine units were requested to be sent downtown to protect the business areas.

James H. Bready, a *Sun* editorial writer, "saw kids racing along the sidewalk carrying burning torches on East North Avenue. Several buildings were already blazing." South on Harford Avenue, not far from the havoc on Gay Street, a large dry-cleaning plant was already in flames and would be remembered as one of the worst fires of the night. The incident would eventually be surrounded by three alarms of firefighting equipment, but for now there were no police or firefighters in sight—"all of this in daylight!"[31]

Maryland National Guard Gen. Gelston, now located in his office at the Fifth Regiment Armory, a large three-story stone building bordered by Howard, Hoffman and Preston Streets, contacted his communications officer and ordered "Scramble Oscar." Oscar was the code name for the city's plan to counter racial disorders. In the order "Scramble," all 8,000 Maryland Guardsman living throughout the state were ordered through telephone calls to report to their assigned local armories.[32]

Feelings of fear and uncertainty prevailed among the firefighters and police officers as darkness replaced the fading rays from Baltimore's setting sun. The firefighters, working on the roof of the now-burned-out and steaming Ideal Furniture Store, looked south across and above the rooftops stepping down Gay Street. They could barely make out the upper portion of the historic 234-foot-high dark-red-brick Shot Tower through the haze and columns of smoke.[33] The free-standing tower, built in 1828 for the manufacturing of pistol and cannon balls, almost looked like a castle tower appearing through the smoke in a medieval battle. It was all very strange and unnerving. What would happen next?

At approximately 6:34 p.m., due to the setting sun and the plumes of dark smoke permeating Baltimore's evening sky, daylight came to an end. As twilight set in, the violence in the streets multiplied. By 6:45 p.m., fires were set along a 10-block stretch of Aisquith Street between Baltimore and Chase streets. Numerous stores and dwellings were burning.[34]

All throughout the Baltimore Metropolitan Area phone lines were strained as calls were made to summon fire, police, and guardsmen back to work. One city police officer, who was with his wife enjoying a hearty meal at the Cheshire Inn on Pulaski Highway, just outside the city limits, was notified by the inn's management that the officer's son had called the restaurant and wanted his dad to call home right away. The officer called his 16-year-old son, who was at their home near Catonsville watching his younger sister. "Dad, the police department just called and you are being ordered back to work because riots have broken out in the city," his son told him.[35]

The officer then called his supervisor at police headquarters and stated that he didn't think he should report to duty because he was out having dinner and had been drinking. The supervisor said, "Come on in anyway—when you see all the hell that has broken loose you will sober up real quick!" The police officer drove his wife home, went downtown and reported to work and didn't leave for two days.[36]

On Gay Street, Lieutenant Mueller and firefighters were relieved by a fresh crew. When Mueller accompanied his crew outside in the fresh air, they observed more stores burning up and down the corridor while heavy smoke continued to darken the early evening sky. What they couldn't see was how the violence was quickly spreading northward up Gay Street, extending out in the shape of a "Y" with the left branch running up Greenmount Avenue and the right up Harford Avenue extending to North Avenue by 7 p.m.[37]

During this time period, a 37-year-old-mother of eight was washing clothes in a coin-operated laundry on Gay Street when a rioter threw a Molotov cocktail through the plate-glass window. When the mother realized what was going on and the danger she was in, she picked up her young daughter, quickly left the building, and just "narrowly escaped the flames."[38]

D'Alesandro and Pomerleau in contact with Governor Agnew in Annapolis via a direct phone line at the police command post put their heads together and decided to implement preventive measures that would hopefully put an end to or slow down the violence. They announced that a curfew would be implemented and enforced starting at 11 p.m. and continue on through 6 a.m. Sunday. Immediately a ban was placed on the sale of alcohol, flammables sold in containers, and firearms. As more police officers reported in for duty a police field command post was set up at the Bel Air Market on Harford Avenue.[39]

As the curfew and bans were broadcast over local television and radio stations, approximately 6,000 Maryland National Guard troops entered the city under the command of Gen. Gelston. The City Police headquarters located at East Fayette Street looked like a fortress as shotgun-carrying police officers ringed and guarded the building.[40]

At the fire department fire alarm center, located on the second floor of fire department headquarters on East Lexington Street the dispatchers were inundated with calls. Extra personnel were ordered in to take calls and keep track of the massive amount of equipment now on the street responding to fires. A fire department command center was also set up in the fire alarm center. In the command center Chief Killen and deputy chiefs Frank Trenner, Edward Schneider and Fire Alarm Battalion Chief Francis Webster sat around a table studying the situation at the strategic level and attempted to address a multitude of issues.[41]

As the chiefs in the command center kept a pulse on fire-related activity, engines were sent to the 900 block of East Eager Street to a store set on fire when someone threw a gasoline-soaked flaming broom through the front door of the business. The first death in the chaos was reported when a black man was shot and killed at a bar on Harford Avenue near Lafayette Avenue, although it was not clearly established whether the incident was related to the riots.[42]

At Broadway and Monument Street the Johns Hopkins Hospital, with its red-brick multi-storied buildings trimmed with Cheat River blue sandstone and the facility's administration building, with its Queen-Anne-style dome, looked very out of place surrounded by the drab row homes of the city's poor. The world-renowned hospital was opened in 1889 with money bequeathed by philanthropist Johns Hopkins. Hopkins, born in Maryland's Anne Arundel County Whitehall area, grew up in Baltimore and became a successful businessman and investor as well as an abolitionist.[43]

Now through the big windows in the well-lighted building one could see a beehive of activity as doctors, nurses and orderlies treated the numerous injured who walked through the main entrance in droves or arrived by ambulance or car at the emergency room. The hospital was so busy providing medical care that the emergency room's status was upgraded to a "Code Yellow" (prepare for multi-trauma cases). Hospital management requested that the staff stay on duty throughout the night as patients filed in with bloody noses, lacerations, and other wounds.[44]

Approximately eight blocks north of the hospital on Federal Street, was the location of the only multiple-victim tragedy of the riots as the violence and fires spread throughout the city.

Outside Gabriel's Spaghetti House in the 2000 block of Federal Street near Chester and Gay streets, a loud raucous crowd of at least 75 gathered. Some were shouting, "We're coming in to kill you." The frightened owner, Mrs. Mamie Gabriel, was inside with her bartender and two customers, a married couple by the name of Albrecht who lived on Broadway in Fells

Point—all of which were white.[45] Before too long the front windows of Gabriel's Spaghetti House were broken out. Two would-be looters, an 18-year-old and a 20-year-old, entered the establishment through these openings. The two trespassers were about 15 feet inside the restaurant when the bartender started shooting, killing one and wounding the other in the shoulder. The wounded man made his escape back through one of the broken windows. Moments later, two fire bombs were tossed in through the window opening, setting the interior ablaze. Mr. Albrecht ran to the second floor while the bartender and the two women fled through the back door.[46]

Jerry Alfinito remembered the Spaghetti House fire well. At the time he was assigned as a firefighter with Engine #26 located on the corner of West and Leadenhall Streets in South Baltimore near Hanover Street. The 32-year-old-Alfinito, who grew up in South Baltimore, joined the fire department in 1959 after a three-year stint with an Army artillery communications unit stationed in Munich, Germany.[47]

Aflinito was working his regular shift that night when the violence broke out. As building fires were occurring throughout the Gay Street, Harford Avenue and Greenmount Avenue corridors, Engine #26 was transferred to the empty quarters of Engine #25 at the corner of McCulloh and Gold Streets a couple of blocks off West North Avenue. "No sooner then we backed the engine into Engine #25's quarters, we were dispatched to the Spaghetti House fire," recalled Alfinito.[48]

When firefighters arrived at the restaurant fire, they knocked down the main body of the fire with their attack hose lines. As they searched the first floor fire area and performed overhaul, they found one body. Extending their operations to the second floor apartment area, firefighters continued their search and simultaneously checked for any extension of fire. As they pulled down plaster and lath ceilings and opened up walls they found Mr. Albrecht on the floor burned to death.[49]

As soon as the white-shirt-and blue-pants uniformed city police cordoned off one section of the streets, the multiplying crowds would move up or down the street to another section. At 7:15 p.m., about 50 youths tore down the protective iron gratings of a discount furniture and appliance store in the 900 block of North Gay Street. Once the iron security gratings were removed and the glass was broken from the windows, the kids moved in and looted and ravaged the business that had been serving the community for decades.[50]

Outbreaks were now occurring almost systematically throughout the city. Police and security guards dispersed a crowd of young boys causing a disturbance at the Mondawmin Mall. The three-story retail shopping mall containing approximately 100 stores built in 1955 by Baltimore developer James Rouse is located at Liberty Heights Avenue and Gwynns Falls Parkway.[51]

Built across the parkway from Frederick Douglas High School, Mondawmin Mall was the first-open air mall in the city. It was entirely enclosed in 1963. The mall was anchored by the Sears-Roebuck Company and the Penn Fruit grocery stores. The complex would be heavily protected by law enforcement in the following days. Also, crowds were now gathering in the area of Harford Road and North Avenue and moving south toward the troubled areas and west towards unsuspecting businesses and stores.[52]

Twenty-three-year-old *News American* reporter Larry Carson remembered walking up Gay Street past the burning store fronts. He watched looters take suitcases from a broken display window of a pawn shop. Since the young bold reporter was wearing a white shirt with tie and a sports coat and had his hair cut short, he believed the rioters thought he was a city police detective and didn't bother him. He would later state, "They didn't give me a second thought!"[53]

Moving among the crowds and the police officers, Carson was privy to a number of police officer discussions as they forced away or apprehended rioters on Gay Street. Carson remembered overhearing several officers lamenting "that since the new emphasis was on civil rights they had to arrest suspects instead of taking them around the corner and giving them a beating." Later, while Carson was standing in the street, a black man passed by him and said, "It was a shame what [was] happening all around us."[54]

Sadly, the majority on the streets were not ashamed as they smashed windows and looted stores on Greenmount Avenue between Lanvale and Madison streets.[55] At around 7:23 p.m., reports surface concerning an old 2½ ton surplus army truck driving in the area of Chase and Eager streets carrying persons throwing rocks. Police who were normally assigned to other districts of the city and unfamiliar with "Oldtown" arrived and couldn't believe their eyes as they witnessed the mayhem for the first time.

As on Gay Street earlier, the mayhem promoted a carnival-like atmosphere along Harford, Greenmount and North avenues. It was as if it were the "greatest sale of all time." Each area of the rioting seemed to follow a step-by-step pattern. Initially there was little violence, as crowds of men, women and children laughed and talked as if they had been just introduced to a "new fun pastime." People were jovial as they walked in and out of stores with their arms loaded with stolen goods. They would carry as much "booty" as they could easily pick up and hold on to—floor and table lamps, coffee tables, radios and small television sets. Eventually, strong men would be seen carrying large cushioned easy chairs. Later, looters would pull their cars up to the curb for easy loading "as clerks, managers and owners stood there dumbfounded and helpless."[56]

By 7:30 p.m., the new "fun pastime" atmosphere was subsiding. Three major outbreaks of violence occurred as stores were looted and fire bombed in the 1600 to 1800 blocks of Harford Avenue between North Avenue and Hoffman Street.[57]

It was becoming more and more obvious that Baltimore's firefighters were no longer the good guys in the eyes of the city's out-of-control black youth and young adults. "Firefighters once the champions of the poor; they were the least likely object of civilian indignation. They have [now] become a ready target for the venting of discontent of disadvantaged persons."[58]

Unfortunately, this would not be the first time Baltimore firefighters would be subject to such disrespect. Five years earlier, on a hot humid Saturday night in September of 1963 as firefighters battled a six-alarm fire at the Walbrook Mill and Lumber Company at 2600 West North Avenue, a number of blacks "amused themselves by throwing bottles and rocks at firefighters and police officers, injuring four men."[59]

At the city command post on the fifth floor of police headquarters, Mayor D'Alesandro received a phone call from Parren J. Mitchell, the city's African-American director of the

Community Action Agency and a future U.S. Congressman. Mitchell suggested that the mayor should make a public appeal through the media and public address systems for civilians to "clear the streets." However the mayor's staff recommended postponing the announcement.[60]

Baltimore Police requested assistance from the Maryland State Police (MSP) who set up a command post at the state office building on Preston Street near Howard Street. MSP Colonel Robert J. Lally, Superintendent, who retired as Baltimore County's police chief and had less than two years on the job, arrived shortly afterwards to head the command post. Within half an hour, 300 to 400 troopers were staging at the state office complex. Thirty-five troopers were assigned to guard the office building. The state police officers were placed under the command of City Police Commissioner Donald Pomerleau.[61, 62]

Within time MSP troopers would be deployed as follows: 92 to Greenmount Avenue and 25th Street, 75 to Milton Avenue and President Street, 50 to North Avenue between Greenmount Avenue and Howard Street and 50 positioned throughout Park Circle and along Park Heights Avenue. By 11:35 p.m., 40 more troopers would be assigned to Baltimore's department store complex in the area of Howard and Lexington streets.[63]

At 7:45 p.m. the Baltimore City Police Department realized that it was increasingly losing control. The police did not have enough manpower to guard every store in the area, as rioters used quick hit-and-run tactics. Rocks were being hurled at moving cars on Harford Road damaging windshields and headlights.[64] Sniper gunshot was reported in the 4300 block of Park Heights and North avenues, and large crowds were still being reported throughout the Gay Street corridor.[65]

Although city officials had been making statements all evening to the Governor's aides that the "situation was well in hand," Agnew was not buying it.[66] At 8 p.m. the Governor contacted Major General Gelston to find out when the National Guard would be ready for deployment. The general reminded the Governor that the troops were on their way, but would not be able to be deployed to the streets before 10 p.m.[67]

No business escaped the wrath of the violence. At about 8:05 p.m., a tailor shop was looted and set on fire in the 900 block of North Gay Street. Many of the looters were the youths who ransacked a nearby discount furniture and appliance store only an hour before.[68] Reports were coming in for incidents north of North Avenue and fire engines were dispatched to a building fire reported at 2300 Greenmount Avenue as a second tailor shop burned. Ten structure fires were now burning up and down Greenmount Avenue.[69]

The city's "white" East Baltimore had been alerted to the trouble and citizens there decided to confront the looters and rioters. At about 8:20 p.m. a group of 20 white men gathered on East Baltimore Street between Calvert and Saint Paul Streets. To avert trouble, police dispersed the group.[70] Twenty-five minutes later, Gene Noble of the Community Relations commission was asked to organize the black clergy, who had volunteered their services, to intervene in calming down the crowds on Gay Street.[71]

At 8:45 p.m., Fire Alarm Dispatch sent engines and ladder trucks from across the city to a burning A&P (Atlantic and Pacific) grocery store. The store, just one in a chain of thousands throughout the nation was located in the 1400 block of North Milton Avenue in East Baltimore. The business was looted before it was torched. Engines that had been sent to fill empty stations or dispatched to what were assumed to be less-threatening fires were radioed to cancel their assignments and respond to North Milton Avenue. The A&P and three adjacent stores was the worst fire to be reported yet.[72]

The unprecedented number of fires, the endless looting, the many unruly crowds, the lack of police presence and the limited power of the officers who did manage to show up was like nothing Lieutenant Mueller had witnessed in his 21-year career with the city fire department. It now dawned on him that this could be a nationwide civil war. Up until now he was only focused on the safety of his crew and on assisting crews, but what was happening at home?[73]

Mueller lived in the community of Brooklyn Park very close to the city line. Were unruly crowds of African-Americans attacking his neighborhood? Were his wife and three young sons safe? For firefighters and police officers working on the Gay Street fires that were now extending up Greenmount Avenue to North Avenue and breaking out in other pockets of the city, the thought of what might be happening at their homes and to their families was now an additional weight on them.[74] However, for most firefighters the emotional side of the incident was cast aside, if only temporarily to focus on the problem at hand.

During the few pauses and breaks in between fire calls, firefighters and police would secure coin-operated phone booths that hadn't been destroyed and make calls to their homes. A system of backdoor personnel communications started to shape up to keep firefighters in the fight aware of what was happening with loved ones, so they could focus on their jobs.

In the fire stations, either occupied by fill-in crews or crews that were called back to work, phones were ringing off the hook. The families of the firefighters on duty were calling in to check on the welfare of loved-ones. On the phone, the on-duty crew would ask family members about their safety and if they needed anything. To reduce the number of calls coming into the station, a couple of families were requested to serve as "clearing houses" for the other on-duty firefighter's families. They would call the families to determine their welfare and to share information on the status of the firefighters. As family information was phoned back to the station, it was relayed to members on the fire ground by relief crews or crews staffing ambulances.[75]

Fire department ambulances that were not committed to attending the injured were now the lifeline of information and supplies to firefighters on the front lines. Most firefighters and police officers who reported in for the evening shift Saturday had not had dinner. Now, as fire after fire erupted in the city many hungry, weary, and worried firefighters depended on the ambulance crews for news from home and a half of a baloney-and-cheese sandwich or a honey dipped-donut.[76]

By mid-evening, most of the other engine and truck companies assisting on the furniture store fires on Gay Street had re-racked their hose lines, packed up, and been sent to other fires and assignments. With the blackened furniture store emitting steam and a light haze behind them, Engine #6 with Mueller and his tired crew on board headed to Greenmount Avenue.[77]

7

Greenmount Avenue
"Put Out and Get Out"
Saturday Evening, April 6, 1968

Greenmount Avenue is the west border of one of Baltimore's largest cemeteries, the Greenmount Cemetery. The cemetery is bordered on the north by North Avenue, on the east by Esnor Street and on the south by Hoffman Street. An area the size of approximately 40 square blocks contains the graves of some of the nation's best and worst.

Among the tens of thousands buried there are numerous political and business leaders: philanthropists Johns Hopkins and Enoch Pratt, 10 U.S. senators and congressmen, nine governors, and several attorney generals and Medal of Honor recipients. Also, buried there is Isaac R. Trimble, a famous Maryland Confederate general in the Civil War who lost a leg at the battle of Gettysburg and also built the President Street train station when he was a superintendent for the railroad before the war. Lastly, the cemetery contains the graves of John Wilkes Booth and two other conspirators in the assassination of President Abraham Lincoln.[1]

As Engine #6 made its way up Greenmount Avenue past the historical cemetery, the turmoil and damage "seemed like a summer television rerun" of what they had just experienced on Gay Street.[2] A corner mom-and-pop grocery store exploded into flames as Mueller and crew passed by. So many fires were occurring on Greenmount Avenue that as engine companies snuffed out one structure fire, firefighters just moved their attack hose lines to the next fire on the same block or added more sections of hose and dragged the lines and equipment to the fire across the street. The engines were never relocated. It was unlike anything ever witnessed before in the city's firefighting history.

By the time the off-duty shift had been called back to work, many firefighters had already had a difficult time reporting to their stations because of roadblocks and detours set up by police or because the streets were taken over by unruly crowds. In stations that contained "second line" fire apparatus, the off-duty shift personnel reporting in placed the units in service. Now with the off-duty battalion and division chiefs ordered in, the battalions were divided into smaller, more manageable geographical subdivisions in order to improve fire ground safety and efficiency and to enhance incident command and control.[3]

Although there were now 1,200 to 1,500 police officers working the disorders throughout east Baltimore, the violence continued to escalate. By 9:30 p.m., the blazing A&P located on North Milton Avenue, along with nearby stores, had reached four alarms of firefighting apparatus and equipment. Crowds of youths, young adults and elderly people, looking on curiously, hindered the movement and placement of emergency apparatus. Some onlookers threw stones and bottles at the firefighters. Police officers responding to protect the firefighters needed to be diverted some seven blocks to the south, as the Levinson and Klein furniture store located at Monument and Chester Streets was being looted.[4]

At 8:55 p.m., the Army surplus truck, reported earlier to be full of rioters throwing rocks and debris up and down city streets was finally intercepted and stopped by a city police detective at Madison and Forrest streets. Six rioters were ordered off the truck and arrested. At 9:15 p.m., rioters threatened to move northward up Harford Road and a structure was burning out of control in the 4700 block of Park Heights Avenue.[5]

Governor Agnew stated at a press conference that the situation was under control. However, with that said, Agnew didn't really believe it to be true.[6] Although Police Chief Pomerleau had advised the governor that nothing would get out of hand and the earlier declaration of emergency had been just a "precautionary measure," Agnew thought otherwise.

In addition to the field command post set up near the Bel Air Market, the city police had set up two additional field command posts by 9:30 p.m., one at Gay and Aisquith streets in the heart of the violence, as rioters nearby had chanted, "We shall overcome." The second post was established at Park Circle on the west side of the city as a precautionary measure, since earlier in the day there were a few scattered incidents reported in the area.[7]

At the command post, a police commander would dictate the law enforcement strategy and tactics to be used to clear the streets. He would also devise methods to apprehend rioters creating the biggest problems and determine measures to protect the firefighters. As additional officers arrived, the commander would stage them temporarily and deploy them to the trouble spots. The command post also provided a location to load up the paddy wagons with rioters that were arrested.[8]

A pair of fatalities was reported during a 30-minute period. One, the second murder of the night, occurred at the Lucas Tavern in the 400 block of North Carey Street on the west side of the city. The victim was a 37-year old man who was shot in the head. It was uncertain if the killing was related to the riots or not. The man died upon arrival at Johns Hopkins Hospital at 9:30 p.m.[9]

The second fatality was the result of a vehicular accident. A 20-year old woman, Lois T. Majette, was a passenger in a car driven by her husband that accidentally crashed into the side of a city police cruiser. The accident occurred at the intersection of North Avenue and Barclay Street.[10]

Engine #24 arrived in the 1900 block of Greenmount Avenue in front of a blazing three-story house with an attached store. It was 9:35 p.m. Over the past three hours the weary four-person crew had worked its way to this block, fire by fire, beginning with the original call to the Ideal Furniture Store fire on Gay Street. Crew members were now some 40-plus blocks away from their station house, at Patterson Park Avenue near Fayette Street, where they had begun this marathon earlier in the evening.

Throughout the city, rocks, bottles and debris were thrown at busy firefighters as they worked the scenes or when they arrived seated or standing on the tail boards on their fire engines. At times the firefighters would motion as if they were going to chase the rioters or throw a tool at them. When threatened, the rioters, mostly kids, ran away, only to regroup a block away and typically return in greater numbers. On Greenmount Avenue, projectiles flew through the air until the police arrived. Police received additional reports of rock throwing throughout 14 blocks of Gay Street between Orleans and Chase Streets.[11]

The crew of Engine #24 laid out a supply line hose from a hydrant located on a corner at Greenmount and North avenues. The driver-operator disconnected the hose line from the hose bed in the rear of the 24-year-old Mack open cab pumper. As he placed the end of the hose line into the inlet coupling located on the driver's side of the engine, he looked up at the west side of the block. From his position, he watched in fascination as a young rioter threw a Molotov cocktail into a store just north of Engine #24's location. As the driver-operator made the connection he waved to the two firefighters standing at the hydrant to open the fire hydrant and charge the supply line. The large supply hose line, laying in a zigzag fashion in the street, briefly snarled and jumped an inch in the air as water forced by 80 pounds of pressure quickly snaked its way through the now-hardened hose line to Engine #24's 1000-gallon-per-minute pump. People standing nearby could hear the sound of the "Mack's" engine roaring as the driver-operator throttled up the pump to increase the pressure and opened the gate valve to allow the water to flow into the attack line.

For the firefighters inside the building who were responsible for getting the water on the fire, the sound of the water and pressure making its way through their attack line was very reassuring. To cut the fire off, the firefighters, working as a team pulled the now-charged line up an enclosed stairway separate from the store but near the blazing store's display window. They attacked the fire now appearing from a second-floor window over the store's front door.

The half-exhausted crew members, who were now on the second floor, crawled on the floor down the hallway to the front room. The nozzle-man directed the nozzle into the front room which was now burning fiercely, and pulled back on the nozzle's control handle with his gloved hand. The pressure in the hose kicked back at the crew as a powerful 100-pound narrow fog pattern of water shot out and within seconds blackened the fire. The men were not wearing any air masks and when the hot steam banked down on top of them, those who had not pulled their helmet ear flaps down and their heavy coat collars up felt a stinging pain on the tops of their ears.

The engine is the work horse of a firefighting operation. Once it secures a water source from a hydrant, a hose wagon or another pumper, it can drop an additional line or two lines simultaneously to the fire. The more supply hose lines connected to it, the more water the engine can pump. It's the crew's job to get water onto the fire. Fire crews can operate hand lines of 1½ and 2½ inches in diameter to deliver up to 250 gallons of water per minute or they can employ the cannon-like deluge gun located and mounted on top of the vehicle, behind the cab in front of the hose bed, to flow 500 to 800 gallons per minute.

If a ladder truck is not on the scene, the engine company does have either a 24-foot or 35-foot extension ladder that can be used to make a rescue from an upper-story window. Otherwise the firefighting crews concentrate on putting out the flames.

An assortment of tools are carried on the engine in small compartments or mounted on the vehicle—an axe, pike poles (a long wooden or fiberglass pole with a steel hook on one end for pulling ceilings and walls down), pry bars, and a haligan forcible entry tool (a steel tool about three feet long with a heavy duty claw on one end and a pry fork on the other). The "Baltimore Basket," a large metal box resembling a "horse trough," hung lengthwise over a portion of the hose bed to carry buckets, tools, salvage covers and rope. A fire extinguisher is mounted to a step alongside the engine or on the tailboard to extinguish small flammable liquid fires or fires involving energized electrical equipment.

Engines are also equipped with Self-Contained Breathing Apparatus (SCBA) air mask that are stowed in compartments or covered and mounted to walls on the side of the engine. The apparatus are enclosed in wide yellow rubber/plastic bags with zippers running vertically along their length. Inside is the

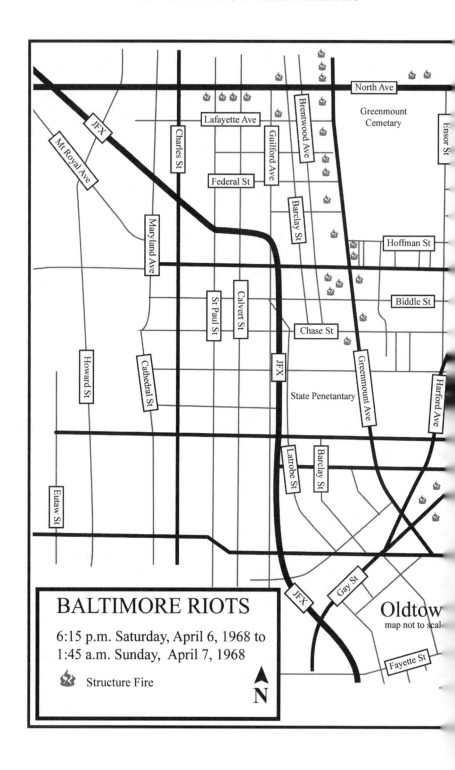

BALTIMORE RIOTS

6:15 p.m. Saturday, April 6, 1968 to
1:45 a.m. Sunday, April 7, 1968

Structure Fire

N

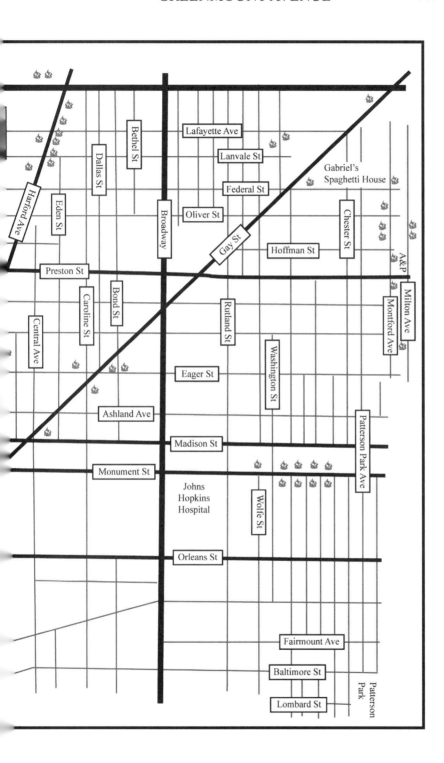

SCBA apparatus with a rubber face piece, attached air regulator and heavy steel bottle connected to a metal back plate with shoulder straps. The SCBA will typically provide a firefighter with approximately 30 minutes of fresh air.

However, on this fire, SCBAs are not being used. Either the firefighters didn't have the time to put them on or their yellow-painted air bottles were empty from the evening's previous fires.

As two other engines and a ladder truck appeared, the captain sent them up the street to the other fires. In the course of three minutes, there were two stores and a tailor shop burning in the 1900 to 2300 blocks of Greenmount Avenue, while two other stores burned below the North Avenue intersection in the 1200 block.[12]

As the crew of Truck #16 from the Calvert Street fire house stood on the roof of the store in the 2300 block of Greenmount Avenue they saw a huge glow in the sky to their east. A warehouse on the corner of Federal Street and Milton Avenue was burning. The call for the warehouse fire that had gone out at 9:33 p.m. was now three alarms and the fourth had just been requested over the radio by the battalion chief in-charge.[13]

An "alarm" consists of three to four engines and one to two ladder trucks. The system dates back to the late 1850s when there were no telephones or radios. A "run card" is assigned to each fire alarm pull station throughout the city. The run card lists the responding companies on each alarm depending on the particular company's fire station distance from the alarm box location (see Appendix B).

Alarm boxes installed throughout the busy Howard Street shopping district would have four engines and two ladder trucks assigned for each alarm. For alarm boxes located along a block of row homes on Eastern Avenue the assignment would be three engines and a ladder truck.

The companies assigned are the closest (by street mileage) to the box. If an officer arrives on the scene and needs additional apparatus, he requests, via radio, a Second Alarm and the next closest three engines and ladder truck are dispatched to respond. On the run card used at the communications center, notably known as "fire alarm," every company throughout the city is listed according to its proximity to the street box. If a call is received by a fire alarm operator at central fire alarm on Lexington Street by telephone, then operators look up the closest street intersection to the alarm box and pull out the corresponding run card.

At Federal Street and Milton Avenue the huge multi-story warehouse continued to burn. On the side of the building where the fire was most threatening to other businesses or homes, three ladder trucks were operating as water towers. Huge white streams of water were cascading from these giant 50-foot towers by ladder-mounted deluge gun nozzles delivering 500 to 600 gallons per minute forced out by 50 to 80 pounds of pressure.[14]

The towers' main objective was to create a wall of water between the heavy fire and any valuable exposures while occasionally turning to assist in the extinguishment of the fire. It was these large building fires for which the large diameter deluge nozzles mounted on top of the engines and attached to the aerial ladders were created.

In water tower operations, the aerial ladder attached to the turntable is typically extended to 50 feet in height and angled slightly towards the fire. When delivering large volumes of water from an aerial ladder, the higher and greater the slope or angle of the ladder to the ground from an upright position (90 degree angle), the more dangerous the operation. Under high pressures and with large volumes of flowing water, the aerial ladder, at unsafe heights and angles, could twist, snap, fall to the ground, and kill or injure firefighters.

Usually, a firefighter is assigned and secured to the tip of an aerial ladder to control and direct the stream, but not tonight. A firefighter attached to the end of a ladder would be an easy target for a sniper. Tonight all ladder pipe operations would be conducted from the ground using ropes to raise or lower the nozzle tip.

Most ladder trucks carry a heavy 100-foot metal three-section extension aerial ladder. The ladder is mounted flat in the bed of a long trailer pulled by a tractor. Ladders in smaller sizes of 65 to 85 feet are mounted on trucks with a straight chassis and no trailer is needed. The tractor-drawn aerials also have a steering wheel in the back of the trailer called a "tiller," so a second driver or "tillerman" can manuever the rear wheels of the trailer around the tight corners of city streets or assist in the positioning of the truck for water tower or general aerial operations.

On the leather helmet shield that is inserted at the front of a firefighting helmet the company number is attached, e.g., 5, 6, 24, or 27. On the shields of firefighters assigned to truck companies there is also a display of a pike pole (or hook) and a ladder crossed underneath the number and extending out past all four corners beyond the number. This display is also known as a hook and ladder. Since truck company firefighters wearing the "hook and ladder" symbol on their shields arrived on the scene on tractor-drawn aerials, the trucks were misnamed "hook and ladders" by the public.

A water tower operation is one of a number of functions carried out by truck companies, but their number one priority is to rescue people. The 85-foot to 100-foot aerial ladders provide quick access to people trapped in upper stories and on roofs of buildings. The truck company's second priority is to provide ventilation for the firefighters working inside a structure. This is usually accomplished by breaking windows in the upper stories or by cutting large holes in roofs for smoke and heat release.

At times the smoke is so thick and dark the crews cannot see their hands in front of their faces, which makes ventilation paramount. Truck companies that properly ventilate a building can significantly improve conditions for crews operating in the interior.

As truck company members crawl through the heat and smoke in a building, searching for victims, the engine company crews follow, dragging one or more fire attack hose lines to protect all operating crews and to suppress the fire.

Truck companies carry an assortment of tools that enable them to perform their fire ground duties. In compartments on the vehicle, there are power saws, chain saws and K-12 circular saws for opening roofs. An assortment of pike poles are attached to the truck for opening up plastered walls and ceilings. A good truck man, with a medium-sized pike pole, can tear out a wall or ceiling in a 15-by-15-foot room in a few minutes to find hidden smoldering fire or check for fire extension.

Another vehicle compartment contains porta-powered hydraulic spreaders which are used to pry open doors and move steering wheels when extricating victims trapped as a result of motor vehicle accidents. Trucks also carry stationary and portable generators to power large smoke removal fans, and bright portable circle "D" lights that can be set up in any part of a building or accident scene. Under the main aerial ladder there are storage racks for an assortment of ground ladders—28-foot straight and 35-foot and 50-foot extension ladders.

It is normal procedure to have the first-due ladder truck report directly to the front of a burning structure and the second-responding ladder truck to report to the rear. It is similar to setting up two large tool boxes for ease of access. In many incidents, because of narrow alleys, a ladder truck or pumper cannot locate directly behind the building. In those situations the companies are still responsible for carrying out their assignments. Crew members park their vehicles on the roadway closest to the alley and carry the equipment, ladders and hose to the fire.

However, tonight—with the violence, the extreme number of fires, the flying projectiles and uncertainty—normal procedures are being modified as engines use quick hit-and-run-tactics in order to knock down one structure fire and move quickly to the next. In a hit-and-run operation, the big ladder trucks have a tendency to get in the way and are mostly reserved for ladder pipe operations.

"It was put out and get out...go to the next fire or become available as soon as possible," said Charles S. Urban, a firefighter who was very knowledgeable about truck company operations. Just 12 days shy of his 25th birthday, Urban was assigned to Truck #25 that shared quarters with Engine #44 at the fire station located on #2 Upton Road in Roland Park.[15]

A graduate of Glen Burnie High School and a member of the Green Haven Volunteer Fire Department in the Pasadena area of Anne Arundel County, Urban grew up on Montpelier Street in East Baltimore and spent a period living on East 22nd Street off of Greenmount Avenue before eventually moving to Pasadena.

Urban was assigned to Truck #25 when he graduated from the fire academy in November of 1966. The first day he walked into the station he was startled when he saw the 1943 Seagrave-built 85-foot straight ladder truck for the first time. He later recalled, "I was shocked looking at this old antique open cab fire truck…It [felt] like it was staring back at me. I thought, 'this thing is as old as I am!'"[16]

A month later, on December 12, Urban would be responding on Truck #25 to one of the biggest and most dangerous fires of his young career. The fire broke out in the administrative building of the College of Notre Dame in the 5100 block of Charles Street in North Baltimore at 7:06 a.m., just after shift change.[17]

Urban recalls, "It was one cold ride, hanging on the side of the Seagrave…The day was cloudy, cold and windy…Heavy smoke was pouring out of the first floor of the multi-storied building when we arrived." Urban remembers that he and firefighter John Sommerville searched various rooms on the fourth floor for faculty and students. Fortunately the 200 women who worked there were able to flee the blaze. Unfortunately 44-year-old city Fire Lieutenant John Hockstedt, collapsed and died at the scene, possibly as the result of a heart attack.[18]

On this Saturday during the early evening, Urban, Truck #25 and crew responded with Engine #33 from #33's Gorsuch Avenue Station to a vacant dwelling fire on Aisquith Street off of North Avenue. While responding west on North Avenue, Urban, hanging on the side of Truck #25, remembers seeing people standing along the roadway "watching us…One guy raised his arm to throw a glass bottle of whiskey at us." With nowhere to move to, recalled Urban, "I prepared to duck and while I was lowering my head the perpetrator took a second look at his half-filled bottle and to my relief decided to finish it rather than waste it… By the time he finished the bottle we were long gone."[19]

"Later that evening," Urban said, "We were assigned to a task force consisting of Trucks #25, #5, Engine #33 along with others. My crew and I were ventilating a glass skylight on the roof of a Harford Avenue row house. From the roof we could see the carnival-like atmosphere of the crowd-filled street. It was like a big party as cars were playing loud music and people were laughing and shouting. At one point as we stood on the roof and turning full circle we could see the columns of smoke silhouetting the downtown tall buildings mixed with the rays of the evening sun setting behind them. Closer to me there were pillars of smoke dotting the city in a 360-degree circle. It was amazing. I have never seen anything like it, except for [in] disaster-related movies with computer-generated enhanced backdrops."[20]

"At another location we responded to a trash fire under a stairway in an apartment building. Since the bottom of the stairs was burned away, we placed a ladder up to an exterior window and climbed into the second floor to perform a search and check for fire extension. We found an old man in a wheelchair who couldn't thank us enough for saving his life...This incident made us think of all the local citizens who suffered at the hands of the rioters. They [rioters] didn't know they endangered the old man's life and it was only by the grace of God we were able to be there." Urban, who would retire as a lieutenant in 1999, would fight many more fires in the next 2½ days.[21]

The violence that started on Gay Street, slowly worked its way up Greenmount Avenue, where more than a dozen stores were burning, and Harford Avenue simultaneously. Almost four hours after the first outbreak of violence on Gay Street, lawlessness and fire bombings were spreading west along North Avenue as large bands of youths and roaming young adults broke out glass in storefronts on both sides of the of the wide boulevard. Between 9:35 p.m. and 10:00 p.m. a fire broke out in a store at North Avenue and Calvert Street as a larger business burned three blocks away at Lafayette and Guilford avenues.[22]

Back on Gay Street it was approximately 10:30 p.m. The violence was declared out of control. Area merchants, armed with rifles, boarded up their stores. However, for many it was too late. Their stores were smoldering shells.[23]

Although hundreds of blacks were rioting, thousands of blacks were staying put in their homes, guarding stores, helping to diffuse the volatile situation or just standing around watching the chaos. In an incident on Gay Street at around 10:45 p.m., one black couple actually saved lives.

A jewelry store in the 900 block was firebombed and burning furiously next to the Jacob's Variety Store which was also starting to burn. When police arrived on the scene they were told by an African-American couple who lived across the street that the owner and his sister were inside the Jacob's store. Police officers kicked down the door, entered the variety store and seconds later found Jacob Shilarod and his 69-year-old sister, Mary Eisenberg. Both were led out of the building to safety.[24]

A reporter observed a black Green Beret soldier proudly wearing his uniform with his beret atilt at the correct angle standing on a corner watching a structure fire on AisquithStreet. As youths rioted at will, the soldier shook his head and said to no one in particular, "This is no way to do it— not for the man." "The man" he was referring to was the slain Dr. Martin Luther King Jr.[25]

As a fire bomb flew through the air and ignited a car parked near the intersection of Aisquith Street and Lafayette Avenue, the curfew mandated earlier in the evening went into effect. Because of the curfew, throughout the town, places of public assembly such as movie theaters and dance halls and clubs were emptied of their patrons. As a result, more people were on the city streets. Violations of the curfew, which would remain in effect until 6 a.m., Sunday, carried a maximum $1,000 fine and six months in jail or both.[26]

Near the intersection of Preston and Howard streets at the Fifth Regiment Armory, Maryland's Nation Guard was preparing to be deployed and confront the rioters on Baltimore's dangerous streets. Guardsmen would form and line up in their platoons on the assembly floor where they were given ammunition for their M-1 rifles, chemical grenades and a stern briefing on the use of force.

They were issued two clips of ammunition of 10 rounds each clipped conspicuously to their field jackets. The 175th Infantry was one of the first to arrive and be deployed. "The regiment was made up mostly of soldiers from Baltimore, Glen Burnie, Centreville, Denton and Chestertown. Company B from Chestertown remained in the Cambridge-Easton area on stand-by in the event hostilities would break out there."[27]

By 11:30 p.m. 2,000 guardsmen moved into two areas. One was bordered by Greenmount Avenue and Calvert Street, between North Avenue and 25th Street. The second area was Park Heights Avenue near Park Circle.[28]

IN MOST FIRE departments, the driver-operators rarely wear the heavy protective firefighting turnout gear since the heavy-bulky material can interfere with the operation of the steering wheel and they rarely participate in the hands-on firefighting. In the city at the time, firefighter work uniforms were khaki-colored with no insignias or arm patches. Most driver operators wore a fire department uniform dress caps with the metal ring removed to give them the "30 mission crush" aviator cap look. Once the engine's hose lines were connected, valves opened and lines charged, the operator had little to do but stand and watch the needles in the glass covered-pressure gauges located on the pump panel.

Driver-operators had auxiliary duties to perform also. They made up additional hose lines and sometimes placed ladders against buildings. They could be very helpful in removing a 30-pound empty SCBA bottle from a firefighter's back and replacing it with a full bottle so the firefighter could go back and join his crew. But, not in this fight. These "new" types of fires required a "run and gun" type of operation. There was no time to put on the protective SCBA unless there was a possibility of a rescue. Firefighters typically entered dangerously toxic atmospheres without protective masks.

While battling a structure fire on Greenmount Avenue, Lt. Mueller looked out of the second floor window of a now-burned-out room over an appliance store to the street below. Down at his Engine #6, National Guardsmen, who were now being deployed to the hotbeds of violence throughout the city, were trying to arrest Mueller's black driver-operator.[29]

The guardsmen had observed the black driver-operator standing next to the pump panel in his khakis and mistook him for a rioter and tried to usher him away. Mueller quickly ran down the stairs and outside to the street and explained to the reluctant young white guardsman that the black man was part of the crew and to leave him alone. From that point on the black driver-operator wore his protective turnout coat and aluminum helmet while in the street operating the engine.[30]

Actually, it wasn't too long after the incident that "all" driver operators and firefighters wore their helmets due to the pelting of rocks, bottles and other by the rioters. Police officers spent most of their time protecting the firefighters from the barrage of projectiles and as a result were not able to disperse the crowds or guard the businesses, which caused more stores to be broken into, looted and set on fire.

According to a number of veteran firefighters, black firefighters were harassed by the crowds more than the majority of white firefighters. African-American firefighters were called "Uncle Toms" and "Honky N____ers" or encouraged by their black brothers to join the ruckus. Engine and truck company officers put many of the black firefighters in the engines with enclosed cabs, battalion vehicles and ambulances for their safety.

African-American firefighters also protected their white fellow firefighters. When Doug Shanks was first assigned to Truck #18, located in the Walbrook section of town, he tried to get along with all members of his shift. When he would journey across North Avenue to go to the store or sub shop he would ask the black firefighters if they wanted or needed anything. Some of the older white members were appalled at Shank's courtesy.[31]

So when Shanks was across the street at the store or sitting in the barbershop for a quick haircut and the station received a call or the battalion chief returned to the station it was only the black members who ran across the street to alert him to the situation. The white members wouldn't do it, nor would they alert any of the black firefighters either. But Shank's courtesy would be repaid.

On one of the fires in the North Avenue corridor during the riots, Shanks was in the back of the ladder truck by himself, pulling out one of the ground ladders from the trailer. A black rioter walked up to him and said if he didn't get back on the truck, he would kick Shank's "white ass." One of Shank's fellow black firefighters, hearing the assault, hustled around and got in between the two. He told the rioter, "the only "ass" here that is going to be kicked is yours and I am going to kick it." He added, "Get out of here and I don't want to see you around here anymore tonight." The rioter took off and they not only didn't see him for the rest of the night, they didn't see him again for the duration of the riots. Shanks was relieved.[32]

It borders on miraculous that a 20-mile-per-hour April Maryland wind didn't kick up to accelerate and spread the fires throughout the city. No one understood this better than city Fire Chief John Killen. About 9 p.m., the chief realized that if he lost the city and there were fire engines from the surrounding counties with full crews ready and willing to respond, he would never hear the end of it.

It would be the first time that the city called for outside help since the Great Baltimore Fire of 1904. Although Killen only wanted paid professional crews he took whatever he could get. Baltimore County's Fire Department is made up of either completely paid or completely volunteer stations. Killen made the request and Baltimore County sent seven of its fully paid companies as well as several volunteer companies to Engine #21 located at Roland and Union avenues in Hampden to stand by.

Anne Arundel County was a different story. The Anne Arundel County Fire Department was still a very young organization. It was created in 1965 when the new charter government went into effect. Prior to charter government, the department had been a loose confederation of 24 volunteer departments with a county-paid driver-operator "engineman" on duty around the clock. Many of the enginemen were sponsored by the particular community department they volunteered with and after a test, monitored by representatives of the county's firemen's association, and an interview, were hired. Enginemen were made officers by their volunteer outfits and provided needed leadership during the day when the higher echelon volunteer officers were out working their full-time jobs.[33]

At the time Anne Arundel's career fire service did not have the large numbers of paid personnel as that of neighboring Baltimore city or county. However, Anne Arundel did have an established professional Fire Marshal's office since 1954, which was presently staffed with a handful of inspectors and investigators. (The fire marshal's office had expanded greatly after the tragic fire at Arundel Park only 12 years earlier)[34]

Anne Arundel County was in the initial stages of building the outstanding fire department that it would someday become. It had opened its state-of-the-art fire alarm operations center, fully staffed around the clock, in the basement of its new headquarters building in Millersville in the fall of 1966, less than two years before. A training division had been established and a chief officer assigned, and the first class of 28 professional firefighters was in the process of being hired.

Plans had been laid out to have the new class trained at Baltimore City's Fire Department Training Academy located out on Pulaski Highway, until Anne Arundel's new training center, under construction in Millersville, could be completed. Captain Lester Helfrich, assigned to Baltimore City's Training Academy, was assisting Anne Arundel's Division Chief Raymond Smith with carrying out the training plans.

Helfrich, himself a former volunteer officer with Anne Arundel's Brooklyn Volunteer Fire Department, was very familiar with the capabilities of Anne Arundel's volunteer firefighters since as a part-time instructor with the University of Maryland's Fire Service Extension training program (now the Maryland Fire and Rescue Institute) he had trained many of them.

As the city's fire training officer, Helfrich responded to all multiple-alarm fires throughout the bustling city in his departmental response vehicle. He would typically respond to multiple alarms to support the fire suppression operations if necessary. Upon arrival, he would not only assist wherever needed and look out for firefighters' safety, but also determine if the firefighters were operating in a fashion as prescribed in the training program doctrine. Helfrich observed, evaluated and critiqued the operations to capture new ideas and concepts that would foster improvements in the way fires were fought.

Helfrich would make observations, take pictures and make mental notes. On this Saturday, Helfrich had been busy all evening, mainly with the Lewis and Ideal furniture store fires on Gay Street. Later, he had stopped by the Lexington Street fire alarm center, which was a bee hive of activity, to see if he could assist there.

Earlier in the evening at the fire alarm center Helfrich had suggested to Chief Killen the use of mutual aid companies in assisting with the fires, particularly those from Anne Arundel County. Killen didn't want to hear it, so Helfrich backed off for the time being. There were many other activities to perform. However as the fires increased throughout the evening, Killen called not only for off-duty personnel to return to work, but also for the Anne Arundel County Fire Department crews.

Eight stations sent engines to Baltimore's Engine #35 and Truck #21 station located in the Brooklyn section of the city. Anne Arundel's Communications Division Chief David Mentzel arrived at Baltimore's fire alarm center with portable county radios so the city would have a direct link with any of the county engines.

Firefighter-engineman Burton Phelps drove Anne Arundel's Chief Harry Klasmeier, Deputy Chief Paul Haigley and Training Division Chief Raymond Smith in Klasmeier's chief's car. They planned to visit the city stations that county units would be transferred to and assist with communications and supervision. They also looked forward to learning as much as they could through observation in the event that Anne Arundel County experienced similar riots.[38]

After all of the decision making, attention to details, moving of apparatus and arrangements, the county units parked at the Brooklyn station all night and didn't turn a wheel. They were sent back to their county stations in Linthicum, Brooklyn, Ferndale, Glen Burnie, Marley Park, Orchard Beach, Lake Shore and Rivera Beach around 4 a.m.

As Linthicum's Engine #321 completed backing into the fire station located on Camp Meade Road near Friendship Airport (now BWI-Thurgood Marshall airport) a box alarm was sounded through the radio dispatch system that the Moma Mias' Restaurant on Camp Meade Road near Baltimore-Annapolis Blvd. across from the Bon Fire Restaurant had been fire bombed. Units from the Linthicum station, as well as the Brooklyn and Ferndale stations, responded.

When units arrived on location, after laying lines from fire hydrants and equipping for fire attack, they found a smoking steaming kitchen. Someone had thrown a Molotov cocktail through the kitchen window and set the kitchen on fire. An alert, sharp-eyed and nearby county police officer saw the fire, called it in and extinguished it with a portable fire extinguisher. Moma Mias was located about two miles south of the Baltimore City/ Anne Arundel County boundary line.

The fire resulted in minor to moderate damage to the restaurant's kitchen. No one knows who actually threw the Molotov cocktail. Was it a black rioter from the near-by African-American community of Pumphrey? A white person who wanted it to look like it was a black rioter from Pumphrey? Or just a random act? No one knew the answer, but fortunately it was one of only two firebombing incidents in Anne Arundel County during the entire Baltimore riots.

FINALLY AT 11:30 P.M., A HALF AN HOUR after the citywide curfew went into effect, Mayor D'Alessandro took the earlier advice of Parren Mitchell and appeared on television. The mayor appealed to citizens to obey the curfew and pleaded for peace.[39]

Although more than 100 rioters had been arrested, the violence and looting that had started approximately six hours earlier on Gay Street and traveled along the corridors of Gay Street to Greenmount Avenue, from Greenmount to North Avenue, west along North Avenue and along the streets in close proximity, continued. Now there were reports of looting throughout the 1200 to 2000 blocks of Pennsylvania Avenue. Police Chief Pomerleau requested that National Guard soldiers be sent to that area.

As the guardsmen of the 175th Infantry were deployed to the city's streets, they carried their M-1 rifles with bared bayonets at high point to be used in moving out the crowds. The guardsmen's company commanders were advised to use whatever tactics necessary to mitigate the situation, with one "confusing caveat—use only the minimum force necessary" to get the job done. Due to the ambiguousness of the order, many guardsmen and their officers were uncertain of what they could do and what they could not do. In addition they were ordered not to load their weapons unless ordered to do so, unless a sniper or gunman could be clearly identified, or unless their lives were in danger.[40]

Typically two companies of infantrymen, about 200 men, would walk down the street with bayoneted guns pointed out ahead, stretched in lines from sidewalk to sidewalk. A reserve company of 100 men would follow and usually guard the closest intersection to the first group's backs. A platoon of Maryland State Police officers would follow, four abreast carrying shotguns and bandoliers, filled with shot gun shells, over their shoulders. One jeep carrying five guardsmen would accompany each company.

John J. Peterson states in his book, *Into The Cauldron*, "With each company was a selected marksman with rifle and sniper scope for anti-sniper fire. This one weapon under the control of the company commander was carried loaded but could only be fired by direct order."[41]

On many streets the guardsmen found that the crowds were gone, leaving a mess in their wake. Windows were knocked out of stores and bars. The interiors of businesses were totally burned out, many still smoldering; burglar alarms were indiscriminately ringing off and on; the streets were filled with damaged merchandise; bent wire mesh was pulled from the window frames; and everywhere shattered glass laid in the street.[42]

On Saturday night, the 175th Infantry encountered occasional harmless rock and bottle throwing and infrequent shouted obscenities from the doorways and upper-story windows of the row houses that lined the streets. Cars occasionally drove by filled with hooligans who shouted out obscenities and taunted the soldiers by throwing rocks or empty glass bottles at them. Although a number of people became belligerent upon being forced inside their homes, most reluctantly obeyed. Small groups of agitators tried to break the soldiers ranks, but would ultimately run down a side street to escape capture.[43]

Maryland State Police officers were now being deployed to guard a large liquor secured-storage facility at Hillen and High streets. Thirty more troopers were sent to Federal and Harford avenues, while 35 were sent to the Civic Center on Baltimore Street to break up a dance. Within an hour-and-a-half after midnight, city officers joined 300 national guardsmen and together the taskforce swept Pennsylvania Avenue.[44]

As if things hadn't been bad enough "Murphy's Law" (if anything can go wrong it most likely will and at the worst time) was in full effect at the Fifth Regiment armory, now a humming fortress of activity. As radio commentators, television news reporters, cameramen, and light and sound personnel were preparing to do "live shots" for the 11 p.m. news in a designated area on the first floor, guardsmen were in the basement preparing the chemicals to make the tear gas that would be dispersed in quantities unheard of for the first time ever on the streets of Baltimore.[45]

As guardsmen prepared the gas containers, one toppled over, smashing onto the basement floor and immediately vaporizing the chemicals. Soldiers, chased by the potent vapors, ran up the stairs and outside into the fresh air very near to where the live newscast was about to take place. For the reporters it was show time and too late to move from their set-up positions. Now in the mist of the potent chemical vapors, the sneezing, runny-nosed, teary-eyed news reporters gave their account of the night's events to the amazement of the Baltimore metropolitan area's television viewing audience.[46]

Sometime after midnight, Lt. Mueller, Engine #6 and crew, now located on the ravaged North Avenue, finished up fighting a fire that had burned through an entire half block of buildings before they had stopped it. They left their last of over two dozen fire responses for the shift and headed back to the Gay Street station in the early morning hours of Palm Sunday. Now in addition to the fire crew, there were a few national guardsmen armed with rifles with fixed bayonets hanging on the sides or sitting on the top of the engine to protect the firefighters from projectiles.[47]

Since the start of the riots, five civilians had been killed and 70 hurt including a fire captain who was pelted in the face with a glass bottle while battling a fire in the 1000 block of Gay Street. Two hundred and seventy-three had been arrested and over 250 fires had been reported.[48]

Most of the violence had occurred throughout the Gay Street and Greenmount Avenue corridors, and in an area bordered by North Avenue to the north, between Greenmount Avenue and Chester Street and Baltimore Street to the south. The most ravaged areas were located in the 1900 and 2300 blocks of East Monument Street, the 700 and 900 blocks of North Gay Street and the intersection of North Avenue and Greenmount Avenue. At 4:15 a.m., the field force commanders of the police department reported that Baltimore City was relatively calm.

8

Palm Sunday
"A Hair's Breath"
Sunday, April 7, 1968

It had been an extraordinarily busy night for police officers and firefighters. Even with a curfew in place the looting and fires had started up again after midnight. Drivers of a dozen troop carriers parked at the Fifth Regiment Armory, started their engines and in a convoy trucked 400 to 500 guardsmen to Aisquith and 25th streets to break up a crowd near the railroad tracks. Once out of the trucks, the sergeants barked out orders and the soldiers, clothed in traditional army olive drab, quickly assembled and with bayonets fixed on their M-1 rifles, moved towards the crowd. Seeing the bayonets, the crowd quickly dispersed before all of the guardsmen could get out of their vehicles.[1]

In between midnight and 1:45 a.m., rioters looted and torched a food market and a nearby five-and-dime at Milton Avenue and Preston Street. The stores were located about two blocks away from the quarters of Ladder Truck #15 located on Montford Avenue. On the Westside of town, city police officers reported a sniper firing at their cruisers at North Fulton and Lafayette avenues.[2]

Considering the violence and destruction that had occurred the night before, it was a relatively calm, cool and sunny Palm Sunday morning. A reporter would later write, "Sunday morning, bathed in bright sunlight, the city seemed deceptively peaceful."[3]

Twenty-six years earlier, on Palm Sunday, March 29, 1942, a 22-inch wet snowstorm hit and entirely blanketed the Baltimore area. Unfortunately, it happened a score and six years too early. Right now even an inch of snow would have been considered a miraculous response to the many prayers being recited for a divine intervention to end the violence. But it would not happen.[4]

Thousands were attending or preparing to attend church, especially those in the residential communities surrounding the riot-stricken areas of Saturday night. There was a lull in the looting. Authorities were hoping that during church services, ministers would request restraint from the unsettled and angry young black men and teenagers. Although many ministers made the request, after church services the riots resumed.

An early morning tour of the shattered riot areas was made by Mayor D'Alesandro and General Gelston. They drove through the glass-and debris-covered streets in Gelston's jeep guarded by a convoy of four National Guard jeeps. The devastation was remarkable. At the scenes "scared by violence, crowds of sullen, unfriendly blacks watched usually wordlessly from street corners."[5] The mayor and general were informed by the fire department that more than 47 major fires had been set throughout the city overnight and that 32 civilians were treated for injuries.

By mid-morning city policemen, now working 12-hour shifts, were staging units at strategic points around the city.[6] White-painted police patrol cruisers were lined up one behind the other at least 30 deep along the narrow Gay Street, near the intersection of Aisquith Street. Along the Gay Street sidewalk outside the damaged stores under store signs marked, "Furniture Fair—Easy Credit," "Epsteins," and "Queen Dress Shop," police officers gathered in small groups discussing the previous night's antics and sharing ideas on crowd control tactics that would be tried on this day.[7] The city's emergency management center, located in the old civil defense compound in the reinforced basement of Engine Company #4 on Cold Spring Lane, was activated. The center contained liaisons from all of the city's agencies and supporting organizations: fire, public works, police, repair shops, transportation, public schools, the Baltimore Gas and Electric Company, Red Cross, hospitals, etc. The center was connected by telephone with the command posts of the fire department, police department, and Maryland

National Guard. If the police needed buses to transport people or the fire department needed a crane or bulldozer to demolish a burned-out shell of a structure creating a safety hazard, all requests would be made through this center.[8]

D'Alesandro decided to call in the city's African-American leaders, moderate and militant, to explain the "gravity" of the situation. D'Alesandro stated, "We came within a hair's breath… It's bad, but not as bad as it could have been." D'Alesandro wanted to know what actions his administration needed to take to avert a second night of violence. After the meeting, the mayor sent the black leadership back into the streets in an attempt to stop small bands of youths from creating more destruction.[9]

Although the riots could have been worse, the damage was still very bad. City Comptroller Hyman Pressman believed that law enforcement needed to crank up the level of effort and toughness. He believed too many were getting away with far too much. Pressman requested that a reasonable amount of restraint be applied to the rioters, adding the caveat that "restraint should not be stretched to the point where crime can be committed with impunity."[10]

Baltimore *Sun* reporter Ernest F. Imhoff would report years later that "the strong odor of smoke was everywhere as people went to church while others looted. People were curious or scared to death. The skies were sunny blue in one direction and black with smoke in the other. Tulips had replaced daffodils in backyards and federal troops patrolled the streets with bayonets on their guns."[11]

At 8:53 a.m., the lootings picked up again in the 900 block of Pennsylvania Avenue and the 600 block of Gay Street as the National Guard requested more assistance to control a large crowd forming there. As city, state and federal officials re-evaluated the situation and planned for another day of hostilities, the question was not whether there would be any more fires. The question now was "how big will the fires be?"

Since the riot had started, "it hopscotched from east to west to east again in an area mostly bordered by North Avenue, Pennsylvania Avenue., Gay Street and Monument Street. The downtown business district had not been affected."[12]

No one understood this "hopscotching" effect better than 40-year-old Fire Lieutenant Fred Riedel. He and his Engine #12 crew had been sent to empty fire stations and fire calls throughout the city the night before. Riedel loved the fire service longer than he could remember. As a youngster, Fred followed fire engines and fires throughout the city. The Clifton High School graduate was destined to enter a career in the Baltimore City Fire Department.[13]

When Riedel was only 6 years old, he received terrible news. On May 15, 1934, his father, Frederick L. Riedel, a member of the fire department's Salvage Corps, was responding on Wagon #3 to a fire at Box 842, located on the corner of Saint Paul and 20th streets. At Gold and Division streets, Wagon #3 collided with a police cruiser. The impact caused Frederick, who was riding on the back step of the unit, to be thrown into the street and fatally injured. When units arrived at the location of the pulled fire alarm box they found a car on fire.[14]

Fire Lt. Fred Riedel had joined the Baltimore City Fire Department on November 17, 1951 and approximately one year later had been drafted into the Army where he saw action as an infantryman in Korea. Two years afterwards he returned to the fire department and as a firefighter assigned to Truck #11, located at 401 West North Avenue, would participate in firefighting operations at the 12-alarm fire that occurred at Martin Motors located on Cathedral Street and Mount Royal Avenue.[15]

On Saturday April 6, Riedel had been painting all day at his home in Towson. When alerted to the riots and ordered back to work, he reported to his regular assignment station at Engine #12 located on Fort Avenue in South Baltimore. He arrived there after navigating a number of road blocks and detours because of the disorders.

Once at the station and making preparations with his crew and equipment, Fred received a phone call from one of his best friends, John Kelly, assigned to Truck #4, located at the 405 McMechen Street fire station. The famous "Captain Kelly," a firefighter's firefighter, was legendary for wild and humorous fire station antics. Kelly told Fred about the fires burning along North Avenue and advised him to get his men ready because things were "really getting crazy."[16]

ABOVE - The BCFD Training Center located in the rear of Engine #36 on Edmondson Ave. It was here that most of the firefighters mentioned in this book trained as rookie firefighters. (Circa 1938)

RIGHT - Engine #6 responded with Lt. Mueller and crew to the first structure fire at the Ideal Furniture store on Gay Street on the evening of Saturday, April 6 (All photos courtesy of Michael Defina)

LEFT - Engine #6 station located at the corner of Ensor and Gay streets (looking north - circa 1960) was constructed in 1853. It was one of the original volunteer fire stations. It was in this building that Lt. Muller and crew heard the roar and the crash when the large plate glass display window of the Sun Cleaners in the 400 block of Gay Street exploded. Gay Street (pictured here on the right side of the station) would be the scene of some of the city's worst rioting.

ABOVE - Captain Phillip Waldner walks to Engine #34 while his crew makes preparations to enter a burning Sylvan Pharmacy, Eager Street and Broadway.

BELOW - Less than a block away, a woman pleads for people to stay out of the area. Saturday, April 6, 1968.

(All photos courtesy of Hearst Corporation)

ABOVE - Teenagers and young adults run from the ravaged Shurfine Market, at Aisquith and Eager streets.

LEFT - Police officers force a group of rioters up against the wall in the 2400 block of Greenmount Avenue Saturday, April 6, 1968.

(All photos courtesy of Hearst Corporation)

ABOVE - Youngsters scurry from Needles Food Market, near Biddle Street and Greemount Avenue. Sunday, April 7, 1968.

(All photos courtesy of Hearst Corporation)

ABOVE - A soldier speaks with a shot gun carrying city police officer.

LEFT - Soldiers guard a damaged "Little Willies" bar at Whitelock Street and Druid Hill Avenue, Sunday, April 7, 1968.

ABOVE - On Sunday afternoon, North Avenue looked like a war zone. On the south side of the wide boulevard looking west towards Linden Avenue an armed city police officer stands by as a soldier tries to advise a youngster to discard his souvenirs and go home. April 7, 1968.

(Photo courtesy of Hearst Corporation)

LEFT - Engine #20 in front of the Walbrook Station at W. North Ave. was where F.F. Doug Shanks was assigned.

RIGHT - Truck #13, a 1957 Peter Pirsch, 100' tractor-drawn aerial, was very similar to Truck #18, a 1962 model Shanks tillered.

(Photos courtesy of Michael Defina)

LEFT - The U.S. Army 18th Airborne sets up camp on the grounds of Druid Hill Park. There were similar scenes of tents, vehicles and soldiers at Carroll, Clifton and Patterson Parks. April 8, 1968.

(Photo courtesy of Hearst Corporation)

ABOVE - Teenagers and adults overwhelm Asquith Liquors on Eager Street.

BELOW - Adults watch out for police as youngsters raid the self-service store at Eager Street and Broadway, Saturday, April 6, 1968. (All photos courtesy of Hearst Corporation)

It wasn't long before Engine #12 with Riedel and crew transferred to the quarters of Engine #13 and Truck #4 at the McMechen Street station. Later the engine and crew transferred to Engine #20, quartered with Truck #18 at the North Avenue station located in west Baltimore's Walbrook section. While transferring they went through the intersection of Eutaw and Lexington streets, where Fred never saw so many city and state police in one place in all of his life.[17]

Later as darkness fell, fire alarm ordered Engine #12 and crew to vacate Engine #20 and to transfer to Engine #4 out on Cold Spring Lane. During one of the transfer assignments the engine and crew passed a blazing warehouse on McCulloh Street. Although Riedel reported the incident to fire alarm and crew members prepared to fight the fire, they were ordered to continue with the transfer since other companies had already been dispatched to the McCulloh Street fire.

Around 11 p.m., Engine #12 ended up at the quarters of Engine #9, located on 1220 East Oliver Street and finally dispatched to the fires on North Avenue. Riedel would later state that the carnival atmosphere on North Avenue seemed like a crazy dream as he watched groups of rioters made up of men, women and children carry small television sets, radios and other stolen goods up and down the street. He remembers one looter pushing a wheeled store clothes rack filled with shirts, pants and jackets right down the middle of North Avenue.[18]

Riedel recalled that rioters and looters verbally abused and harassed black firefighters. He said, "the white guys protected the black firefighters" and remembers escorting one black firefighter into the battalion chief's vehicle to get him out of harm's way. Riedel would finally go home on Monday, only to be called back again. On Monday, he fought fires at 25th and Saint Paul Streets, a candy company located at Harford Avenue and Federal Street and along Broadway on the eastside.[19]

AS THE PALM SUNDAY SERVICES finished up and churches were let out, there was more activity on the streets. Crowds were now much larger than they had been on Saturday. They were uglier and more boisterous, made up of mostly young African-American males between ages 14 and 19 as well as adults in their early 20s.[20]

Despite the redeployment of National Guardsmen, city, and state police officers, Baltimore's second wave of violence in less than 24 hours was again surging throughout the city as violence now broke out at 42nd Street and York Road as well as at Walbrook Junction.[21]

Around 8:50 a.m., the city had dispatched a dump truck with a crew of sanitation workers to the intersection of Gay and Eager Streets to start clean-up. As the workers started sweeping and shoveling up the glass and debris, a crowd formed and started to harass and threaten them. By the time the guardsmen arrived to protect the shaken workers, they said "the hell with this," and left the scene.[48]

In fire stations throughout East Baltimore the tired city firefighters were opening the bulky and weighty fire engine house doors, putting on their heavy canvas bunker coats still damp from Saturday night's firefighting, and starting up the engines on the big rigs. The engine's hoods covering the motors were still warm from pumping all night.

The sound of sirens and bells were heard for the second straight day as responding engine and ladder trucks headed to a reported building fire at Federal Street and Milton Avenue. Within minutes, building fires broke out within two blocks apart; one at Federal and Holbrook streets and one at Harford Avenue and Lanvale Street.[22]

More soldiers were now being deployed to hot spots around the city. At about 8:53 a.m., at the intersection of Fulton Avenue and Baker Street, nearly 300 angry youths threw stones and bricks at passing cars. Guardsman cordoned off the area with fixed bayonets. Some of the kids took off running upon seeing the armed soldiers. Others played chicken with the guardsmen, yelling obscenities and then quickly running away. The more defiant youths raised their arms and hands and displayed their middle finger while standing unfretted in the center of the street.[23]

A few kids acted as if they were going to throw things at the soldiers, egging them on. As guardsmen approached, the kids would hold out as long as they could and then take off in a sprint, running down alleys and scurrying through pedestrian tunnels between the row houses. Safe from the soldiers, the youths would regroup about a half a block away and start the frenzy all over again.[24]

Companies from the National Guard's 115th Infantry arrived in the city and were immediately deployed to Pennsylvania Avenue to relieve guardsmen who had been there through most of the night. One hundred and eighty men were split in pairs and assigned to street corners. The soldiers were stretched ridiculously thin, had no ammunition and were required to keep scabbards over their bayonets. "They couldn't even use cold steel as a threat."[25]

The situation that the guard commanders put their soldiers in was highly questionable at the least. According to John J. Peterson's, *Into the Cauldron*, guardsmen along Pennsylvania Avenue had no ammunition and no tear gas canisters. One soldier claimed, "If you were on Pennsylvania Avenue during the riot and not scared, you were a dammed fool." [26]

As far as the soldiers were concerned, Pennsylvania Avenue was scary enough in the daytime under normal conditions. Groups of a dozen or so young thugs would surround the soldiers and taunt them by saying, "What are you going to do with that toy gun mother f___er? We know you ain't got no bullets." The young adults, who were about the same age of most of the guardsmen, would try to grab their rifles, hit them in the shins with leather belts and spit in their faces. A threatened guardsmen stated, "I couldn't swing at him, [swat] him with a rifle butt or [gorge] him with a bayonet, only stand there and let him have fun. Never have I felt so helpless.[27]

Mike Kernan was an 18-year-old senior at Loyola High School when the riots broke out. He remembered going to church on Palm Sunday and driving by the military encampment at Clifton Park. "Seeing the hundreds of tents in the camp, the activity of the armed soldiers along with the army trucks and jeeps driving up and down the streets, it was like we were at war," Kernan would later remark.[28]

During the weekend Kernan was staying at his aunt's house near Greenount Avenue and remembers seeing the numerous columns of smoke rising from the fires throughout the city. Two years later, Kernan would enter the Baltimore City Fire

Department as a firefighter and would quickly be promoted through the ranks to chief officer. He retired in 2002 as an assistant chief. However, even at 18, Kernan had a keen interest in the fire service.

As a young teenager Kernan would hang out at the 3123 Greenmount Avenue fire station, the quarters of Engine #31 and Truck #7. Kernan would run errands for the firefighters and would eventually become the station's official "door closer" securing the large bay doors when the apparatus would leave the station for a call. At his aunt's house, Kernan had a fire department and police radio monitor which he listened to from morning to night during the riots. Around 9:30 a.m. on Sunday, the first of many "assist a police officer" requests to be communicated that day were broadcast across the radio for Greenmount Avenue and Biddle Streets. Kernan would later remark, "Before the riots it was rare that the police would send out a signal "13" to have all nearby officers' respond to a police officer in trouble at a particular location. But during the riots there seemed to be signal "13s" like every 20 minutes. And when they were announced [police] dispatchers would give not just one, but up to a half-dozen locations where policemen were calling for help. It was unbelievable."[29]

White firefighters, police officers, and guardsmen took their share of verbal abuse, but the black firefighters, police officers, and guardsmen got it twice as bad. The rioters considered them "Uncle Toms" and "House N___ers." One such African-American guardsman was taunted while guarding a store in downtown Baltimore. More than once the rioters called him a "traitor" and stated, "You're no soul brother." Later interviewed by a reporter who witnessed the taunting, the guardsman said, "It's tough to say how you react to this violence — I guess you have to be one of us to feel it."[30]

On North Avenue, stores were looted "mercilessly."[31] Looting was heavier along this mainstay of shops, stores, bars and restaurants than anywhere else in the city. Guardsmen would later say that there were mobs the full length of the boulevard. People were carrying furniture, televisions and unbelievably, heavy refrigerators. Most paid no attention to the soldiers and some even waved to them.[32] Just south of North Avenue, the

Western District police station looked like an armed camp. Guardsmen surrounded the guarded structure as handcuffed looters and curfew violators were ushered in by city cops for a trial in makeshift courts set up in the building.

There were so many people under arrest that school buses were now being used for transport instead of police paddy wagons and patrol cars.[33] Guardsmen now closed down Pennsylvania Avenue sealing off all traffic from North Avenue to Mosher Street. Other streets were shut down in a similar fashion: Harford Avenue from Monument Street to North Avenue and Gay Street from Orleans Street to Preston Street.

R.B. Jones, a freelance writer, would later write, "Riding on the bus Sunday morning [I] saw parents looting with their children in tow. When I saw that, I knew that they were going to have trouble reasserting their authority. The 1968 riots [were] a time when parental authority and respect for adults in the African-American community began to erode. In my house, my parents told me that if I brought any stolen property into the house, I was going back out the door with it."[34]

There were additional fires burning in east Baltimore, one in the 1700 block of Harford Avenue and one on Gay Street. Crowds were now chanting "We've got the key to the city" and "We shall overcome." As fires increased, a call went back out to the Baltimore County and Anne Arundel County Fire Departments to standby and make preparations for moving fire companies into the city for a second day.[35]

In a ravaged store on Gay Street near Eden Street a large crowd cornered two guardsmen against a back wall while others looted. A city police canine unit arrived and before long most of the rioters scrambled. However, there was one woman who was pushing a shopping cart full of merchandise. She was adamant that the cart "in no uncertain terms" was hers and that she was going to keep it. One of the police officers stated, "in no uncertain terms" that the cart was as much the dogs as it was hers and added that he would let the dog and her fight over it. The women left the building without the cart.[36]

Police officers understood that their job was dangerous. They could deal with the disrespect and most of the insults as they persuaded looters to go home, apprehending and handcuffing the ones that didn't. However, what scared the police officers the most, next to dying, being seriously injured, or being shot at by a lone sniper from a window or on a rooftop, was the prospect of killing someone else.[37]

Shots were now being fired in west Baltimore as city police responded to reports of sniper fire at Lafayette and Fulton avenues. At around 10 a.m., clouds rolled into the Baltimore area and rain began to fall. The looting slowed down and in some areas took a break.

Although a small rain shower dampened the area and many children, youths and young adults withdrew from the popular "hit sites," it didn't take long for them to re-emerge after the rain stopped. Violence after an hour's break would now rear its ugly head along the west side of the city.

About five blocks north of North Avenue near Druid Lake, a store on the corner of Brookfield Avenue and Whitelock Street was being looted. The white sign with black letters above the store's now-broken-out large windows said: STEAKS, CHOPS, BORDENS ICE CREAM; on a smaller sign was a picture of a bottle cap with the famous red and blue PEPSI COLA logo.[38]

The signs seemed meaningless as scores of looters, crawling through the now-large window opening, ransacked the store. Young boys and older men were now carrying out cartons of cigarettes, large jars of mayonnaise and mustard. The cigarettes could be later sold and the glass jars would be squandered by being smashed in the street.[39]

In the 900 block of Whitelock Street, in the area bordered by McCulloh Street and Madison Avenue, was being looted. Ten small stores were wrecked and looted as National Guard troops cordoned off the area.[40] Lines of troops, now being deployed in gas masks with bayonets fixed on their rifles, swept down Whitelock Street all the way to where the street intersected with North Avenue. It looked like a scene out of a futuristic science fiction movie.[41]

At Brown's Food Market located at 1901 Chase Street near Broadway, a 55-year-old mother of six was arrested by city police as she and others emptied the store's shelves. When asked "Why?" by the judge at the Eastern District Police Station, she replied that she didn't know; she went grocery shopping "only the day before." She would receive a suspended 3-month jail sentence and 6-months probation.[42]

Approximately 10 blocks south of Brown's Food Market in the 1400 block of East Madison Street, near Eden Street and Central Avenue, was Flak's Food Market. The slightly-built black-haired 45-year old James Flak moved to the area from Argentina to seek a better life for himself and his family. Flak's little 250 square-foot mom-and-pop store crowded with counters and display cases was where he worked 12 to 14 hours a day, six days a week.[43]

On Saturday, Flak was assured by local blacks that he would have "no problems" at his store since he was a nice man. One of the blacks said, "You're our Soul Brother." However, by mid-morning, the business was broken into, looted, and firebombed. Flak fled out the back door in tears.[44]

Around 11 a.m., at the Zitto Buick Service garage on Whitelock Street and Callow Avenue in Reservoir Hill, firefighters were battling a stubborn fire. As the fire raged out of control, an unruly crowd emerged and threatened the firefighters. Troops were requested to quell the crowd.[45]

Fires were now breaking out in several buildings along the 2200 block of Fulton Avenue near Pennsylvania Avenue. About 10 blocks south down Fulton Avenue, 50 looters broke into an abandoned liquor store on Presstman Street. Included in the crowd were many kids not older than age 6—where were their parents? [46]

As the fires burned along Fulton Avenue, incidents of violence surfaced throughout the city. At 11:30 a.m., on the corner of North Avenue and Chester Street about five blocks north of Gay Street, soldiers used CS tear gas for the first time. The soldiers used the gas to clear out approximately 300 young blacks who had gathered and were smashing out the windows of the H&E self service grocery store.[47]

The "tear gas" also known as "CS," a riot agent, is made from Potassium Chlorate and when dispersed creates a pungent, pepper-like odor. The gas produces an extremely harsh burning sensation in the eyes, causing the person exposed to it to cry and involuntarily close their eyes. The gas stings when it comes into contact with moist skin areas. If it comes into contact with the sinus it brings about nasal drip. It also causes coughing, difficulty in breathing, and chest tightness. In large concentrations CS can cause nausea and vomiting. Unlike a bullet shot from a gun or a puncture of the body with a bayonet, CS does not cause death or seriously endanger health. Its effect is temporary. Once an exposed person is in a CS-free environment for about 15 minutes, the adverse effects will cease. To disperse the gas, guardsmen would throw the one-pound canister, about the size of a hand grenade, over the heads of the crowd. A timed fuse would detonate the canister within two seconds of its release. The canister would burn for about 15 to 35 seconds, releasing the gas throughout an area with a diameter of 100 feet. The odor could be detected at greater distances but with less effect. The canisters could be carried by the guardsmen clipped to their belts or their harnesses or in their field jackets. A larger unit weighing about 55 pounds and operated by three guardsmen sprays the CS gas in the form of a fog. The unit looks like a flame thrower.[48]

Youths continued to play games of "Cat and Mouse" taunting the soldiers, than at the last minute, would run away. Sometimes the guardsmen would attempt to run after them, but being in full battle dress the guardsmen could never keep up. As the young vandals started looting the stores, the troops swarmed in with their tear gas and drove the unruly crowds away.[49] In many instances, some of the older senior African-American residents watched the movement of the vandals from their third story row home bedroom windows and alerted guardsmen to the trouble. In some cases their vigilance led to arrests.[50]

At 11:20 a.m., crowds threw rocks at police officers and guardsmen working on Preston Street and Greenmount Avenue. Tear gas was used to disperse hostile groups looting on Gay near Ensor Street. Radio speakers on fire department apparatus were blaring out dispatch acknowledgement for requests for police assistance at Lanvale Street and Guilford Avenue, as well as numerous other locations.[51] As if there wasn't enough trouble to deal with, there were now reports of problems at the city jail. At the jail, near Eager Street, after the noon meal, prisoners in support of their brethren rioting in the streets, refused to go back to their cell blocks.

Around noon the first major fire erupted at the two-story brick furniture warehouse belonging to the Chernock Transfer Company, located a half block west of the 1700 block of Guilford Avenue between Lafayette and Lanvale streets. National Guardsmen arrived first to greet a surprised looter carrying a new double mattress on his back out of the front door who was quickly apprehended. The fire quickly grew to four alarms. The situation became more dicey when a roof and wall collapsed in an alley almost killing a number of firefighters.

City firefighter Walter Lemmon remembers this fire well. Lemmon, with three years on the job was assigned to Engine #19 located in the two-story fire station at North Avenue and Bond Street. As Engine #19, a 1944, 80 Model Mack open-cab pumper, pulled up to a fire hydrant, two firefighters hopped off the rear tailboard to make the hookup with the supply fire hose. As the engine traversed the street towards the burning warehouse and hose slid out of the hose bed, an unruly crowd gathered around the hydrant and threatened the two firefighters with bodily harm if they turned the hydrant on.[52]

Engine #19's African-American driver-operator, Larry Pully, parked the engine near the warehouse to begin firefighting operations. As he connected the supply hose from the hydrant into his pump, he wondered why the hose had not been charged with water. The two firefighters ran up the street and reported the crowd's angry threats to Pully.

A very furious and determined Pully ran back down the street to the hydrant, challenged the crowd, and then placed the hydrant wrench on top of the hydrant. After 14 turns, the needed water was on its way to the engine. Years later Lemmon retired as a lieutenant and Pully retired as a Shift Commander.[53]

Pully, Lemmon and Engine #19's crew spent most of their time during the riots fighting structure fires throughout the Greenmount Avenue corridor. Lemmon said, "It was crazy... As we entered the structures with hose lines, rioters were running out with stolen goods."

Fires on any given day that would normally be fought with two alarms' worth of apparatus, equipment, and men (6-8 engines and two ladder trucks) were handled with two engines and one ladder truck. Pully, Lemmon and the Engine #19 crew worked the day shift Saturday, had gone home, and had been called back to duty when the riots broke out earlier on Gay Street. They wouldn't go back home until Tuesday.[54]

PRIOR TO THE CITY'S ANNEXATION of sections of Baltimore County in 1888, North Avenue was the boundary line between the most northern part of the city and the county. It runs approximately seven miles from the Baltimore Cemetery near Belair Road to the east and west to Hilton Street in Walbrook. Large three-story row homes were erected along its tree-lined boulevard. In these beautifully styled homes lived wealthy German brewers, printers, merchants and manufacturers. Corner units were constructed with an additional one-story spiraling tower with an attached cone shaped roof.[55]

On the northwest side of North Avenue is a section named Reservoir Hill. In the late 19th century picturesque homes "began to line the fashionable streets" that ran from North Avenue to Druid Hill Park. These lavish structures, mostly large elegant row homes, displayed an "amazing richness, creativity and detail," and provided elegant living spaces for "Baltimore's new mercantile Jewish elite, department store owners and clothing manufacturers."[56]

In 1907, advertisements for row homes on the 3000 block of West North Avenue ran: Attractive Section, No Soloons, No Colored, Up to Date Three Story Houses, Every Convenience.[57] In less than 50 years, this would all change as African-Americans moved in from the North Upton areas on the west side and the Oldtown areas on the eastside. Up and down North Avenue, in addition to the residences there were now numerous stores and businesses many black-owned.

On the North side of the boulevard at Maryland Avenue stood the historic North Avenue Market with its Spanish-mission-style towers. It was anchored on its west end by a "Run Right to Reads" drugstore. A large Sears-Roebuck Store was located on North Avenue, between Harford Road and North Broadway. At the southwest corner of North and Greenmount avenues, one of the busiest transit stops of the city, a large white sign displayed "SODA - DRUGS - CARRY OUT" over the large windows of Clayman's Pharmacy.[58]

Another North Avenue pharmacy was owned by the Singer family who lived in the building's second floor apartment. On Sunday morning, Sharon Singer and her mother went out shopping and picked up Sharon's older sister at the Baltimore Hebrew College located in the Park Heights section of northwest Baltimore. Sharon, a 16-year-old student at Western High School, located near Cold Spring Lane, had grown up on North Avenue, enjoying Oriole games at Memorial Stadium on 33rd Street and taking ballet lessons at the Peabody Institute.[59]

After picking up her sister, the three were driving in the mother's Oldsmobile on Jones Falls Expressway. As they drove off the exit ramp onto North Avenue they couldn't believe their eyes. "It was just an inferno," stated Sharon. "Buildings were on fire and smoke filled the sky." The eastside riots that had occurred the day before had now spread down North Avenue.[60]

When the three reached the pharmacy, Sharon's father, was waiting. They picked him up and headed to a relative's home in northwest Baltimore. When the family returned to their home on Monday everything was looted—the pharmacy and their second-floor apartment. The next day the building was burned —"there was no going back." Before the fire the Singers were a part of the community, now they weren't.[61]

At the 900 block of West North Avenue, a fire broke out in a Lee's Military Surplus Store. The fire quickly spread to three other buildings which together stood in a "V" shaped pattern where Linden and North avenues meet. A half a block away east of the surplus store fire, looters hit and set fire to Sagel's Market. When the first engines arrived, the battalion chief stated to reporters, "This is a one alarm fire because that's all the trucks we've got to fight the fire with."[62]

The fire in Sagels spread to a boarded-up store and restaurant. There were some 400 bystanders watching the fire when someone called out, "Let's go over to D.C. and get the White House." An hour later the National Guard arrived to disperse the crowd.[63]

Guardsmen, although deployed all along Pennsylvania Avenue from Preston Street to North Avenue, three at each corner and a number stationed in the middle of the block, still couldn't stop the looters from vandalizing the Tommy Tucker

Five and Dime store located in the 1600 block. Looters were calmly walking out with varied merchandise.[64]

Looters on the eastside were not as lucky, as police arrested 10 looting a pawn shop at Bond and Monument streets. The pawn shop was like most of the businesses hit since the riots started. It consisted of a three-story brick row house with the first floor converted into a business with apartments and storage or offices occupying the upper floors. As police placed their unlucky captives in nearby police cruisers, the lucky rioters that got away struck back and torched the pawn shop.

At 12:25 p.m., the Maryland State Police reported that 12 cars with D.C. and Virginia license plates loaded down with five or six African-Americans in each car were traveling north towards Baltimore on the Baltimore-Washington Parkway. Police would be on the lookout.

During the afternoon the looting and burning continued. National Guardsmen responded to hundreds of fires where they protected the firefighters. Looting was reported in the 1800 block of Greenmount Avenue. City police worried that the National Guardsmen were not protecting all critical spots.

In the blue-collar mostly white Hampden section of the city located well north of the North Avenue turmoil and sealed off geographically by Jones Falls on the west and the John Hopkins University campus to the east, fire engines were combating a fire on the corner of Falls Road and 41st Street. As a grocery store at Federal and Barclay streets west of the Greenmount Cemetery burned, thieves used the distraction of the riots to jack up cars parked on numerous east Baltimore streets to steal parts and tires.

The downtown department store shopping area was quiet as additional law enforcement personnel were moved in to protect the big-name department stores such as Hutzlers, Hochschild Kohn, Stewarts and the Hecht-May Company. At approximately 1:46 p.m., 50 Maryland State Police troopers were assigned to Baltimore and Franklin streets between Calvert and Howard streets.

The Southern Christian Leadership Conference (SCLC) had a number of its members working the streets trying to convince rioters and looters to go home. As police were attempting to apprehend three black youths for looting, a group of SCLC officials tried to intervene. This bold attempt by SCLC members to control out-of-control youths only created friction with police and almost ended in the arrest of the SCLC members. Once cooler heads prevailed, police reluctantly gave in and allowed the group to escort the young teenagers home.[65]

After almost 24 hours of looting and arson, the rioters seemed to have set down a pattern to the madness. Most looters would break a window of a business, run, hide a short distance away and await the arrival of law enforcement. If the police officers or guardsmen didn't show, they would start to loot the store.

Once all of the worthwhile merchandise was removed, someone would set the structure afire. This pattern occurred repeatedly in the 1600 block of Pennsylvania Avenue and finally ran its course in the 900 block of Whitelock Street, as a grocery store burned after it was looted.[66]

At 1:44 p.m. firefighters were requesting assistance due to sniper shootings and the throwing of rocks and bottles by rioters. State police officers and soldiers were sent into the trouble areas to protect firefighters. Although the firefighters seemed to be successful in battling the fires, the looting got worse. Teenage looters were reported as far north as the Pimlico area.

As another fire broke out at a liquor store at Federal Street and Milton Avenue, the east Baltimore area between Gay Street on the west and Broadway on the east appeared to be a hotbed of problems. Around 1:30 p.m., State's Attorney Charles Moylan Jr. was quoted as saying, "The looting in the eastern half of Baltimore has reached terrible proportions." Large crowds were starting to gather on Baltimore Street in the famous "block" of strip clubs and bars. Two hours later the police moved in with the K-9 Corps and dispersed the crowd.[67]

The riots were now spreading north, south and west throughout the city. Dozens were arrested each hour and school buses continued to be used to transport the vandals to jail.[68] By mid-afternoon, the city ran out of police officers on the eastside—all policemen were committed and there were no reserves. The availability of shelters for the disabled and homeless became a concern since they were now being filled by many that lived near or above businesses that were burned.[69]

At 2 p.m., authorities made the decision to enforce an earlier curfew and moved the curfew hour from 11 p.m. to 4 p.m. Sales of gasoline and other inflammables were banned (except for fuel dispensed in vehicles). No alcohol was to be sold in Baltimore City, Anne Arundel, Baltimore and Howard Counties and the bans went into effect at this new time. It was decided that state, city and county offices would be closed on Monday. Throughout the city, special municipal courts were set up to handle nearly 2,000 cases of possession of stolen goods and curfew violations. To add to the city's problems, it was reported that there was a second flare up in the city jail—approximately 250 prisoners were involved in series of altercations.[70]

IN 1968, THERE WERE FIVE FIRE STATIONS located along and within the busy North Avenue corridor between Hilton Street and Broadway; three were located on North Avenue and the other two within two to four blocks away. On Sunday afternoon, as were many other stations in the east side and west side communities north of Baltimore Street, they were empty. Ten minutes after the Fire Alarm center downtown at Lexington Street received reports from on-scene battalion chiefs that all of the structure fires were under control and maybe, just maybe, the chiefs could send a couple of engines back to the empty stations, four blocks of Harford Avenue, from Federal Street to North Avenue, hard hit by Saturday night's arson and looting, erupt in flames again with new fires.

Around 2:30 p.m., a luncheonette at Harford Avenue and Federal Street that had been looted in the morning was burning. It took up to two dozen state police troopers and another dozen guardsmen to protect the firefighters working there from an unruly crowd.[71] Two blocks north from the fire-and-rock-throwing melee, a delicatessen was torched along with three nearby houses. Firefighters dragged charged hose lines across glass shards and loose bricks and tried not to trip over ruined vending machines lying ripped apart in the street. Police officers also tried to maneuver around the debris-ridden street as they restrained, captured, and handcuffed rioters. After some 18 hours of mob violence and multi-alarm fires, four blocks of Harford Avenue south of North Avenue looked like a war zone.[72]

As the fires and lootings continued, the only good news, announced at 3:10 p.m., was that the Baltimore Transit Company would continue with its normal bus runs after the new 4 p.m. curfew went into effect.[73] Rioters celebrate the start of the early curfew by torching a dry cleaning business located at Ashland Avenue and Broadway. The blazing cleaners, which had been vandalized the night before, was quickly attacked by responding firefighters who confined the fire to the building.[74]

The curfew celebration continued as two more blazes broke out in liquor stores between 4 and 5 p.m. The Cut-rate Liquors and Rico's Package Goods Stores located a block apart, burned in the 800 and 900 blocks of Caroline Street.

Throughout the eastside lootings and fires rambled uncontested. At approximately 3 p.m., the police command post at Gay and Aisquith streets reported that between 400 and 500 people were looting stores near Monument and Bond streets and Cold Spring Lane. Police Command personnel downtown were attempting to concentrate law enforcement personnel in a large area bordered by Maryland Avenue on the west side, Milton Avenue to the east, 25th Street to the north and Orleans Street to the south.

At the National Guard Command Operations Center located at the Fifth Regiment Armory, requests were being communicated to "deploy all troops." An editorial in the following night's *Evening Sun* summed up the situation: "Baltimore, once charmed, has fallen apart like the rest. Baltimoreans had tended to congratulate themselves that it couldn't in any way happen here."[74]

National Guardsmen were using tear gas to displace rioters around the American Brewery complex located on Gay Street, five blocks below North Avenue. However the Guard's attempts were futile as the building was looted and burned.[75]

Major looting was reported on Lamont Street and Harford Avenue. Five police cruisers transported a number of Maryland State Police Officers with K-9 dogs to address the chaos.[76] By this point more than 30 offenders had been arrested in the Western District alone. Most were charged with looting and burning. At 3:30 p.m., the eastern command post, set up earlier along Gay Street, ran out of police cars—they were all committed to incidents and there were no reserves. However, "there [was] a bright spot in the darkly turbulent afternoon" as black and white youths worked together to quell four brush fires beside the B&O tracks near Howard, Sisson, and 26th streets on the west side.[77]

The *News American* would report the next day that "Youth packs roamed and prowled the glass littered streets from curb to curb. Police radios blared out assist-an-officer calls continuously."[78] As police dispersed a crowd on Baltimore Street at 3:40 p.m., three stores were looted at Guilford Avenue and 21st Street and at Fayette and Gilmor streets. "It was the young negroes, often teenagers, who smashed the plate glass, set the fires, [and] dashed out laughing with a dozen pairs of shoes they couldn't wear."[79]

On the West side, police officers assisted a fellow patrolman lying in Gilmor Street with a bloody head wound caused by a "flying brick." Like other injured police officers, he would be transported to Mercy Hospital. As police assisted the downed officer, Gilmor Street was ravaged from Baltimore to Franklin Street as a string of drug and liquor stores were looted. At the corner of Lexington and Gilmor streets, 50 people looted a drug store, as another 200 cheered them on.[80]

Between 3 and 4 p.m., numerous reports of violence and fires were flooding the fire and police communications centers. A fire was reported in the 500 block of Robert Street; rioters looted a pawn shop burned-out the night before at Bond and Monument streets. The near-by Club Savoy was burning. More violence was reported at Hoffman and Dallas streets and at Bond and Lanvale streets.[81]

Police had their hands full, as an unruly mob gathered in the 2400 block of Barclay Street and a crowd of looters moved in on a warehouse at Guilford Avenue and Biddle Street. Most of this violence occurred just 20 minutes before the 4 p.m. curfew began. At approximately 3:45 p.m., there was renewed looting at Ashland Avenue and Aisquith Street, North Avenue and Wolfe Street, and Preston and Ensor streets. Fires and unruly crowds were reported in the 1700 and 1800 blocks of Harford Avenue.

At 4 p.m., the police were stretched to the limit. Police paddy wagons along with school buses were extremely busy hauling offenders to city jails and temporary lock-ups. Since officers were required to guard prisoners at the command post and waited for considerably long periods before the wagons and buses returned, the police couldn't be deployed to the streets.[82] As a result, all cars were ordered back to the scenes of reported violence, leaving prisoners jailed unofficially in the hands of the National Guardsmen patrolling the posts.

It seemed that liquor stores were the hardest hit of all the available opportunities to loot and burn. Despite the 4 p.m. curfew, the west side looting quickened; more problems were reported in the 1500 to 1700 blocks of Pennsylvania Avenue as youths hit more liquor stores. Police tried to seal off the area, but teens circled back to loot sought out-stores serving alcohol. Dark brown smoke could be seen billowing in the sky as a liquor store located on the corner of Laurens and Stricker streets went up in flames.[83]

At Ashland Avenue and Broadway, a drycleaners that was looted on Saturday was torched. At Madison and Gay streets, windows were kicked in at the Midway Gas Station. Over on the eastside, twenty shotguns were ordered to be sent up from the armory, and four cruisers were sent to disperse a crowd of hundreds of youths at Ashland Avenue and Central Avenue. The Eastern Police District was severely running short of officers.[84]

As reports were received indicating that approximately 300 people were milling around the 2400 block of Barclay Street, six stores were looted in the 2000 block of Edmondson Avenue near Payson Street. Weary, tired and exhausted, city police officers complained that the National Guardsmen were refusing to intervene in the hostilities making the officer's jobs more difficult.[85]

At 4:30 p.m., mobs were reported congregating all along Pennsylvania Avenue from the 700 block to the 2000 block. At Bond and Madison streets a liquor store was burned and looted. As the late afternoon sun began to descend in the west, Red Cross workers set up a refugee center at 758 Dolphin Street in west Baltimore. The city jail was pushing its capacity with 500 offenders now confined.[86]

Streets normally deserted on a Sunday afternoon were filled with hundreds of African-Americans. Some were looting, some were watching, some were throwing rocks and bottles at firefighters and police officers, and some were wandering aimlessly.[87] A structure fire was reported at Lanvale Street and Guilford Avenue, near the Mildred Monroe Elementary School. Flames leaped from the vacant dwelling's windows on the second floor.

As the out-of-control dwelling fire spread, firefighters endured and prevailed through unprecedented conditions. Engine company and truck company personnel working in teams of two and three, raised extension ladders, and pulled and advanced hose lines. Driver-operators set up and maneuvered the large deluge nozzles, capable of pumping hundreds of gallons per minute, mounted on the tops of their engines. The brave men ducked and dodged rocks as hundreds gathered. It was hard to read the ever-growing crowd.

The three-story dwelling fire produced a dark grey smoke combined with a brownish-black billowing smoke as the structure's roof began to cave in. The billowing smoke ascended to join the many other plumes accumulating over the sunny Palm Sunday sky of Baltimore. The fire quickly accelerated to three alarms before it was considered under control approximately two hours later.[88]

Firefighters, although they know their profession is one of the most dangerous in the world, generally enjoy fighting fires. It's why they join up with the fire department and it is what they have been trained to do. Over the years, firefighters have shared with one another the danger of battling fires especially firefighting with the adversity of the weather's unpredictable elements. In many companies that experience has bonded the men together into one strong cohesive team where no job is too big.

Firefighters that needed to be alert, aggressive, and simultaneously look out for their own safety as well as the safety of those working with them. Being on the nozzle of an attack line was the best, being the backup person was good. Being the backup person pulling the slack of the hose line was not as good. Pulling hose up from the ground, while standing on a ladder was the worst; especially while being pelted by rocks and bottles.

The leadoff man's responsibility was to hook the hydrant fitting attached to the supply line hose to the fire hydrant. Although it was one of the most important jobs, to get much needed water to the fire ground, it was the least liked by firefighters.

During the riots the job was even less desirable since a lone firefighter was left at the hydrant to fend off the crowd and put up with the taunting while the driver-operator drove the apparatus and remaining crew some distance away towards the burning structure.

As they gained experienced in battling fires under hostile conditions, two firefighters would be left to hook up to the hydrant. At times, rioters would shut down hydrants or use sharp objects such as axes to cut holes in the hose lines. For firefighters down on their knees in a dark smoky superheated atmosphere fighting an interior fire, having their water cut off was a terrifying experience. During the riots, the conditions firefighters fought under in Baltimore as well as in the other burning cities in the nation were scarcely equaled anywhere.

At 21st Street and Greenmount Avenue, two stores and three dwellings were burning. One, a military surplus store, was ransacked before it was torched. Firefighters were working tough and making headway to protect the other adjacent structures threatened by the raging blaze.

Three blocks south on Greenmount Avenue near North Avenue, the Baltimore Police Community Relations Center's plate glass window was busted out. It appeared that it took one hit in the exact center of the large display window. One could just make out the painted words now missing some letters as a result of the damage which had said, "LET'S TALK IT OVER." Maybe seeing the sign and taking a few seconds to contemplate and to reflect on the sign's message kept looters and arsonist from completely ravaging and burning the facility.[89]

For a period on Sunday afternoon there was not one single police officer or military officer in the North Broadway section of East Baltimore and as a result the violence spread as fast as a California wildfire.[90] Now, fire engine after fire engine raced down Monument Street between Broadway and Patterson Park Avenue as a string of 15 stores and businesses were looted and some set on fire. Hardest hit were Penn Optical and Provident Savings and Loan. All three floors of a cleaning establishment were burning.[91] While dwellings burned nearby on north Broadway, two separate structure fires were started at Monument and Bond streets, and a tavern and package goods store were looted.

CITY SCENES NOW TOOK ON THE LOOK of televised reports from Vietnam as Army helicopters flew over and patrolled the stricken areas. The helicopters circled the riot areas and radioed their reconnaissance back to the National Guard command post located at the Fifth Regiment Armory. As choppers chattered overhead, firefighters below were wearing down. It took many companies two hours to battle a fire that destroyed four dwellings in the 1800 block of Harford Avenue near North Avenue.[92]

In one of the Army choppers hovering above, sat Lieutenant General Robert H. York. York had arrived in the city around 8 a.m., straight from his regiment's arrival at Andrews Air Force Base in near-by Prince Georges County. From the chopper, the general observed the rioting, the damage, and attempted to get a handle on the situation. He had a gut feeling that at some point the President would deploy his Federal troops, the 18th Airborne Artillery unit. Like any good commander he wanted to understand the lay of the land below and familiarize himself with the tumultuous situation in the event he was placed in charge.

York was a professional soldier. He was a West Point graduate from the class of 1938. The general had seen action in World War II, Korea and Vietnam.[93] The 54-year-old Army veteran fought battles in North Africa, Sicily and Normandy. More recently, York had commanded the 18th Airborne during the four-day Detroit riots in the summer of 1967. York knew what needed to be done to quell the racial unrest. As some of his soldiers at Andrews were unloading planes and loading trucks, 1,900 men of his airborne unit were already in a convoy of Army deuce-and-a-half trucks headed for Baltimore.

In the event the President gave the order to deploy if requested by Governor Agnew, York wanted to be ready. Preparedness was the General's middle name.[94]

By 5 p.m., the majority of the fires were under control as firefighters wet down the smoldering debris lying throughout the burned out structures. Policemen were now driving through the riot-ravaged sections of the city with megaphones broadcasting "The curfew is now in effect — anyone caught on the street will be locked up."[95] Policemen wisely permitted an unofficial one-hour warning period starting at 4 p.m. to allow those on the street to get back home. Police officers did not actually start apprehending curfew violators and making arrests until 5 p.m.[96]

There were so many people arrested and brought to the Western District Police Station, it was decided that judges would hold court throughout the night. Since the building could not hold all of the offenders awaiting hearings, many of the defendants had to be lined up in the station's parking lot until their cases were heard. All of this guard duty at the police stations took police officers from the streets, which allowed the violence to continue.

Guard duty at the Western District Police Station would only get worse at 5 p.m. as police officers would now be arresting curfew violators.[97] The situation was compounded when 50 additional rioters were brought in. In one sweep, they were picked up while looting a clothing store in the 2000 block of Edmondson Avenue. More rioters were picked up at stores located along Baltimore Street from Pine Street west.[98]

In addition to the all-night courts, other high-level decisions were being made. At 5 p.m., Fire Chief Killen ordered all firefighters back to work. Sixty percent of the department's fire apparatus (or 50 engines and ladder trucks) were committed throughout the city on numerous fires; the likes of which the Baltimore City Fire Department had never seen before.[99]

9

North Avenue
"A Match Waiting to be Struck"
Sunday Evening, April 7, 1968

As the sun started to go down in the burning and smoking city, it seemed a new fire occurred every 30 seconds. In a period of six minutes over a dozen structure fires were set throughout town. At 5:05 p.m., units responded to a fire in the 600 block of Barnes Street near Aisquith Street. A minute later another fire was reported at Myrtle Avenue and Mosher Street near the Pennsylvania Avenue corridor, a third at North Gilmor and Laurens streets near the Gilmor Elementary School and a fourth two blocks north in the 1500 block of Gilmor Street.

A minute later a fifth fire broke out in a structure in the 1900 block of North Rosedale Street near Hanlon Park. Not far from Fulton Avenue, two more fires erupted in the 1000 block of West Lombard Street and at Calhoun and School streets respectfully. Further north engines and ladder trucks were responding to an eighth fire at Liberty Heights Avenue not far from the Mondawmin Mall. Three more fires were reported, the ninth in the 2000 block of East Biddle Street, the tenth in the 800 block of North Port Street and at the 600 block of East Eager Street the eleventh. The twelfth fire occurred 10 blocks east at the 1600 block of Eager Street at 5:11 p.m. As the dozen fires burned another fire would break out at the 1000 block of East Lombard Street.[1]

"As the afternoon turned to evening, the violence escalated… Young blacks and crowds of spectators were heard singing the famous civil rights song—We Shall Overcome." Crowds seemed larger and uglier than those that roamed the streets Saturday night approximately 24 hours earlier.[2] City Police

Colonel Frank J. Battaglia, in charge of operations, stated, "That 95 percent—almost all of the offenders were teenagers or younger."[3]

Michael Olesker was a reporter for the *Sun* walking the streets and making observations for the paper. In his discussions with African-Americans from the neighborhood, he found that there was animosity between the blacks and the white store owners. According to Olesker's observations, "there were white store owners everywhere in the neighborhood, who had no blacks working for them. When the owner got sick, rather than hire a black to keep the store open, he closed it."[4] The white owners thought the blacks would rob them or give things away.

Olesker remembered, "Standing on the corner of Eager and Ensor streets, about five blocks east of the State Penitentiary, and looking in every direction of the city and seeing fire everywhere."[6] He would later report from his contacts in the neighborhood, he wrote, "In the barbershop, months before the murder of Martin Luther King, there was talk of the riots. The assassination was just an excuse. The riots were a match waiting to be struck."[5]

More violence continued as police officers responded to assist other police officers working the looting now occurring at North Poppleton and Saratoga streets and to a shooting reported at Poppleton and Lexington streets, not far from the home of one of America's most famous poets and writers, Edger Allen Poe.[7]

Between 5:17 and 5:21 p.m., structure fires broke out in the 1600 block of Eager Street, the 1000 block of East Lombard Street and the 1800 block of Baker Street.[8] At 5:31 p.m., Engine #28, from its station located at Guilford Avenue near Mount Royal Avenue was dispatched to a liquor store fire in the 1200 block of East Preston Street.[9]

As orange flames and dark smoke billowed from a broken out display window the white-with-red-trim open-cab Peter Pirsch built Engine #28 slowed down to make its way through the crowds now moving towards Harford Avenue. The engine paused at a fire hydrant near the corner of Preston and Aisquith streets and two firefighters jumped off the backstep to hook the connection to the hydrant.

On Preston Street, the "wingman" firefighter waved down a police officer to assist in getting the crowd back and out of the way of the hydrant. Once the supply hose and firefighters at the hydrant seemed secure, the engine moved up the street to a spot near the front of the burning liquor store. It is wise to park the engine so it does not block the front of the building so the ladder truck can maneuver in and set up there. Unfortunately on this fire, for the time being anyhow, the men would not be seeing a ladder truck anytime soon since nearly all in the area are already committed. In its place would be Engine #15 responding approximately two and one-half miles away from its station located on Lombard Street near Eutaw Street.[10]

The officer, who was now standing on the floor in the front seat area of Engine #28 with the radio microphone in one hand and holding on to the top of the windshield with the other, radioed that they had heavy fire showing from the structure and requested two additional engines and a ladder truck. As the officer sat down his radio microphone, he could now see flames breaking through the second-floor windows of the converted store/row house. The fire was extending to the second floor which usually contained apartments. The officer observed a second engine proceeding through the crowd and moving toward the fire building from Harford Avenue. Crew members on that engine too had laid supply hose from another hydrant north of the blaze and the driver/operator was positioning the large firefighting vehicle at the row house adjacent to the fire.[11]

Firefighters were now pulling hose lines out of Engine #28's hose bed to attack the fire. Normally, the crew would put on SCBA and crawl into the structure from the unburned side. From the unburned side they would try to drive the fire out with high-pressure water spray from the attack hose line, but not today or any time soon. The firefighters, now adapted and, utilized "hit and run" tactics similar to the rioters. These tactics consisted of knocking down or controlling the fire by firefighters using hose lines in the street. Firefighters only moved into the interior once the heat and smoke turned to steam and they typically entered without breathing apparatus.[12] Similar scenes were taking place across the city as dozens of engine and truck companies were dispatched to fires.

The fires were wearing down the firefighters. At 5:34 p.m., engines were dispatched to structure fires at East Chase Street and Lakewood Avenue and four minutes later to a fire at North Milton Avenue and Preston Street. For most firefighters the next hour's objective was to move to another fire across the street or a block away. At many fires only one engine was all that existed in the street for a block or two surrounded by police officers and guardsmen. At 5:50 p.m., units responded to a reported building fire at North Washington and Eager streets.[13]

As firefighters continued with their hit-and-run tactics, sometimes not even checking for fire extension and/or smoldering hot spots, fires broke out around 6 p.m., at Gay and Eager streets, in the 200 block of East Biddle Street, in the 700 block of East 20th Street, at 30th Street and Jennifer Avenue, in the 200 block of South Bethel Street, at Bond and Gay streets, at Madison and Caroline streets, at Caroline and Dallas streets, and at Ensor and Preston streets. Additional fires occurred at Warwick Avenue and Presbury Street, at Biddle Street and North Collington Avenue, and in the first block of North Poppleton Street. Basically there was one fire every five seconds.[14]

As dusk set in over the smoking city, authorities realized that the number of troops and police officers were insufficient to quell the disturbances. Riots were spreading west and intensifying. A spokesperson for the National Guard stated, "The fires are better, but the looting is worse. We are doing everything we can but we are stretched thin."[15] At approximately 5:46 p.m. Mayor D'Alesandro was at the police command post for a briefing with Police Major William Armstrong. Armstrong was considered one of the best of Chief Donald Pomerleau's commanders. The efficient, by-the-book police officer was always prompt, professional and impeccably dressed in his uniform. However, on this early evening, when the major entered the conference room to begin the briefing his uniform was unkempt and his hair was mussed as if he had been in a scuffle. Observing that, and seeing a look of despair in the major's face, D'Alesandro knew in that instant that it was time to bring in the Federal troops.[16]

D'Alesandro conferred with Police Chief Pomerleau and generals Gelston and York regarding the increased violence and the thinning of available law enforcement. They all agreed that additional assistance was needed. D'Alesandro then contacted Governor Agnew to make the call to President Johnson and request the President to deploy the Federal troops. Fortunately, by order of the President, Federal troops had been arriving in the city since mid-morning for stand-by. Once notified, Agnew contacted U.S. Attorney Ramsey Clark and the deployment process was discussed over the phone.[17]

At 6 p.m., Governor Agnew sent a telegram directly to the White House. It said:

President Johnson—*"Under existing circumstances the law enforcement resources of the State of Maryland are unable to suppress the serious domestic violence in and near the City of Baltimore. Federal troops requested."*—Governor Agnew

The President replied quickly. At 6:04, Agnew received a telegram from President Johnson. It said: Governor Agnew— *"I have already directed the troops you request to proceed to Druid Hill Park. They will be available on arrival for immediate deployment as required to support and assist the National Guard."*—President Johnson[18]

The 1,900 members of the 18th Airborne unit would be the first Federal soldiers called into the city since the Railroad Strike at Camden Station in 1877. They were flown into Andrews Air Force Base about 50 miles south of the city and bused or trucked to Baltimore.[19] General York was now in command of the National Guard and the 6,000 guardsman were officially federalized at 10:15 p.m. Task Force OSCAR became Task Force Baltimore, the federal designation.[20]

In order for National Guard units to be federalized, there is a formal procedure that the guardsmen perform that requires them to swear an oath to the President of the United States. The officers carried out this procedure among the enlisted men. The irony of it all was that there were rumors among the guardsmen that the federalization of the guard was a ploy and that they would be sent to serve in Vietnam after the riots were under control.[21] Some guardsmen were understandably more worried about going to Southeast Asia than they were about getting killed on the streets of Baltimore.

Dust stirred throughout the fields near the Baltimore Zoo as the big duce-and-a-half army trucks and buses drove in and soldiers started setting up camp in Druid Hill Park. Within a couple of hours the huge area encompassing the camp was protected by barbed wire. Hundreds of traditional Army pup tents were pitched neatly and orderly throughout the grounds. Large cooking and supply tents were set up to support soldiers. As troops worked at setting up the camp, others were immediately moved out to riot areas.[22]

At 6:05 p.m., the city fire alarm office announced for the second time that day that all fires were under control for the time being. As soon as the announcement was made, a fire broke out in a three-story building at the corner of Preston Street and Central Avenue. The building contained two vacant apartments, an income tax service and a confectionary store on the first floor. Looting continued as a liquor store located at Baker Street and Fulton Avenue was hit by rioters. Rioters were also looting various businesses in the 3500 block of Park Heights Avenue. City jails were overflowing with prisoners within two hours after the curfew. The downtown city jail typically houses 1,700 inmates. But due to the curfew violators, it was filled to 2,200 and nearing its maximum capacity of 2,500.[23]

City police responded to an unprecedented number of incidents. In the 36 hours between 7 a.m. Saturday and 7 p.m. Sunday, the Baltimore City Police Department received 7,647 calls for service.[24] By 7:30 p.m., the conflict had spread across the city, especially to the west, with 95 percent of the offenders estimated to be teenagers.

As authorities worried about sabotage to the city's critical infrastructure, five Baltimore Gas and Electric substations were placed under guard. Surrounding counties were now also implementing curfews as Governor Agnew directed Baltimore County to implement a curfew starting at 9 p.m. and ending at 6 a.m., Monday morning. Since mid-night Sunday morning there had been 248 reports of looting and 67 fires.[25]

A meeting was held at the Fifth Regiment Armory at 7:40 p.m. between Chief Pomerleau and Generals York and Gelston to discuss plans for the next 24 hours. The Civil Defense reported that 234 persons had been treated in area hospitals since the start of the disturbance.[26]

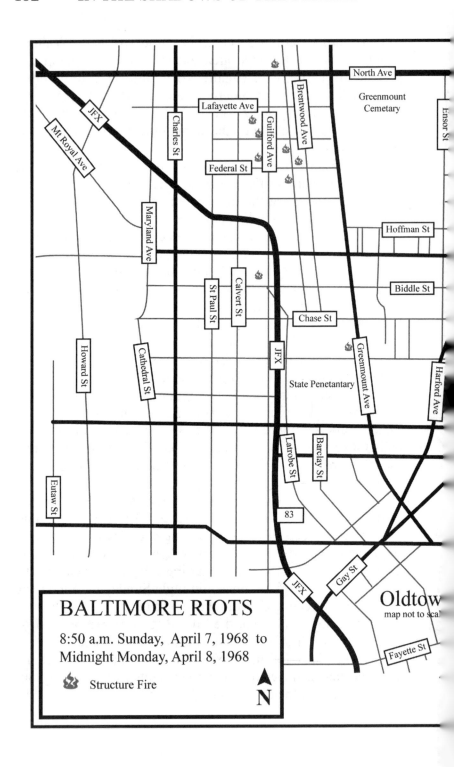

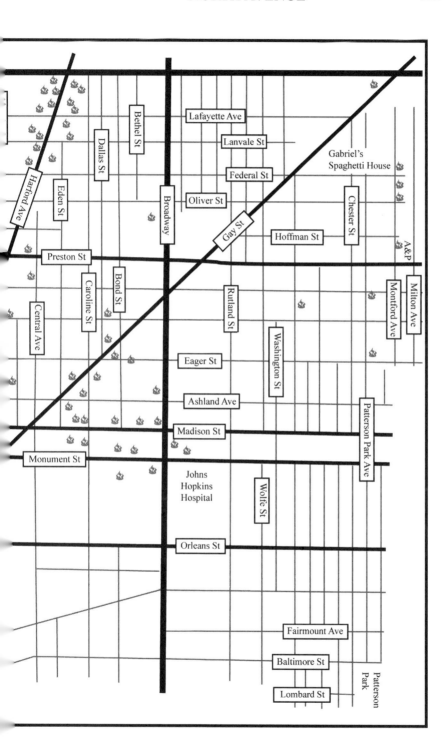

Harford Ave

Bethel St

Lafayette Ave

Lanvale St

Dallas St

Federal St

Gabriel's
Spaghetti House

Eden St

Broadway

Oliver St

Chester St

Gay St

Hoffman St

Preston St

A&P

Caroline St

Bond St

Rutland St

Montford Ave

Milton Ave

Central Ave

Eager St

Washington St

Ashland Ave

Madison St

Patterson Park Ave

Monument St

Johns
Hopkins
Hospital

Wolfe St

Orleans St

Fairmount Ave

Baltimore St

Patterson
Park

Lombard St

ANNE ARUNDEL COUNTY FIRE ENGINES were sent to the city for a second night. Unlike Saturday when they had been parked all night in front of Brooklyn's Engine #35 station on Maude Avenue near Fourth Street, tonight they were immediately dispatched to calls. Henry "Butch" Lawall, a Friendship Airport career firefighter volunteering as a lieutenant with the Linthicum department remembered that he and county driver/operator Melvin Morrison and crew responded to a brush fire with Engine #321.

The fire was located approximately eight miles from Brooklyn in a wooded area near Hilton Parkway on the west side of the city. A city firefighter was riding "shot gun" in the engine's cab as a "bird dog." [27]

A "bird dog" is a regular firefighter who is assigned to a vacated fire station and assists the mutual aid company with directions. The mutual aid company is typically unfamiliar with the area.

Lawall would later state that on this night the city firefighter bird dog assigned to them had never worked on the west side before. It was the first time in his career that he had ever responded to a fire out of the South Baltimore area and he wasn't sure on the directions.

Morrison and Lawall eventually figured out the direction they needed to take. They responded and arrived at the fire, which was burning very rapidly due to the dry April weather on a hill in Gwynns Falls Park.

As Morrison positioned the engine on the side of the Hilton Parkway near the fire, in order for the riding firefighters to deploy the hard rubber booster attack lines, the bird dog city firefighter ran up to Lawall and exclaimed, "Where do you keep your brooms?" "Brooms? " Lawall questioned.[28]

It was a tactical issue. In the city, it took way too much time to re-rack and manually hand crank the booster line back onto many of the engines. It was easier for the city firefighters to beat out brush and field fires with brooms. The Linthicum crew members quickly put out the fire with their "automatic rewind" booster attack lines and returned to Engine #35's station in Brooklyn.[29]

At 8:30 p.m., Governor Agnew appeared on all three major Baltimore television stations to explain the mobilization of federal troops. He also commended the overwhelming majority of the city's citizens, both white and black, who had remained calm during these hours of crisis.

He said, "I ask you to continue this example to remain at home and obey the curfew — even during the daytime hours...I urge all parents to exercise vigilance over their children. In the affected areas much of the lawlessness to date has been caused by unruly and unsupervised youths...Other youngsters whose conduct has been responsible and admirable could be endangered by even the most innocent sightseeing." Agnew went on to promise aid to victims of ravaged businesses and for those made homeless. Finally he stated strongly, "For those who loot and burn will be shown no sympathy."[30]

The Maryland National Guardsmen were now re-forming, concentrating and making a coordinated sweep through the east side of town. As the east side calmed, the west side exploded into what was described as a "liquor crazed frenzy of looting and carousing."[31] Between 8 p.m. and 9 p.m. looting peaked; 128 incidents were logged and fires continued.

On Lexington Street, in the protected area of the city, in a large room on the second floor of the Baltimore City Fire Department Headquarters was the operations "nerve center," the fire alarm office. About a dozen or more alarm operators were fiercely trying to hold things together. Some of the staff (all either on regular shift or on call back) were answering phone calls from frantic citizens reporting fires. Others were handling requests reported in from the city's police department and from the firefighting units on the street.

A large Motorola hard plastic electronic map of the city was mounted on the wall behind the outside center of the U-shaped alarm operator's console. The colorful map, with all of the fire stations noted geographically throughout the city, clearly indicated the tough spot the firefighters were in this night.

Just about all of the station location lamps were lit red, indicating that the stations were vacant. Others were lit in green. Green lights denoted that the stations were in service with staffed second-line apparatus. On the sides of the map were more lights showing the status of the individual ladder trucks, engines, ambulances and battalion chiefs. The alarm operators had a good handle on which units were working on fires and which units were available for a growing list of additional reported fires.[32]

Operators sitting inside the U-shaped operator's console were extremely busy keeping track of the units and the incidents they had been assigned and whether or not they were available for new reports of fires. Brush, dumpster, trash and auto fires were placed on the bottom of the list unless they threatened structures. Since Saturday night, Chief Killen had directed the center operators not to answer any of the city's 2,072 manual fire alarm pull boxes, since most of these were being pulled by rioters simply to create distraction.[33]

A confident alarm operator not only knows the geography of the city, but more importantly has a working knowledge of company fire suppression tactics and capabilities of the fire apparatus. Operators also need to be familiar with the size of various buildings in the city, how various city buildings are constructed, and what parts of the city might be particularly crime-ridden. Armed with this knowledge, an operator might dispatch two engines when on the surface one engine would appear to be sufficient. The operators were also very aware of the dangers in the riot areas and knew when two or more units were dispatched to an incident it enforced the old organizational maxim of safety-in-numbers.

Operators also understand that certain parts of the city have old vacant warehouses or structures that are close to hospitals, nursing homes and other occupancies that contain large numbers of non-ambulatory people that could be harmed by a fast spreading fire. Operators adjust the response to these areas with great care. The operators are experienced enough that they know at times they can send only a couple of engines that must do the work of a half dozen. Ladder truck responses are kept to a minimum since when employing "hit and run" tactics the long tractor-drawn-aerial rigs have a tendency to get in the way of a quick attack. Sometimes operators must send everything that is available at that particular moment in time.

It is the responsibility of individual truck and engine companies to radio in their locations, whether or not they are committed, and if committed how long before they will become available for the next fire. Unfortunately as a result of approximately 150 mobile units attempting to report on the one-channeled radio system, it became overloaded with communications traffic and some units became lost in the confusion. Many units needed to wait for a break in the transmissions before they could make a report. The operators were working extremely hard to keep the confusion to a minimum.

By 8:50 p.m., Federal activity perked up as troops arrived at the Mondawmin Shopping Center en-route to Druid Hill Park. The 18th Airborne was deployed to sweep the western and southwestern districts due to widespread looting and fires in those areas. Other Federal units were sweeping Edmondson Avenue from Hilton Street east to Pennsylvania Avenue. The military deployment strategy was to assign Federal troops such as the 18th Airborne to the west side of the city starting at the Jones Falls Expressway and deploy the National Guard to the east side. Due to the increased disturbances at the city jail, approximately 50 National Guardsmen were deployed there.[34]

Although the violence was increasing and more widespread than on Saturday night, Baltimore hospitals found that they were treating fewer patients. Reports were now coming in for scattered looting at Baltimore and Pine streets. Rioters were becoming more sophisticated in gathering booty as stolen taxi cabs were being used to transport stolen goods in the 900 block to the 1200 block of West Baltimore Street. In the first block of North Caroline Street., a pawn shop owner was ordered by police to hand over all his store's shotguns. Officers carried them to the Pikesville Armory.[35]

On North Avenue, firefighters would later comment that the destruction resembled scenes in World War II news reels of the "London Blitz" in the fall of 1940 during the outbreak of the war. It appeared that every store between Mount Royal Avenue and Monroe Street on both sides of North Avenue had been hit. Fire engines responded to North Avenue and Barclay Street as additional fires were reported.[36]

At Laurens and Stricker streets another liquor store went up in flames. The 909 Club in the 900 block of North Calhoun Street was set on fire. As firefighters pulled up in front of the blazing building, they observed ripped apart pinball machines and a pried open cigarette vending machine, contents missing, lying abandoned on the sidewalk.[37]

Firefighters in the streets noticed that there were isolated cars full of extremely noisy black youths, with the words "soul" or "soul brother" whitewashed on the side doors. Many of these cars had black flags hanging from their antennas.[38] Doctor Louis L. Randall, who lived in West Baltimore in 1968, stated that black doctors put a "soul brother" sign in their office windows and on their office doors to keep from being looted. In many small shops without the "soul brother sign," owners watched as their entire life savings went up in smoke.[39]

Looting and arson continued for four hours after the curfew. Pillaging was taking place on Edmondson Avenue, especially in the 2000 block, and rioting was beginning in the 900 block of Whitelock Street. In the 1800 block of Greenmount Avenue, still smoking from the night before a liquor store was looted. The city jail remained filled beyond capacity. Three municipal courts were severely overcrowded and a race riot involving 400 black prisoners broke out at the Maryland Training Center.[40] Baltimore's riot area comprised 1,000 square blocks, bounded roughly by 23rd Street on the north, Poplar Grove Street on the west, Baltimore Street on the south, and Broadway on the east.

Since the bungled firebombing of the shopping center in Cherry Hill late Thursday night, Baltimore City south of the middle branch of the Patapsco River had been fairly quiet. So it was quite a surprise when minor looting broke out in Brooklyn Heights at Sixth and Church streets in Anne Arundel County just a stone's throw from the city line. Anne Arundel County Police as well as city police responded.[41]

On North Avenue near Linden Avenue a firefighter received an eye injury moments after he relieved his lieutenant. The lieutenant was being transported to Maryland General Hospital in a fire department ambulance experiencing what was described as a minor heart attack.[42] As other firefighters were pulled from their positions to tend to the firefighter's eye injury, a crowd of

150 people gathered to watch three stores and several vacant buildings burn.

The crowd could hear other fire engines racing to a reported fire at Falls Road and 41st Street. Simultaneously, a grocery store was set afire at Federal and Barclay streets, as another crowd of 300 looked on. More looting was now being reported at Guilford Avenue and 21st Street. On the west side along Gilmor Street from Baltimore Street to Franklin Street, a string of discount drug and liquor stores were burglarized. Three more stores were looted on Edmondson Avenue, and another six stores located near Edmondson Avenue and Payson Street. Everywhere streets were covered with broken glass.[43]

North of North Avenue there was looting at 21st Street and Greenmount Avenue. On Sunday, unlike on Saturday night, teenagers and young adults were now joined by adults "who had stood on the fringe the night before uncertain of the risks."[44] These adults now joining the ruckus were older, in their 50s and 60s. They could be seen "casually" entering stores, broken into only minutes earlier, and "clamoring" alongside youth for the expensive hardware.[45] "Apparently the success of the street leaders and their cohorts emboldened the older generation." The looting widened to include fathers and their sons.[46]

Off duty city firefighter Lloyd Marcus and his family had attended Palm Sunday services earlier that morning. When the family returned home, one of his young daughters told him that the fire department had called and ordered him back to work. He reported to Engine #6 and had been battling fires throughout the business corridor all afternoon.

Around 5 p.m., Engine #6 and crew members responded to a dwelling fire on Gay Street near Chester Street. When they arrived they found flames leaping out of the windows of a corner row home. The flames covered the width of the sidewalk. Marcus recalled that a cheering crowd of about 100, standing in front of a liquor store across the street started heckling and throwing bottles, bricks and debris at the firefighters as they prepared to fight the fire.

When the Engine #6 officer was hit in the face and temporarily blind in one eye, he shouted to the firefighters to leave the area. The firefighters dropped whatever they were doing and bolted down Chester Street abandoning the running engine in the middle of the street. A second engine that was assisting uncoupled its water supply line and departed the area with the firefighters hanging onto the sides.

A few minutes later, the state police arrived, broke up the crowd, and secured the area. The firefighters returned to suppress the out-of-control fire. Approximately one hour later, as darkness set in and the fire was well extinguished, Marcus and crew members were on the row house roof checking for fire extension and possible hot spots. When he looked out and up into the night sky, "There was fire and smoke everywhere" Marcus said, "It looked like the apocalypse, the end of the world."[47]

On North Broadway a home was burning, while in the 1800 block of Harford Avenue fires were set in trash cans. Laurens, Riggs and Stricker, all side streets off of Pennsylvania Avenue, were consumed by looting. Pennsylvania Avenue took on the appearance of a "ghost town." Now looting was occurring south of the Upton area at Baker Street and Fulton Avenue. Weary police officers were investigating reports of looting in Baltimore Street stores from Pine Street to the west. In the 2000 block of Edmondson Avenue and in the 900 and 1200 blocks of West Baltimore Street there was heavy looting.[48]

As darkness set on the ravaged city, shootings were reported at Lennox Street and Callow Avenue and at Franklin Street and Warwick Avenue. At Division and Wilson Street two more structure fires broke out. Rioters armed themselves after breaking into a pawn shop in the 1300 block of Edmondson Avenue and stealing 73 rifles. A couple of miles west in the 4800 block of Edmondson Avenue, a service station was looted. City police arrested four looters at Laurens and Stricker streets. Police officers confiscated a loaded pistol from a man at Monroe Street and Wilkens Avenue.[49]

At 9:30 p.m., a fire broke out in the Chinese-American Restaurant located in the 1300 block of Pennsylvania Avenue, between Lanvale Street and Lafayette Avenue. After receiving reports of people trapped on the second floor, firefighters set up numcrous ground ladders and entered the second floor through window openings to conduct a coordinated search. As much as possible, they worked in pairs, crawling along the floors with their shoulders or hands always making contact with the walls. In thick smoke, the walls or a hose line are the firefighters only reference points in the event they have to retreat from the building. Hose lines were also pulled up the ladders and the fire was checked before it could penetrate the second floor apartments, which were occupied by a least 11 family members. The owner of the business, Tim Ching, said that everyone escaped from the fire.[50] The fire badly damaged the restaurant as well as the adjacent Big Value Supermarket.

Four pieces of equipment and 30 firefighters were able to control the fire in an hour. Battalion Chief Godfrey Rys stated, "[The fire] looked like all the others." The adjacent supermarket was looted and the first floor burned, however received less damage than the Chinese restaurant.[51] When firefighters arrived about 50 blacks stood around the street watching the operation. Soldiers arrived later, announced to the crowd that the curfew was in effect, and ordered everyone to leave. They all left.

Between 8 p.m. and 11 p.m., the greatest amount of looting and fire incidents since the start of the riots was reported.[52] At 10 p.m., a drug and liquor store at Windsor Mill Road and Chelsea Terrace was looted repeatedly in the two hours leading up to midnight while the Bolton Hill Shopping Center at McMechen Street was ransacked. Back at the police stations, Special Municipal Courts convened—more than 1,800 faced charges of curfew violation or possession of stolen property.[53]

There were people living in the riot torn areas who were ashamed of the out-of-control violence. They stayed indoors and took no part in it. There were clergy who thought they failed their congregations. Father Joseph Gallagher, a Catholic Priest, would later write for the Baltimore *Sun* about a fire that broke out in a junkyard on Pennsylvania Avenue around 11p.m. He could see the flames from Saint Gregory's Seminary, where he lived, not far from North Paca Street. He recalled, "With a brisk wind blowing, the flames looked threatening. As the firefighters fought to control the fire, they were pelted from projectiles from the out-of-control crowd."[54] The next day, at afternoon mass at Saint Gregory, a young negro woman approached Father Gallagher and said, "Please don't feel responsible [for this]. If you blame yourself, it will make me feel worse."[55]

At 11:45 p.m., Chief Killen made a decision to free up needed ambulances. From this point on, the department would refuse ambulance service for non-emergency sick cases. Ambulances would only be used for and respond to life-threatening injuries. Chief Killen also stated that the fires in Baltimore were "the worst since 1904."[56]

The Johns Hopkins Hospital claimed that the majority of the injuries that were coming in were minor. These injuries consisted of small cuts on heads, hands, and legs. Many wounds were the result of rioters hurling stones, trash cans, and bottles at passing motorist and pedestrians. Most persons injured in East Baltimore over the weekend were black teenagers and young adults. The Johns Hopkins emergency room admitted 121. Out of that number, only six were admitted overnight or longer. They had either been shot or stabbed.[57]

During the riots, many teenage to young adult African-Americans had been attacked by other blacks. It was an opportunity to settle old scores between rivals such as vengeful pay backs for unresolved conflicts or issues that occurred between members of the city's youth before the assassination. To make sure the violence did not spread into the hospital, security guards were placed at every door. As far as Johns Hopkins Hospital was concerned, the movement of patients and application of medical treatment ran very smooth.[58]

At midnight a major fire destroyed a furniture store at Guilford Avenue and Lanvale Street. About the same time a store in the 900 block of North Avenue went up in flames spreading to three buildings.[59] In the four blackened blocks of Harford Avenue between North Avenue and Federal Street another fire broke out.

Sunday's police reports included 400 episodes of looting, for a two-day total of 600. Most of Sunday's looting took place between 2 p.m. and 11 p.m. A 40-block swath (of the east and west mid sections) of the city had been severely impacted by rioting. More than 700 businesses had been robbed. Looting had increased and surprisingly the number of fires had decreased from Saturday.

By late Sunday night, the combined force of Federal troops and National Guardsmen equaled more than 9,000 soldiers and it was evident that the looters and arsonist continued the hit-and-run tactics developed on Saturday. There were 300 people injured, 420 active fires, 550 verified cases of looting, and 1,350 arrested.[60]

However unlike Saturday, there were clashes between looters and troops. When the National Guardsmen hit the streets, many of them had fixed bayonets to their rifles. Although they carried 20 rounds of ammunition just in case they were fired upon, the rifles were empty.

The guardsmen were now assigned to the fire department engine and truck companies. They would ride on top of the engines in the hose bed or the main aerial ladder of a truck company with bayonets fixed to their rifles.

Lloyd Marcus would later say, "My biggest fear with the guardsmen riding on the engines was that the vehicle was going to be involved in some kind of accident and I was going to land on one of those sharp bayonets."[61]

For the first time since the riots started, there were reported clashes between whites and blacks. On Sunday, it was reported that fights developed between white and black youths in the area of Broadway near Bank Street after whites heard rumors that blacks were going to burn areas around South Broadway. White youths were arrested for throwing a Molotov cocktail into the street from a speeding car.[62]

Although, General Gelston stated, "It is difficult to believe that this [the riots] could be completely spontaneous. However there is no hard evidence of any conspiracy behind the rioting." Authorities were still looking for a Ford Mustang with Broward County Florida tags, rumored to be driven by H. Rap Brown. Brown was suspected of assembling large groups of angry protesters and agitating them into violence.[63, 64]

10

West Baltimore

"The Flames Were On Their Own"

Monday, April 8, 1968

During the early morning hours between midnight and Monday's sunrise the violence in Baltimore continued. Six sniper incidents had been reported at Gilmor and Baker streets, the 1600 block of Calvert Street, Lombard and Lloyd streets, Monroe and Baltimore streets, Biddle Street and Argyle Avenue, and in the 2900 block of the Alameda. At 1:55 a.m., police officers believed they had caught some of the culprits as two suspects were arrested in the 900 block of North Fulton Avenue.[1]

Many more fires broke out during the night at Frederick Avenue and Millard Street, in the 1200 block of Central Avenue, and on Franklin Street near Allendale Road. At all of the fires, large crowds continued to gather and watch the action despite the curfew. Firefighters did not get any rest as additional fires broke out on North and Patterson Park avenues, the 100 block of East Lanvale Street and the 2100 block of Normandy Avenue.[2]

On North Hilton Street and the 600 block of Mount Holly Street, there was looting and burning of grocery and liquor stores. A furniture store in the 800 block of West Baltimore Street, a jewelry store on Eastern Avenue, and a tavern on Longwood Street in the Westwood neighborhood were looted.

Fire engines responded to the 1600 block of Warwick Avenue where a house was burning. In the 2300 block of Hollins Ferry Road, between the communities of Morrell Park and Westport, firefighters laid hose in the street, hooked up hose and nozzles, applied water streams and raised extension ladders at a store that was looted and burned. In the 200 block of East Preston Street, a mom and pop food market was broken into. Rioting was reported near the Murphy Homes housing projects at Myrtle Avenue and Hoffman Street. On the east side there was more trouble in the 2100 block of North Calvert Street as flames blew out of a structure's windows and dark smoke billowed into the night sky.[3]

Unbelievably, the number of lootings had actually died down. There were 14 lootings reported between midnight and 1 a.m., as opposed to the 128 incidents that had occurred between 8 p.m. and 9 p.m. In the 3800 block of Clifton Avenue, looters were spotted and police officers were dispatched. Additional looting was reported in the 1800 block of Linden Avenue, and on Division Street near Lanvale Street.

At 1:30 a.m., U.S. Army General York stated, "The curfew seems to be having an effect. The city is generally under control."[4]

The hot spot area of the night was in the western district, where fires and looting were reported in an area bounded by Druid Park Lake Drive and Gwynns Falls Parkway on the north, Poplar Grove Street on the west, Baltimore Street on the south, and Greene Street to the east.

City firefighters would find that one day's firefighting was overwhelmed by that of the next. At dawn on Monday morning, the day started off with three dwelling fires, several lootings, and a two alarm building fire at a liquor store located on Federal Street and Milton Avenue. As 6 a.m., approached, and the violence continued; authorities made a decision to close Baltimore City schools for the day.

The city reported that since 6 p.m. Saturday night, when the hostilities had begun at the 400 block of Gay Street, until 6:30 a.m., Monday morning, April 8, 1968, the fire department logged a total of 764 fires.[5]

City police were now working 12-hour tours with 1,100 officers assigned to each of the two shifts.

Even with the reported 764 fires over the past two days and nights, the fire department had been responding and performing outstandingly. Chief Killen reported that on-duty strength was normally 600 men; now it's double that number. He also stated that Anne Arundel County officials sent eight engines to Engine #35, at Fourth Street and Maude Avenue in Brooklyn, and Baltimore County officials sent seven engines to Engine #21, at Roland and Union Avenues.[6]

Firefighters that had gone home on the day shift on Saturday afternoon were called back into work at 9:30 pm. that evening. Fifty pieces of second-line equipment, mostly engines, were placed back into service at the city's fire stations.[7]

The typical day-to-day practices of providing fire protection to a city of 970,000 were temporarily shelved as Chief Killen instituted modifications to deal with the multitude of fires. Fire Alarm discontinued the practice of sending units to brush, trash and dumpster fires unless near-by structures were endangered. Also, the practice of fire ground officers requesting multiple-alarms; where prescribed companies were due to respond (2nd, 3rd, and 4th alarms, etc.), was discontinued.[8] From here on in, Fire Alarm would send whatever was available.

The firefighters were wearing down. Many who were working on Saturday at the start of the riots were still on duty and needed rest. They had been fighting one fire after another. Some crews were on engines transferring from one side of the city to the other to fill empty fire stations. As a result many firefighters found themselves fighting fires in sections of the city that they were not that familiar with. The multitude of fires, the stress created from the hostile crowds, the unfamiliarity and the uncertainty of what would happen next weighed heavily on the firefighters' minds. To address firefighter fatigue and to deal with the additional firefighters now living in the stations, cots from the city's civil defense stores were moved into the fire houses and firefighters dined on K rations provided by the National Guard.[9]

Monday was a sunny day with temperatures approaching the lower 70s. The fair weather just meant more violence in the streets as a "whirlwind tour" of the devastation was conducted by the mayor, accompanied by U.S. Senator Joseph Tydings. All schools, most businesses, and almost all offices in the city were closed.[10]

The inhabitants living on the city's east side awoke to the sounds of gunfire at about 7:40 a.m.; a 47-year-old looter was shot in an alley near the 800 block of North Aisquith Street. The looter was chased four blocks by a lone police officer. The looter, suspected of robbing Mike's Cut Rate Liquor Store in the 800 block of Gay Street, entered an alley behind the 1200 block of East Madison Street where an "out of breath" policeman shot him. As the police officer, standing next to the downed body, called for help on his hand-held radio, a hostile crowd gathered around him. Before the situation could get out of hand, 15 to 20 uniformed city police officers arrived to assist the officer.[11]

Upon arrival at Johns Hopkins Hospital, the victim was pronounced dead as a result of a gunshot wound to his right side. The victim had lived in the 1100 block of Thompson Street. Although the account was disputed by neighborhood residents, the patrolman stated that the victim had threatened him with a knife and a rock.[12] At approximately 7:40 a.m., illegal activities continued as looting was reported in the 800 block of Somerset Street, between Biddle and Madison streets on the east side.[13]

An hour later a bomb was found on North Avenue near Charles Street. The area needed to be evacuated. By 9 a.m., police reported that looting had picked up again in the western district and was causing more devastation than what had been experienced on the city's east side, which had been heavily damaged by the rioting of the previous two days. Once police officers left an area, looters would swoop in and start anew. Gangs were rumored to be using walkie-talkie portable radios to keep tabs on the location and numbers of police officers and troops. The downtown business area was still spared as National Guardsmen and members of the 18th Airborne Division patrolled the high-value district.[14]

Police spokesmen reported that between 9 a.m. and 9:40 a.m., the number of reported lootings were already double the number reported during the same time period on Sunday - a good indicator that Palm Sunday church services had a positive impact in keeping the violence low.[15]

Unfortunately there would not be any church services today. At 10:25 a.m., Chief Pomerleau directed the following teletype to be sent to all police districts:

"You are reminded that the established firearms policy remains in force. Police personnel will only shoot in defense of their-selves, fellow officers, military personnel and citizens. Looters will not be shot except in self-defense as described in the previous sentence. No warning shots will be fired. No gas will be used without direct authority of the chief of patrol, deputy commissioner of operations, or the police commissioner."[16]

Between 10 a.m. and 11 a.m., the lawlessness in the West Baltimore area was picking up. Reports were being received for extensive looting in the 800 to 1100 blocks of West Baltimore Street. To improve law enforcement communications and organizational effectiveness in combating the increase of crime on the west side, a new police command post was set up in the center of the Upton community at Pennsylvania Avenue and Laurens Street.

There was no doubt that Chief Pomerleau was very concerned about the mental health of the overworked and weary police officers. One of the things he worried about was the possibility of law enforcement personnel taking matters into their own hands. Pomerleau sent out a second communiqué at 11:55 p.m. which was transmitted across the city's police teletype system. The communiqué emphasized that police were not to use unauthorized personal firearms. As these communiqués were being reviewed and digested by the city's police officers, the central command post at city hall was in the process of contacting the Civic Center Commission to request permission to use the facility as a temporary holding jail.[17]

Blood pressures rose among officers working the central command post at approximately 1:40 p.m., when they received reports of rioters breaking into and looting Franklin Square and Provident hospitals. Police officers turned up the heat and rushed to these facilities only to find out that the reports were bogus. However, later in the afternoon the west side hospitals did make arrangements with the police department to assign officers to protect these very busy medical facilities.[18]

Rioting spilled out from the "Negro slums east and west of the downtown area along main streets in all directions," according to one newspaper headline. "For the first time, unruly groups of whites and blacks confronted each other in the streets and posed the threat of race rioting," another news account reported. Since Saturday at 5:30 p.m., there had been 510 injured, more than 900 fires reported, more than 1,700 cases of looting called in, and more than 3,450 blacks arrested.[19]

Authorities decided that the 4 p.m. to 7 a.m. curfew mandate was to be ordered again. As General York, Mayor D'Alesandro, and Chief Pomerleau spent more than two hours traveling through the city to check out conditions, there were reports of more looting on Fremont Avenue and along Edmondson Avenue.[20]

During the riots for many Baltimoreans, it was important to move on and continue with their lives. They went to their jobs, shopped downtown, and took advantage of public transportation. Thomas A. Ward, a retired judge of the circuit court, was in private practice at the time and handling a settlement in Bolton Hill just south of North Avenue.

Judge Ward would later tell a *Sun* reporter, "Fires were breaking out all around... While we were sitting [in the office] doing the paperwork, you could see columns of smoke going up and the couple buying the house became nervous looking at all these fires all around us... The couple asked Ward what in the world was going on...Ward tried to appear calm; [telling them], oh it's just the riots."[21]

THE CITY FIREFIGHTERS WERE REQUIRED to wear their dress blue uniforms with caps to work. The policy was a throwback to the 19th century; firefighters in dress blues could ride city trolleys free of charge. Many firefighters living in or near the city still took advantage of this perk and now rode for free on the city's buses. Unfortunately some of these bus riding uniformed firefighters were threatened by angry blacks. One firefighter was told, "We're going to find out where you live and burn down your house." Some firefighters were intimidated to the point where they actually started carrying concealed handguns on the bus and to the fires. Others discontinued the practice of wearing uniforms.[22]

Some of the most outrageous "tall tales" recounted during the first three days of the riots were stories about numerous sightings of H. Rap Brown possibly driving a red Ford Mustang with Broward County, Florida, license plates.

There is no doubt that the young militant, based on his past experiences, would have enjoyed being a pivotal force in the violence and excitement in the streets, but he was not in Baltimore. Nor had he taken part in the Washington, D.C. riots only 40 miles to the southwest. However, Brown wasn't too far away. The militant activist was 140 miles to the south in the city of Richmond under the guard of federal marshals.

As a result of the Cambridge riots the previous July, Maryland's Governor Agnew had issued a warrant for Brown's arrest for inciting the riot. Brown, now a fugitive, was eventually found and arrested in Virginia in September. Freed after posting bond, he continued his journeys to meetings and speeches and was later arrested in Louisiana for transporting a firearm, a 30-caliber carbine, while under indictment, a violation of his bail. After sitting in a New Orleans jail cell for seven weeks, Brown was "whisked [away] without notice" and extradited under the supervision of Federal marshals to Richmond, his $30,000 bail revoked.[23, 24]

Brown was notorious for making outrageous statements such as "If President Johnson is worried about my rifle, wait until I get my atom bomb."[25] In August, before being arrested in New York City for another charge, Brown gave a speech in Florida where he stated, in front of a mixed audience of blacks and whites, "If you're gonna loot, loot a gun store."[26, 27]

Two months previously, the deadly "Orangeburg Massacre" had occurred in South Carolina. Local police officers had fired into a crowd of young people protesting local segregation at a bowling alley, killing three and injuring 28. Brown would say, "For each colored killed by a white policeman, there must be 10 dead racist cops." Brown had continued, "We must move from resistance to aggression, from revolt to revolution."[28, 29]

Now, on Monday morning, Brown sat in a Federal courtroom as his famous defense attorney, William Knustler, pleaded for his release. Brown, "clad in blue denims and a new pair of paratrooper boots," was now looking worn-out and weak due to a self-imposed hunger strike. He "sat impassively" throughout the hearing.

Knustler, in front of the court with Brown's mother and other family members looking on, stated, "Free him in the interest of racial harmony…we may be fiddling while our cities are burning." U.S. District Judge Robert Merhige fired back, "Assuming the cities are burning, that makes it more important that the law be obeyed. I'm not going to be bullied by kooks on one side or the other." The request for bail for H. Rap Brown was denied.[30]

As afternoon approached, violence in the city's streets continued. Mom and pop stores throughout the city were taking an unbearable beating. Tear gas was used by law enforcement officers to disperse a crowd of approximately 300 youths who smashed into a mom and pop grocery at the corner of North Avenue and Chester Street, near the worst area of destruction on Saturday night.[31]

Looting stepped up and the west side's first major fires began shortly before noon. At the Channel 13 Studio on Television Hill near the Hampden area, Gwinn Owens, former editorial director of Channel 13, would write, "From Television Hill, the highest point in Baltimore, the Channel 13 staff had a panoramic and frightening view of some 300 fires. [It was] a city going up in smoke and anger."[32]

Federal troops and National Guardsmen were now busy in West Baltimore as soldiers with bayonets affixed to rifles blocked the intersection of Fulton Avenue and Baker Street, where earlier crowds of black youths had been throwing bricks and bottles at passing cars.

By noon, 400 blocks on the west side, from North Avenue south to Pratt Street, from Gwynns Falls Parkway east to Fulton Avenue, were a "no man's land." As the riots continued to head west, a bar, a loan company, a drug store and a cleaners were looted at the corner of North Avenue and Pulaski Street.[33]

On Baltimore's west side, Pennsylvania Avenue was considered the mainstay for African-American shopping and nightclubbing. It had emerged as "the center of black culture in the 1920s as the spirit of the Harlem Renaissance came to Baltimore." It was during this period that the "Avenue" flourished. It was where famed playwright and musician Eubie Blake got his start and wrote the first black musical for Broadway entitled "Shuffle Along."

There was the Douglas Theater in the 1300 block that featured big name musicians like Cab Calloway and Duke Ellington.[35] Years later the theater was renamed the "Royal," featuring performances by Ella Fizgerald, Nat "King" Cole, and Billy Holiday, and in the 60s The Supremes and James Brown. There were also a number of flashy clubs like Gambys, the Ritz, the Casino and the Comedy Club where television personality Redd Foxx got his start.[36]

At times long black limos would line up one after the other along Pennsylvania Avenue as performers such as Dizzy Gillespie visited and performed at the "Avenue's" black restaurants and nightclubs.[37] Pennsylvania Avenue, from the 1930s through to the early 1960s, became the African-American "Howard Street." Since blacks were unwelcome in the big Baltimore downtown shopping districts, like Howard Street, they opened up their own businesses—like movie theaters, restaurants and clothing shops.

A business association in the area sponsored an Easter parade every year for the children.[38] Many of these businesses, such as hardware stores, saloons, a Tommy Tucker five & dime and some shabby clothing shops, were mixed within the blocks of brick rowhomes that lined the street.[39]

Baltimore's African-Americans launched a campaign entitled, "Don't buy where you can't work." The campaign forced stores, many owned by whites, and located on Pennsylvania Avenue, to hire black workers. This program brought a multitude of black shoppers to the area in the evenings and on the weekends.

However, there was no shopping on Pennsylvania Avenue on this afternoon with the riots in full bloom. Channel 13 had assigned its reporter Gwinn Owens and a television news crew to report the violence, and Owens would later describe what they saw. She said, "The atmosphere was an eerie combination of resignation and Roman holiday."[40]

The news crew observed "several burly men climbing through a window of a liquor store, loading their loot in the trunk of a car." On another part of the street the news crew observed firefighters battling a building fire while a block or so away another building burned unattended—"the flames were on their own!"[41]

Now in the 2700 block, closer to North Avenue, five stores were burning ferociously. Dark smoke and red and orange flames emanated from the first-floor windows. The flames would eventually spread to apartments on the floors above. Simultaneously down the street, structures were burning along the 1300-1500 blocks between Lanvale and Pitcher streets.

Many vacant houses as well as stores were burning. At the corner of Lafayette and Pennsylvania avenues the only legible sign remaining over the broken-out windows of a burned-out drug store said "Money Orders." Before the week was out, three blocks of Pennsylvania Avenue would be completely destroyed. Only the 1200 block would contain a few stores left intact. In the 900 block a gun shop was broken into and looters took guns from the store.

Due to all of the violence breaking out on the west side, police officers were very scarce in the areas south of North Avenue. On West Baltimore Street, between Monroe and Smallwood streets, cars were pelted with rocks and bottles by gangs of youths. People looted at will along Monroe Street. The police department's call center was receiving an unprecedented amount of calls. By noon the center was receiving reports of one a minute "and the pace was yet to pick up."[42]

THE EDMONDSON VILLAGE SHOPPING CENTER located in the 4500 block of Edmondson Avenue was the most modern shopping center in Baltimore City when it was constructed in 1947. One of the first planned shopping centers in the nation, the commercial complex, was built by Baltimore builders Joseph and Jacob Meyerhoff on 11 acres.

The commercial buildings were designed to aesthetically blend into the quaint little row home village with a Colonial Williamsburg look and featured brick walls, slate roofs, and dormer windows. The stores sat back off of Edmondson Avenue. A tree-lined parking lot was located between the highway and the structure. The 29-store shopping center included a Hochschild

Kohn Department Store along with a Food Fair, a Tommy Tucker five and dime, a pet store, Hess Shoes, a bowling alley, and the 1,205 seat Edmondson Village Movie Theater.[43]

In the late afternoon around 3 p.m., the popular shopping complex was vandalized by youths who shattered display windows at Reads Drug Store, Princes Shops and the Arundel Ice Cream store.[44] Ten blocks to the east in the 3500 block of Edmondson Avenue, the sandwich shop belonging to Colt Football Hall of Famer John Mackey was broken into and looted.[45]

The Westside Shopping Center located on Frederick Avenue near Bentalou Street was thought of as a neutral zone between the black areas to the north and east and the small white enclaves along the Frederick and Wilkens avenue corridors. Around noon a band of 75 black youths, armed with clubs and rocks, marched down Pratt and Frederick avenues to the Westside Shopping Center. The young group had plans to wreck the shopping center; however, four very courageous and fearless police officers blocked the assault and were able to turn the angry crowd back.

Throughout Baltimore, as soon as rioters and arsonist were driven from one city intersection by law enforcement officers and soldiers, they would just find another to ravage. As the violence continued to accelerate on the west side, trouble rekindled on the city's east side as a two-alarm fire broke out in a liquor store at the corner of Federal Street and Milton Avenue near the Sinclair Cemetery about seven blocks east of Gay Street. As companies responded to the liquor store fire, a three-story brick warehouse was burning to the west at Federal and Holbrook streets a block east of the Greenmount Cemetery. Five blocks to the north, a small mom and pop grocery burned at Harford Avenue and Lanvale Street.[46]

Due to the unprecedented number of fires, it was not unusual for a responding fire company to be dispatched to one location then via radio be redirected to another. The idea was to send at least one engine to every reported structural fire as soon as possible. In what was now a "hit and run" firefighting operation, if a fast response could be accomplished, many fires in their initial stages could be contained or controlled by one company, thereby reducing the possibility of the incident escalating into a fully involved or multi-alarm fire.

Doug Shanks and his fellow firefighters were dog-tired. Shanks had been working on Truck #18 since being called back to work on Saturday night. In his teenage years as a volunteer firefighter he had dreamed of responding to fires like this, but now it all seemed so crazy. Like other fatigued firefighters, Shanks slept whenever and wherever he could; between fires, at the fire station, or in his tiller seat mounted in the rear of Truck #18's tractor-drawn-100 foot-aerial. Fires were one thing, but life was getting worse; during the last 12 hours he and his coworkers had been dining on nothing but Army K rations.[47]

Truck #18 crew members, with their West North Avenue station in Walbrook now protected by National Guard soldiers, responded to and fought fire after fire along the North Avenue corridor. They were dispatched to the warehouse fire located on Federal Street near Holbrook Street and were first to arrive.

Other than to pre-position ladders, truck companies, unless there is a rescue, typically do not go to work to open up the structure until charged hose lines are available and ready to be advanced by the engine companies. As the truck company positioned itself in a location so the firefighters could raise their 100 foot aerial ladder to the roof, the light-colored smoke that had appeared when they arrived was now turning to dark gray. The building was still closed up and the fire was now getting hotter![48]

The officer tried to contact Fire Alarm for assistance, but the radio traffic chatter was too heavy for them to report the situation. In the distance, with the many sirens, emergency apparatus bells, and air horns sounding, the firefighters heard one that sounded as if it was getting closer and closer to their location. The truck officer, believing this one siren sounded from an engine dispatched to assist them, ordered the anxious truckmen to "open up!" And the experienced veterans went to work.

Firefighters employed a gasoline-powered K-12 circular saw on the rooftop to cut a large hole. Shanks and a fellow firefighter moved around the structure quickly, dropping the tip of a heavy 35 foot extension ladder into the upper windows and smashing the glass to allow for quick ventilation of the now dark smoke. As the team of firefighters congratulated themselves on successfully completing the ventilation tasks and the dark smoke started to vent upward, revealing flames, they realized that the siren of the engine company they were counting on was now starting to fade away. The red flames in the building were growing and the fire was spreading as a result of the man-made fresh air supply.[49]

Realizing the engine that the firefighters had anticipated was going to another fire, most likely the fire at the corner of Harford Avenue and Lanvale Street, the firefighters quickly changed tactics. All ladder trucks carry a metal ladder pipe equipped with a mechanical locking device to secure it on the end of an aerial ladder. Using the ladder pipe, firefighters can deliver large quantities of water (at least 600 gallons per minute or greater) at major fires. The truck also carries 100 feet of supply hose that is attached to the pipe and lays in the bed of the raised ladder. From the ground an engine company can hook-up to the hose and provide water and pressure since ladder trucks do not have a pump or a water tank.

With the limited 100 feet of hose, Truck #18's crew attached the large pipe to one end and was able to connect the other end to a nearby hydrant. One firefighter attached a three foot steel hydrant wrench to the nut on top of the hydrant and started turning it clockwise. After a couple of turns the hose was charged with water. All five truck firefighters held the heavy pipe that normally would be attached and locked to a heavy ladder rung, and tried to do everything in their power to direct the water onto the now-accelerated fire. They are probably the first lone truck company to ever apply a handheld master stream device on a well-involved structure fire in the history of the department. Help would finally arrive in the form of many companies about 10 minutes later.[50]

Around 1 p.m., violent activity picked up in West Baltimore. Telephone lines were jammed because so many people were trying to call and report incidents to the police and fire departments. Reports of looting were being received at police headquarters at the rate of one per minute. Edmondson Avenue from Fremont Avenue all the way west to the shopping centers located near the city line had been scourged by looters; only a few stores burned, but almost all were looted and vandalized.

In the Upton area, in the 500 block of Robert Street between Pennsylvania Avenue and Druid Hill Avenue, soldiers and police officers dispersed a mob carrying torches. A group of 40 guardsmen set up a roadblock at Pennsylvania Avenue and Franklin Street to block westbound traffic on U.S. 40.

THE UNION SQUARE and Hollins Market section of West Baltimore has been made famous by Baltimore's H.L. Mencken, who lived in the 1500 block of Hollins Street. Mencken was a successful author, editor, and newspaperman. In the mid 1950s the famed critic of the American scene died of natural causes at his house at the age of 75.[51]

Also on Hollins Street, is the location of Baltimore City Engine Company #14. The dark brick two-story one bay station, built in 1888, is located near the middle of the block on the north side between Monroe and Payson streets, adjacent to (two-and-three story) row houses. The station blends into the community so well that if you drive past at night when the station's doors are closed, it can easily be mistaken for a residence.[52]

On the west side of the station was a blacktop area just large enough to park the company's two-year-old American La France pumper when the four firefighters assigned to the station washed and hosed out the engine bay. For the first time in the 88-year history of this little fire station with the high hose tower located to the rear of the building, a non-city company, Anne Arundel County Engine #321 from the Linthicum Station, was assigned and parked on the adjacent blacktop.[53]

The Anne Arundel Fire Companies that were assigned to Station #35 in nearby Brooklyn on Saturday night and didn't end up turning a wheel were called for again on Sunday and were actually sent out to various fires throughout the night. Since there were no problems with these volunteers from the county and it seemed they could make a valuable contribution in assisting the weary city firefighters, Chief Killen decided to send them out to the stations to team up with city engine companies. This could easily become a city with more fires than firefighters, but not on John J. Killen's watch.

Engine #321, manned by county pump operator Tom German, volunteer firefighters Sonny Harvey, Charles (C.J.) Wright, and others, were ordered to the Hollins Street station on Monday early in the afternoon. German backed the 1960 Ford, an enclosed cab forward American Fire Apparatus built pumper truck onto the blacktop area adjacent to Station #14. The fence enclosing the blacktop space had a gate opening, which was so narrow that there were only a couple of inches to spare on each side of the engine.[54]

Engine #321, like most engines in northern Anne Arundel County, was set up very similarly to the city engines. In the back it had a split hose bed with approximately 1500' of three-inch supply hose on each side. This allowed the engine to drop and lay dual lines simultaneously to increase the water supply from a fire hydrant as the engine proceeded to the fire. The engine was also equipped with 1½-inch and 2½-inch attack lines that were connected to the pump via a water-thief appliance equipped with control valves. The attack lines with attached nozzles were laid and folded in a partition separating the two supply hose compartments. The attack lines could be charged quickly after being pulled off the back of the engine and advanced by the firefighters into a structure fire.

Located on each side of the pumper, near the top behind the cab, was a 200 foot reel of rubber-covered booster line. The inch diameter red colored booster line was light (similar to garden hose but heavier) easy to advance, and typically used on vehicle, brush and trash fires. Unlike the booster hose carried over the rear step on many of the city engines, Engine #321 had an automatic electric motor rewind feature. The city engine booster line had to be hand-cranked back onto the reel.

Unlike the many city engines built by apparatus manufacturers such as Mack, Seagrave, and Ward La France, Engine #321 had an enclosed cab. Behind the cab where the driver and officer rode, there was a metal canopy that extended from the cab roof and sides, partially enclosing a jump seat bench where the self-contained breathing apparatus (SCBA) mask and bottles were mounted. Firefighters riding in this position, encapsulated in full protective gear and facing towards the back of the vehicle, with their backs up against the rear of the cab would strap the SCBA on their backs similar to a knapsack. When the engine arrived at the fire, these SCBA equipped firefighters were ready to make entry into the dangerous smoke-filled structure.

Tom German was no stranger to the city where he had grown up. As a child he had attended Boy's Latin Catholic School, Baltimore Public High School #46 and Edison Vo-tech. In his last year of high school his family moved to Harmans, about 10 miles south of the city, and Tom finished his last year at Glen Burnie High School in Anne Arundel County. After a four-year stint in the Navy in the early-to mid-fifties Tom joined the Linthicum Volunteer Fire Department and became an Anne Arundel County Engineman (driver-operator) in 1963. Initially assigned to the county's Cape Saint Claire Station located near Annapolis, German eventually was reassigned to the Linthicum station sometime in 1964.[55]

Now introducing himself and the crew to Engine #14's captain and crew, German felt very confident that he and the Linthicum crew were up to the task. He had a number of years behind him and was considered a very competent driver and pump operator. His cadre of firefighters were trained and experienced also.

Engine #14 and crew had just returned from a multi-alarm military surplus store fire in the 1000 block of West Baltimore Street in the Hollins Market area. One could still smell the stench of smoke from the city firefighters' turnout coats and the wet, ashen-covered hose hastily laid, folded and placed back into the hose bed of the engine. Engine #14s' crew was tired, but they perked up upon seeing the firefighters from the county. Although grateful, the city firefighters wondered how these county volunteers would perform on their first trip to the big city.[56]

It was decided that Engine #321 would follow Engine #14 everywhere it was dispatched and that its primary mission would be to back up the city firefighers. Talking and mingling with the city firefighters, the Linthicum crew was amazed that there were still markings on the engine bay walls and ceilings from the days of horse-drawn engines. They could still see where the horses chewed on the wood window sills near the location of the horse stalls and where the tack (headgear, halters and bridles to control the horses) was hung in the ceiling that would be lowered onto the horses when the alarm bell sounded. While the excited county firefighters exclaimed over the building's historical signs and impressions from 80 years of firefighting, the city firefighters marveled at the electric rewind booster hose on the Linthicum engine.

Engine #14's driver/operator looked rather old with his white hair and weather beaten face. He had probably experienced thousands of fires over his career and was no doubt close to retirement, thought German. Now German believed, because of the city driver's age, the driver would probably be slow and take his time responding to a fire and German would have no problem keeping up with Engine #321. German was relieved.

Around 2 p.m., the gongs went off in the station for a reported grocery store fire in the 1400 block of West Baltimore Street. As German jumped up into the driver's seat of Engine #321 to start the engine and the crew members put on their protective gear and climbed aboard, Engine #14's American La France, according to German, flew out of the station with the force of a Navy jet fighter catapulting from an aircraft carrier. The old man had put the pedal to the metal and was quickly shifting through the five-speed gear stick on the floor of the cab. He was just about turning onto Fulton Avenue when German pulled out from the little parking spot onto Hollins Street. "That old pump operator was flying," German would say later.[57]

As they made their way through the city's west side streets, it was everything German could do to keep up with the speedy Engine #14. Driving east on West Baltimore Street, Engine #321's crew could see the firefighters hanging on the rear step of Engine #14 and the heavy billowing smoke about seven blocks ahead. The fire, on West Baltimore Street very near to Calhoun Street, consisted of a number of building fires. Engine #14 crew members chose the fire that was the closest to the exposed unburned structures and started their attack there. The closest truck company, Truck #13, had just left the earlier surplus store fire only a few blocks east. The truck was now positioned at the corner of Calhoun Street and West Baltimore Street and the crew members were raising ladders.

LEFT - The fire station of Engine #9 and Truck #5 located on E. Oliver St. near Harford Ave was the location of B/C Burt Bedford when Lt. Mueller advised him of the "carnival atmosphere" on Gay St.

BELOW - Engine #10, a 1946 Seagrave is the same model as Lt. Riedel's Engine #12 which he and his crew manned transferring throughout the city on Saturday night. (All Photos courtesy of Michael Defina)

RIGHT - Engine #26, the engine F.F. Jerry Alfinto was assigned, responded to the deadly Gabriel's Spagetti House fire in the 2000 block of Federal Street. Engine #26 was a 1960 FWD, 1,000 gpm pumper.

ABOVE - Heavy smoke billows from a fire bombed business in the 700 block of Whitelock Street as firefighters try to get a handle on the situation.

BELOW - Federal soldiers with bayonets at the ready, assemble at Brookfield and Whitelock streets to clear out a crowd in the background. April 7, 1968.

(All Photos courtesy of Hearst Corporation)

ABOVE - Approximately eight minutes after the picture was taken on the left, the heavy smoke subsides as the fire ventilates itself at the fire bombed business in the 700 block of Whitelock Street. April 7, 1968. (Photo courtesy of Hearst Corporation)

BELOW - Engine #24, a 1944 Mack (Model 80), the same model as Engine #19, that F.F.'s Walt Lemmon and Larry Pully were assigned when they battled the Chernock Transfer warehouse fire on Guilford Ave. (Photo courtesy of Michal Defina's Collection)

LEFT - Truck #16, 1964 Seagrave 100' tractor-drawn aerial.

BELOW - Engine #8, a 1954 Peter Pirsch 1,000 gpm pumper is the exact model as Engine #28. Engine #28 and Truck #16 responded and worked many fire incidents on North Ave., Calvert St., Greenmount Ave. and Guilford Ave. (Photos courtesy of Michael Defina).

BELOW - A circa 1940s open cab Mack fire engine sits on North Avenue as firefighters prepare to re-enter a steaming Clayman's Pharmacy on the corner of North and Greenmount avenues.

(Photo courtesy of Hearst Corporation)

ABOVE - An alone African-American Guardsman with M-1 and bayonet at the ready keeps an eye on a city police patrol car on East Baltimore Street.

BELOW - In the 800 block of Gay Street, police nab a suspect. Notice SOUL BROTHER painted on the display window. April 7-8, 1968. (Hearst Photos)

ABOVE - Firefighters operated a master stream from a deluge gun in the street as they battle a stubborn fire at Lee's Military Surplus store on the south side of North Avenue near Linden Avenue.

(Photo courtesy of Hearst Corporation)

LEFT - Engine #14's station located on Hollins Street between Monroe and Payson streets, opened on June 6, 1888. The one bay two-story station housed Engine #14 and Anne Arundel Engine #321 parked on the gated lot to the left of the building during the riots.

(Photos courtesy of Michael Defina)

LEFT - Engine #32, a 1966 American La France 1,000 gpm pumper, was an exact replica of Engine #14, which teamed with Anne Arundel Engine #321.

(Engine #32 Photo courtesy of Michael Defina)

RIGHT - Both engines responded to many structure fires in and around West Baltimore during the riots.

(Engine #321 photo courtesy of Tom German)

BELOW - A company of Federal troops protect firefighters from flying rocks and bottles as they pick up after a fire at the corner of Gay and Eden streets.

(Photo courtesy of Hearst Corporation)

ABOVE - After making a quick knock down of the fire and searching the floors above, firefighters prepare to enter the ground floor of the burnt out business on the corner of Wolf and Chase streets. April 7, 1968.

(All Photos courtesy of Hearst Corporation)

LEFT - A 1963 Chevrolet "Box" fire department ambulance. City ambulances that were not committed to attending the injured were the lifeline of information and supplies to firefighters on the front lines.

(Photo courtesy of Michael Defina)

As Engine #14 laid out a supply hose line from a nearby fire hydrant, a large crowd assembled and started to follow the engine towards the fire. By the time Engine #321 arrived, German had to drive very slow as the crowd filled the street and would not yield. Slowly the crowd allowed Engine #321 to continue. Engine #321 was now inching its way down West Baltimore Street completely surrounded by a "sea of black people." German pulled Engine #321 up and past the city firefighters operating the hydrant that Engine #14 had laid out from and made his way to the rear of Engine #14.[58]

As his crew stepped out of and off the engine and made its way to assist the Engine #14 firefighters, German, now by himself, felt very uneasy. Although the crowd never threatened him, the numbers were very intimidating. Having never experienced a situation like this, German grabbed a steel pry bar and held it in his hands as he stood by the engine's pump panel and guarded the unit.

Within 10 to 15 minutes after the firefighting started, German heard a horn sounding and the onlookers standing around in the street started to disperse. It was the horn on an olive drab army truck, loaded with soldiers from the 18th Airborne and located a half block away on West Baltimore Street. The troops, just in from Georgia, and many fresh from Vietnam, jumped out of the back of the truck in their army drab military clothing and started to form up. Before all of the soldiers could get out of the truck the crowd left the area. German felt relieved as peace seemed to be restored in the street and steam was now coming out of the buildings—an important sign that the fire was under control.[59]

While the Engine #14 and Engine #321 crews and about a half dozen other engine and truck crews were working on the corner of West Baltimore and Calhoun Streets there was more trouble happening on West Baltimore Street and Poppleton Street about six blocks to the east.

Thirty-eight-year old Father Thomas Donellan, a Catholic priest out of the Church of Saint Peter the Apostle located at Hollins and Poppleton streets, was walking the streets to talk with the looters and rioters and ask them to go home. The Hollins Market area was his "spiritual" domain and as a man of the cloth, he strongly believed he was responsible for bringing about peace on the streets. The good Father, witnessing hundreds of people walking on the streets, including whites trying to protect their little clusters of stores and homes in the mostly African-American community, did not know that he would be a hero on this day.

Three blocks north of the church, at the corner of Poppleton and West Baltimore streets, both sides of West Baltimore Street were on fire and other stores were being looted. The police were helpless as the rioters and looters continued on.

Kleins Shoe Store had been on the corner for 40 years. Father Donellan liked and had great respect for the shoe store's owner. Father Donellan knew very well that when poor kids showed up at the Catholic school without any shoes, they would be sent to the store. Klein would give them shoes and the church would reimburse Klein at a later date. When Klein arrived and saw his store on fire and being looted, he ran in to try to put the fire out. Father Donellan and others ran in and pulled Klein out possibly saving him from serious injury or death.[60]

Back on West Baltimore and Calhoun streets many of the engines were being sent to a major warehouse fire that was underway in the 500 block of Wilson Street near the quarters of Engine #8 and Truck #10 on West Lafayette Avenue in Upton. The warehouse belonged to the Chernock Company, the same owners of the furniture store warehouse that had burned down the day before on Guilford Avenue. It would take six city and three Baltimore County engines an hour to bring the fire under control.

As Engines #14 and #321 and their crews headed back to Engine #14's quarters they had to stop at Fulton Avenue. The intersection was blocked as truck after truck of a military convoy headed north. Additional Federal troops had arrived and were en-route to the grounds of the Baltimore Zoo, near Druid Hill Park, to join the the approximately 2,000 that had arrived the day before and set up a camp and field headquarters.[61] As the two engines' crew members arrived back at the Hollins Street fire station they heard the dispatch chatter on the fire radio that not far from the warehouse fire in nearby Upton, a grocery store was burning at 1700 Madison Avenue near Laurens Street. Engine #14 and #321 were not dispatched since other engine companies were closer.

The grocery store and apartment located at 1700 Madison Avenue, looted heavily Sunday night, was blazing with red flames and billowing heavy dark smoke at around 2:30 p.m. An elderly black man reluctant to leave the apartment above the store was dragged out of the building by firefighters just as the front wall of the store collapsed into the street. Next door lived 69-year-old William Fund, a retired porter from the railroad. As Fund watched the firefighters using the hose line streams to knock down the leaping flames now searing his home, he just shook his head and said, "All of my life's savings—50 years [worth]—are gone."[62]

The firefighter's main objective was to get an engine to the fire quickly. Time was critical — a fire once started will make great headway. Furniture stores, clothing stores, drugstores and grocery stores, which traditionally have a number of combustible products on display or on shelves, were often fairly involved by the time firefighters arrived. Large broken display windows which provided additional air flow along with the use of accelerants like gasoline made the store fires worse.

At this point, the firefighters' challenge was to address possible occupants trapped in the upper-story apartments whose exits were blocked by the flames. They also needed to make sure the fire did not extend to upper floors through vents and pipe chases or to attached buildings by way of common attics and attached rear porches.

ONE OF THE BALTIMORE County units sent to Engine #21's Roland Avenue Fire Station staging area on Saturday and Sunday nights was Engine #321 from the Pikesville Volunteer Fire Department. By Monday afternoon, the all-volunteer crew had experienced a good deal of firefighting. Twenty-year-old John Berryman, a Baltimore County firefighter, was also a volunteer captain with the Pikesville organization at the time.[63]

Berryman recalls that on Monday afternoon a call was put out over the city fire radio system for Engine #14 and Engine #321 to respond to a dwelling fire in Cherry Hill near Brooklyn. Upon hearing the dispatch, Berryman and crew responded with lights and siren over 80 city blocks from the Hampden area.

Berryman said that "It was the longest and one of the most exciting rides in a fire engine in my 35 year career."[64]

It took the engine at least 25 minutes to get to the Cherry Hill location, and upon arrival crew members discovered that two city engines and Linthicum's Engine #321 were already on the scene. It then dawned on Berryman that they had been mistakenly dispatched. Berryman later said, "I had no idea there was another Engine #321 in the Baltimore region." He added, "There was so much confusion during the riots, no one noticed, so we drove on back to the Roland Avenue Station to fight more fires."[65]

The Pikesville Volunteer Fire Department was a very progressive volunteer organization. They were always looking for new ideas on how to improve their firefighting operations. They trained and prepared for tough firefighting challenges. One of the members was a Baltimore City police officer who informed the company that based on recent intelligence, the city was expecting an outbreak of violence during the summer of 1968.

The police officer predicted that there would be a large number of fires as experienced in other cities throughout the nation during the 1967 summer riots. Berryman, who had been studying the reports from the Detroit Fire Department's riot experience the past summer, pulled a page out from the report. Detroit's fire crews had experienced numerous Molotov cocktail attacks, where the fire bombs hit the hose beds of the engines and set them on fire. As a result, Detroit's firefighters had attached canvas salvage covers over "A" frames constructed of 2-inch x 4-inch wood framing to protect the hose beds. When the fire bombs hit the canvas they would bounce off the vehicle and if a fire did happen to start it would be one that could be quickly extinguished with a fire extinguisher. Berryman believed Pikesville volunteers could modify their engine with an "A" frame too.[66]

Pikesville's 1956 Seagrave pumper was the pride of the volunteers. The vehicle was equipped with an enclosed sedan cab with jumpseats and was powered by a V-12 gasoline engine. Sometime between the summer of 1967 and April of 1968, the firefighters made modifications to the Seagrave pumper. They drilled holes in the engine's cab and bolted a 500-gallon-per-minute deluge gun to the cab's roof to better position the large nozzle for hit-and-run operations. They built a portable "A" frame, and cut a large canvas salvage cover to fit over it.

Straps were made out of old tire inner tubes to secure the cover to the sides of the engine. The portable "A" frame could be quickly attached if the engine was called upon to respond to the city.[67]

On Saturday night, when crew members received the word that they would be going to the city, the volunteers quickly outfitted the engine with the deluge nozzle and wagon cover in addition to putting all of the tools normally carried outside the engine into secured compartments. With the "A" frame canvas cover installed, Berryman said Pikesville's Engine #321 looked like "a covered wagon."[68]

When Engine #321 and crew arrived at the city staging area, the city battalion chief was so impressed with the modifications that he moved them up to the front of the line. "A few minutes later a city engine arrived at the fire station where they were staged." According to Berryman, "It was an open cab Ward La France with a smashed windshield." The driver, Berryman said, "had a bloody face…It was then, that we were all glad that we had equipped ourselves with various hidden guns and ammo."[69]

Berryman remembers that on Sunday night, his engine and crew, along with a city engine, battled a group of stores burning on 25th Street. Normally, due to the size and number of structures involved, this would be a two-alarm fire. However, under the circumstances, the city was fortunate that it had the two engines to spare.[70]

Back on the east side, the whites were fired up. A large crowd formed on the east side of the roadway near Perkin's Homes. Across from the southeast Baltimore housing project, whites were now shouting and taunting. As the white mob entered the predominantly black apartment project, guardsmen arrived, forcing the white mob east of Broadway and the blacks west to create a three-block buffer zone. Even with a buffer zone in place, whites exchanged insults with black youths, bottles and bricks were thrown, and four cars driven by blacks were damaged by rocks.[71]

In the area of West Baltimore from Popular Grove Street on the west to Fulton Avenue on the east in between North Avenue and Pratt Street on the south was referred to as an "ugly no-man's land" by reporter Richard Basoco in Wednesday's *Sun*. During a two-hour period, "there were no cops" and chaos ruled as "black kids roamed the streets, threw rocks at cars driven by whites at Monroe and Franklin streets, and looted stores."[72]

"On the north side of the side streets," wrote Basoco, "Intersecting Pratt [Street] and Frederick avenues, groups of blacks most of them young, stood and waited. On the south side the white residents looked on nervously."[72]

As some whites and blacks looked forward to the possibly of a confrontation, a number of African-American community interest groups were doing everything within their power to stop the riots. As a Luskins store was looted in the 4600 block of Park Heights Avenue, a car belonging to a member of one of the groups drove by with painted words daubed on the side. The words said, "That's Enough Brothers."[73]

Around 3 p.m., the 50 guardsmen that had been sent to West Baltimore and Calhoun streets earlier to disperse crowds were redirected to the area of Fulton Avenue and Baker Street as a store was being looted. In the 3400-4000 blocks of Edmondson Avenue, six blocks west of Hilton Parkway, hundreds of people were on the street and 10 stores in the area were broken into and looted. Fortunately, no structures were set on fire in this area which was very near to the Baltimore City and Baltimore County boundary line.

As crews at Engine #14's Hollins Street station cleaned up and discussed how they would improve their operations on the next fire, a few blocks away at Pratt and Pulaski streets about 250 whites gathered and shouted "white power!" and blocked the streets. Two blocks away on Frederick Avenue, a smaller crowd of blacks gathered. Police began arriving and were working very hard to keep the two crowds apart. The last thing they wanted was an all out brawl between the whites and blacks.[74]

Despite the efforts of the police, a block away at McHenry and Payson streets; a fight broke out between several whites and two blacks. A police officer arrived and prevented a serious confrontation by firing his pistol into the air. Two white youths were arrested. Nearby a black driver ducking from rocks thrown by whites lost control of his car and caused a three-car collision.[75]

Though law enforcement officers were under strict orders not to use deadly force, police operations were inconsistent. In many cases soldiers stood by in clusters, watching those who kicked in doors and looted stores. While guardsmen stood at the end of the block, stores were looted in the middle of the block. In other cases, guardsmen and police officers would respond to a scene of looting, arrest anyone in the vicinity, and hotly pursue fleeing subjects.

Some stores had police protection, including Sears located on North Avenue and the Mondawmin Mall at Liberty Heights Avenue and Gwynns Falls Parkway. Other stores stood alone, vulnerable to vandalism or arson. The types of businesses targeted by the looters were locally owned and operated appliance stores, corner groceries, pawn shops, clothing stores and furniture stores. Schools and churches were unharmed[76]

"No group experienced so much property damage as businesses operating in the riot-torn areas." Although most of the businesses were white-owned, a good number of blacks were employed at those businesses. By 1968, the relations between the residents and the inner city merchants, many of them Jewish immigrants who had come to America from Europe after World War II, were breaking down.

The typical store owner was in his 50s or older, was financially unable to move or improve his store, and was unable to purchase insurance because of the high rates applied to the inner city areas. Many of the owners had invested their entire lives and small fortunes into these little stores. A number of stores had been purchased decades earlier by relatives of the current shop owners before the neighborhoods became predominately black.[77]

Critics of the stores charged shop owners with "almost every imaginable abuse:" "price gouging, the sale of shoddy merchandise, and ruthless credit card collections." Radical Malcolm X once declared that "all stores are run by the white man, who takes the money out of the community as soon as the sun sets." Stokely Carmichael believed that the whites were "exploiters who come into the ghetto from outside, bleed it dry, and leave it economically dependent."[78] Although a number of the mom and pop stores were targeted, many untargeted which included stores that were black-owned were hit because they were in or near the hot bed areas of the riots.

Despite a citywide curfew that had gone into effect at 4 p.m., looting and burning continued in the 1400 block of Druid Hill Avenue. However, overall there seemed to be a decrease in the violence as the curfew moved through its first hour. A shooting was reported at the 1200 block of James Street between Carroll Park and the B&O Railroad Mount Claire repair shop.

There were additional reports of looting in the 1000 block of Lombard and the 800 block of North Gay streets. At York Road and Woodbourne Avenue, a window was smashed by a gang of roving youths. Downtown, the commercial section was threatened as looting broke out in the 500 block of Washington Boulevard between Greene and Paca streets. Two white men were shot during an alleged sacking of a small grocery store in the 100 block of East Lanvale Street.[79]

Areas on the fringe of the hard-hit areas were reporting violence as a store emblazoned with a "Soul Brother" sign in the 2900 block of Garrison Boulevard was looted. At Garrison Boulevard and Windsor Mill Road, windows were smashed at a drug store, and a store was looted in the 4600 block of Park Heights Avenue just south of Pimlico Race Course.

Monday's lawlessness seemed to take a toll on bars and drinking establishments as taverns along Harford Road opposite Clifton Park were looted by north-going rioters from the east side. In the 2600 block of Harford Road, a bar that refused to serve blacks was broken into and looted. In the 100 block of East Lafayette Avenue, another bar was looted. Looting was now spreading out of poor areas into middle-class shopping centers serving racially-mixed neighborhoods.[80]

At 5 p.m., additional Federal troops arrived from Fort Benning, Georgia and reported to the Druid Hill Park assembly area.[81] Would these troops be assigned quickly enough to halt the lawlessness throughout west Baltimore's "ugly no-man's land?"

11

Lombard Street
Snipers and Flag Court
Monday Evening, April 8, 1968

As the sun began to set, there were reports of rioters hurling bricks and bottles at cars traveling on Fulton Avenue and Baker Street a few blocks south of North Avenue. Near South Broadway on the east side tensions mounted again between whites and blacks. As city police officers broke up the crowds, a man objected to being frisked and was arrested. Police officers were now spraying mace to subdue uncooperative curfew violators.

It was hard to believe that neither the violence nor the citywide curfew had deterred people from driving their vehicles on the city's streets. Throughout the black residential communities and riot torn business areas, the words "Soul Brother" or "Black Brother" had been painted on some vehicles' windows and doors. These randomly organized packs of cars, driven by blacks and with their headlights on, joined in neighborhood funeral salutes to King by driving one behind the other in funeral possession formation.[1] Other cars had black rags tied around the antennas in solidarity. However in the downtown business areas there was no traffic as roadblocks were set up by law enforcement officers at intersections, and all motorists were forced to turn back.

People who had to conduct official business or had emergencies were directed to attach white cloths to their car antenna in order to be allowed through the roadblocks. Carol McNally, who lived in Brooklyn Park at the time, was expecting a child at any minute. Per the doctor's orders, her husband tied a white cloth to their Volkswagen Beetle antenna and when she went into labor, he rushed her to Saint Agnes Hospital with no hassles at any roadblocks.[2]

In the late afternoon light, the rising plume of smoke from dozens of fires hovering over the city was now a striking rust-orange color. Sporadic fires would burn throughout the night, many between 10 p.m. and midnight. The fires were concentrated in a single square mile bounded by North Avenue, Preston Street, Harford and Milton avenues. Teenagers still roamed the streets and were reported to be throwing rocks and bricks at cars driven by whites along Monroe Street near Franklin Street and on West Baltimore Street near Smallwood Street.

National Guardsmen were now reporting to the fire stations, to not only guard them, but to ride with the firefighters on the engines and ladder trucks. At the Hollins Street fire station, guardsmen, having the advantage of monitoring the military radio traffic, informed the firefighters that looting was breaking out again nearby on Monroe Street just below Franklin Street. Radio transmissions described the looters, not as teenagers but "middle aged."[3] Hearing this, the firefighters started preparing themselves for the next call by grabbing quick meals, making last-minute runs to the bathroom, and quick phone calls to home.

On the station's television, firefighters watched as a very serious Governor Agnew released a statement on the control of the city's looting. News commentators were informing viewers that Red Cross food stations would be set up throughout the city and the U.S. Department of Agriculture would be sending in trucks with nonperishable food at night. One commentator reported that the city's yellow taxi cabs were being removed from the streets.

THE BALTIMORE CIVIC CENTER was a well-known landmark and source of pride to the people living in the Baltimore Metropolitan area. The large multi-level structure's main entrance was located on the south side of Baltimore Street between Howard Street and Park Avenue. The enormous structure was part of the famed "Charles Center" revitalization effort that took place in the early 1960s and was built on the site of the old Congress Hall where the Continental Congress met in 1776.[4] The 14,000 seat-arena, which had opened in 1962, was the site of many memorable events.

In September of 1964, the famed rock-and-roll quartet the Beatles played to a packed house of screaming teenagers. The band played many hit songs from their new movie, "A Hard Day's Night." Other British bands had played at the Civic Center: The Rolling Stones, The Dave Clark 5, and Herman's Hermits. The center was also home to the city's professional basketball team, the Bullets; the hockey team, the Clippers; and held many boxing and wrestling events. In 1966, the center hosted a gathering of Methodist clergymen who listened to a speech entitled "Race and the Church" presented by Dr. Martin Luther King.[5]

Today, Monday, April 8, the Civic Center was being used in a manner that would never have been dreamed of by city planners when the plans were laid down in 1955. It was now a jail, a jail that within 24 hours since the beginning of the riots held approximately 800 persons who had been arrested. An additional 3,300 prisoners had been warehoused at the city jail during the night. The rioters arrested and charged with felonies were transported to the city jail and those arrested for misdemeanors were sent to the Civic Center.[6] Inmates, handcuffed to the arena seats, were hungry, and many needed to use the bathroom facilities.[7,8] According to John J. Peterson's, *Into the Cauldron*, prisoners were packed so tightly into the Civic Center's holding area that many slept standing up. "The air reeked with the smell of urine and human waste from those who could not wait to get to the rest rooms." "The odor of vomit added to the smell permeating the already foul air" as prisoners who were gassed prior to their arrest threw-up their stomach's contents.[9]

School and city transit buses, commandeered to transport the prisoners, were driven by police cadets from the city's police training academy. Two guards were assigned to each bus. The buses could transport approximately 20 to 30 prisoners at a time.[10] Many of Baltimore's famous African-American sports legends rose to the occasion and tried to help. Colts' football legends Lenny Moore and John Mackey were summoned to the Civic Center to help calm things down and work with city police to address the basic needs of the prisoners. Moore, Mackey, and others negotiated with the officers in letting the prisoners use the restrooms in small numbers accompanied by security—it worked and calmed things down. They also brought in food and made sandwiches which were handed out to everyone in the building.[11]

Colts great Jim Parker, who recently retired after the 1967 season, was now a successful black businessman. Baltimore's *News American* sports writer John Steadman, whose father had been a highly respected Baltimore Fire Department Deputy Chief in the late 1930s, wrote a column on Monday revealing Jim Parker's thoughts about the riots and fires.[12] In his column he quoted Parker as stating, "Only a small percentage of rioters and looters are causing the trouble."[13]

Parker loved Baltimore and he pleaded with the rioters to stop. "The riots won't prove anything," Parker had said to Steadman, "People must work together in the community to make things better.[14] "It [the city] has been progressive where the black and white were concerned. Schools were integrated and the general feeling is that most get along and live [amicably] together." Parker had stated further, "I'm embarrassed and ashamed. I feel sorry for the children coming up who have to witness a city that is kept under guard by troops to keep it from being set on fire."[15]

By late afternoon, soldiers with M-1 rifles slung over their shoulders could be seen in small groups guarding most of the key intersections of the city's major arteries. Some drivers were stopped a dozen times as they drove their vehicles out of communities or returned to communities in or near the prime riot areas. Pedestrians trying to traverse from one community to another were halted at each intersection and during curfew their passes were closely scrutinized.[16]

As Monday evening transitioned into late night, the violence continued along the North Avenue corridor and throughout the west side of the city. "The lawless element, after being run off the street [by] the Federal troops, moved indoors and vented their rage and anger with blasts from the shadows."[17]

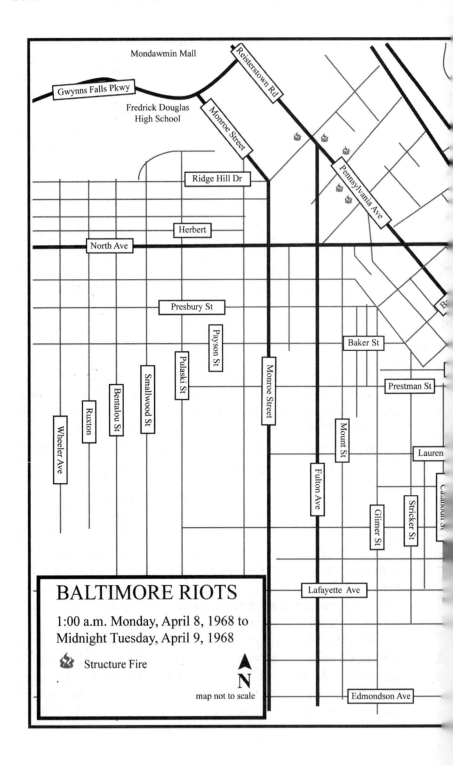

BALTIMORE RIOTS

1:00 a.m. Monday, April 8, 1968 to
Midnight Tuesday, April 9, 1968

Structure Fire

N

map not to scale

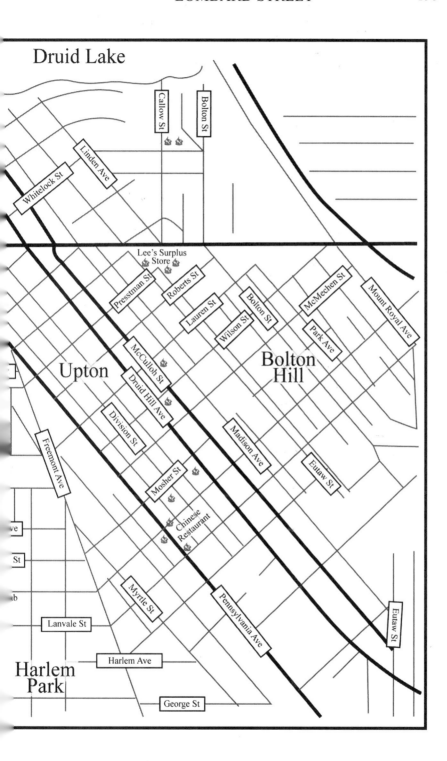

Druid Lake

Callow St

Bolton St

Linden Ave

Whitelock St

Lee's Surplus Store

Presstman St

Roberts St

Lauren St

Wilson St

Bolton St

McMechen St

Mount Royal Ave

Park Ave

Upton

McCulloh St

Bolton Hill

Druid Hill Ave

Division St

Madison Ave

Eutaw St

Freemont Ave

Mosher St

Chinese Restaurant

Myrtle St

Pennsylvania Ave

Eutaw St

Lanvale St

Harlem Ave

Harlem Park

George St

Sniper incidents were now increasing at a higher rate than during any period since the disturbances had begun on Saturday. Sniper fire was now reported at Calvert and Lanvale Streets. The shootings would continue throughout this area until after midnight.

As Baltimore's *News American* hit the streets, the evening's readers, hungry for the latest news concerning the riots, read the editorial "Halt the Holocaust." The editorial stated, "Only the Great Baltimore Fire of 1904 provides a comparative to the devastation of the last two days. Few people consider this any longer a battle for civil rights. It is simply hooliganism perpetrated by those who have no respect for themselves or their race let alone the laws many had helped make."[18] Another editorial in the morning's Baltimore *Sun* was very supportive of the city's policemen and firefighters: "The firmness, strength and discipline of the men in the front lines of this city's battle for law and order should stand as an example to all of us."[19]

Looters and fire bombers struck hard in West Baltimore around 8 p.m. where some looting and fires were reported at Reisterstown Road and Edmondson Avenue. Seven people in Pikesville were arrested for violating the curfew. On the east side rioting spilled up Harford Road as far as Clifton Park and on the west side all the way out to the Edmondson Village Shopping Center.

IN 1953 THE FLAG HOUSE COURT public housing apartment complex had been constructed between East Lombard and East Pratt streets near Exeter Street. It had been built on a site where approximately 350 structures comprising one of the worst urban slum areas in the country had been torn down. The new complex was named after the nearby two-and-a-half story brick Star Spangled Banner Flag House located on the corner of Pratt and Albemarle streets and built in 1793.[20] In the Star Spangled Banner Flag House, Mary Pickersgill had made the large U.S. flag that flew over Fort McHenry during the Battle of Baltimore with the British in 1814 and inspired Francis Scott Key to write the Star-Spangled Banner.[21] The $4.5 million project, modeled after a similar complex in Chicago, consisted of three 12-story high-rises and 13 3-story low-rises and was a welcome sight when it opened in 1955 for 487 low-income and poverty-stricken families.[22]

Originally the new multi-storied apartment complex was occupied by the city's Italians, Poles, and southern whites displaced by the demolition of the slums. Within two years it would be integrated with African-Americans. For many, the complex was a new lease on life. Its new inhabitants found it a 100 percent improvement over the slum rentals in nearby Oldtown and other run-down areas of the city. Many successful families got their starts at Flag House and as family members gained meaningful employment, they moved out to houses miles from the ghetto areas. Other families chose not to move out and some just couldn't afford to.[23]

By 1968, the newness of the high-rises had been replaced by severe wear and tear similar to that at the city's other 15 high-rises in sister public housing projects throughout Baltimore. Graffiti covered the exterior walls and interior hallways were in need of painting and patching. Many of the buildings' elevators would break down routinely and occupants would have to climb numerous flights of stairs in the trash cluttered stair towers. Children playing in the elevators would be injured by moving parts. Drug dealing and robberies within vacant apartments and unsecured stair towers would become a common occurrence.[24]

In his book "*Journeys to the Heart of Baltimore*," Michael Olesker summed up the area as follows: he said, "The old street stalls and the push carts and the curbstone businesses were long gone, but Lombard Streets delis and bakeries still had some zest…On Lombard Street behind the old storefronts were the housing projects that shadowed everything. They were half-century disasters borne out of semi-honorable intentions. The city had attempted to move black people from the ramshackle slums to high-rise filing cabinets. But the buildings had an isolating effect, [and] drugs and family breakdowns made everything worse."[25]

The city firefighters hated to respond to Flag House Court. Occupants would throw bags of trash from their upper floor balconies into the street and parking lot below. After the Christmas holiday, it was not uncommon to see discarded holiday trees with tinsel and bulbs hanging on to the dried-out branches chucked from the upper-floor balconies. In one incident, the discarded Christmas trees were stuffed into an elevator and set afire. Tenants were fortunate that no one was injured or overcome by the resulting fire and heavy smoke.[26]

When the city's fire engine and ladder companies would pull up in the court's parking lot to combat an apartment fire, investigate smoke from burnt food on the stove, or respond to a pulled fire alarm, rookie firefighters were cautioned never to look up to the upper floors. It wasn't long before the puzzled rookie firefighters would find out why: kids and young adults would sometimes urinate off of the balconies onto the vulnerable firefighting crew members walking along the sidewalk.[27]

Earlier Sunday afternoon, on April 7, firefighters had been fighting a blaze in the 1000 block of East Lombard Street near the Flag House Court complex. Someone had poured kerosene into the street and an entire block where the road met the curb produced a four-foot wall of red and yellow flickering flames. As the firefighters pulled hose lines, raised ladders and worked the fire ground, tenants leaned over the upper story balconies of Flag Court, hooting, making catcalls and shouting "We shall overcome" and "Wait until tonight!"[28] Rioters also set trash cans on fire along Lombard Street at the Flag House Court facility.

At around 8:30 p.m. Monday, sniper fire rained down on firefighters trying to extinguish a fire in the Smelkinson's Dairy store in the 1000 block of East Lombard Street. The shots seemed to be coming from the upper floors of the Flag House high-rises. Glass bottles were being hurled down also. The shots from the sniper(s) forced city firefighters to dive underneath their fire apparatus to protect themselves. Firefighters refused to fight the fire until the sniper(s) was located. *News American* Reporter Christopher Hartman slid under one of the ladder trucks in the firing zone on Lombard Street to interview a few of the hunkered-down firefighters. He asked one of them, "When are you going back in?"[29] The shaken firefighter replied, "We're not going back in until they get everybody [the snipers] out. I don't care if the whole block burns to the ground. If that's the way those people want to play games let them. I'm tired of risking my life to save them."[30]

Lieutenant Robert Mueller, with not as much as a few hours' sleep was now back working with Engine #32 and crew from the fire station located on lower Gay Street. While fighting the Smelkinson's Dairy store fire, he too hit the street and crawled under the apparatus when the shots rang out. While underneath one of the ladder trucks, Mueller witnessed one rioter run over to an engine, take the axe off the unit, and use it to cut the fire hose lines in the street. He had never witnessed anything so outrageous, deadly and thoughtless in his entire career.[31] Firefighters withdrew from the area, leaving their apparatus and hose lines unattended in the street. They refused to fight the fire until the sniper fire was terminated. During the lull the fire spread to Attman's Deli and another store. Guardsmen and police officers actually used the fire equipment and manned the hose streams in an attempt to suppress the fire. Policemen struggled to reopen a fire hydrant that was turned off by one of the rioters.

Approximately 100 police officers and guardsmen flooded the projects and for the first time since the start of the riots, a guardsman fired the only shots by a military man in the streets of Baltimore—three shots in all. Under cover of police shotguns, the soldiers rushed across the street into the high-rise building. On the fourth floor, a guardsman noticed an exit door opening. A man stuck his head out. Thinking the man was a curious tenant, the soldier momentarily put his guard down and ordered the man back to his apartment. The man pulled out an automatic rifle and fired three to four bursts at the soldier at point-blank range. As chips of plaster flew about "knee high" out of the hallway walls, the guardsman opened up and fired at him but the perpetrator ducked back inside the door and fled the scene possibly by jumping across the balconies.[32] For approximately 30 minutes, police officers and guardsmen searched for the perpetrator. However he was never found. The sniper fire ceased.

The three shots were fired by a guardsman from the 121st Engineer Battalion. When the guardsmen arrived at Lombard Street, they could actually see the gun flashes from the upper-story windows. Bullets were striking the pavement as chips of concrete were flying through the air very close to where the soldiers were gathering. Although there was a standing order to keep their weapons unloaded, a number of guardsmen ignored it.

Firefighters returned to their positions at Lombard Street but the Attman's Deli and the adjacent store were lost. The sniper fire along with the shutting down of fire hydrants and sabotaged hose lines, contributed greatly to the damage to businesses in the 1000 block of East Lombard Street. A total of nine shots were fired by the sniper or snipers.

Another firefighter who remembers the events of that day is Bud Chaney. Entering the fire department as a rookie firefighter in 1966, Bud was no stranger to the city. He grew up in a section of South Baltimore along Washington Boulevard named "Pig Town" located not far from Carroll Park and graduated from Southern High School in South Baltimore.

The incident he remembers best on Monday was an earlier fire at a deli on Lombard Street near the Flag Court projects.[33] Twenty-eight-year-old Chaney was assigned to Truck #1 out of the downtown Gay Street station. Riots were not unfamiliar to him as he was in the National Guard and had worked the riots in Cambridge, Maryland, that previous summer. At Cambridge, he didn't participate in any "real" action; he just teamed up with state troopers and secured and patrolled the city after the hostilities ended.[34]

However, on this day two events would occur that were so traumatic they would be forever etched in his brain. On Monday afternoon Truck #1 and crew were responding eastward on Lombard Street. In the front seat of the cab were the driver and officer with Chaney stuffed in between. There were two firefighters crammed into each of the two jump seats behind the cab and about six firefighters hanging on to the side of the trailer along with the tiller-man. There were also a couple of guardsmen riding in between the beams of the large aerial ladder.[35]

As the cruising ladder truck approached Attman's Deli, Chaney notice an African-American youngster standing on the side of the road. Before Chaney could holler "Look out!" the youngster threw a brick at the front of the truck. "It was like slow motion," Chaney would later say. "It was like the brick was suspended in the air and the three of us in the cab of the truck were paralyzed [and could not] say anything for a split second, anticipating [the brick hitting and smashing] the windshield and showering us with glass and lord knows what else."[36]

Fortunately, the youngster's timing was off and the brick hit and dented the front bumper of the truck. Chaney would remark, "I'll never forget the incident or the determined look on the kid's face. I will remember it until the day I die."[37] Chaney, who would retire years later as a battalion chief of the city's Hazardous Materials Response Unit, stated that the incident was the second worst thing that happened to him that day. The worst had been when he was underneath the ladder truck hunkered down with his colleagues as the sniper shots rang out from Flag Court. Even the guardsmen, he said, initially hid under the vehicles until they realized that they were the ones who were equipped and trained to assault buildings and put an end to the madness.[38]

Captain Lester Helfrich was also on Lombard Street that night to keep the fire command post up to speed on events there. When the shots first rang out, he dove into a doorway alcove of one of the stores, hitting three or four wooden cartons of live chickens and sending feathers flying. He would later state, "I don't know who scared who the most, the chickens [me] or me [the chickens]."[39]

At 9 p.m., at Calvert and Lanvale streets, sniper fire was pouring out of the darkness and pinning down police officers as they tried to move a truckload of curfew violators. During this incident a white man was shot. Three suspects were arrested; however, it was found out later that they were not snipers. The injured white man was taken to the hospital in serious condition. Guardsmen were brought into the area. It was not clear if the guardsmen shot back or not. Many of the reported sniper incidents occurred in the areas of the city's various housing projects.

Joe Nawrozi, of the Maryland National Guard, said, "For a while I wondered if the jungles of Vietnam wouldn't be safer."[40] In the vicinity of Greenmount Avenue and 26th Street, guardsmen were searching houses for snipers after a number of reports of sniper fire. Guardsmen didn't find any snipers but did find an 80-year-old woman in the basement of one of the residences manufacturing Molotov cocktails.[41]

Since there was very little fire activity between 9:30 p.m. and 10 p.m., firefighters assumed the arsonists had taken a break. In the Mount Winans section of the city, west of Westport and basically unscathed from the three days of disorders, there were reports of looting in the 2400 block of Hollins Ferry Road at a grocery store. At 10:15 p.m., there were four reports of fires in the 1000 to the 1100 block of East Lombard Street.

Approximately 15 minutes later, there were reports of sniper fire in the 4000 block of Edmondson Avenue and at Baltimore and Monroe streets. In the 600 block of North Carey Street, a man was seized after he pointed a gun at a soldier.

On this night there seemed to be waves of flying Molotov cocktails sailing through the air. In the Reservoir Hill section near North Avenue, the firebombs smashed through glass pane windows of businesses lighting fires. Fires set by Molotov cocktails were also reported on Guilford Avenue, in the Forest Park Avenue area, along Harford Road to Clifton Park, and west along U.S. 40 to Edmondson Village and on Hilton Street south to West Baltimore Street.[42]

At 705 Whitelock Street, an auto garage and the City Wholesale Drug Company burned, as well as a nearby black-owned barber shop. The fire at the drug company was so intense that portions of the roof collapsed. It would take 30 firefighters and seven pieces of apparatus to extinguish the fire.[43] In the 900 block of Whitelock Street there was reported looting and troops were sent in to cordon off the area. At 11 p.m. in the 2300 block of Callow Avenue in Reservoir Hill, a drugstore was vandalized and looted.

AROUND 10:30 P.M., ENGINES #14 AND #321 were dispatched to a structure fire in the 2200 block of Fulton Avenue, north of North Avenue. A drug store and several small stores had been firebombed and had erupted into flames.[44]

Normally this was Engine #14's second alarm area, but the first due or fire companies that were closer to the area were all out fighting other fires. As the pair of engines crossed the war-torn North Avenue littered with debris, Tom German and Sonny

Harvey, riding in the cab of the Engine #321, could see the flames blowing out of the front of the store. Since Engines #14 and #321 were the only engines dispatched, German, concerned about the water supply, decided to lay an additional hose line from the same hydrant that Engine #14 laid out from.[45]

As Engine #321 pulled up and positioned in front of the three-story converted row house store, firefighters Harvey and Charlie Wright pulled a pre-connected attack line off of the rear of the engine. Engine #14's crew was trying to hit the fire with hose lines from the exterior, but was making little headway in beating down the flames. Harvey and Wright quickly sized up the situation and believed that they could make a clean interior fire attack in addition to Engine 14's crew's actions.[46]

Harvey, Wright and additional Linthicum firefighters, all equipped with SCBA, entered the building through a side door to the store. German quickly charged the hose line with pressure and water and the crew members, anxious to prove themselves, crawled about six feet through a hot and smoke-filled storage room and then opened their attack hose nozzle. Wright, who was on his knees, with his head down, rotated the nozzle. The nozzle, set to a narrow fog stream pattern, was rotated in a clockwise fashion. A loud crackling sound was heard as hot fire and smoke quickly turn to steam. The Linthicum crew quickly suppressed the fire and started the process of wetting down the burned area. Tom German would say later that Engine #14's crew was impressed with the volunteers' actions.[47]

Unfortunately, a battalion chief standing in the street who observed the fire suppression operation did not approve of Engine #321's gutsy performance. Possibly worried that the crew could be injured from exterior hose streams or possible booby traps, he lined up the Linthicum crew members which included the officer of Engine #14, and forbade them from making entries into burning buildings. They were to terminate all future interior firefighting operations.

As the crew members started picking up their hose lines to be placed back on the engines, Engine #14's officer and the battalion chief walked over to an alley and entered into a serious discussion. The officer attempted to explain to the chief that on some fires in their initial stages, it would be wiser to enter the structure and quickly extinguish the fires rather than setting up for an exterior knockdown, especially for fires located on upper floors. Exterior fire suppression operations would require the companies to remain on location for an extended period of time.

The two officers continued discussing the pros and cons and how to integrate the county firefighters into a coordinated fire suppression operation. Finally German noticed the battalion chief leaving the company officer and then turning around and pointing his finger at him and saying, "if one of those volley's gets hurt, you will do all the paper work bunk!" The chief stepped into his vehicle and sped away to another fire.[48]

When both engines returned to the Hollins Street station the Engine #14 company officer assembled all the crew members together in the little kitchen. He congratulated the Linthicum crew for a job well done, but said henceforth the tactics that they would use on a structure fire would be different.

From here on in, Engine #321 would continue to follow Engine #14 to the fire. When Engine #14's crew members located the closest fire hydrant, they would pull off to the side, allowing Engine #321 to pass. Engine #321, not stopping to put a supply hose line in the street, would quickly proceed to the fire location. If it was found that the fire was small and located in the interior of a structure with little smoke, Engine #321 crew members could enter with a booster line and knock down the fire. In the event that occupants were trapped on upper floors, crew members could also enter and if more water or manpower were necessary they would signal to Engine #14. Engine #14 crew members would then lay a supply line hose from the hydrant to Engine #321's location and both crews would join in a rescue or coordinated fire attack.[49]

This idea proved to be best. As the pair of companies responded to over a dozen vacant dwelling fires throughout the night, Engine #321 would proceed into the fire location. Harvey would pull off the rubber booster line while Wright and others donned SCBA and grabbed axes and pry bars. As Harvey advanced the line into the burning structure, German charged the line immediately with water and pressure from the engine's pump panel. On most fires, Harvey was able to put out the smaller

ABOVE - A private police officer checks out a ravaged grocery store in the 2200 block of West North Avenue.

(Photo courtesy of Hearst Corporation)

ABOVE - On Sunday afternoon, a flammable liquid is poured down the gutter of the 1000 block of East Lombard Street and torched.

BELOW - Engine #321 of the Pikesville Volunteer Fire Department set up with the "cover wagon" tarp over the engine's hosebed. From left to right are Lt. Donald Bull-Driver/Operator, F.F. Kenneth Morris, Capt. John Berryman and Lt. William Kehne.

(Photo courtesy of John Berryman)

BELOW - As sniper fire rained down from the Flag Court Housing high rise, into the 1000 block of East Lombard Street, firefighters ceased suppression operations. Until the National Guard could get a handle on the situation, the Smelkinson's Dairy store continued to burn eventually spreading to Attman's Deli and other ajoining businesses. April 8, 1968.

(Photo courtesy of Hearst Corporation)

City police officers in riot helmets make an attempt to knock down the fire with a fire department hose line at Smelkinson's Dairy store in the 1000 block of East Lombard Street. Firefighters refused to operate until the sniper fire ceased. April 8, 1968.

(Photo courtesy of Hearst Corporation)

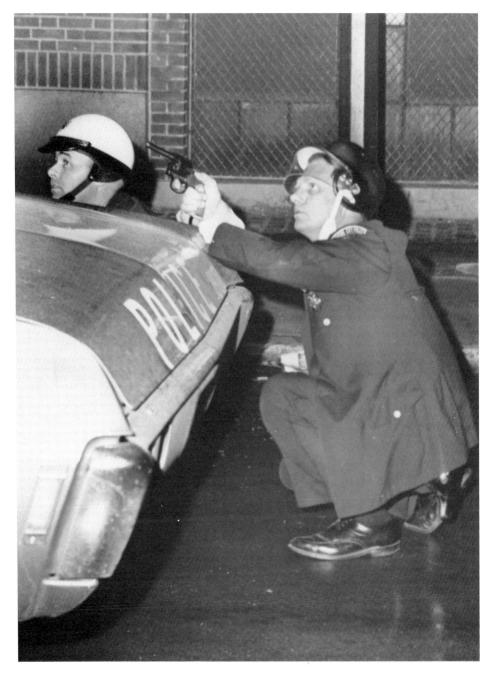

City police officers hunker down behind a patrol car and look for snipers as shots are fired from the Flag Court Housing high rise in the 1000 block of Lombard Street near Exeter Street. April 8, 1968.

(Photo courtesy of Hearst Corporation)

LEFT - Engine #35 and
Truck #21, located at 430
Maude Ave. in Brooklyn.
Anne Arundel Co. fire
engines would stage
here before being sent to
downtown fire stations to
team up with city engines.

(Photo courtesy of
Michael Difina)

LEFT - On Friday,
April 12, 1968 the riots
ended. Crowds stroll
down Greenmount Ave.
near 20th St. to check
out the damage.

(Photo courtesy of
Hearst Corporation)

Federal soldiers with bayonets at the ready, assemble at Brookfield and Whitelock streets to clear out crowds. April 7, 1968.

(Photo courtesy of Hearst Corporation)

ABOVE - Truck #6, a 1954 American La France tractor-drawn 100' aerial was assigned to the station at 1227 S. Hanover Street. Truck #6 along with Truck #21 and Engines #58, #35, and #26 would respond to the first outbreak of violence three hours after Dr. King's assassination. An arsonist tried to set the doors on fire in the rear of a shopping center located in the 600 blk of Cherry Hill Rd. It would be the only fire in the community of Cherry Hill during the riots.

(Photo courtesy of Michael Difina)

Baltimore City Fire Department cites Baltimore and Anne Arundel County fire departments for services provided during the Baltimore riots.

FRONT ROW (from left) Joseph Repp of Rosedale VFD, John Berryman of Pikesville VFD, John Killen, Chief, Baltimore City, Chief Winfield Mineholt, Baltimore County Fire Dept., Harry Klasmeier, Chief, Anne Arundel County Fire Dept., W.Donald Schaefer, President, City Council, Richard Keagle Jr. and Jim Doran, Lutherville VFD, Gordon King, Ferndale VFD, Joseph Morris, Pikesville VFD.

(Photo courtesy of Hearst Corporation)

BACK ROW - (from left) Ed Crooks, Owings Mills VFD, Smith Stathem, President Pikesville
VFD, Clem Bosley and Lewis Smith, Providence VFD, John Corcoran, Glen Burnie VFD, Thomas
German, Linthicum VFD, Charles Doegen, Brooklyn VFD, Unknown, Joseph Sank, Rivera Beach
VFD, Walt Snyder and Walt Myers, Orchard Beach VFD.

Guardsman watches as city firefighters operate water towers from their ladder trucks.The 4 alarm fire was at the Broadway Storage Company warehouse located at the corner of Broadway and Orleans Street. Thursday, April 11, 1968.

(Photo courtesy of Hearst Corporation)

Truck #1, a 1962 Seagrave ladder truck was the unit F.F. B. Chaney was assigned which responded to the Broadway Storage warehouse fire and shielded firefighters from bullets raining down from Flag Ct. high rises. on 4/8/68.

(Photo courtesy of Michael Defina)

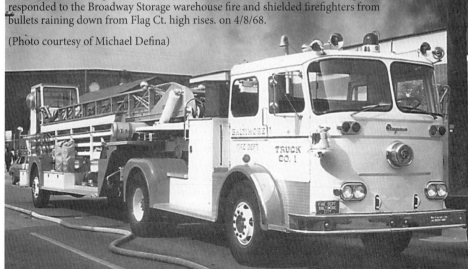

ABOVE - Firefighters work to extinguish a fire that extended to the upper floors of five stores located in the 2700 block of Pennsyvania Ave. April 8, 1968.

(Photo courtesy of Hearst Corporation)

BELOW - Engine #19's station located on the corner of 1601 E. North Ave. and Bond St. F.F. Walt Lemmon and a colleague would sneak out of the station to make a phone call from a pay phone across the street at the Sears-Roebuck Retail store complex, only to be apprehended by National Guard soldiers. Today the building is "The National Great Blacks In Wax Museum."

(Photo courtesy of Michael Defina)

LEFT - Anne Arundel Engine #331 teamed with Engine #38 and spent 3 days and 3 nights fighting fires.

(Photo courtesy of Joseph MacDonald)

LEFT - Engine #21's and Truck #9's station, located at 3724 Roland Avenue, Hampden, is where the Baltimore County fire units would stage before being sent to downtown fire stations to team up with city engines.

(Photo courtesy of Michael Defina)

ABOVE - Truck #25, a 1943 Seagrave, 65' service aerial truck responded to fires up and down North Ave with F.F. Charles Urban.

(Photo courtesy of Charles Urban)

fires by himself while the Engine #14 crew members watched the backs of the county firefighters. These new tactics were quick, less risky, and allowed the crews to go back into service quickly. As soon as the booster hose was rewound on the hose reels by the electric motors and the equipment and tools were placed back on the engine, the firefighting crews were ready to respond to the next fire. Although they had little sleep, resting on the engine's back step or running boards when they could, it had been an exciting tour for the Linthicum firefighters. The action-filled assignment would continue for two more nights with different crews.

Sometime before midnight, three National Guardsmen were assigned to each engine and were now riding by sitting on the top of the engine's hose bed. The guardsmen would assist the firefighters when they could by pulling hose or feeding hose to the firefighters inside of the burning structure. They did not, nor were they expected to go inside burning buildings, but more importantly, their presence at the scene kept the crowds back.[50] During one of the few 10-minute lulls between responses back at the Hollins Street Station, one of the black city firefighters sat at a table, German remembers. The tired firefighter bent over, his forehead on his crossed arms on the table top, and was heard saying repeatedly, "They don't know what they're doing, they just don't understand."[51]

It is not really clear how the city's black firefighters, police officers, and National Guardsmen felt seeing their brother African-Americans defy the law and loot and burn the city. On Monday the *News American* reported that a black police officer had commented, "I hope they realize what they have done. They've burned down their own neighborhoods and the decent citizens are going to suffer for it."[52] Chief Herman Williams Jr., Baltimore's first African-American fire chief, grew up in West Baltimore and was a firefighter during the riots. He would later write in his book *Firefighter*, "The rioters who committed arson were like kids playing with matches, setting loose a force they didn't understand. A community was wrecking itself, and it broke my heart to see it.[53]

Many soldiers were victims of jeers and catcalls, as had been police officers and firefighters. Some of the black kids joked with soldiers but some talked seriously with them. Others were openly hostile, daring them to "come out and fight." Others told the soldiers to go back to Vietnam "where you belong." [54] Later Monday night at the Hollins Street fire station, extra mattresses were brought in for the county firefighters and the off-duty city firefighters, who were ordered back to work. Firefighters tried to sleep wherever and whenever they could. The stations were actually getting crowded. Two of the city's fire department shifts were now in the stations manning the first-line and second-line engines and ladder trucks while the third shift slept upstairs in the bunk room. There were also a number of National Guardsmen at the stations providing security and assisting in the distribution of army "K" rations.

One fire fighter would later comment, "There were so many men working in the fire stations, we were starting to get on each others' nerves. If you would leave your spot on the couch while watching TV to go to the rest room or grab something to eat, someone would take it. If you were lying in a bed and got up to go to the bathroom, when you got back someone was snoring in your spot. If you were sitting and eating at the kitchen table and left for a moment, there would be two others arguing over who was going to take your chair. The toilet paper was running out and if you could get in the shower stall at all, there was no soap and you were lucky if you had any hot water. Plus for those of us who couldn't shower or wash our clothes, we were all getting mighty smelly." "Hell," another firefighter added, "If the men wouldn't have been so dead tired there may have been a riot in the fire station."[55]

Dozens of police officers continued to guard key intersections including: Calvert and Fayette streets, Baltimore and South streets, and Calvert and Baltimore streets. Three food distribution centers were setup at Eden Street and Ashland Avenue, North Avenue and Barclay Street, and North and Pennsylvania avenues. Phone booth service was out in the riot areas — most of the fully enclosed glass/aluminum booths were totally destroyed. At midnight, the mopping up of the earlier fires in the Smelkinson's Dairy store, Attman's Deli and attached structures in the 1000 block of East Lombard Street was the only fire suppression activity going on. Reports of looting and fires cooled down for the first time since early evening. Personnel at the fire alarm and the police communications centers took much-needed breathers during this lull. The dispatchers actually had time to view the center's television sets, that were now broadcasting national news anchormen reporting on the approximate 110 communities across the country that were hit by post-assassination violence.

Interestingly, later studies showed that at this point approximately 29 percent of all arrests made nationwide were made in Baltimore.[56] The last incident of the night involved two white men who were shot during an alleged sacking of a small grocery in the 100 block of East Lanvale Street. At 2:30 a.m., in an effort to enhance military control and communications, the lst Battalion of the 29th Infantry Maryland National Guard set up a command post at North Avenue and Caroline Street. Two police patrol cars were assigned to the new command post to act as liaisons with the city police department. The 29th's responsibility was to cover the area from Patterson Park east to Guilford Avenue West and from Chase Street south to North Avenue north. The 31st Infantry reported to the police command post at Pennsylvania Avenue and Laurens Street.

As of midnight, the start of Tuesday, April 9, the worst of the rioting appeared to have taken place on the west side of the city. Two thousand and one hundred firefighters had fought 900 fires in three days. During Monday alone, 332 fires had been fought. Chief Killen would later state, "I feel as though I've been in the trenches for a long time."[57] Four hundred and sixty-six arrests had been made. Later studies would reveal that the rioters did not stray too far from their home base since most who were arrested were picked up within 10 blocks of where they lived.[58] Johns Hopkins Hospital reported 74 lacerations, 12 gunshot wounds, one tear gas inhalation injury, three fractures, four stabbings, one bout of hysteria and two burnings resulting in death. Since the start of the riots on early Saturday evening fewer than 40 persons had been injured seriously enough to warrant admission to city hospitals.

Most of the devastation occurred in the Western Police District from Druid Hill Park south along Pennsylvania and Fulton avenues and in the Northeastern Police District along

Greenmount Avenue. The total complement of Federal and National Guard troops in the city was 10,848.[59]

Many statistics were being gathered during the disturbance. As a matter of fact, Baltimore became the first city to plot this information as the riots were going on. A graph by police statisticians showed that most riot activity occurred in the city's high-crime areas. The rioting appeared to decline at normal meal times. It was also found that television and radio reports influenced the locations and frequency of the sniper shootings. When television and radio broadcasts reported that sniper fire was under control in one area of the city, it would pick up in another. There were seven reports of snipers after the 4 p.m. curfew.[60]

Throughout Baltimore schools, offices and businesses remained closed. By early Tuesday morning, it was believed that 4,424 arrests had been made since the riots had begun.[61]

12

"That's Enough Baby"
Tuesday, April 9, 1968

By Tuesday morning, the riot numbers were still escalating. Since midnight, there had been 76 lootings and 10 fires. To date, there had been six deaths, 1,075 lootings, and 1,032 fires. The number of injured, who had reported or were transported to hospitals since the start of the riots, reached approximately 600. The city jail was filled beyond the maximum capacity and the overflow, of approximately 800 prisoners, were being held at the Civic Center.

Around 12:01 a.m., gunfire erupted again at the Flag House Housing Project, bringing police back to the complex. Although additional sniper shots had been reported by the police, they found no suspects.[1] Reporter Mark Miller, of the *Evening Sun*, would later comment, "They said it wouldn't happen here [in Baltimore]. Rocks, bottles and Molotov cocktails flew. Fires flared. Stores were looted. Gangs roamed the streets. Anarchy prevailed. Alas, rioting had become an ugly reality here too."[2]

Fifty-five thousand U.S. troops were now seeing action in American cities as they assisted law enforcement personnel in putting a stop to the riots. Never before had so many military troops been simultaneously deployed to aid in law enforcement. Another 302,540 soldiers were assembled at armories and other areas, ready to deploy in more than 40 states.[3]

In deploying elements of the 197th Infantry Brigade from Fort Benning, GA to Baltimore, the Army had committed virtually all of its available troop strength in the eastern states to the efforts of combating the riots in Baltimore and Washington, D.C. There would eventually be 11,000 troops, including the federalized National Guard, in Baltimore.[4]

Tent cities were now going up across Baltimore as the "Army of Occupation" settled in Patterson Park, Carroll Park, Clifton Park, and Druid Hill Park, and a grassy area near City College on 33rd Street. The cost of assigning and maintaining a force of troops in Baltimore was costing taxpayers about $100,000 a day with an additional cost of $25,000 a day for food.[5]

On the southwest side of the city lies the 117-acre Carroll Park. Consisting of little league baseball diamonds, soccer fields, playgrounds and colorful gardens, the park was named for the wealthy Baltimore landowner and delegate to the Continental Congress Charles Carroll Barrister, whose beautiful Mount Clare estate is also located there.[6]

Mount Clare, today a noted historic building, sits in the middle of the park, bordered by Monroe Street to the west, Bayard Street to the east, Washington Boulevard to the south and the Baltimore and Ohio (B&O) railroad tracks to the north. Carroll's Georgian mansion, built in 1756, was in April 1968 surrounded by the pup tents, mess tents, supply tents, command tents, trucks, and troops of the Maryland National Guard's 121st Engineer Battalion of the 29th U.S. Army Infantry Division.

One of the battalion members assigned to the 121st Engineer Battalion headquarters company, Pfc Kenneth Klasmeier, would later recall that the federalization of the guard was a "significant emotional experience for all of us." He said, "It was bad enough [that] when federalized, our pay dropped from $10 to $7.20 per day. But, the biggest worry, even more than going out to the violence in the city's dangerous streets, was the rumor that we were only federalized so the Army could send us to Vietnam when the riots were over."[7]

Klasmeier grew up in the "Pig Town" section of Baltimore along Washington Boulevard near Carroll Park. Other than going off to Missouri for his basic training, of all the places in the world he could be deployed through the Maryland National Guard, his only military tour would be located just a few blocks from his home in the 1200 block of West Cross Street. As a kid, Klasmeier had played in Carroll Park and knew the southwestern section of the city as well as the back of his hand.[8]

Twenty-year-old Klasmeier had his entire life before him and he had prepared well. He graduated in 1965 from Mount Saint Joseph High School on Frederick Avenue and was attending the University of Baltimore. At age 16, Klasmeier had become a volunteer firefighter at the Lombardee Beach Fire Department located in a little waterfront community on the west side of Stony Creek in Anne Arundel County. His family had a summer cottage there. He decided that he would make a career out of firefighting and applied for a firefighter's position with Anne Arundel County.[9]

Like millions of young American men in the late 1960s, Klasmeier joined the Guard so he wouldn't be drafted into the Army and be sent to the war in Vietnam. Now, after taking an oath to serve the U.S. President and being federalized, he and his battalion companions were wondering if they had all been tricked.[10]

But, if he wasn't sent to Vietnam, Klasmeier would shortly be fully employed. He had already been accepted and was looking forward to working at the Anne Arundel County Fire Department. He was to become a member of the department's very first probationary firefighter class to be held at the Baltimore City Fire Department Training Center, located on Pulaski Highway. The training was scheduled to start in 10 days.[11]

On Saturday night, when the Maryland National Guard was activated, Klasmeier had been notified by a phone call. He reported to his assigned post at the battalion's headquarters in Ellicott City, located about 14 miles west of Baltimore. There, the troops formed and mustered. Later in the evening when they arrived at Carroll Park, the battalion members quickly set up camp, climbed back into the Army "duce-and-a-half" trucks, and were transported in a convoy to Aisquith Street.[12]

On Aisquith Street near Orleans Street where buildings were already burning, Klasmeier took part in the battalion's clearing of rioters. The guardsmen, equipped with full army gear, gas masks, helmets and "no bullets" walked shoulder-to-shoulder about three lines deep, with fixed bayonets on their M-1 rifles. The width of line of guardsmen extended fully from one side of the street to the other.[13]

The troops were an impressive and intimidating sight and most of the rioters, upon seeing them, took off running. The rioters that stayed were quickly captured and moved back behind the lines where city or state police would arrest them and transport them to one of the holding areas.

On Sunday morning, the battalion's officers formed the troops and asked if any of the soldiers were familiar with the city and if so, would volunteer for a special assignment. Klasmeier raised his hand and was quickly assigned as Major Rzepkowski's jeep driver.[14]

For the majority of the time during the hostilities, Klasmeier sat in the jeep's driver seat outside of the Southern District Police Station located at Ostend and Light streets. Major Rzepkowski was now the Maryland National Guard liaison with the Southern Police District command unit and would be inside most of the time attending meetings. Outside, with his steel helmet slanted forward to shield his eyes from the bright sun, Klasmeier watched throughout the day as city police brought in rioters in groups of four or five, all handcuffed together, to be locked up. At times during Klasmeier's tour, the major would let him slip home with the jeep to take showers, change into clean uniforms, and indulge in his mother's delicious home-cooked meals. Klasmeier would recall, "It wasn't a bad assignment."[15]

South Baltimore, compared to the inner city with its violence and fires, was relatively quiet. Baltimore City Firefighter Jerry Alfinito remembers that in the black pockets of communities near Engine #26's station at West and Leadenhall streets, mourners tied black ribbons around their doorknobs out of respect for the slain King. Many believed the ribbons also were displayed so the residents wouldn't be harmed by the rioters. However, most of the African-Americans living in the area remained calm; they didn't want to get involved.[16]

The only structure fire Alfinito recalls responding to during the riots from the Engine #26 Station was at Parker Metals. The old three-story factory, constructed of brick and heavy timber is located on the southeast corner of Ostend Street, at the foot of the bridge over the B & O Railroad tracks. According to

Alfinito, "It could have been a "real burner," He said, "As we were fighting a small fire on one side of the factory, rioters set a second fire on the other side of the building." Fortunately, the firefighters aggressively attacked the fires and they were quickly extinguished.[17]

On South Charles Street approximately 10 blocks northeast of Parker Metals is the Shofer's Furniture store complex. It is the site of one of the most dangerous fires that Alfinito ever responded to. The fire occurred during the early 1960s on a frigid New Years Day in the furniture store's warehouse. A onetime ice house, the warehouse filled with furniture, was constructed of heavy timber. Initially Alfinito and his crew members made an interior attack on the fire. However, as the fire became more intense, the firefighters withdrew their interior positions just as the roof fell in. The hose lines froze in the streets. It would take a couple of days to thaw out all the lines.[18]

Shofer's Furniture, established in 1914, was an icon in South Baltimore and still is today. The main showroom store, located at 930 South Charles Street on the former site of a Hecht's department store was also heavily damaged by a destructive fire in 1953.[19]

The store's owner and manager Henry Shofer says that he was very young when the warehouse burned. He recalls, "At that time I was desperate to be a fireman myself. So I got into my Halloween firefighter costume expecting to have the firemen allow me to participate in putting out the fire. I remember going into the first floor of the warehouse with my Dad and not seeing any fire, but lots of water pouring out especially from the elevator shaft. We quickly ran into the battalion chief and he angrily ordered me out of the building. I was naturally upset that the chief kicked me out, but now as an adult, I realize that it was for my own personal safety."[20]

Shofer says he believes the hard-working blue collar African-Americans living in the Sharp-Leadenhall section of South Baltimore were very proud of their neighborhood and looked out for one another. According to Shofer, they were above the violence that was occurring throughout the inner city. Shofer does suspect, however, that his father, to be on the safe side, hired a security guard who remained on the store's roof and watched over the structures on South Charles Street.[21]

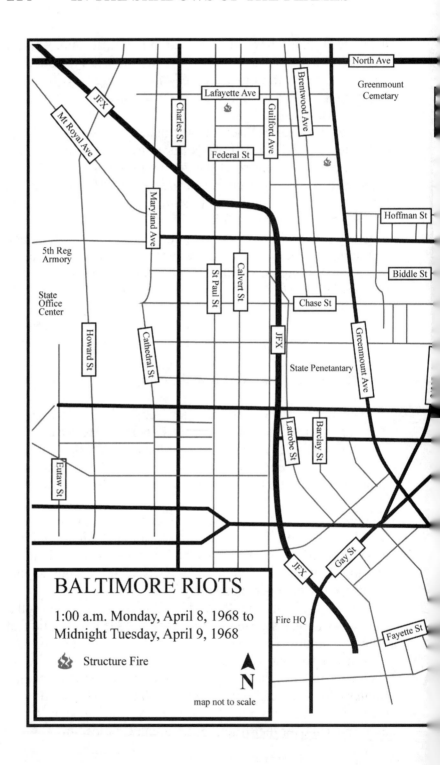

BALTIMORE RIOTS

1:00 a.m. Monday, April 8, 1968 to
Midnight Tuesday, April 9, 1968

Structure Fire

N

map not to scale

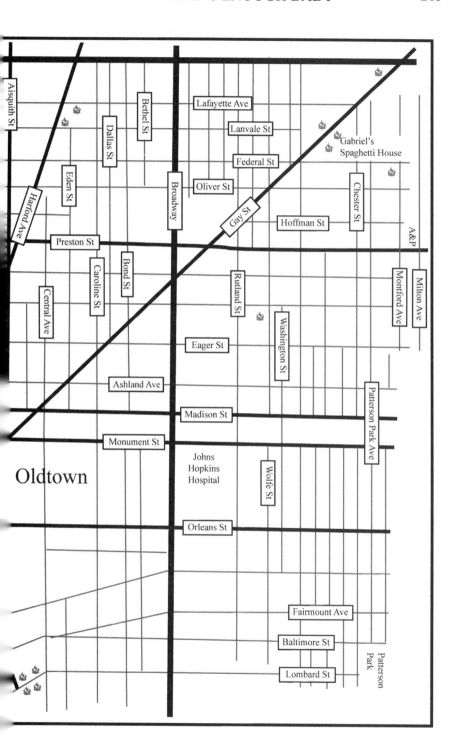

Maryland National Guardsman Pfc Kenneth Klasmeier remembers driving Major Rzepkowski to an appliance store incident on West Baltimore Street. Klasmeier says he will never forget what happened when he and Rzepkowski arrived at the scene. As police officers were trying to get a handle on the crowd of looters, an Army jeep from one of the airborne units came in quickly and screeched to a halt, and a soldier positioned himself behind one of the 50-caliber machine guns mounted at the back of the jeep.

The soldier didn't even flinch as he held on to the gun, pointed it at the group of wide-eyed lawbreakers, pulled back on the clip, and hollered "freeze!" The group froze. It is unknown if there was any ammo in the clip or not, but the ploy worked, and the city police arrested the would-be looters. Klasmeier would later say, "Some of these guys were just back from Vietnam, [and] they were capable of doing just about anything. For me it was the scariest moment that I can remember during the riots."[22]

In order to improve communications and coordination, the federalized National Guard, 18th Airborne Corps and 197th Infantry Brigade were re-organized as "Task Force Baltimore." The task force consisted of three brigades and a reserve.[23]

Since Friday night at Baltimore's Fifth Regiment Armory, a central operations headquarters had been activated to manage "Oscar," the code name for operating plans that were laid down by General Gelston, Chief Pomerleau, MSP Superintended Lally and Federal officials months before in the event of a city riot.[24]

In the armory's 1,000-square foot Tactical Operations Center, or "war room," large maps of the city hung along the green painted walls. Army officials placed green and red tags and stickers on the maps to keep track of troop deployment and areas of violence. Huge green chalkboards lined the other walls in the room, noting numbers of troops, companies to which the troops belonged, and the location and status of the troops.[25]

The war room was a beehive of around-the-clock activity. Outside of the war room in one of the hallways was a huge sign proudly displaying an enlargement of the paratrooper's patch, the "Blue Dragon."[26, 27]

There seemed to be a high degree of selectivity in riot targets. On block after block some stores were hit and some stores were spared. A number of stores were hit more than once. Homes were not typically damaged with the exception of apartments over stores or dwellings next door to targeted structures.[28]

For a store not spared, tragedy would strike. Earlier at 3 a.m. on Tuesday, firefighters responding to the 400 block of Myrtle Avenue near Harlem Park, found the body of a 74-year-old man who died from smoke inhalation. He lived in a second floor apartment above a grocery store which was looted and burned. He was the sixth fatality of the riots.[29]

AT 7 A.M. THE BALTIMORE-WASHINGTON PARKWAY entering the city from the south was backed up about seven miles, all the way to the Friendship International Airport (renamed Baltimore-Washington International Airport in 1973) cutoff near the Linthicum/Hanover area. The backup was a result of the road-blocks and car checks on the major arteries running through the city.[30] However, once the curfew was lifted, and motorists from outside the city were allowed in, the looting began again, as 10 stores were hit and another two were burned.[31]

Most incidents were now occurring on the east side of Baltimore as the west side rested after two busy nights. It had been determined that tear gas seemed to be having a positive effect. The tear gas was now used extensively by troops and police officers. Eventually, the troops began to gas stores and then immediately board them up. The tear gas (CS gas) suspended in the air, would last for hours and keep looters out. One clever rioter, after looting a Sunny's (Military) Surplus Store, stole a gas mask and used it to loot the stores that contained the choking gas. However not to be outsmarted, guardsmen quickly caught up with him and the culprit was arrested by city police.[32]

The "wave of looting" appeared to hit liquor stores, then move on to appliance stores, then food stores, followed by pawn shops for firearms, then jewelry stores and loan shops for money and valuables. City Council President Donald Shafer asked that special attention be given—such as police protection and other assurances—to the neighborhood grocery stores which he had requested to be reopened.[33]

In an attempt to get the city's youngsters off the streets the public schools were opened. However there would be no bus transportation. Surprisingly, approximately 50 percent of the student population returned. Unfortunately among the absent were many teachers and the class day in some schools was disturbed due to reports of bomb threats. The fire department received reports of four threats in city schools. All proved to be false.[34, 35]

After dealing with over 900 fires in three days and seeing 17 of his firefighters injured, Fire Chief John Killen was furious with the restraint the soldiers were demonstrating. The veteran fire chief said to reporters that his men had been subject to constant harassment and wanted to know what the guard and the Federal troops were doing.[36]

"I don't know what the hell they've been doing," Killen stated. "My men have been pelted with bottles, bricks and stones and everything else they [rioters] can throw." Killen said that most of the trouble had occurred at the smaller fires.[37]

The problem was that fire engines were typically the first to arrive at incidents. In the early stages of the incident, there were no police or troops on location, leaving the firefighters vulnerable to flying projectiles. Once guardsmen were assigned to and riding on the engines, this problem diminished.[38]

It wasn't just the firefighters who were dissatisfied; the police were also unhappy with the guard's performance. Police officers, many on duty since the outbreak of the riots on Saturday evening, were severely critical of those giving orders to the guardsmen. "They [the guardsmen] stand around and watch and wait until we get there," said one police lieutenant. A guardsman replied, "We can't do anything but watch. What in the hell are we doing here? If they [military superiors] would let us go, we could quiet down the situation."[39]

Store owners, on the other hand, were not satisfied with the performance of the police. At a store on North Avenue near Robert Street, it was everything one of the owners could do to keep the looters out of his store. He had barely survived since the riots broke out on Saturday. Now, with all of the extra troops in town, he might just make it, he thought.[40]

Youths were kicking down the door of the store and breaking the display windows as older men sat on steps across the street and kept an eye out for police. Police officers would not arrest a kid for breaking and entering—during the turmoil it wasn't worth the effort and they would just be sent home. Plus there were no police or soldiers in sight anyway. The owner told his son to run down to the command post at Pennsylvania Avenue and Laurens Street and ask the police officers for help.[41]

Exhausted after running more than 15 blocks to the command post intersection, the son was advised by authorities that if he and his father were in danger they should leave the building—authorities had no one to send. By the time the son arrived back at the store it was filled with flames. The father said, "After the kids broke down the security [steel bars and cages], the men waiting across the street (who were in their 20s and older) moved in, looted the store and set it on fire. The owner and son were devastated.[42]

On Tuesday, April 9 the *News American* reported that on Sunday at the Fifth Regiment Armory many troops of the Maryland National Guard were seen lounging on the lawns or standing in groups while elsewhere, police officers in the street were "screaming" for assistance.[43] It was later established that many of these soldiers had been up all night and were resting. Other guardsmen were being assembled to be sent back out to the streets to assist the police officers.

AT THE SEARS-ROEBUCK COMPLEX, located on North Avenue near Harford Road, the guardsmen were doing an outstanding job of guarding the shopping center. They were not allowing anyone anywhere near the three-building complex. Once the site of an orphanage, the store had a three-story high showroom window covering approximately one complete side of the building. Sears boasted of having the largest display window in the country when the store was constructed in 1940. Prior to the arrival of law enforcement someone had broken out an area of the glass big enough to try and steal a row boat that was set up in a sporting display. When the guard and police arrived the boat was partially hanging out of the window. Miraculously, it would be the only damage to the huge display window.

Walter Lemmon of Engine #19 remembers asking his captain if he and another firefighter could walk across the street over to the Sears parking lot and use one of the public telephone booths (still standing) to call home. The captain authorized them to make the call, but with one caveat. "If the battalion chief catches you," he said, "you're on your own." With that, Lemmon and his partner walked over to the Sears parking lot.[44]

While in the telephone booth talking to their wives, who they had not seen in days, a jeep filled with armed guardsmen drove up and skidded to a stop. The guardsmen threatened to arrest the pair if they couldn't identify themselves. After the firefighters explained their sad predicament, the now sympathetic guardsmen drove them back to the rear of Station #19 so the firefighters could sneak back in the station now that the Battalion Chief #3 (who shared quarters at Station #19) was back.[45]

At this point in the crisis, it was obvious that Killen's firefighters' "Hit and Run" tactics were working. Chief officers had greatly benefited from information gleaned from the fire instructor's conference in Memphis less than a month before. As a matter-of-fact, the chief had already instituted a number of modified operational guidelines prior to the conference as a result of watching and reading about the previous summers' riots.

Baltimore's firefighters would not turn hoses on rioters as was done in Birmingham, AL, during civil protest in the early '60s unless they were acting in self-defense. Firefighters would not carry firearms (although a number actually did). As soon as a reported incident was determined to be located in an area experiencing civil disorders, fire engines and ladder trucks would not use sirens, bells, horns or flashing lights.

Another recommendation from the fire instructor's conference that would not be put into effect was to discontinue white coats and white helmets for chief officers. The light colors could very easily single out the chiefs as targets for snipers. In the previous summer riots, one city department took the unheard of step of spraying flat black paint on the reflective stripes and identification letters of the black turnout gear.[46]

In some other cities during the '67 summer riots, it was found that firefighters, in addition to watching out for flying projectiles and sniper's bullets, had an additional worry—as some rioters had sinisterly put acid in toy squirt guns and fired the irritant at public safety officers.[47]

The Memphis conference also highly recommended that city fire departments more often request mutual aid from fire departments outside metropolitan areas. Ideas such as pairing out-of-town units with city units or putting a city "bird dog" up front in the cab of the out-of-town unit were emphasized during the conference meetings. Killen instituted both of these recommendations.[48]

Across the country, as hundreds of cities burned, fire departments were now evaluating their operating procedures. There were changes in firefighting methods. Instead of single engine and truck company responses to a given fire whereby all units arrived piecemeal before interrelating and working together, units would now respond as task forces. Engines and ladder truck companies would meet at a safe staging area, a couple of blocks away from the fire, and arrive as one large protected group. It became evident that rioters would be less likely to attack 18 firefighters with many trucks arriving at the same time than five or six vulnerable firefighters on a single or dual company response.[49]

Mentally it was becoming very difficult for the firefighters to adjust to the fact that their dedication to the saving of life and property was directly opposed by the rioters whose goals were to rob, loot and destroy.[50] However, the firefighters continued to perform their duties in the most professional manner possible and to adapt to new methods of fire attack.

Instead of performing interior attacks wearing self-contained breathing apparatus and full protective gear, and fully ventilating the fire structure and checking for fire extension in walls and ceilings, firefighters employed quick attack methods. They would quickly knock down the fire from the street with heavy hose streams, rapidly disconnect, pack up, and go to the next fire.

Firefighters would also heavily soak unburned areas in the structure so an arsonist could not light additional fires. Very little equipment was taken off the fire vehicle and no firefighter was left alone. All firefighters worked in groups of at least two. In those incidents when company members were threatened, they just uncoupled the hose and left the area leaving the hose in the street. Fortunately, most of the fires were started in the front of the structures on the first floor, making them much less difficult to put out than fires located in the depths or upper floors of a building.

At approximately 9:30 a.m. frustrations and tempers flared on Dukeland Street and Lafayette Avenue as looting started to pick up. In the street, damaged vending machines stripped of their contents and money laid upon shrouds of broken plate glass. Ripped packages of napkins, damaged bottles of vitamins, alcohol, mineral water, and hydrogen peroxide, and canned goods lie indiscriminately on the sidewalks in front of looted and damaged stores. The discarded loot, "too small to be of interest" laid innocently on the ground trampled by scrambling rioters and gun totaling soldiers as tear gas, for the third day, was being used to disperse rioters.[51]

On Aisquith Street, a bullet from a sniper ripped through a car carrying office workers to their downtown jobs. Fortunately no one was hurt.[52] Additional firings were reported along nearby Curtain Street as dozens of police officers raided the area. Pennsylvania and Lafayette avenues were now involved in more looting. Three dwellings at Pennsylvania Avenue and McMechen Street were destroyed.

On Pennsylvania Avenue, a police officer and a firefighter complained about the offending stench emitting from one of the burned-out vacant dwellings. The three-story red brick row house had seen its share of vagrants, malicious destruction, and other fires. The two men felt it would have been better to let the row house burn all the way down. However, by letting the dwelling burn it would tie up more fire companies; worse, a slight wind could transport embers onto someone else's home and set it on fire perhaps an occupied home where the inhabitants were law-abiding citizens, staying indoors and mourning their lost civil rights leader instead of engaging in the mayhem.[53]

Between 10 a.m. and 11 a.m., a dozen lootings and one fire were reported, along with 49 arrests. Addressing the intentionally set fires and the reporting of false alarms, Deputy Chief John T. O'Malley stated that "There is no complete pattern to these fires." He believed that there was "no original group setting them." (However, there was a pattern as most fires seemed to be started by an arsonist breaking a window and throwing in a torch.) According to O'Malley, the fires were sporadic and unprofessional. "If professionals were at work, O'Malley said, "The fires would be larger." At the fire department's Central Fire Alarm Center on Lexington Street, O'Malley talked with reporters and continued, "People aren't bothering with false alarms, there's too many real ones going on."[54]

The country was witnessing, in Atlanta, GA, the largest gathering of prominent public figures for a funeral of a private citizen in the nation's history. Over 150,000 mourners walked in a funeral procession through Atlanta's streets as the slain body of Dr. Martin Luther King was delivered to the Ebenezer Church for the final eulogies.[55]

In Baltimore, however, as mourners were praying and paying their last respects to Dr. King, a drugstore at North and Greenmount avenues and a liquor store at Wolfe and Chase streets were destroyed. At Lexington and Gilmore streets, three blocks east of Fulton Avenue, apartments were burned as sporadic looting took place on the west side. Although the violence continued, many businesses reopened along with public schools. Downtown stores were opened. In some areas taverns opened, but were subsequently ordered to stay closed until further notice. In an attempt to calm angry citizens, Federal troops were instructed to bare rifles but tuck away bayonets.[56]

To the dismay of angry citizen complaints, a line of soldiers, many with reddened eyes from the tear gas, and with unloaded guns displaying bayonets, and carrying live ammo in their pockets, followed General York along the 2000 block of Edmondson Avenue. The general and his troops were conducting a walking tour of the western section of the city. However, 18 blocks to the east of the tour in the 200 block of Edmondson Avenue and six blocks to the west near the intersection of Dukeland Street and Edmondson Avenue, there were still reports of disorderly crowds.[57]

Police, guardsmen and Federal troops were now gearing up for the worst since it was rumored that a former leader of Baltimore's Congress of Racial Equality (CORE) was reported to be on Federal Street telling residents "wait until the funeral is over and we will start."[58] At noon, authorities at the city jail requested that the National Guard send in soldiers due to disturbances created by inmates.

Around mid-day a major breakdown in communications occurred between Federal troops and city police officers. Apparently, the city police department had approved a peaceful march at Lafayette Square, on Lanvale Street and Carrollton Avenue for 1 p.m. Unfortunately, Federal troops never received the word and the marchers were dispersed. As a result, angry crowds scattered and regrouped at Mosher Street and Pennsylvania Avenue. Fortunately, cooler heads prevailed and the masses broke up and went home. On the city's east side a white mob gathered at Patterson Park to protest the rioting. In the 1400 block of North Monroe Street, around 1:37 p.m., a person was shot by a sniper.[59]

At approximately 2 p.m., at Harford and Lafayette avenues, a saloon was looted and one man was arrested by city police officers. Later city authorities made the decision to postpone the Baltimore Orioles home opener against the Oakland Athletics at Memorial Stadium on 33rd Street that was scheduled to be played today.

Three engine companies and one truck company were heavily engaged fighting a liquor store fire at the corner of Chase and Wolfe streets on the city's east side at approximately 2:10 p.m. Once the main body of the fire was knocked down, a quick search for any hidden fire began. As the smoke started to clear and the hot steam dissipated, a firefighter shut off the leaking 1 1/2" fog nozzle. Through the haze one could just make out the nozzle's chrome plating that was blackened from years of exposure to high heat. The nozzleman stood by with the charged hose line as the truck firefighters pulled some ceiling areas to check for fire extension. Broken wood lathing strips and chunks of plaster fell to the floor with every pull from the firefighters' eight-foot long pike poles.[60]

Normally, in a well-kept dwelling or business, canvas salvage covers would be draped over the floor like painters' cloths to collect the debris and protect the hardwood floors or soft carpeting. This was not the case during the riots. There were too many fires to fight. As city firefighters put out one fire,

Fire Alarm sent them to another. Now as firefighters started to put their equipment back on the engine and pick up the hose in the street, they can hear fire alarm dispatch acknowledging various units responding to another fire at a drug store on the corner of Greenmount and North avenues.

A growing restlessness existed in white neighborhoods bordering inner-city black areas, especially on the west side. Groups of whites would gather at intersections very near to these borders. These groups became very frustrated over the past three days of rampage. They believed they needed to do something about all of the violence—and they did. Around 4:20 p.m., at the intersection of Monroe and Pratt streets this frustration was vented out as group of whites attacked a black family. The black family, was in a vehicle just passing through the city.[61]

At first the vehicle was stoned. When the driver got out of the car, he was assaulted by the whites. As the mob increased in size, it was reported that a tall white man fired shots at the children in the back seat of the besieged sedan. The shooter then ran in a southwardly direction and dropped the pistol. Members of the mob were now jumping on top of the car.

The mob kicked in the car's hood and windows just as several guardsmen intervened. A few minutes later police officers arrived to reinforce the guardsmen who were now in the process of pushing back the white crowd. The driver, finally having freed himself from the crowd, jumped back into the driver's seat and drove to the nearest hospital according to reports. The crowd began jeering and surged against the police officers. However, police officers and guardsmen would prevail and two men and one woman were arrested and booked.[62]

"Baltimore is ravaged," wrote Steve Garvin, in his "Man About Town" column in the *News American*, "Sparkled broken glass littered the narrow streets like confetti."[63]

Between 4 p.m. and 6 p.m., 30 store lootings and five fire bombings were called in to police. Later, it would be said that many black spectators claimed to know of white store owners who after being looted set their own stores on fire in order to collect the fire insurance.[64]

As Chief Killen of the fire department decided to send one of his three shifts home, a curfew for the city of Baltimore was mandated to start at 7 p.m. and end at 5 a.m. Wednesday morning.[65]

In Atlanta, the burial of Dr. Martin Luther King was concluded and as the sun started to set in the Baltimore sky, it was beginning to look like the worsted of the urban nightmare was subsiding. Possibly contributing to this perception was the rumor that black militant leaders had left Baltimore for Philadelphia. Even though there were still small and isolated outbursts, things seemed to quiet down between 5 p.m. and 6 p.m., only to start up again as looters took to the streets hitting 18 stores and lighting 9 fires.[66]

By 8 p.m. the imposed curfew that went into effect an hour earlier seemed to be working as the reports of trouble seemed to drop compared to the same time period during the past three days. A number of black community leaders patrolled trouble spots with black plainclothes police officers in an attempt to get people off of the streets. Non-violent civil rights organizations sent out sound trucks to drive through riot-torn areas urging residents to remain in their homes. In other areas, crowds started chanting, "That's enough, baby."[67]

Although the violence and illegal activity were scaling back across the city and troops were ordered to tuck away bayonets, plans were announced for at least one more night of curfew. Authorities believed that the worst was over. The bulk of the lootings and fires seemed to peak at 2 p.m. Monday. There were fewer police and fire responses to calls since then. Unfortunately, snipers were still about. One sniper held firefighters at bay for 90 minutes at Lombard and Exeter streets earlier in the day. Sniper activity was also reported at a fire at Fayette and Pulaski streets at around 3:00 p.m.[68]

Although the worst was over, there was still disorder during the evening. As lethargic gangs, drained and worn-out from three nights and four days of mayhem, gathered at Broadway and at Gay Street, police heard gunshots from along West Baltimore Street, in the block between Mount Street and Fulton

Avenue, and also near a row house on Longwood Street near North Avenue. More looting and arson was now taking place on Division Street and in the 1700 block of Madison Avenue. In the 1400 block of Presstman Street, there were reports of looting while a liquor store at the corner of Presstman and North Calhoun streets was robbed. Mace was used by police officers to disperse a crowd in a store in the 1300 block of Pennsylvania Avenue, one of the hardest-hit areas of the city.[69]

Between the hours of 9 p.m. to 11 p.m. there was a sharp drop as only three incidents of looting and two fires were reported. Two nights before there had been 94 lootings and 26 fires within the same time period. Monday, 53 lootings and eight fires had been reported between the hours of 9 p.m. and 11 p.m.[70] There was now a scarcity of milk and gasoline throughout the inner city because so many grocery stores had been attacked and the mandatory ban on gasoline closed a number of city gas stations.[71]

Baltimore's telephone communications were strained as its inhabitants called in reports of looting and fires, emergency personnel called relatives to keep them apprised, and authorities called one another to strategize. It could have been much worse. Originally, a strike had been planned for Friday, April 5. The AFL-CIO had called for all communications workers in the Middle Atlantic area to go on strike. The strike by 200,000 workers was put on hold until April 18 when the union called on the Bell Telephone System to reach a new contract agreement.[72]

At an 11 p.m. news conference, planned to coincide with Baltimore's late night news, Mayor D'Alesandro said, "Life in our city is returning to normal." Within an hour of Mayor D'Alesandro's vote of confidence in the city, 48 were arrested, 19 lootings were reported and three new were fires set.[73]

As of Saturday evening, riot losses had been estimated at $10 million, enough to classify Baltimore as a catastrophe area—although federal disaster relief did not cover riots and civil disorders. It only covered natural disasters. But, there would be some relief for merchants. It was announced that merchants would receive some form of tax relief in the future due to the destruction of their businesses. In anticipation of this relief, authorities began compiling a list of affected merchants in the riot areas. Also as a result of the riots, taxpayers would be permitted to file their income tax after the April 15 deadline without penalty.

There had been 1,150 fires, 1,150 lootings, and nearly 5,000 arrests since the riots' beginning. Lootings dropped to less than 10 per hour during the night. With the makeshift courts set up in the district police stations and working around the clock, more than 80 percent of those booked since Saturday had already been tried.[74]

On Tuesday, the east side's center of violence seemed to be concentrated in a rectangular section bounded by North Avenue on the north, Monument Street on the south, Guilford Avenue on the west and Washington Street on the east. The west side's center of violence seemed to be concentrated to a triangular area bounded on the south by Mulberry Street, on the west by Monroe Street, and on the north to northeast by Pennsylvania and Fremont avenues.

By late Tuesday night large sections of Federal, Gay, Monument, Aisquith streets, and Pennsylvania Avenue above Biddle Street had been cleaned out by the rioters. Of the 600 treated in hospitals since Saturday, only 19 had injuries serious enough to require admission.

Scattered reports of gunfire and snipers were still occurring and were investigated by police. Due to heavy usage, many city phones still had no dial tones. Cooperation between police and the Army was said to have greatly improved.

The riots had prompted some citizens living near or around the city to arm themselves. A check by the police department of sporting goods and gun stores in the surrounding counties revealed that residents were purchasing firearms and ammunition at an above-average rate on the previous Friday and Saturday as the threat of rioting in Baltimore mounted.

Fortunately, in 1966 Maryland legislators had passed a law requiring a background investigation on anyone purchasing a handgun. No doubt there would have been more guns on the city streets if this law had not been in effect.

In Baltimore County requests for ammunition and firearms had been pouring in since Monday and on Tuesday even though sales had been forbidden. One hundred and fifty-nine applications had been received since Friday, April 5. Most of the applications were from citizens living in the Dundalk and Essex areas of Baltimore County. Substantial increases in applications were also seen in Howard County, as 44 applications were submitted.[75]

On early morning Wednesday, April 10, 1968, around 1:20 a.m., sniper fire was reported in the 1400 block of East Oliver Street. The sniper was not found. However, a suspect was arrested. At 6 a.m., it seemed as if everything was taking a turn for the better. "The people are exhausted on both sides," claimed Furman L. Templeton, Director of the Baltimore Urban League. County firefighting units providing mutual aid were sent back to their suburban fire stations.[76]

As Anne Arundel's Glen Burnie Engine #331, a 1964 forward-open cab 1,000 gpm Ward La France, left its assignment at Engine #38, located on the corner of Baltimore Street and Fremont Avenue, engineman (driver-operator) Forrest "Bunky" Wharran was dog tired. He was glad to be returning to Glen Burnie.[77]

Thirty-year-old Wharran had joined the Glen Burnie volunteers in 1951 at the age of 14 as the department mascot. His family had lived in the third-floor apartment over the original fire station located between Central Avenue and the B&A railroad tracks across the street from today's current station.

Although Wharran had been hired by the Glen Burnie Fire Department at age 21 as an engineman, he was now an Anne Arundel County Fire Department employee.[78]

Over the years Wharran had responded to and battled many large fires throughout Glen Burnie and northern Anne Arundel County, but the previous five-day assignment to Engine #38 would be his greatest firefighting experience ever. With the exception of a couple of short breaks on Sunday morning and afternoon, Wharran had been driving and operating the engine's pump on fires continuously since Saturday night. His crew of six volunteers included future Anne Arundel County career firefighters John Miller and Donald Schultheis, who slept on the engine tailboard, on the running boards, in the engine cab, and on top of the hose bed in between fighting fires.[79]

Wharran would later say, "We followed Engine #38 on a multitude of incidents everywhere." Engine #331 had a Baltimore City firefighter assigned as a "birddog"—to assist the out-of-city crew with directions and operating procedures. Eventually National Guardsmen with firearms were assigned to the engine. On Monday the engine and crew were placed in "task forces" with other city engines.

Engine #331 was equipped with a 2,000-gpm monitor pipe, water cannon like-appliance that was used on at least two large building fires. Baltimore City firefighters, in addition to being impressed with the professionalism of the firefighters on Engine #331, were also very impressed with the engine's high volume monitor pipe. All the equipment mounted to the outside of the apparatus had to be removed and stowed in the compartments. Ladders were tied down. The city had provided chicken wire to build a makeshift enclosure around the open cab to protect the driver, the officer and the crew riding in the jump seats (all encompassed within the open cab) from airborne projectiles, many of them red bricks that would come to be to be known as "alley apples."[80]

Now all of the Anne Arundel and Baltimore County engines and crews were returning to their home stations with stories of heroic deeds and unbelievable descriptions of the events that they had experienced since the fires broke out on Saturday evening. None of the firefighters would ever forget the experience.

WEDNESDAY WOULD TURN OUT TO BE THE FIRST DAY since the riots started on Saturday that people could walk the streets without treading on shattered glass. A small army of 1,120 city public works employees and 97 dump trucks were sent throughout the riot-torn areas to sweep the streets and board up damaged buildings.[81]

All banks were opened today. The Lafayette, North Avenue, Bel Air and Lexington markets were all opened for business as a new curfew was announced for this day.[82] The only city market that didn't open was located on Broadway which had been damaged by a small fire.

Fire Chief John Killen stated to news reporters that the numbers of fire incidents were dropping because military personnel and the police officers were now strictly enforcing the evening curfews and as a result there were fewer people on the street. Killen, who on Monday was furious over the lack of protection for his firefighters, was now complimenting the soldiers and police officers for stepping up their enforcement obligations.[83]

Around 11 a.m., Mayor D'Alessandro, with the latest intelligence from law enforcement agencies in hand, stated that he believed Baltimore's riots were organized in advance. The mayor said that there was evidence that some of the street gangs had acted under the direction of leaders working with well laid plans. Yet, Assistant U.S. Attorney Fred Vinson stated, "There is no hard evidence of any outside [of the city] agitation."[84]

Later in the afternoon, curious sightseers took the place of street gangs, as they walked in crowds to examine the devastated stores and businesses. Workers cleaned up debris from lootings and fires on the west side. The city's phone service that had been severely impacted since Saturday night was still struggling to get back to normal—at times there was still no dial tone.[85]

The city inhabitants who relied on public phones throughout the riot torn areas would be greatly inconvenienced. Over 1,500 outside glass-and-aluminum stand-alone phone booths had been demolished, their coin boxes pried out, opened, and looted. Telephone repairmen would not be sent out to replace or make repairs until the areas were completely secure.[86]

At 4 p.m. Governor Agnew made an announcement that conditions in the city had improved enough to possibly modify or remove entirely the ban on the sale of alcoholic beverages in the city and five surrounding counties.[87]

AT BALTIMORE'S MEMORIAL STADIUM, located on 33rd Street north of the war-torn corridor along North Avenue and west of the devastation along Harford Road, the Orioles' opening day game that had been canceled on Tuesday was about to start.

Enthusiastic applause broke out as baseball stars Brooks Robinson and Frank Robinson ran across the infield in their bright white home uniforms adorned with the orange Orioles' logo on the front of their shirts and black caps with bright orange brims to begin the team's warm-ups—two superstar athletes, one black and one white, worked together.[88]

The opposing team was the new Oakland Athletics (A's). The batting coach, famed Yankee Clipper Joe Dimaggio, in his light gray road trip uniform with a green number "5" and the teams' city, Oakland, in green letters across the front of his shirt, ran over to the mayor's box and shook Mayor Tommy A'Dlesandro III's hand—the two had been friends for years. The handsome 39-year-old mayor threw out the first ball to Oriole catcher Andy Etchebaren, "who promptly handed it back."[89]

The Oriole's new relief pitching hopeful, left-hander Pete Richert, would not be available for today's opener. Richert, a national guardsman assigned to Washington, D.C.'s 163rd Military Police Battalion, had been called up over the weekend and federalized on Sunday morning. Oriole Manager Hank Bauer said, "It's going to hurt us some, but we should be able to cover [for] him without much trouble." The starting pitchers for today's game were Tom Phoebus for the Orioles and Jim "Catfish" Hunter for the A's.

Compared to the year before when approximately 39,000 fans attended the home opener, today's attendance of 22,050 was somewhat low. Unfortunately, after the first inning D'Alesandro was summoned back to city hall. The Orioles would defeat the Athletics in the home opener, 3 to 1. Brooks Robinson would seal the game by hitting a home run in the eighth inning.[90]

By 8 p.m., the day's fires were limited to a few vacant houses and previously looted stores. Most of these structures were located in or near the city's west side. Newspapers would label these incidents as "One last little fling."[91]

At 9:15 p.m., Governor Agnew's spokesman announced that the ban on liquor sales still stood. The Governor, who four hours earlier had considered modifying or removing the ban altogether, decided, for the time being, to leave the ban in place.

On West Lanvale Street shots rang out in the night as police exchanged gunfire with suspected snipers on a roof. Officers used tear gas to disperse crowds in the area. A fire was reported on Fayette Street east of Broadway.[92] Three white men were arrested in southwest Baltimore and charged for procession of or throwing Molotov cocktails.[93]

Arrests on Wednesday from midnight to 1 p.m. numbered 105, bringing the total for the riots to 5,316. Trials were still being held in the makeshift courts set up at the district police stations. Juvenile court cases were postponed until the upcoming Monday, April 15. Miraculously, there were only 10 lootings on Wednesday. The total number of reported lootings during the riots was now listed at 1,214. It was also announced on Wednesday that applications for aid from the state insurance commission were now available at the Enoch Pratt Library downtown and at its branches.[94]

Most of damage was in the city's "poverty belt," officials reported. Student attendance in city schools rose on Wednesday but remained below normal. Plans were announced by a white interfaith group for a walk of penance on Saturday. Courts processed the last of more than 5,300 criminal cases.[95]

Eleven thousand Army and National Guard troops remained in Baltimore to assure that the relative peace was kept. Since lootings were occurring less frequently and there was far less crime in the daylight hours than usual, this day marked the end of the marathon duty hours for troops, policemen, and firefighters. (There was less crime during the light hours as one would find on a Sunday afternoon.)[96]

Some 1,000 to 1,500 business owners were expected to meet at the Pikesville fire hall to discuss ways of getting help and protecting against future disturbances. As merchants returned to their stores, the downtown shopping areas were opened for holiday gift buying until 9 p.m., and some shopkeepers along Pennsylvania Avenue and Gay Street were open. Merchants in the 2100-2200 blocks of Monument Street reported business was almost back to normal.

In Annapolis, Governor Agnew sent telegrams to President Lyndon Johnson and the Maryland Congressional Delegation requesting that quick action be taken to bring damage caused by the riots within the terms of Federal disaster relief. Only natural disasters were covered under Federal disaster relief and Agnew was hoping that the president and congress would pass emergency legislation to include riots.[97]

13

The Smoke Clears

Thursday, April 11, 1968

On Thursday morning, 50 trucks and 200 men were sent out from the city's Department of Public Works to continue the work of boarding up looted and burned-out buildings. Baltimore was in its second day of cleaning up. Considering the fact that the union, that represented more than 5,000 of the city's municipal employees, had been looking at a possible strike just before the riots started, the appearance of the workers in the streets was a "bright face in a city with a black eye."[1]

The union members had complained about a "lousy proposed two and half percent pay raise" on their hourly rate that was in the process of being negotiated between union leaders and the city's administration. The raise was to go into effect on July 1, 1968. Many workers only took home about $50 per week and a higher raise was anticipated. James D'Claxton, president of the Amalgamated Municipal Employees Union, Local 1231, strongly believed that 75 percent of the membership would strike if called upon.[2]

The city's health department also was very busy this day. Businesses that sold food such as grocery stores, drug stores, restaurants and sub shops destroyed or partially damaged had to be inspected for contaminated and spoiled food. Some stores were unscathed by fire, but had been totally damaged by vandalism, and the rotten food smelled. The city had just survived the worst riot in its history, and health department officials were going to make sure no more injuries or deaths would occur as a result of a city-wide health epidemic.[3]

Health department officials noted one positive outcome of the fires—they may have killed a huge number of rats. And while the surviving rats were running between habitats, it was an opportune time to set up traps and kill even more.[4]

Baltimore now seemed to be emerging from the nightmare that had plagued the city since Saturday afternoon. As the smoke cleared, activity besides that of responding police officers and firefighters started to take effect. The city was beginning to see signs of normalcy.

And to encourage that normalcy, at 4 a.m. Thursday when the curfew was lifted, Governor Agnew announced an end to the ban on liquor sales, and allowed gasoline in containers to be sold at filling stations. Agnew did not lift the ban on sales of guns and explosives, but he did decide that there would be no more curfews after this day. As the bars started to open and were visited by customers, police officers entered tavern after tavern to force the customers out. The police officers had never been informed of the lifting of the ban. The tavern busting only lasted for about a half-hour as news of the regulation change finally made its way down the rank and file.[5]

At noon, city fire units were dispatched to a building fire at the corner of Broadway and Orleans Street. By the time units arrived, the red brick multi-level building was completely engulfed in flames and three more alarms of equipment were quickly summoned. The fire produced a large column of dark smoke that could be seen from every corner of the city.

The raging fire was located at the Broadway Storage Company warehouse. Earlier in the morning, Baltimore Gas and Electric troubleshooters had been inside repairing electrical lines that apparently were damaged during the week's riots. Two of the workmen saw a small group of children playing on the elevators and chased them out of the building. Approximately 25 minutes or so after the workmen went back to work they noticed that the building was on fire. There were two separate fires, one on each end of the building.[6]

Flames reached 100 feet into the afternoon sky. One of the 500 or so spectators who watched the fire was Mayor D'Alesandro. The mayor stood on the corner of Broadway and Fayette Street as firefighters smartly took a defensive position and applied large streams of water from their large-diameter ladder pipes and engine deluge nozzles into the flaming structure.[7]

Bud Chaney remembers the fire well. As a firefighter assigned to Truck #1, Chaney and fellow crew members operated on the fire. After the main body of the fire was extinguished, all that remained of the warehouse was the burned-out shell. Chaney and crew were ordered to knock down the high free-standing and damaged brick walls that posed a danger to the public. The crew members actually used the tip of the truck's 100-foot aerial ladder as a battering ram. Using an aerial ladder as a battering ram and possibly damaging high-pressure hydraulic lines and the ladder's stabilizing struts, goes against every standard operating guideline when operating fire department ladder trucks.[8]

Chaney would later comment, "We knew we shouldn't do it, but we were too dogged tired to tear the walls down any other way. If Chief Killen would have been there, he would have locked us up too." Bud also remembers a brand-new car parked across the street from the burning building. "It was smoking due to the extreme heat being radiated by the fire…so we broke out the side window, opened the door, released the brake, and moved the vehicle to a safer place."[9]

Later in the afternoon, city and Baltimore County units responded to a fire in a carryout shop in the 1600 block of Ingleside Avenue, in Baltimore County just over the city line. Other than the fire in the carryout shop, all was quiet.

AT 2 P.M. ON THURSDAY AFTERNOON a very agitated Governor Agnew held a press conference at the state office building located on Preston Street. He had summoned news reporters, city department heads, city councilmen, judges, state officials, African-American community and religious leaders, and politicians. It was perceived that he wanted to speak about the riots and civil rights in general. Maryland State Police officers guarding the complex refused admittance to any of the city's militant leaders trying to attend.[10]

After the approximately 100 members of Baltimore's moderate African-American leadership showed up, Governor Agnew started his speech. He made some opening comments, but before long the true reason that he had called the gathering became apparent. Agnew could not hold back his contempt for the militant leaders who he believed had initiated the turmoil. Agnew started to scold and admonish the gathering. He criticized and called the militant leaders "Circuit riding, Hanoi visiting, caterwauling, riot inciting, burn America type of leaders" and told the African-Americans in the audience that the black community had not done enough to put an end to the disturbances. Agnew accused the African-Americans of yielding to the militants for fear of being called Mr. Charlie's Boy or Uncle Toms.[11]

Agnew continued on: "The fires were not lit in the honor of your great fallen leader [Dr.] Martin Luther King. Nor were they lit from an overwhelming sense of frustration and despair. The fires were kindled at the suggestion and with the instruction of advocates of violence."[12] Agnew's speech intimidated, humiliated and polarized the attendees.[13]

Within a couple of minutes after the governor started to speak, the black leaders, many who had supported Agnew's campaign for governor, started walking out. Most of the members of the African-American community eventually walked out of the meeting before Agnew could finish. Fire commission board member Reverend Bascom, a supporter of Agnew during his 1966 campaign for governor, was one of the first to walk out.[14]

Although Agnew gained support among people who felt that there were too many concessions and pardons made to looters and arsonists during the riots, liberal critics felt Agnew had alienated the African-American community—the same community that had turned out for him at the voting booths just two years before.[15]

In admonishing the group, Agnew knew he was committing political suicide. He understood very well that the black community had supported him during his election for governor. However, Agnew believed his views clearly needed to be stated and felt that no apologies were needed.[16]

The blacks charged that the governor had sought to "divide us."[17] They condemned him for failing to demonstrate enlightened leadership. It wasn't long afterwards that Baltimore's black leadership considered Governor Agnew a "wolf in sheep's clothing."[18] Leaders would interpret from the speech that Agnew implied that "fleeing looters ought to be shot and the Kerner Commission's report did not hold any weight and may even encourage further rioting."[19]

The city's black leadership drafted a statement denouncing the governor's comments. The statement concluded by saying, "We call upon all people of goodwill black and white to demonstrate enlightened and concerned leadership today."[20]

It had only been six days since the breakout of the city's racial unrest and Mayor D'Alesandro did not want Agnew's speech to reignite the turmoil. D'Alesandro understood that "there was a fine line between the end of the riots and the possibility of another."[21] Two blocks away from the Preston Street state office building at the Fifth Regiment Armory, D'Alesandro hastily called a press conference.

The mayor read a prepared statement responding to the governor's afternoon speech. The mayor requested that "all citizens of the community to exercise calm and restraint in action and [at] public attendances." The mayor termed the governor's remarks as "somewhat inflammatory" and said, "we should be emphasizing reconciliation and harmony, not divisiveness.... This is a bad time to say what he [the Governor] did. Most of the people reject the extreme aspects of both sides." The mayor continued, "The city and the whole community was [were] hard hit by the force of the disturbances, but I believe that it [they] absorbed the punch with remarkable resiliency."[22]

Friday's Baltimore *Sun* editorial stated that "Agnew insulted the Negroes who had been working all week to mitigate the violence. The *Sun* emphatically disagrees with Mr. Agnew."[23] An editorial in the Baltimore *News American* stated, "One thing we like about the governor is his determination to put the blame where it belongs. Our governor is a man with the courage of his convictions." The paper complimented Agnew for trying. "His motives were sound," editors wrote, but "he may have picked the wrong time and the wrong place."[24]

Governor Agnew would receive 1,117 telegrams and 312 phone calls from citizens praising his speech to the black leadership. He also received 69 telegrams and seven phone calls in opposition to it—including an open letter from 30 of the city's Catholic priests.[25]

Based on undercover reports from the Maryland State Police, Agnew knew that on April 3, 1968 some members of the city's black leadership held a secret meeting with Stokley Carmichael in a café on Pennsylvania Avenue. As a result, Agnew had convinced himself that the black leaders with whom he was trying to work with were ignoring his efforts to bring about peace in the community. He couldn't understand why they would deal with extremists like Carmichael. According to Maryland State Police Colonel Robert Lally, "[the thought of] it perturbed him to no end.[25] The secret meeting coupled with a death threat, Agnew had received only the day before, perpetuated his lashing out against the black leadership.

In the evening, there were still signs that the violence was not completely over. Around 7:40 p.m. fire engines and ladder trucks responded to a fire in a loan office in the 1900 block of Greenmount Avenue. The business had been repeatedly hit throughout the six days of violence.[26] Approximately two hours later, a tailor shop was torched in the 900 block of Whitelock Street. Four engines and a ladder truck with a total of 25 firefighters responded. While battling the blaze, firefighters had to evacuate 25 patrons from an adjoining bar which had received a great deal of smoke.[27]

As Governor Agnew lifted all executive orders with the exception of that night's curfew and bans on firearms and explosives, the city's powerless victims of the devastated inner city businesses started to voice their dissatisfaction with law enforcement during the riots.

No group experienced so much property damage as the businessmen operating in the riot-torn areas.[28] Many of the store owners "recognized the looters and vandals as customers of long year's standing and couldn't believe what was happening to them."[29] The store owners offered extra services to the customers and residents of the ghetto such as contributing to local churches and helping customers fill out government applications and forms for jobs and credit.[30] Most of these stores and offices were white-owned, though many of the employees were black.[31] In nearby Washington, D.C., more than one-half of workers displaced as result of the riots were black.[32]

Representatives of small merchant associations claimed that government officials neglected the impacts on the small mom-and-pop stores and embraced an ideology that focused sympathetic attention on rioters.[33]

In some cases when mobs were ravaging the stores, the store owners would call for National Guard or police assistance. The police officers would arrive and apprehend the looters only to let them go free when the store owner refused to sign the complaint because of fear of retribution. It was all very frustrating to the police as they looked very foolish trying to hold on and handcuff the looters after the store owners refused to press charges. When the culprits were let go, the crowds in the street became even bolder and more intimidating.[34]

Many looters appeared to be in the melees for fun and profit. They stole consumables such as liquor, cigarettes, drugs, and clothing. They generally avoided stealing merchandise that would have to be sold.[35] Typically rioters struck poorly lit, unguarded stores first, then moved against other business establishments in their neighborhoods.[36]

Black radicals defending the riots argued that nonviolent tactics of the civil rights movement had failed to produce real economic gains for the inner-city poor.[37] Others, mostly whites who deplored the disobedience of blacks claimed that the riots were not rebellions but giant shopping sprees.[38] Black moderates believed the violence hurt the cause of Civil Rights.[39, 40]

For the first time since Saturday, the city's firefighters could get a good night's sleep and the police officers would have easy, incident-free patrols. There were no incidents of fires, vandalism or looting between midnight Thursday and 7 a.m. Friday.

ON FRIDAY MORNING, APRIL 12, 1968 Lt. Gen. Robert York declared that order was restored in the city and returned responsibility for control back to Governor Agnew as some of the Federal units started to move out. Governor Agnew called President Johnson and advised the president of the general's declaration, and informed him that 3,800 Federal troops could be withdrawn.[41]

In the opinion of Lt. Gen. York, there was no riot. He wanted to play down the hostilities. The general stated, "We did not have a riot, a race riot as such and it was my job to prevent that." He added, "Is a life worth a loaf of bread or a pint of whiskey?" York reminded reporters that the Army guidelines in these circumstances call for minimum use of force for protection of life and property. The general said, "Indiscriminate firing takes the lives of more innocent persons then guilty ones." York made it clear that his soldiers were not going to shoot anyone for looting.[42]

Considering the violence experienced throughout the week, Friday was a cakewalk. At 2:30 a.m., Saturday, it was reported that since 8 p.m. Friday, four outbreaks of violence had occurred: three fires and a shooting. One of these fires was at a public school in the 2700 block of Shirley Avenue.

Sometime around 8 p.m. an arsonist broke a window in one of the annex buildings, of the school, climbed through, and poured a flammable liquid over a teacher's desk, setting it on fire.[43] A vacant house was torched in the 1200 block of East Madison Street around 9 p.m. At 1:30 a.m. Saturday, a vacant building in the 800 block of North Gay Street was set afire. The last fire occurred at 2:40 a.m. at the Union Food Center at 1500 Harford Avenue—a building that had been set afire a number of times during the past week.

Despite the few fires, the city was getting back to normal. A sign that things were getting better was that police were now responding to reports of rape and numerous assaults and robberies. No stores had been looted or burned on Friday.[44] From noon Friday until noon Saturday there would only be 43 arrests. The amount arrested was considered normal for a typical Friday night and early Saturday morning in Baltimore.[45]

On Saturday morning, April 13, 1968 the tent cities quickly set up less than six days previously were taken down and packed away. The barbed wire fence was rolled up and stacked in the backs of trucks. The dust-covered "Deuce and a half" army trucks were started up as tired and weary but somewhat happy Federal troops began to leave the city. The deadline for Federal troops to be out of the Fifth Regiment Armory was 9 a.m. About 5,700 National Guardsmen would remain to patrol the streets. However, to assist in maintaining the new calm the Guard's presence would only be evident at the Fifth Regiment Armory and the city's nine police stations.[46]

Many praised the police officers and firefighters for their work during the riots. Of the police officers Lt. Gen. York said, "I have been most impressed by their leadership, their competence, by their understanding of the problem and their dedication." The general also praised the firefighters.[47]

Police Chief Pomerleau sent a message to all of the city's police stations over teletype. It read, *"Each of you can be extremely proud of the job that this department has accomplished during the past several days. Your individual and collective efforts have been truly professional. Your dedication and devotion to duty and your demonstrated restraint under the most trying conditions possible have been outstanding....We can all be proud being members of the Baltimore City Police Department. I can assure you its performance has established standards for these occurrences that will be most difficult to equal."*[48]

Beer sales rocketed Saturday as establishments untouched by the violence were selling three times the normal rate. Local breweries like Carlings and National Beer were swamped with calls for deliveries. Normally drivers didn't work on Saturdays, but today they did. Customers were running up to the beer trucks trying to bribe the drivers to let them buy six-packs.[49]

On the front page of Saturday evening's *News American,* there was not one headline or column concerning the riots. The news was about U.S. Air Force B-52 bombers bombing the Mekong Delta and killing approximately 200 Vietcong soldiers.[50]

On Easter Sunday at 10 a.m., Governor Agnew announced that the emergency was over and Maryland's National Guard were to be sent home.[51] However, the sounds of piercing sirens and ringing bells on the city's fire engines and ladder trucks began again when a fire broke out in Oldtown.

This time, it was a fire burning out of control at the Peterson Lumber Company located on Fayette and Chester streets. The fire grew to five alarms within 30 minutes. Firefighters weathered by a week of "hit and run" firefighting tactics now dug in to protect many row homes across the street from the lumber yard. Homes were evacuated. The fire spread to the roofs of five row homes on Chester Street but was eventually extinguished.[52]

The burning lumber yard capped what had been the busiest eight days of fighting fires in the history of Baltimore.

14

A Divided Community

Mark Miller of the *Evening Sun* would remark, "The rioting divided an already divided community even more, accentuating the hostility, the mistrust between blacks and whites. What would we say to each other? Could the friendship endure?"[1]

What could anybody say? It was very unfortunate that the riots happened at all. It was even worse that a great African-American leader, Dr. Martin Luther King, was cut down in his prime. But as stated earlier, the riots were just waiting to happen, "a match waiting to be struck."[2]

But the important questions to be asked now were: What could be salvaged from this tragedy? What lessons could be learned from the violence, fires, looting, injuries, deaths and arrests of that stormy week in April 1968? Were there any positive outcomes?

For starters, there were a number of accolades handed out. "Negro leaders were quick to praise the effort of General Gelston, a veteran of five Maryland riots. He did not isolate himself among white members of the power structure. He and his staff devoted long hours to studying the needs and desires of the slum dwellers," said an editorial in the Baltimore *Sun*.[3]

The editorial continued, "The familiar cry of police brutality was virtually unheard of in Baltimore."[4] The Maryland National Guard under Gelston won the respect of white and black leaders in communities throughout the state.[5] Another positive worth noting was that the death rate in Baltimore was very low compared to those of other cities where rioting had occurred. This miracle was a result of a combination of restraint, tolerance, and law enforcement ideologies advocated by Gelston and Baltimore City Police Chief Donald Pomerleau.

However, not all were pleased. Many police officers were outspoken critics of how the riots were handled. According to police officers, Chief Pomerleau originally had approximately 50 officers trained in riot control methods. These men had been set up into two units equipped with riot gear to be deployed upon an outbreak of hostilities. Unfortunately, Pomerleau had deactivated these units about a month before the riots began. The officers claimed that had the members of the unit been deployed immediately to Gay Street on the first evening of the disturbances and permitted to use tear gas, they could have stopped the riot or controlled it more quickly.[6]

City Comptroller Hyman Pressman was outraged and very vocal in his criticisms of how the Federal soldiers handled the rioters. He said, "Orders came from Washington not to shoot. The lawmakers were weak-kneed." Pressman accused the soldiers of dereliction of duty.[7]

Lt. Gen. Robert York, U.S. Army, disagreed as he posed the question, "is a life worth a loaf of bread or a pint of whiskey?"[8] City police officers, however, had a different motive for holding back on pulling the trigger of their side arm. Many police officers, possibly all of them, at one time or another over the past week had either lost or came close to losing their tempers. But, they continued to remind themselves, and it was no doubt a thought process that lingered continuously in their collective minds, that if they did shoot a looter, they would be made a "whipping boy" for the civil rights groups and they would be "thrown to the wolves" by the city's bosses to set an example.[9]

The important point, however, was that the only shots fired were fired when an officer felt his life was in danger. This attitude was paramount in keeping the injury and death rates very low considering the thousands of people who participated in the Baltimore riots.[10]

Regarding shots fired by the Guardsmen, Gelston claimed that it had only happened once. He said one round was fired by a Guardsman over the head of a suspected looter at a shopping center.[11] However, he never addressed the shots fired by a Guardsman at the Flag Court mid-rise apartments on Lombard Street which had occurred on Monday night.

A final positive worth noting is that it appeared that only a small percentage of the city's 400,000 African-Americans were involved in the vandalism, looting, and burning as most stayed indoors.[12]

A good many of the rioters were juveniles and they didn't stray too far from their inner-city homes. The youngsters were used by the older teenagers and young men to perform the initial action of breaking-in businesses and stores. As stated earlier, once the juveniles broke the glass and gained access to the business, the experienced teenagers and young men took over. Of the thousands that were on the streets, 500 juveniles were taken into custody and later sent home to their parents.[13]

It would be found out that most looters lived within 10 blocks of the businesses they broke into and looted.[14] Baltimore's experience was similar to Washington D.C.—teenagers started the action and by the second day, young men in their 20s had also joined the ruckus.[15]

There are those who believe that even if Dr. King had not been assassinated, there still would have been riots during the summer of 1968. According to Maryland State Police reports, a meeting was held on April 3, 1968 just one day before Dr. King was assassinated. In a café on Pennsylvania Avenue, Stokely Carmichael met with certain members of the area's black leadership. An undercover officer sitting in the next booth heard Carmichael say among other things, "The only way to deal with a white man is across the barrel of a gun." Carmichael was also heard to say that riots were "part of the war against the white power structure."[16]

The riots were part of a bigger problem. Harry L. Goldberg, city attorney, would say, "The riot and crime in general is part of a cancer eating at the heart of the city."[17] Blacks lived in and sometimes worked in deplorable conditions. It's interesting that

Baltimore did not immediately erupt into riots upon receiving the news of Dr. King's death as did nearby Washington, D.C. and other cities. There was an almost 48-hour lull before the riots began in Baltimore.

It's been said that the facts leading up to an accident happen slowly but the accident happens fast. What caused the riots—what were some of the "slow" processes that evolved to create the pent-up hostile state among African-Americans that existed in Baltimore's inner-city?

Residential segregation and racism created most of the hostility. Unemployment was also a critical factor. Between World War II (1945) and 1968, Baltimore's African-American population increased from 220,000 to 400,000 and blacks needed jobs. Although new construction soared in the areas surrounding Baltimore during the 1960s, it was light to non-existent in the city.[18]

Blacks were lowly represented in city jobs and construction projects, many of which were subsidized through Federal funding. Time and time again Gay Street was slated for urban renewal, but there was always a reason to push the renewal back. Blacks had less access to well-paying jobs and decent housing. They wanted to have the "good" life that was characterized on the TV shows like "Leave it to Beaver" and "Donna Reed" which was not happening.[19]

Maryland's U.S. Congressman Parren Mitchell believed the riots were a result of the unfair conditions endured by African-Americans. After the riots, Mitchell would simply state that, "the riots were a reaction to the way it was."[20] Similarly, others believed the riots were rooted from the rotten ruins of the ghetto —business as usual.[21]

Robert Holt, executive director of Baltimore's Opportunity Industrialization Center, an African-American job training organization, stated that there was a "particular pattern" of destruction aimed primarily at liquor, drug and small grocery stores and bars and taverns. According to Holt, these businesses had exploited the black man, and the pattern of destruction led Holt to believe that the riot was planned.[22]

Holt said these businesses exploited black customers by charging high check-cashing fees. Many of the businesses charged 10 percent of the amount of the check for check cashing, even if the check casher had an account at the store. The stores would shortchange kids when they purchased merchandise. The owners increased prices on goods and sold inferior, damaged, and surplus products at inflated prices. The business owners lived outside the city and didn't do anything to try to improve the neighborhoods. Holt said that furniture and appliance stores would set up charge accounts at 12 percent interest for whites and 18 percent for blacks.[23]

Additionally, Holt pointed out that there were some things that defied explanation: an untouched business in a block of devastated stores or an unmarred telephone booth in an area of grave destruction. According to Holt, the businesses spared "received assurances in advance." He also stated that, the fires were "highly controlled...they were extensive enough to involve the fire department, but not so intense [that they] would burn down the entire block." In contrast to the observations of others, Holt stated, "The adults would do the breaking in and initial looting and then leave it to the youngsters."[24]

In regard to human life, the fires were not "highly" controlled. A week after the fires, an article appeared in the Sunday *Sun* entitled "The Changing City—The Fire This Time," written by James D. Dilts. Dilts interviewed a 21-year-old rioter who was raised in the Greenmount Avenue corridor. The young man said that he helped 17-and 18-year-olds set fires in businesses. His only condition, he said, was that they "burn white men's stores only." He added, "The minute we set the fire, we [knocked] on the doors and would tell them that their building was on fire. If they don't come out, it's too bad."[25]

The young man also stated that there was a "white lady" on Greenmount Avenue, who was told that her residence was on fire. He said, "She wouldn't come out—the fire department had to drag her out." What was troubling was the fact that the young man was not the typical uneducated, unemployed, high school dropout out in the streets as identified in the Kerner Commission Report. He was employed as a lab technician with three years of college.[26]

Mayor Tom D'Alesandro III also believed that the riot was planned and outside agitators had encouraged it. His belief was based on the fact that riots did not break out in Baltimore immediately following Dr. King's assassination as they did in Washington, D.C. and other cities. The programs that he and his predecessors, Acting Mayor Goodman and Mayors McKeldin and Grady, had or were in the process of implementing over recent years were working. D'Alesandro also believed that if he had been in office for a year, the riots wouldn't have occurred at all.[27]

"I was bringing in the money," said D'Alesandro in a recent interview with this author. "I was able to convince the city council to float an $85 million bond for new school construction."[28]

In the summer of 1968, D'Alesandro cinched the deal of the century for the city's youth. His staff had found that Federal funding for 26,000 summer positions was awarded to New York City. However, the New York City administration did not have the organization set up for the payment process or the bureaucracy to manage the positions for the youngsters when they were hired and turned down the offer. When D'Alesandro was able to verify the rumor, he immediately contacted William Millard Wirtz, President Johnson's Secretary of Labor and was able to have the funding redistributed to Baltimore. The program provided part-time jobs for 15,000 of the city's youth from July through September of 1968.[29]

D'Alesandro also believed that he would have had a better police intelligence or undercover operation in place after a year in office. This intelligence organization would have been better able to identify the agitators and filter information to head off violence before it had a chance to start. D'Alesandro would serve one term as Baltimore's mayor and return to private law practice in 1973.[30]

The riots would affect Baltimore for decades and still do today. Merchants whose businesses were looted or burned left for the suburbs. The blight of abandoned homes led to the "scourge of drugs and crime."[31] Affordable insurance for merchants located in the inner city was not available.[32] Baltimore is still recovering.

Baltimore had begun losing residents in the 1950s as middle-class families left the city for "bigger homes, greener lawns and safer streets."[33] This white flight escalated after the riots. Baltimore lost 13 percent of its population—104,000 residents—between 1970 and 1980.[34] From 1969 to 1980 the city lost 35,000 jobs. As a result, Baltimore was added to the list of the nation's 10 poorest cities.[35] The schools lost 50,000 students in the 1970s "most of them white."[36]

The riots would affect the fire department by bringing about changes in operational policy and personnel protection. During the riots firefighters responded to more than 1,000 fires. Approximately 1,000 businesses were looted and burned, resulting in $13.5 million in property loss.[37] Twenty-five firefighters were injured, four serious enough to be taken off duty and retired. Two firefighters sustained eye injuries when they were smashed in the face by thrown objects. Despite sniper shootings at several fires, no firefighters were struck by bullets.[38]

While Baltimore's 1968 riots subsided into history, incidents of mobs harassing firefighters responding to alarms continued. Under a new policy a police squad car would now be dispatched with firefighters to all fires."[39]

In October 1968 in Cherry Hill, only six months after the riots, firefighters were stoned by a large crowd of 17-to 22-year olds during a fire response. (According to many firefighters, that worked the Cherry Hill area, rock-and-bottle throwing incidents by residents occurred quite often and months before the April 1968 riots.)[40]

As a result of these rock-and-bottle throwing incidents the city fire department installed clear plastic face and neck shields on firefighters' helmets along with hard ear flaps. In addition to protecting firefighters from flying stones and bottles, the hardware prevented debris from hitting the face when a firefighter pulled ceilings or broke glass.[41]

Hard hats (the type worn by construction workers) were issued to driver/operators to protect them when they worked alone at the engine. Fiberglass and wooden covered enclosures were installed over the open cab engines and ladder trucks. Shatterproof clear plastic enclosures were installed on the rear of the apparatus to protect firefighters riding on the tailboard. Tillermen operating the steering wheel on the back of the long tractor-drawn ladder trucks were protected by 14-gauge steel enclosures and shatter proof clear plastic. The combined protection gave the appearance of a small telephone booth on the back of the vehicle.[42]

It is believed that the riots strengthened the bond between the city's white and black firefighters. During the riots, the African-American firefighters performed their duties to the fullest. They tolerated the catcalls and obscenities from the rioters and watched the backs of their white counterparts.

Lloyd Marcus, firefighter assigned to Engine Company #6, remembered that a couple of days after the riots ended he was upstairs in the sewing room of the fire station reading his bible, when the company driver-operator said over the station intercom, "Marcus, get down here to the dinner table before your dinner gets cold." For the first time in his career Marcus sat at the station dinner table and ate with the white members of his shift. He never ate alone in the firehouse again.[43]

Nationwide, as a result of the riots, there were 46 deaths in 12 cities. Chicago had the highest number of deaths, twelve. Eleven were killed in nearby Washington, D.C. Six died in Baltimore and six in Kansas City. There were two deaths each in Cincinnati and Detroit. Finally there was one death each in Highland Park, Michigan; Trenton, New Jersey; Jacksonville and Tallahassee, Florida; Saint Louis, Missouri; and Minneapolis, Minnesota.[44]

In Baltimore, 4,500 had been arrested: 391 for disorderly conduct, 13 for arson, 955 for larceny and 665 for other crimes. (The 2024, unaccounted for were most likely arrested for curfew violations.)[45] Of those arrested, 443 were white. Of the 13 arrested for arson, only a few were ever convicted.[46]

In addition to the businesses that were suspected of exploiting African-Americans, the mom-and-pop stores had been hit most severely and frequently. The little shops, liquor stores, and corner taverns were easy and inviting targets. The larger businesses in Baltimore, like those in Detroit and Newark, the previous summer, were not affected.[47]

Eighty percent of all destroyed businesses were owned by whites. They were mostly Russian Jewish immigrants. Many were Holocaust survivors.[48] Some of the black-owned stores that were hit were targeted because the owners lived outside the city—they didn't contribute to the community and they lacked "soul."[49] As the Jewish merchants moved out in 1968 following the riots, a small amount of Korean merchants moved in.[50]

One-third of all the stores destroyed during the riots never reopened at or near the same location. According to a police department study, 1,049 privately owned businesses and two transit company buses were burned, looted or otherwise damaged.[51]

Approximately 50 businesses, mostly grocery stores, liquor outlets, drug stores, carry-outs and other small retailers, were successfully transferred to blacks from white businessmen through the Business Opportunities Administration which was established as a result of the riots. It was easier and less painful for the burned-out owners to transfer their licenses than to rebuild. "It is evident that the riot had a serious effect on the small businessmen of Baltimore, many of whom simply suffered losses and made no attempt to regain their former livelihoods."[52]

Businesses that remained began to take extraordinary precautions against future damage. Storefronts were boarded up, equipped with bars, bricked up and/or screened in with heavy metal cages. "There are few stores operating today in the [former] riot areas that do not look like miniature fortresses."[53] Many store operators now keep guns on their premises. [54]

After the riots more than $6 million in civil suits were filed claiming that the city failed to enforce the law diligently and exercise its police powers authoritatively during the riots, thereby permitting extensive fires and looting. Subsequently, the efforts of "budding" black businessmen were hampered as they encountered difficulty and unanticipated expense in starting up new businesses due to costly insurance, credit, loans and other necessities.[55]

Actually, a number of Baltimore area wholesalers were already looking at plans to build "64/40" stores throughout the East Baltimore riot-torn areas and were optimistic about transitioning the little mom-and-pop stores to better ones. The new stores would be better equipped and have more aisles and cashier lines as well as a wider range of merchandise.[56]

The "64/40" stores were so-called because the average building would encompass 6,440 square feet of selling space and equal space outside for parking. These grocery stores would be one-third the size of most suburban market stores and would be more economical and efficient than the, only marginal profitable, mom-and-pop stores. It was also believed that the larger chains like "A&P" would enlarge their inner city stores.[57]

Although the large downtown stores along Baltimore's Howard Street shopping corridor were not damaged during the turmoil, the riots had a severe impact on their business. Within two years of the riots, business at the downtown Hutzler's store, the "pride of the company" declined by 50 percent. 1968 would be the store's last high profit year.[58] Prior to the riots, Baltimore's downtown stores were "real estate rich," but following the riots, their values "plummeted 50 to 80 percent."[59]

The downtown Hutzler's department store, "once bustling with shoppers, became eerily quiet almost overnight. The riots of 68 were a large turning point for downtown," said George Hutzler Bernstein.[60]

The city police department needed to make changes in how it responded to disturbances and riots. As a result of the riots, changes in policy and procedures brought about a new program and it is believed that the city is better prepared to address small disorders and keep them from escalating into full blown riots.[61]

The new program was set up to deploy a total combination of 3,000 city and state officers, and Guardsmen at the scene of a disturbance within one hour of being alerted. And a force of 10,000 could be put on the ground within four to six hours of any outbreak of violence. "It is agreed that a show of strength is necessary to maintain order," stated Colonel John S. Edwards Jr., Chief of Staff for the Maryland National Guard.[62]

Annapolis was also trying to do its part in establishing tougher laws to assist police and firefighters. New "anti-riot legislation" passed by the general assembly would assist in preventing small disorders from turning into riots. Police officers would be able to arrest people hindering the work of firefighters, and police would not be required to obtain warrants before making arrests on misdemeanor charges during an emergency.[63]

Members of the police force would also need to find a way to tighten up on information sent to the media. It was found that television broadcasters unwittingly informed potential looters where they might join the mobs and enjoy safety in numbers (28 years later in Los Angeles during the Rodney King riots, lawbreakers would once again use information gleaned from broadcasts for their own nefarious purposes). And when it was announced on television that police had addressed a sniper problem in one part of the city, sniper activity would just break out in another part.[64]

During the riots, courts held marathon sessions to handle the large number of individuals arrested. If an offender was charged with breaking and entering and there was no proof of breaking, it was necessary to reduce the charge to a curfew violation unless the offender was carrying looted property.[65]

All defendants had legal advice available; no questions were raised as to whether the defendant could afford personal counsel. Sixty percent of cases were tried on stipulated facts and agreement between opposing attorneys to simplify and expedite trials by dispensing with the need to prove formally uncontested factual issues.[66, 67]

In some instances, there was confusion regarding the identity of defendants as they used false names. The defendants forgot the false name that they had given to the booking officer so when the name was called out hours later, no one would respond. And when inquiring relatives or friends of the defendants tried to locate them, their real names were not on the list of those arrested.[68]

Baltimore's nine municipal courts conducted 3,446 trials which resulted in 2,193 convictions. There were also 778 acquittals and 389 of the arrested were given probation before verdict.[69]

Only eight of the nine city courts kept track of what happened to the convicted. Of the 1,836 accounted for, 81 percent, or 1,487, received fines ranging from $5 to $300. The 349 remaining defendants were jailed for 10 days to one year. About 80 percent of the crimes were considered curfew violations; the remaining cases were for petty larceny, disorderly conduct, and assault.[70]

The heaviest penalty was the life-plus-10 year's sentence imposed on a man for firebombing the Gabriel's Spaghetti House which caused the death of a man inside. Two other persons were tried for the same arson-murder. A 22-year-old man was sentenced to 10 years for firebombing a furniture store on West Baltimore Street. (There were two other co-defendants still waiting for trial during that period)[71]

"Since the riot, the city of Baltimore, more than any other city in this country is beginning to make real progress in such areas as housing, recreation, employment and education," stated, Kalman Hettleman, administrative assistant to Mayor D'Alesandro. However, not everyone felt as positive. "Baltimore is a sick city. In fact it's worse. It's a dying city. And the riot speeded up the disease. The riot really sent the city to hell," stated Harry L. Goldberg, former spokesman for a small businessmen's organization.[72]

The riots created, in the public imagination, an urban wasteland of shattered storefronts and bombed-out buildings. Later, even the rioters stated that what they did really hurt the neighborhood, especially the "mom-and-pop" stores that supported the community. It would be over a month before Lombard Street would come back to life. As a result of the destroyed stores, Baltimore would lose $345,000 in tax revenue.[73]

The riots accomplished nothing and only increased the divide between races in a dying city. According to Louis L. Randall a doctor who lived in west Baltimore, the black businessmen and professionals, such as doctors and lawyers were making progress quietly—there was no need for disturbances. The riots put all progress for black businessmen and professionals on hold.[74]

IN JULY 1974, SIX YEARS AFTER THE RIOTS, shades of April 1968 would cast their ugly shadows again on the city's streets. However, this time the discontent would not be triggered by an assassination. City employees and police officers, in response to negotiations between the administration of Mayor William Donald Schaefer and the city's labor unions, engaged in a wildcat strike.

City workers had been negotiating for a 50-cent-per-hour pay raise. The city was only offering 20 cents. Although the membership of the labor union, the American Federation of State, County and Municipal Employees (AFSCME), had voted for the 20-cent-per-hour raise, many changed their minds after the vote and decided that a 20-cent raise was not enough. The average garbage worker's take-home pay was $85 a week. The workers were fed up with what they perceived to be meager salaries and announced a wildcat strike. On July 2, 1974, 1,500 workers walked off their jobs.[75]

When the garbage workers left their jobs, so did many of the other city union workers. Within a few days many more—including 300 jail guards—would walk off their jobs. Striking members included utility workers, highway workers, school groundskeepers, and zookeepers. On July 3, 1974, the union leadership had officially sanctioned the strike after a vote by 500 of its members.[76]

Within a couple of days, trash was piled high in the city's streets and alleys attracting flies and rodents in the 90°F heat. The smell of garbage permeated the city's humid air. The city transferred utility workers and highway crews to the sanitation department to drive the garbage trucks, but many refused. Fights began to break out at landfills as workers in garbage trucks tried to crash picket lines set up by the union. New employees hired were being harassed by striking members. Piles of trash and overloaded dumpsters were set on fire throughout Baltimore, keeping the city's fire engines busy throughout the nights. It would get worse.[77]

On the ninth day of what became known as the "garbage strike," a very large portion of police officers who, like the striking municipal members, were also members of AFSCME walked off their jobs. When it came down to union membership, the city's 3,300-strong police department was much fractionalized. The majority of the officers were members of the Fraternal Order of Police and about 1,000 were members of Local 1195, AFL-CIO (also part of AFSCME). The striking police officers, not satisfied with an approximately $1,200 yearly raise slated to go into effect on July 1, 1975, wanted more money.[78]

At 8 p.m. on Thursday, July 11, 457 police officers, many veterans of the 1968 riots, walked off the job. Patrol car radios were turned off and the vehicles were left in the streets. Calls for backup from non-striking police officers patrolling the city streets went unanswered until Central Police Communications was able to get the situation under control. The wildcat strike was in full swing.[79]

The country's first police officers' strike since Boston's police officers had gone on strike in 1918 was having a drastic effect on Baltimore's police protection. Within hours the Southwestern District police station was closed down. The Central District was severely undermanned. Only five police officers reported for the midnight to 8 a.m. shift in the South Eastern District. The Western District was almost completely closed down. When news of the strike reached city residents all hell broke loose.

Now, not only were there burning piles of trash in the streets and in the alleys, but also mobs starting to gather in some of the same places where the 1968 riots had occurred. It was reported that a mob of around 500 roamed near the intersection of Gay and Orleans streets. Firefighters battling the trash fires were now being pelted by rocks and bottles.

At the intersection of Lafayette and Gilmor streets a liquor store was broken into and looted. On Gay and Aisquith streets several liquor stores were looted. There was no police protection. On West Baltimore Street, four businesses were looted and structures were set on fire. More unruly crowds were forming and continued to throw rocks at firefighters. A furniture store in the 2100 block of East Monument Street and a warehouse in the 900 block went up in flames. Many vacant buildings in these areas were also set on fire.[80]

Windows were broken at Fedderman's Furniture store, located on Gay Street near Aisquith Street. On two occasions during the night, looters stormed in and stole furniture. Fedderman, a veteran of the 1968 riots whose store took a number of hits, rented a German shepherd to keep looters out. It worked and there were no more break-ins during the disturbance.[81]

Mayor Donald Schaefer and Police Commissioner Donald Pomerleau were furious. However, in anticipation of the strike, they had put a number of contingency plans into effect. Off-duty police officers not participating in the strike were called back to work.

One-hundred Maryland State Police officers were immediately assembled at their Pikesville, MD barracks. The state troopers were sent into the city in one large column of patrol cars which resembled a parade driving down Reisterstown Road. The Maryland National Guard was ordered to be prepared if necessary, but was not put on alert.

Since Chief Killen's retirement, veteran fire officer Thomas Burke was now the city's fire chief. After the Anne Arundel County and Baltimore County Fire Department engines had been brought into the city during the riots of 1968, demonstrating remarkable assistance, the Baltimore Fire Department would call for the counties' support increasingly in the years that followed. Chief Burke called for them again on the night of July 11. Anne Arundel sent six engines and Baltimore County sent two. The engines were distributed throughout the city mainly to cover stations that were vacated.

By midnight of July 11, police and fire communication lines were jammed with hundreds of emergency calls. Although the heavy volume of fire calls was taxing the fire department, Chief Thomas Burke was confident.

Based on lessons learned from the 1968 riots, Burke had quickly brought in additional off-duty personnel and increased the department's protection from the normal shift strength of 550 firefighters and 90 engines and ladder trucks to 800 firefighters and 115 engines and ladder trucks. Because of this buildup of city fire units along with assistance from surrounding counties, Chief Burke had the fire situation under control even as hundreds of fires broke out every night.

During the strike the fire department would respond to more than 1500 fires—a 150 percent increase over a normal six day period. The incidents consisted of mostly trash fires, dumpster fires and vacant building fires.[82] By Friday night, it was estimated that approximately 600 policemen were on strike. City crime surged up to 33 percent of what would typically occur in a 24-hour period before the start of the strike.

After the first night of the strike, the Maryland State Police were able to cut back on their assistance to the city's problem areas. Due to the quick response by off-duty city police officers in filling the vacated positions left by the strikers, the Maryland State Police officers only needed to send 55 officers per night to assist with law enforcement.

By the end of the strike 200 stores reportedly had been looted. At the 300 block of South Fulton Avenue a young white girl was injured while she was sitting on a doorstep. She was shot by a black man driving by and randomly firing a gun. There was only one death attributed to the disturbance caused by the strike.[83]

The city's saving grace was that the majority of the city police force did not strike. Many police officers were also members of the Fraternal Order of Police, an organization made up of sworn law enforcement officers in the United States that lobbies and provides legal support to police officers.[84] Members of this group believed they had a higher calling to the city's police protection.

The non-striking police officers strongly believed in the "No Strike Cause" in their contract. Although some of the police officers assigned to the south and west sides of the city participated in the strike, the majority of the police officers assigned to the Eastern District's station reported in and refused to participate. Many of these police officers were transferred to the problem areas of the city.

The police strike would end on July 16. The worst period of the strike lasted from 8 p.m. on July 11 to 4 a.m. July 12. During this critical time period, the number of major crimes committed in the city increased by 258 percent over the number committed during same time period the day before.[85]

According to Baltimore *Sun* reporter Doug Struek, "Officers participated in an illegal strike which bitterly divided officers between those who picketed and walked out and those who proclaimed loyalty and professional dedication sticking to their post."[86]

Police Commissioner Pomerleau would fire the union president of Police Local 1195, AFL-CIO for his role in calling an illegal strike. The president was a 17-year veteran of the police force. He was fired four days before his planned retirement.[87]

In addition, Pomerleau would fire 82 probationary police officers who took part in the strike and demote 18 other police officers. The striking municipal employees and police officers ended their strike on July 16. Although many lost as a result of the strike, the municipal employees did end up with a 19 percent raise. Firefighters and teachers were the only other members of the city's bargaining units as a whole who did not strike.[88]

THE ONLY OTHER MAJOR CITY disturbance following the riots would occur during a snow blizzard that started on a Sunday afternoon, George Washington's birthday, on February 18, 1979. The storm dumped 22 inches over the Baltimore area by the following morning. The city was paralyzed. "Movement around the city ground to a halt."[89]

Disorderly conduct broke out throughout the city again in many of the areas that were the scene of the 1968 riots eleven years earlier. Before Baltimore's police department could mobilize and get their officers in to quell the disorder and looting, mainly by four-wheel drive vehicles driven by Maryland National Guard (which was called in to assist), approximately 374 businesses and offices were broken into and looted. Approximately 827 were arrested during the disturbances that occurred from Monday, February 19 to Thursday, February 22, 1979.[90]

Most of the break-ins and looting occurred at mostly grocery and liquor stores in the Pennsylvania Avenue, North Avenue, and Gay Street areas of the city. Of the number arrested, 25 percent were junveniles.[91]

The most momentous incident during the four-day disorders occurred when Police Commissioner Pomerleau, wearing a heavy overcoat and cowboy hat, mounted a horse and "like the perfect sheriff to lead a small posse," led a small mounted police force into the deep snow-covered North Avenue corridor to put a stop to the violence.[92]

IT HAS BEEN 44 YEARS SINCE BALTIMORE'S April 1968 riots. There have been many changes in the city since—some for the better and some for the worse. Downtown Baltimore today is a thriving tourist attraction and convention city. Although the majority of the major industries and big department stores have either shut down or moved out, the department stores have been replaced with luxury hotels. Many industrial buildings have been torn down or renovated into offices or spacious apartments.

People travel from all over the world to the revitalized downtown harbor area and visit the Convention Center, National Aquarium, Science Center, and Harborplace. They also visit historic Fort McHenry, art, history, and industrial museums, and the city's many monuments. The uniquely designed Orioles' Camden Yards baseball stadium and the enormous Ravens' M&T Bank football stadium have been the sites of many momentous sporting events which bring thousands of sports fans into the city in the evenings and weekends. World-famed hospitals, universities, and colleges thrive in the city and provide employment for thousands.

Although thousands of African-American families have moved out of the city into the adjacent Baltimore County communities of Catonsville, Woodlawn, and Owings Mills; today African-Americans make up 63.7 percent of Baltimore's population of 620,960.[93]

Since 1968, the city has seen African-American mayors, fire chiefs, and police chiefs. The police department has very effectively dodged the budget axe over the years. In 1968, the police department had approximately 2,200 police officers; today there are approximately 4,000 strong, including civilians in administrative roles.[94]

Crime shot up after April 1968. In 1968 there were 239 murders.[95] Twenty-five years later, in 1993, the number of violent crime incidents reached and all-time high of 21,799 that included an unheard-of 353 murders.[96]

Baltimore became known as a "murder capital." Television shows such as "Homicide" and "The Wire" flourished and their episodes were based on the city's murders and violence. In 2010, the number of violent crime incidents was down to 9,316. In 2011 the city experienced 196 murders, less than in 1968.[97]

In contrast to the police department, the fire department has been chopped and chiseled by the budget axe. At 1,800 firefighters and officers, the number of personnel has not radically changed since 1968. However, many companies have been disbanded and stations closed. In 1968 there were 53 engine and 29 ladder companies operating out of 66 stations. Today there are only 40 engines/squads and 19 ladder trucks operating out of 36 stations.[98]

The city's blighted corridors along North Avenue, Pennsylvania Avenue, and Gay Street are much the same as they were in 1968. The only difference is that today there are very few business establishments, acres upon acres of vacant lots, and thousands of vacant row homes.

EACH YEAR ON THE ANNIVERSARY of the April 1968 riots, many newspaper writers opine on what little the riots accomplished and how the riots affected the city of Baltimore.

On April 10, 1983, *Sun* columnist Michael Olesker would write, "Fifteen years after the riots of 1968, the faces are different, but the picture was the same. A shabby poverty, and people going nowhere, and anger just beneath the surface because some things never change."[99] Five years later, *Sun* writer James Reston would state, "Violence, while it can destroy indifference, which is the curse of the moderate middle class, cannot choose...It destroys good as well as evil. Brute coercion and savage intolerance of the Negro must be destroyed, but they cannot be burned away by raging demons intoxicated with illusion...Twenty years later the pill box aesthetics is still evident on Gay, Whitelock Streets, on Pennsylvania Avenue and other hard hit areas of the riots"[100]

But there is still hope. Mark Miller of the *Evening Sun* would write in 1988, "Ultimately, though, slowly, brotherhood prevailed over racism and blatant criminality. Through torn asunder, Baltimore's social fabric began to mend, even before the last fire went out. Business people victimized by looting and arson supplied the needy residents—the innocent refugees—with food, clothing and medicine."[101]

Michael Olesker wrote, "In an odd way, [the riots] was the moment the two Baltimore's black and white began discovering each other across the great gaps that had been carved over generations. In the ashes of the riots, Baltimore struggled to find its common humanity.[102]

News American Columnist Louis Azrael put it the best. Azrael said in 1968:

"The fact remains that the Baltimore riots, bad as they were, left the city with less serious scars and with fewer dead or wounded than those of almost any other large city in the nation. This is a tribute to not only law enforcement, but also —and perhaps chiefly—to our white and the great bulk of our colored citizens."[103]

TODAY BALTIMORE IS A CALMER, more modern city than that of the late 1960s. Trendy, upscale waterfront developments, world-class sports stadiums, and a tourist-filled Inner Harbor area have changed the urban landscape. Whole areas that were devastated by the fires of that April have been replaced by modern housing or cleared and never rebuilt. On the surface, Baltimore has been transformed; prosperity has arrived. Innovative fire protection and law enforcement efforts developed in the years following the riots. Yet, in many of Baltimore's neighborhoods, residents face the stark reality of urban problems—poverty, sub-standard housing, joblessness, crimes, and drugs. Until these conditions change, Baltimore will never be fully immune to the violence that ravaged it in April 1968.

Appendix A

Baltimore City Fire Department - April 1968
Inventory of Apparatus and Stations

Rescue #1   1950 Mack 85 Rescue Squad (18 yrs old)
Floodlight #1
Station – Completed 12/21/1908, 1 bay, 2 story brick bldg.
323 N. Paca Street

Engine #2   1963 Mack 95D (5 yrs old)
Station – Completed 12/21/1920, 1 bay, 2 story brick bldg.
800 Light Street

Engine #3 1951 Ward La France U-34 (17 yrs old)
Ambulance #13
Air Cascade #1
Station – Completed 12/10/1951, 2 bays, 2 story brick bldg.
6714 Pulaski Highway

Engine #4   1953 Ward La France (15 yrs old)
Truck #29 1967 American La France tractor-drawn 100' aerial
Station – Completed 2/26/1954, 2 bays, 2 story brick bldg.
1201 E. Cold Spring Lane

Engine #5   1960 FWD (8 yrs old)
Truck #3   1956 Peter Pirsch tractor-drawn 100' aerial (12 yrs old)
Ambulance #10, HI X #1
Station – Completed 4/13/1964, 4 bays, 2 story brick building
2120 Eastern Avenue

Engine #6   1967 American La France D (1 yr old)
Station – Completed in 1853, 1 bay, 2 story brick building
416 N. Gay Street

Engine #7   1965 Mack 95 D (3 yrs old)
Station – Completed 1/7/1860, 1 bay 2 story brick fire station
700 N. Eutaw Street

Engine #8 1954 Peter Pirsch (14 yrs old)
Truck #10 1957 Peter Pirsch tractor-drawn 100' aerial (11 yrs old)
Ambulance #15
Station – Completed on 11/20/1967, 4 bay 1 story brick bldg.
1503 W. Lafayette Avenue

Engine #9 1942 Mack 80 (26 yrs old)
Truck #5 1961 American La France tractor-drawn 100' aerial (7 yrs old)
Station – Completed 11/27/1905, 2 bay, 2 story brick bldg.
1220 E. Oliver Street

Engine #10 1946 Seagrave (22 yrs old)
Truck #28 1964 Mack 85' (4 yrs old)
Station – Completed 2/26/1952, 2 bay 2 story brick building
1302 E. Chesapeake Avenue

Engine #11 1961 Ward La France (7 yrs old)
Truck #24 1965 Mack 19 tractor-drawn 100' aerial (3 yrs old)
Ambulance #2
Station – Completed on 4/9/1962, 4 bay, 1 story brick/cinder block bldg.
5714 Eastern Avenue

Engine #12 1946 Seagrave (22 yrs old)
Station – Completed on 1/1/1875, 1 bay, 2 story brick bldg.
399 E. Fort Avenue

Engine #13 1963 Ward La France (5 yrs old)
Truck #4 1963 Seagrave tractor-drawn 100' aerial (5 yrs old)
Ambulance #4
Station – Completed on 12/4/1963 4 bay, 1 story brick bldg.
405 McMechen Street

Engine #14 1966 American La France D (2 yrs old)
Station – Completed on 6/6/1888, 1 bay, 2 story brick bldg.
1908 Hollins Street

Engine #15 1948 Mack 85 (20 yrs old)
Engine #27 1947 Ward La France (21 yrs old)
Station – Completed on 11/29/1891, 2 bay, 2 story brick bldg.
308 W. Lombard Street

Engine #16 Fireboat P.W.Wilkinson, 85' 12,000 gpm
803 Lancaster Avenue

Engine #17 1946 Seagrave   (22 yrs old)
Truck #19   1967 Mack 19 85' aerial (1 yr old)
Ambulance #3
Station – Completed on 3/15/1895, 2 bay, 2 story brick bldg.
1426 Fort Avenue

Engine #18   1961 Ward La France (7 yrs old)
Station – Completed on 2/15/1893, 2 bay, 2 story brick bldg.
105 W. 21st Street

Engine #19   1944 Mack 80 (24 yrs old)
Station – Completed on 3/1/1895, 2 bay, 2 story brick bldg.
1601 North Avenue

Engine #20   1951 Ward La France (17 yrs old)
Truck #18   1962 Peter Pirsch tractor-drawn 100' aerial (6 yrs old)
Ambulance #8
Station – Completed on 12/21/1896, 2 bay, 2 story brick bldg.
3130 W. North Avenue

Engine #21   1944 Mack 80   (24 years old)
Truck #9   1964 American La France tractor-drawn 100' aerial (4 yrs old)
Ambulance #11
Station – Completed 12/15/1897, 2 bay, 2 story brick building
3724 Roland Avenue

Engine #22   1947 Ward La France (21 yrs old)
Truck #17   1966 American La France tractor-drawn 100' aerial (2 yrs
old), **Station** – 2 bay, 2 story brick building
1030 S. Linwood Avenue.

Engine #23   1949 Mack 85 (19 yrs old)
Ambulance #1
Station – Completed on 12/1/1903, 2 bay, 2 story brick bldg.
220 W. Saratoga Street

Engine #24   1944 Mack 80 (24 yrs old)
Station – Completed on 7/28/1904, 1 bay, 2 story brick bldg.
214 N. Patterson Park Avenue.

Engine #25   1947 Ward La France (19 yrs old)
Station – Completed on 1/5/1904, 1 bay, 2 story brick bldg.
2140 McCulloh Street

Engine #26 1960 FWD (8 yrs old)
Ambulance #5
Station – Completed 1/26/1906 1 bay 2 story brick bldg.
140 W. West Street

Engine #28 1954 Peter Pirch (14 yrs old)
Station – Completed 11/6/06, 1 bay 2 story brick bldg.
1312 Guilford Avenue

Engine #29   1953 Ward La France (15 yrs old)
Truck #22   1961 Seagrave tractor-drawn 100' aerial (7 yrs old)
Station – Completed 8/1/1907, 2 bay 2 story brick bldg.
4312 Park Heights Avenue

Engine #30   1947 Ward La France (21 yrs old)
Truck #8   1962 American La France tractor-drawn 100' aerial (6 yrs old)
Ambulance #12
Station – Completed 7/6/1907, 2 bay, 2 story brick bldg.
3220 Frederick Avenue

Engine #31   1965 Mack 95D (3 yrs old)
Truck #7   1964 American La France tractor-drawn 100' aerial (4 yrs old)
Station – 2 bay, 2 story brick bldg.
3123 Greenmount Avenue

Engine #32   1966 American La France D   (2 yrs old)
Truck #1   1962 Seagrave tractor-drawn 100' aerial (6 yrs old)
Ambulance #7
Mobile Hospital Unit
Station – Completed 6/20/1907, 2 bay, 2 story brick bldg.
14 S. Gay Street

Engine #33   1957 Peter Pirsch   (11 yrs old)
Station – 2 bay, 2 story brick bldg.
1749 Gorsuch Avenue

Engine #34   1963 Mack 95D (5 yrs old)
Station – Completed 7/8/1910, 1 bay 2 story brick bldg.
316 S. Caroline Street

Engine #35 1946 Seagrave (22 yrs old)
Truck #21 1967 American La France tractor-drawn 100' aerial (1 yr old)
Ambulance #9
Hi X 2
Station – Completed 10/9/1961, 4 bay one story brick/cinderblock bldg.
430 Maude Avenue

Engine #36 1957 Peter Pirsch (11 yrs old)
Station – Completed 11/5/1910, 1 bay 2 story brick bldg.
2249 Edmondson Avenue

Engine #37 1943 Mack 80 (25 yrs old)
Station – Completed 5/27/1910, 1 bay, 2 story brick bldg.
1202 Ridgely Street

Engine #38 1955 Ward La France (13 yrs old)
Station – Completed 12/10/1910, 1 bay 2 story brick bldg.
756 W. Baltimore Street

Engine #39 Fireboat Mayor J. Harold Grady, 85' 12,000 gpm
2609 Leahy Street, Fort McHenry

Engine #40 1967 American La France D (new)
Station – Completed on 5/29/1922, 1 bay, 2 story wood frame bldg.
5200 Liberty Heights Ave.

Engine #41 1947 Ward La France (22 yrs old)
Truck #20 1962 Seagrave tractor-drawn 100' aerial (6 yrs old)
Chemical #1
Station – 3 bay, 2 story brick building
520 Conkling Street

Engine #42 1955 Peter Pirsch (13 years old)
Truck #14 1954 Mack 85 service aerial 65' (14 yrs old)
Ambulance #6 **Station** – Completed 5/27/1963 4 bay one story brick/
      concrete bldg.
4522 Harford Road

Engine #43 1942 Mack 80 (26 years old)
Station – Completed prior to 1/1/1918 annex of Balt.Co.FD stations, 1
bay, 2 story brick bldg.
414 Lyman Avenue

Engine #44   1958 Peter Pirsch (10 yrs old)
Truck #25   1968 Peter Pirsch service aerial 85' (new)
Station – Completed prior to 1/1/1918 annex of Balt.Co.FD stations,
          2 bay, 2 story brick bldg.
2 Upland Road

Engine #45   1951 Ward La France (17 yrs old)
Truck #27   1952 Peter Pirsch service aerial 65' (16 yrs)
Ambulance #14
Station – Completed on 8/23/1951, 2 bay, 2 story brick bldg.
2700 Glenn Avenue

Engine #46 1950 Ward La France (18 yrs)
Station – Completed prior to 1/1/1918 annex of Balt.Co.FD stations,
          1 bay, 2 story brick bldg.
5116 Reisterstown Rd.

Engine #47 1963 Ward La France (5 yrs old)
Station – Competed 9/6/1923, 1 bay, 2 story brick bldg.
2608 Washington Blvd.

Engine #48 Fireboat August Emrich, 85' 12,000 gpm,
Station – Completed 7/12/1965, 1 story station built on Colgate Creek
2700 Broening Highway

Engine #49 Fireboat Thomas D'Alesandro, 103' 12,000 gpm
Station – City pier, Wagner's Point
Asiatic Avenue

Engine #50   1948 Ward La France (20 yrs old)
Station – Completed 5/15/1922, 1 bay, 2 story brick bldg.
4700 Holabird Avnue

Engine #51   1958   Peter Pirsch (10 yrs old)
Station – Completed 7/1/1922, 1 bay, 2 story brick bldg.
646 Highland Avenue

Engine #52   1948 Mack 85 (20 yrs old)
Station – Completed 3/22/1922, 1 bay, 2 story brick bldg.
3525 Woodbrook Avenue

Engine 53   1961 Mack 85 (15 yrs)
Station – Completed 7/1/1922, 1 bay, 2 story brick bldg.
608 Swann Avenue

Engine #54 1954 Peter Pirsch (14 yrs old)
Truck #30 1961 Mack 19 service aerial 85' (7 yrs old)
Station – Completed 11/3/1956 2bay 1 story brick/cinder block bldg.
5821 Belair Road.

Engine #55 1948 Mack 85 (20 yrs old)
Truck #23 1965 Seagrave tractor-drawn 100' aerial (3 yrs old)
Station – Completed 11/15/1923, 2 bay, 2 story brick bldg.
1229 Bush Street

Engine #56 1945 Mack 85 (23 yrs old)
Station – 1 bay, 2 story brick bldg.
6512 Harford Road

Engine #57 1948 Mack 85 (20 yrs old)
Chemical #2
Station – Completed on 8/31/1923, 1 bay, 2 story brick bldg.
4427 Pennington Avenue

Engine #58 1948 Mack 85 (20 yrs old)
Station – Completed 11/15/1923, 1 bay, 2 story brick bldg.
2425 Annapolis Road

Engine #59
Floodlight 2
Station – annexed to the Engine #32, Truck #1 complex
6 S. Gay Street

Truck #2 1962 Seagrave tractor-drawn aerial 100' (6 yrs old)
Station – Completed 1/20/1910, 1 bay 2 story bldg.
Water Tower #1 1961 International Harvester 85 Hi-Ranger Snorkel
        (7 yrs old)
106 N. Paca Street

Truck #6 1954 American La France tractor-drawn 100' (14 yrs old)
Station – Completed on 4/6/1888, 1 bay, 2 story brick bldg.
1227 S. Hanover Street

Truck #11 1957 Pirsch tractor-drawn aerial 100' (11 yrs old)
Ambulance #16
Station – 2 bays, 2 story brick bldg.
401 West North Avenue

Truck #12 1966 American La France tractor-drawn aerial 100' (2 yrs old)
Station – Completed 9/17/1907, 1 bay 2 story brick bldg.
3901 Liberty Heights Avenue

Truck #13 1959 Peter Pirsch tractor-drawn aerial 100' (9 yrs old)
Station – Completed 12/7/1907 1 bay 2 story brick building
43 S. Carey Street

Truck #15 1965 Seagrave tractor-drawn aerial 100' (3 yrs old)
Station – Completed 5/12/1908, 1 bay 2 story brick bldg.
1223 N. Montford Avenue

Truck #16 1964 Seagrave tractor-drawn aerial 100' (4 yrs old)
Station – Completed 2/2/1910, 1 bay 2 story brick building
831 N. Calvert Street

Truck #26 1964 Mack service aerial 85' (4 yrs old)
Station – 1 bay, 2 story brick building
4315 Mannasota Avenue

Appendix B

Fire Alarm Run Card

RIGHT - The Run Card listed all of the Engine, Truck Companies and
Special apparatus, starting with the closest station to the alarm box. This
card is for Box 6448 - Wilgrey and Annor Courts. All apparatus is listed
by mileage.

More information can be found on page 33.

(Photo courtesy of Michael Defina's Collection)

6448

WILGREY and ANNOR Courts

2300 S.
24.00 W.

Engines		Trucks	BC	DC	Special Units
58	47 55	23 13	6	1	R-1 AIR-1 MHU WT-1 SAT. ENG.
37	26 14	8	10		
38	30 15	6	5		
23	2 35	2	4		
12	36 8	21			
7	32 17	10			

Reference

E	13 25 6 34 10 20 53 1 52 28 5 57 18 24 9 22 19 41 29 51 33 31 21 11	E
E	50 40 46 44 27 3 42 4 43 45 54 56	FB.
T	1 19 4 16 28 18 11 3 5 17 15 20 22 12 7 9 24 25 26 14 29 27 30	T
BC	2 7 3 1 11 9 8	BC

SEP 17 1974

References

Chapter 1: The Great Migration

1. Chapelle, Suzanne Ellery Greene. 2000. Baltimore — An Illustrated History, American History Press. Sun Valley, CA
2. Utilization of the National Guard In Coping with Civil Disturbances, Langsdale Library, Special Collections Dept, 1420 Maryland Ave., Baltimore, MD 21201-5779 http://archives.ubalt.edu
3. Baltimore. 2009. Wikipedia, the Free Encyclopedia. http://wn.wikipedia.org/wki/Baltimore_city 2009
4. Chapelle, Suzanne Ellery Greene. 2000. Baltimore — An Illustrated History, American History Press. Sun Valley, CA
5. Ibid
6. Frederick Douglas (1818 - 1895). 2010. Wikipedia, the Free Encyclopedia. http://en.Wilkipedia.org/wiki/Frederick_Douglass
7. 4/20/61. Transit of Massachusetts Volunteers and Other Troops. *Baltimore Sun.* p.1
8. Ibid
9. Toomey, Daniel Carroll. 1988. The Civil War in Maryland. Toomey Press. Baltimore, MD.   pp.11-13.
10. Ibid
11. Ibid pp.62-63
12. Ibid
13. Emancipation Proclamation. 2010. Wikipedia, the Free Encyclopedia. http://en.wikipedia.org/wiki/Emancipation_Proclamation
14. African-American Mosaic — A Library of Congress Resource Guide for the story of black history and culture.
15. Ibid
16. Ibid
17. Great Migration (African-American). 2010. Wikipedia, the Free Encyclopedia. http://en.wilkipedia.org/wiki/chicken_bone_express
18. Ibid
19. Ibid
20. Afro-American newspaper. 2011. Wikipedia, the Free Encyclopedia. http://en.wikipedia.org/wiki/Afro-American_newspaper
21. Baltimore '68: Riots and Rebirth. 4/08. University of Baltimore. Baltimore, MD. (Notes from seminar and website timeline)
22. Williams, Juan. 1/7/1990. Marshalls Law. Washington Post. Washington D.C.
23. Great Migration (African-American) Wikipedia, the Free Encyclopedia http://en.wilkipedia.org/wiki/chicken_bone_express

24. Haywood, Mary Ellen and Belfoure, Charles, 1999. The Baltimore Rowhouse. Princeton Architectural Press, NY. p.125
25. Redlining — http://www.encyclopedia.chicagohistory.org/pages/1050.html
26. Great Migration (African-American) Wikipedia, the Free Encyclopedia http://en.wilkipedia.org/wiki/chicken_bone_express
27. Levy, Peter. The Dream Deferred: The Assassination of Martin Luther King Jr. and the Holy Week Uprisings of 1968.
28. Haywood, Mary Ellen and Belfoure, Charles. 1999. The Baltimore Rowhouse. Princeton Architectural Press, NY. p.165
29. Frey, William H. Central City White Flight: Racial and Nonracial Causes. American Sociological Review, Vol. 44, No. 3 (Jun., 1979), pp.425-448
30. Ghettos. 2009. Wikipedia, the Free Encyclopedia http://wn.wikipedia.org/wki/
31. Keating, Dennis. 1994. The Suburban Racial Dilemma: Housing and Neighborhoods . Temple University Press.
32. Haywood, Mary Ellen and Belfoure, Charles, 1999 The Baltimore Rowhouse. Princeton Architectural Press, NY. p.171
33. Olesker, Michael. 2001. Journeys to The Heart of Baltimore. Johns Hopkins University Press. Baltimore, London. p.117
34. "Racial" Provisions of FHA Underwriting Manual 1938
35. Elizabeth Eisenhauer, GeoJournal Volume 53, Number 2 / February, 2001
36. Olesker, Michael. 2001. Journeys to The Heart of Baltimore. Johns Hopkins University Press. Baltimore, London. p.118
37. Lupo, Alan. 6/24/66. Redistricting issue appears as key solving many racial problems. Evening Sun, Baltimore, MD. p. A-8
38. Haywood, Mary Ellen and Belfoure, Charles. 1999. The Baltimore Rowhouse. Princeton Architectural Press, NY. p.173
39. Gwynn Oak Amusement Park. 2010. Wikipedia, the Free Encyclopedia http://en.wilkipedia.org/wki/Gwynn_Oak_Amusement_Park
40. Gwynn Oak Park — Baltimore Civil Rights — Pat Fish. 2005. http://blogcritics.org/archives/2005/06/18/121501.php
41. African-American Mosaic — A Library of Congress Resource Guide for the story of black history and culture.
42. Brown vs. Board of Education. 2010. Wikipedia, The Free Encyclopedia http://en.wilkipedia.org/wki/Brown_v_Board_of_education
43. Ibid
44. Olesker, Michael. 2001. Journeys to The Heart of Baltimore. Johns Hopkins University Press. Baltimore, London. p.118

45. 2nd Great Migration (African-American) Wikipedia, the Free Encyclopedia http://en.wikipedia.org/wki/second_Great_ Migration_%28African_America%29
46. Ibid
47. "Martin Luther King". The Nobel Foundation. 1964. http://nobelprize. org/nobel_prizes/peace/laureates/1964/king-bio.html. Retrieved 2007-04-20
48. Parks, Michael. 4/7/69. A year later City Officials, Community Leaders Appraise the Impact of the Rioting. *Baltimore Sun*. Baltimore, MD

Chapter 2: Long Hot Summers

1. Molotov Cocktail. 2009. Wikipedia, the Free Encyclopedia http://en.wilkipedia.org/wiki/molotovcocktail.
2. - 4. Ibid
5. Report of the National Advisory Commission on Civil Disorders, New York, E.P., Dutton and Company Inc. NY. April 1968. p.35
6. Ibid pp.203-204
7. Ibid p.201
8. Ibid p.36, p.202
9. Ibid p.205
10. Ibid p.38
11. - 13 Ibid p.39
14. Ibid p.40
15. Ibid p.40
16. 7/12/63. March on Gwynn Oak Park. Time Magazine. New York, NY
17. - 19. Ibid
20. Hiltner, George J. 8/5/66. Court Asked to Lift Ban on Racist. The Sun. Baltimore, Maryland. p.C26.
21. Report of the National Advisory Commission on Civil Disorders, New York, E.P., Dutton and Company. NY. April 1968. p.38
22. Ibid
23. Rap Brown. 2009. Wikipedia, the Free Encyclopedia http://en.wikipedia.org/wiki/H._Rap_Brown
24. Ibid
25. Report of the National Advisory Commission on Civil Disorders, New York, E.P.
    Dutton and Company Inc., April 1968. p.52
26. Ibid
27. Ibid
28. Ibid p.205
29. Ibid pp.55-56
30. Ibid pp.59, 62, 68-69

31. Ibid p.78
32. Ibid p.71
33. Parks, Brad. 4/08. How the good will in a city gave way to good byes. The Star Ledger — A Special Reprint. Newark, NJ
34. Sauter, Van Gordon and Hines, Burleigh. 1968, Nightmare in Detroit, Henry Regency Company, Chicago, IL .
35. Ibid
36. Ibid
37. Detroit — The Twelfth Street Riot. 2009. Wikipedia, the Free Encyclopedia http://en.wikipedia.org/wiki/12th_Street_riot)
38. Report of the National Advisory Commission on Civil Disorders, New York, E.P. Dutton and Company Inc., April 1968. p.93
39. Cambridge - Governor Tawes sent in the National Guard. 2009. Wikipedia, the Free Encyclopedia http://en.wikipedia.org/wiki/ cambridge riot_1963
40. - 43. Ibid
44. Cohen, Art, 4/08, April 1968, Passager, University of Baltimore, Baltimore, Maryland. pp.21
45. Lyden, Jackie. Maryland Town Recalls Racial Unrest in 1967. http://www.npr.org/templates/story/story-php?storyId=12420016 NPR 4/9/08
46. Levy, Peter. Civil War on Race Street
47. Kerner Commission. 2009. Wikipedia, the Free Encyclopedia http://en.wikipedia.org/wki/kerner_commission
48. Cambridge - Governor Tawes sent in the National Guard. 2009. Wikipedia, the Free Encyclopedia http://en.wikipedia.org/wiki/cambridge riot_1963
49. Ibid
50. Levy, Peter. Civil War on Race Street
51. Kane, Gregory. 3/5/08. 40 Years after the Kerner Commission, a question remains. The Sun. Baltimore, MD
52. Maryland Civil Rights. 2009. http://mdcivilrights.org/timeline.htlm
53. Kerner Commission. 2009. Wikipedia, the Free Encyclopedia http://en.wikipedia.org/wki/kerner_commission
54. Report of the National Advisory Commission on Civil Disorders, New York, E.P. Dutton and Company Inc. NY. April 1968
55. Ibid
56. Ibid
57. Ibid pp.110-111
58. Ibid pp.128-203
59. Ibid p.325

60. Jim Crow Laws. 2010. Wikipedia, the Free Encyclopedia
http://en.wikipedia.org/wiki/Jim_Crow_laws
61. 10/4/66. Backlash Victim — Editorial. The Sun. Baltimore, MD.
p.A16
62. Lawrence Shehan. 2012. Wikipedia, the Free Encyclopedia
http://en.wikipedia.org/wiki/Lawrence_Shehan
63. Flamm, Michael William. 1998. "Law and Order": Street Crime,
Civil Disorder, and the Crisis of Liberalism. Ph.D. diss., Columbia
University.

Chapter 3: A Ticking Time Bomb

1. George, Deborah., Executive Producer. 3/31/08 - 4/2/08. The fire next
time. A special WYPR Radio series. Producers Sunni Khalid, Mary
Rose Madden and Fraser Smith, Baltimore, MD
2. White, Jack. 1968. Time Magazine Article
3. Report of the National Advisory Commission on Civil Disorders, New
York, E.P. Dutton and Company Inc. NY. April 1968
4. George, Deborah., Executive Producer. 3/31/08 - 4/2/08. The fire next
time. A special WYPR Radio series. Producers Sunni Khalid, Mary
Rose Madden and Fraser Smith, Baltimore, MD
5. Maryland Civil Rights. 2009. http://mdcivilrights.org/timeline.htlm
6. Haywood, Mary Ellen and Belfoure, Charles, 1999 The Baltimore
Rowhouse. Princeton Architectural Press, NY. p.171
7. Kerner Commission. 2009. Wikipedia, the Free Encyclopedia
http://en.wikipedia.org/wki/kerner_commission
8. George, Deborah., Executive Producer. 3/31/08 - 4/2/08. The fire next
time. A special WYPR Radio series. Producers Sunni Khalid, Mary
Rose Madden and Fraser Smith, Baltimore, MD
9. Melton, Tracy Matthew. 2005. Hanging Henry Gambrill — The
Violent Career of Baltimore's Plug Uglies, 1854-1860. The Press at
the Maryland Historical Society. Baltimore, MD. p.17
10. Williams, Juan. 1/7/90. Marshall's Law. Washington Post Magazine
Article. Washington, D.C.
http://www.thurgoodmarshall.com/speeches/tmlaw_article.htm
11. Murray, William A. 1969. The Unheralded Heroes. E. John Schmitz &
Sons, Inc. Baltimore, MD. pp. 2 - 5.
12. Lyons, Paul Robert. 1976. Fire in America. National Fire Protection
Association (NFPA). Boston, MA. p.27
13. Melton, Tracy Matthew. 2005. Hanging Henry Gambrill — The
Violent Career of Baltimore's Plug Uglies, 1854-1860. The Press at
the Maryland Historical Society. Baltimore, MD. p.167
14. Ibid
15. Murray, William A. 1969. The Unheralded Heroes. E. John Schmitz &
Sons, Inc. Baltimore, MD. pp. 2 - 5.

16. Melton, Tracy Matthew. 2005. Hanging Henry Gambrill — The Violent Career of Baltimore's Plug Uglies, 1854-1860. The Press at the Maryland Historical Society. Baltimore, MD. p.16
17. Murray, William A. 1969. The Unheralded Heroes. E. John Schmitz & Sons, Inc. Baltimore, MD. pp. 2 - 5.
18. Lyons, Paul Robert. 1976.. Fire in America. National Fire Protection Association (NFPA). Boston, MA. p.25
19. Melton, Tracy Matthew. 2005. Hanging Henry Gambrill — The Violent Career of Baltimore's Plug Uglies, 1854-1860. The Press at the Maryland Historical Society. Baltimore, MD. p.172
20. Ibid p.17
21. Ibid p.22
22. Murray, William A. 1969. The Unheralded Heroes. E. John Schmitz & Sons, Inc. Baltimore, MD. pp. 2 - 5.
23. Ibid
24. Ibid pp.7-9
25. 2010. Fire Museum of Maryland. Lutherville, MD
26. Murray, William A. 1969. The Unheralded Heroes. E. John Schmitz & Sons, Inc. Baltimore, MD. Page 8.
27. Ibid p.11
28. Ross, Joseph B. 2008. Arundel Burning. Chesapeake Publishing Company, Baltimore, MD. p.3
29. Welden, George R. 2004. No Reason to Burn-The story of the Great Baltimore Fire. Fire Museum of Maryland. Lutherville, MD. p.56
30. Murray, William A. 1969. The Unheralded Heroes. E. John Schmitz & Sons, Inc. Baltimore, MD. p.46
31. Fredrick, Gary. 7/09. Baltimore City Fire Department. Firehouse. Melville, NY pp.140 -142
32. Ibid
33. Murray, William A. 1969. The Unheralded Heroes. E. John Schmitz & Sons, Inc. Baltimore, MD. p.79
34. Mueller, Robert. 1/10. Interview
35. Murray, William A. 1969. The Unheralded Heroes. E. John Schmitz & Sons, Inc. Baltimore, MD. p.154
36. Ibid
37. Williams, Jr., Herman. 2002. Firefighter. Mountain Press., Carlsbad, CA. pp.78-79.
38. Ibid
39. D'Alesandro III, Tommy. 3/9/11. Interview
40. Williams, Jr., Herman. 2002. Firefighter. Mountain Press., Carlsbad, California. pp.78-79
41. Ibid
42. Ibid p.86

43. Ibid p.91
44. Alfinito, Jerry. 1/10. Interview
45. Ibid p.95
46. Ibid p.98
47. Ibid p.109
48. Ibid p.108
49. Ibid p.127
50. Marcus, Lloyd. 11/09. Interview
51 - 57. Ibid
58. 2/7/60. Firefighter is overcome during blaze. The Sun. Baltimore, MD. pp.24
59. Marcus, Lloyd. 11/09. Interview
60. Ibid
61. Murray, William A. 1969. The Unheralded Heroes. E. John Schmitz & Sons, Inc. Baltimore, MD. p.179.
62. Ibid
63. Marcus, Lloyd. 11/09. Interview
64. Williams, Jr., Herman. 2002. Firefighter. Mountain Press. Carlsbad, CA. pp.128 - 130
65. Murray, William A. 1969. The Unheralded Heroes. E. John Schmitz & Sons, Inc. Baltimore, MD. p.166
66. Alfinito, Jerry. 1/10. Interview
67. NFPA Handbook. 1969. 13th Edition. National Fire Protection Association Quincy, MA. p.10-45
68. Murray, William A. 1969. The Unheralded Heroes. E. John Schmitz & Sons, Inc. Baltimore, MD. p.166
69. Ibid

Chapter 4: Law Enforcement

1. History of the Baltimore City Police Department. 2010. Wikipedia, the Free Encyclopedia
   http://en.wilkipedia.org/wiki/Baltimore_city_police_department
2. - 5. Ibid
6. Olesker, Michael. 4/10/83. The Riots were 15 years ago and nothing has changed., The Sun, Baltimore, MD
7. History of the Baltimore City Police Department. 2010. Wikipedia, the Free Encyclopedia
   http://en.wilkipedia.org/wiki/Baltimore_city_police_department
8. Miller, Floyd. 1968. How Baltimore Fends Off Riots. Readers Digest, 3/68. p.109. Condensed from the Baltimore Sunday Sun, 2/11/68. Baltimore, MD
9. Olesker, Michael. 4/10/83. The Riots were 15 years ago and nothing has changed., The Sun, Baltimore, MD

10. Miller, Floyd. 1968. How Baltimore Fends Off Riots. Readers Digest, 3/68. p.109 Condensed from the Baltimore Sunday Sun, 2/11/68. Baltimore, MD.
11. Ibid
12. 9/3/66. Tawes Ends Police Post Interviews. The Sun. Baltimore, MD. p.B20
13. Ibid
14. History of the Baltimore City Police Department. 2010. Wikipedia, the Free Encyclopedia http://en.wilkipedia.org/wiki/Baltimore_city_police_department
15. Donald D. Pomerleau, Baltimore Police Commissioner (1966-1981) 6/29/09. Wikipedia, the Free Encyclopedia http://en.wilkipedia.org/wki/Donald_Pomerleau
16. Ibid
17. 7/26/66. Police Commissioner Interviews Start. Evening Sun. Baltimore, MD. p.B28
18. 7/11/66. CORE Demonstration Protest Wage Scales. Evening Sun, Baltimore, MD. p. B24
19. Ibid
20. Maryland Civil Rights. 2009. http://mdcivilrights.org/timeline.htlm
21. Lupo, Alan. 6/24/66. Redistricting issue appears as key solving many racial problems. Evening Sun. Baltimore, MD. p.A8
22. 9/3/66. Tawes Ends Police Post Interviews. The Sun. Baltimore, MD. p. B20
23. Donald D. Pomerleau, Baltimore Police Commissioner (1966-1981) 6/29/09. Wikipedia, the Free Encyclopedia http://en.wilkipedia.org/wki/Donald_Pomerleau
24. Miller, Floyd. 1968. How Baltimore Fends Off Riots. Readers Digest. 3/68. p.109 Condensed from the Baltimore Sunday Sun, 2/11/68. Baltimore, MD
25. Ibid p.110
26. Donald D. Pomerleau, Baltimore Police Commissioner (1966-1981) 6/29/09. Wikipedia, the Free Encyclopedia http://en.wilkipedia.org/wki/Donald_Pomerleau
27. Ibid
28. 3/2/68. Pomerleau Agrees with Riot Report. The Sun. Baltimore, MD. p.B20
29. 6/24/66. Gelston Appoints Harris Police Community Aide. Evening Sun. Baltimore, MD. p. B-30
30. Miller, Floyd. 1968. How Baltimore Fends Off Riots. Readers Digest. 3/68. p.109. Condensed from the Baltimore Sunday Sun. 2/11/68. Baltimore, MD
31. Ibid
32. Ibid

33. Cooke, Joseph. 1/10. Interview
34. Ibid
35. Miller, Floyd. 1968. How Baltimore Fends Off Riots. Readers Digest, 3/68. p.109 Condensed from the Baltimore Sunday Sun. 2/11/68. Baltimore, MD
36. Peterson, William, E., Dr., Zumbrum, Alvin, T. A Report of the Baltimore Civil Disturbance of April 1968. The Maryland Crime Investigating Commission. Baltimore, MD
37. 2/17/68. Get Tough Police — Editorial. Afro-American. Baltimore, MD. p.4
38. Ibid
39. Ibid
40. 3/2/68. Pomerleau Agrees with Riot Report. The Sun. Baltimore, MD. p.B20
41. - 44. Ibid
45. History of the Maryland Army National Guard. 2010. Wikipedia, the Free Encyclopedia
    http: llen.wikipedia.org/wiki/Maryland_Army_National_Guard
46. - 51. Ibid
52. Utilization of the National Guard In Coping with Civil Disturbances, Langsdale Library, Special Collections Dept, 1420 Maryland Ave., Baltimore, MD.. 21201-5779 http://archives.ubalt.edu
53. Ibid
54. Ibid
55. 8/8/67. Riot Control Gas Ok'd by Gelston. News American. Baltimore, Maryland. p.2C
56. Ibid
57. Ibid
58. Brugger, Robert J. 1988. Maryland, A Middle Temperament 1634 - 1980. Johns Hopkins University Press. Baltimore, MD. p.619
59. 7/8/66. Eight Alarm Fire at Maryland Penitentiary-blaze Destroys Print/tag Shop. Evening Sun. Baltimore, MD. p.B28
60. Ibid
61. Murray, William A. 1969. The Unheralded Heroes. E. John Schmitz & Sons Inc. Baltimore, Maryland. p.180
62. 7/8/66. Eight Alarm Fire at Maryland Penitentiary-blaze Destroys Print/tag Shop. Evening Sun. Baltimore, MD. p.B28
63. A Civil Rights Hoax Gone Bad — Baltimore, http://soulofamerica.com/baltimore-civil-rights-hoax.phtml.
64. Frames, Robin. 7/22/67. Rioting here is doubted by church civil rights leader. Evening Sun. Baltimore, MD. p.4
65. 4/8/68. End of a Myth-Editorial. Evening Sun. Baltimore, MD. p.A16

66. Streets of Fire: Governor Spiro Agnew and the Baltimore Riots, April 1968. Maryland State Archives, Annapolis, Maryland http:teachingamericanhistorymd.net

67. Brugger, Robert J. 1988. Maryland, A Middle Temperament. 1634 - 1980. Johns Hopkins University Press. Baltimore, MD. p.619

68. Streets of Fire: Governor Spiro Agnew and the Baltimore Riots, April 1968. Maryland State Archives, Annapolis, Maryland http:teachingamericanhistorymd.net

69. Brugger, Robert J. 1988. Maryland, A Middle Temperament. 1634 - 1980. Johns Hopkins University Press. Baltimore, MD. p.619

70. Witcover, Jules. 1972. White Night. Random House, NY. p.10

71. Ibid p.4

72. Ibid

73. 9/20/68. The Counter Puncher. Time Magazine. New York, NY

74. Brugger, Robert J. 1988. Maryland, A Middle Temperament. 1634 - 1980. Johns Hopkins University Press. Baltimore, MD. p.626

75. Streets of Fire: Governor Spiro Agnew and the Baltimore Riots, April 1968. Maryland State Archives, Annapolis, Maryland http:teachingamericanhistorymd.net

76. 9/20/68. The Counter Puncher. Time Magazine. New York, NY

77. Streets of Fire: Governor Spiro Agnew and the Baltimore Riots, April 1968. Maryland State Archives, Annapolis, Maryland http:teachingamericanhistorymd.net

Chapter 5   An Untimely Death

1. 4/4/68. Khe Sanh Relief — Just One Mile Away. News American. Baltimore, MD. p.1A

2. 4/3/68. Assaults In The Streets. News American. Baltimore, MD. p.2B

3. 4/5/68. Off Duty Policeman Rescues 5 In Fire. News American. Baltimore, MD. p.2B.

4. - 6. Ibid

7. 4/5/68. Police Action Taken After "Study-In" at State House. The Sun. Baltimore, MD. p.C28.

8. - 12. Ibid

13. Assassination of Martin Luther King — Lorraine Motel, Memphis, TN. 2010. Wikipedia, the Free Encyclopedia http://en.wikipedia.org/wiki/Martin_Luther_King,_Jr.#Assassination_and_its_aftermath

14. George, Deborah., Executive Producer. 3/31/08 - 4/2/08. The fire next time. A special WYPR Radio series. Producers Sunni Khalid, Mary Rose Madden and Fraser Smith, Baltimore, MD

15. Ibid

16. 1/7/67. Maryland Society — The Baltimore Assembly. The Sun. Baltimore, MD. p.A6

17. D'Alesandro III, Tommy. 3/9/11. Interview
18. Baltimore City History of Mayors, Thomas J. D'Alesandro III, Mayor of Baltimore 1967-1971, http://mdarchives.us/megafile/msa/speccol)
19. D'Alesandro III, Tommy. 3/9/11.
20. Murray, William A., 1969. The Unheralded Heroes. E. John Schmitz & Sons, Inc. Baltimore, MD. p.92
21. Breihan, John R. 4/4/08. Why No Rioting in Cherry Hill? (notes from conference presentation) Baltimore '68: Riots and Rebirth. University of Baltimore. Baltimore, MD.
22. Helfrich, Lester. 1/10. Interview
23. Ibid
24. Ibid
25. Peterson, John J. 1973. Into the Cauldron. Clavier House. Clinton, MD. p.35
26. Baltimore News American — 4/6/68
27. 4/5/68. Mayor Urges Calm — City Joins in Mourning. News American. Baltimore, MD
28. 3/2/68. Pomerleau Agrees with Riot Report. The Sun. Baltimore, MD. p.B20
29. History of the Baltimore City Police Department. 2010. Wikipedia, the Free Encyclopedia
http://en.wilkipedia.org/wiki/Baltimore_city_police_department
30. Ibid
31. D'Alesandro III, Tommy. 3/9/11. Interview
32. Ibid
33. 12/5/67. D'Alesandro to Name Russell as Solicitor. The Sun. Baltimore, MD. p.C24
34. 12/12/67. Mayor Chooses Lacy as President of Fire Board. The Sun. Baltimore, MD. p.C24
35. Ibid
36. Reverend Marion Bascom.
http://www.thehistorymakers.com/biography
37. Brugger, Robert J. 1988. Maryland, A Middle Temperament. 1634 - 1980. Johns Hopkins University Press. Baltimore, MD. p.626
38. D'Alesandro III, Tommy. 3/9/11. Interview
39. Ibid
40. Lupo, Alan. 7/13/66. Tommy III seeks his own identity. Evening Sun, Baltimore, MD. C-1.
41. Murray, William A. 1969. The Unheralded Heroes. E. John Schmitz & Sons, Inc. Baltimore, MD. p.158.
42. Chapelle, Suzanne Ellery Greene. 2000. Baltimore — an Illustrated History, American History Press. Sun Valley, CA. p.87
43. Ibid

44. Weldon, George. 2004. No Reason to Burn — The Story of the Great Baltimore Fire. Fire Museum of Maryland. Lutherville, MD. p.24
45. Ibid. p.50
46. Chapelle, Suzanne Ellery Greene. 2000. Baltimore — An Illustrated History, American History Press. Sun Valley, CA. p.160
47. D'Alesandro III, Tommy. 3/9/11. Interview
48. Ibid
49. Lukas, Anthony. 4/24/62. Grady-Tawes Link Seen as Judge Deal. The Sun. Baltimore, MD. p.36
50. Flowers, Charles. 11/13/62. Council Fight is Shaping Up. The Sun. Baltimore, MD. p.10
51. Lupo, Alan. 7/13/66. Tommy 3d Seeks His Own Identity. Evening Sun, Baltimore, MD. p.C1.
52. Whiteford, Charles. 6/25/67. Official Mayoral Candidacy Announcing D'Alesandro. The Sun. Baltimore, MD. p.24
53. Woodruff, John E. 6/3/67. Police Fire Pension Shift is Proposed. The Sun. Baltimore, MD. p.B20.
54. D'Alesandro III, Tommy. 3/9/11. Interview
55. 1/17/67. Police Union Need Denied. The Sun. Baltimore, MD. p.C7
56. 3/19/66. Fire Stations Request Hit — D'Alesandro Says Other Plans Merit Priority. The Sun. Baltimore, MD. p.A7
57. 5/14/67. $10 Million in Budget Cut Sought. The Sun. Baltimore, MD. p.F20.
58. Lupo, Alan. 7/13/66.Tommy 3d Seeks His Own Identity. Evening Sun. Baltimore, MD. p.C-1
59. D'Alesandro III, Tommy. 3/9/11. Interview
60. Report of the National Advisory Commission on Civil Disorders, New York, E.P. Dutton and Company Inc., NY. April 1968
61. Ibid
62. Runkel, David. 3/1/68. City Developing Program to Soothe Racial Woe. Evening Sun. Baltimore, MD. p.C16
63. Ibid
64. Ibid
65. Lupo, Alan. 7/13/66. Tommy 3d Seeks His Own Identity. Evening Sun. Baltimore, MD. p.C-1
66. 12/5/67. Mayors - A Befogged History. The Sun. Baltimore, Maryland. p.A16
67. 4/5/68. Mayor Urges Calm — City Joins in Mourning. News American. Baltimore, MD.
68. Shanks, Doug. 12/23/08. Interview
69. Ibid
70. 12/6/67. False Alarm Total Soars. The Sun. Baltimore, MD. p.C7

71. Gilbert, Ben W. 1968. Ten Blocks From The White House — Anatomy of the Washington Riots of 1968. Fredrick A. Praeger Publishers. New York, NY. p.16

72. - 74. Ibid

75. Ibid p.24

76. Ibid p.26

77. Ibid p.27

78. Risen, Clay. The Unmaking of the President. Smithsonian Magazine. New York, NY

79. 4/6/68. News American. Baltimore, MD. p.A1

80. Gilbert, Ben W. 1968. Ten Blocks From the White House — Anatomy of the Washington Riots of 1968. Fredrick A. Praeger Publishers. New York, NY. p.46-47

81. 4/5/68. Arming Urged by Carmichael. Evening Sun. Baltimore, MD.

82. 4/5/68 News American. Baltimore, MD.

83. Gilbert, Ben W. 1968. Ten Blocks From the White House — Anatomy of the Washington Riots of 1968. Fredrick A. Praeger Publishers, New York, NY. p.85

84. Ibid p.87

85. Heinl, R.D., Jr. July 1968. Washington's Three Days of Burning. Fire Engineering. PennWell Corp. Fairlawn, NJ. p.38.

86. - 90. Ibid

91. 4/6/68. News American. Baltimore, Maryland.

92. Ibid

93. Peterson, John J. 1973. Into the Cauldron. Clavier House. Clinton, MD. p.35

94. Heinl, R.D., Jr. July 1968. Washington's three days of burning. Fire Engineering. PennWell Corp. Fairlawn, NJ. p.38.

95. 4/6/68. News American. Baltimore, MD.

96. Peterson, John J. 1973. Into the Cauldron. Clavier House. Clinton, MD. p.35

97. Ibid

Chapter 6: Oldtown — The Situation is Well in Hand

1. 4/6/68. News American. Baltimore, MD

2. 4/6/68. Evening Sun. Baltimore, MD

3. 4/6/68. Police Throughout the State Stay on Alert, Evening Sun. Baltimore, MD. p.20

4. Peterson, John J. 1973. Into the Cauldron. Clavier House. Clinton, MD. p.35

5. Lynton, Stephen J. 4/6/68. Baltimore Sad But Peaceful as Negro and White Mourn. The Sun. Baltimore, MD. p.B22

6. Brugger, Robert J. 1988. Maryland, A Middle Temperament. 1634 - 1980. Johns Hopkins University Press. Baltimore, MD. p.626
7. Mueller, Robert. 1/10. Interview
8. Ibid
9. 1/17/51. Multi-Million Dollar Fire Destroys Pier and Ship Here. The Sun. Baltimore, MD. p.1
10. Mueller, Robert. 1/10. Interview
11. - 13. Ibid
14. City Curfew Imposed; Agnew Sends Troops as Unrest Spreads — One Killed. 4/7/68. The Sun, Baltimore, MD. p-1
15. Mueller, Robert. 1/10. Interview
16. Ibid
17. 04/7/68. "Scramble Oscar" the Code to Order all 8,000 Maryland Guardsman to the Armories. The Sun. Baltimore, MD. p.10
18. 4/7/68. City Curfew Imposed; Agnew Sends Troops as Unrest Spreads — One Killed. The Sun, Baltimore, MD. p.1
19. Levy, Peter. 4/4/08. The Dream Deferred: The Assassination of Martin Luther King Jr. and the Holy Week Uprisings of 1968. Peter Levy. (handout from conference presentation) Baltimore '68: Riots and Rebirth. University of Baltimore. Baltimore, MD.
20. 4/6/68. News American. Baltimore, MD
21. 4/7/68. City Curfew Imposed; Agnew Sends Troops as Unrest Spreads — One Killed. The Sun, Baltimore, MD. p.1
22. Mueller, Robert. 1/10. Interview
23. Information captured from photo taken by a Sun photographer on 4/6/68 of Gay Street shopping district.
24. Mueller, Robert. 1/10. Interview
25. Ibid
26. Ibid
27. Ibid
28. Moltz, Jane, Report on Baltimore Civil Disorders April 1968. Middle Atlantic Region American Friends Service Committee, Baltimore, MD
29. Levy, Peter. 4/4/08. The Dream Deferred: The Assassination of Martin Luther King Jr. and the Holy Week Uprisings of 1968. (handout from conference presentation) Baltimore '68: Riots and Rebirth. University of Baltimore. Baltimore, MD.
30. 4/6/68. News American, Baltimore, MD
31. Bready, James H. 4/3/98. Editorial. The Sun. Baltimore, MD
32. 4/7/68. "Scramble Oscar" the Code to Order all 8,000 Maryland Guardsman to the Armories. The Sun. Baltimore, MD p.10
33. Shot Tower. 12/7/09. Wikipedia, the Free Encyclopedia http://en.wikipedia.org/wiki/Phoenix_Shot_Tower_

34. Levy, Peter. 4/4/08. The Dream Deferred: The Assassination of Martin Luther King Jr. and the Holy Week Uprisings of 1968. Peter Levy. (handout from conference presentation) Baltimore '68: Riots and Rebirth. University of Baltimore. Baltimore, MD.
35. City Police Officer (Retired) Interview
36. Ibid
37. Mueller, Robert. 1/10. Interview
38. Kiehl, Stephen. 4/08. When Baltimore Burned — Sun Special Report. The Sun. Baltimore, MD
39. 4/7/68. City Curfew Imposed; Agnew Sends Troops as Unrest Spreads — One Killed. The Sun. Baltimore, MD. p1
40. 4/7/68. "Scramble Oscar" the Code to Order all 8,000 Maryland Guardsman to the Armories. The Sun. Baltimore, MD. p.10
41. Helfrich, Lester. 1/10. Interview
42. Levy, Peter. 4/4/08. The Dream Deferred: The Assassination of Martin Luther King Jr. and the Holy Week Uprisings of 1968. Peter Levy. (handout from conference presentation) Baltimore '68: Riots and Rebirth. University of Baltimore. Baltimore, MD.
43. Johns Hopkins Hospital. 2010. Wikipedia, the Free Encyclopedia http://en.wikipedia.org/wiki/Johns_Hopkins_Hospital
44. 4/08. April 1968. Passager. University of Baltimore. Baltimore, MD. p.21
45. Hiltner, George J.. 11/23/68. Five Years Given in Riot Break In. The Sun. Baltimore, MD. p.B20
46. Ibid
47. Alfinito, Jerry. 1/10. Interview
48. Ibid
49. Hiltner, George J. 11/23/68. Five years given in riot break in. The Sun, Baltimore, MD. p.B20
50. Baltimore '68: Riots and Rebirth. 4/08. University of Baltimore. Baltimore, MD. (Notes from seminar and website timeline)
51. 4/8/68. 5 Dead, 350 Hurt as Few Make Use of Refugee Centers. Evening Sun. Baltimore, MD.
52. Ibid
53. Carson, Larry. 4/6/68. When Baltimore Erupted in Rage. News American. Baltimore, MD.
54. Ibid
55. Levy, Peter. 4/4/08. The Dream Deferred: The Assassination of Martin Luther King Jr. and the Holy Week Uprisings of 1968. Peter Levy. (handout from conference presentation) Baltimore '68: Riots and Rebirth. University of Baltimore. Baltimore, MD.
56. Turner, Harry. 4/08. A City Wide Riot. Passager. University of Baltimore. Baltimore, MD. p.18

57. 4/6/68. News American. Baltimore, MD

58. Casey, Jim, May 1968, Fire Engineering. The crisis in our cities. PennWell Corp. Fairlawn, NJ. p.39

59. Murray, William A. 1969. The Unheralded Heroes. E.John Schmitz & Sons, Inc. Baltimore, MD. p.175

60. D'Alesandro III, Tommy. 3/9/11. Interview

61. Baltimore '68: Riots and Rebirth. 4/08. University of Baltimore. Baltimore, MD. (Notes from seminar and website timeline)

62. Utilization of the National Guard In Coping with Civil Disturbances. Langsdale Library Special Collections Dept. 1420 Maryland Avenue. Baltimore, MD. 21201-5779

63. 4/6/68. News American. Baltimore, MD

64. 4/7/68. City Curfew Imposed; Agnew Sends Troops as Unrest Spreads — One Killed. The Sun. Baltimore, MD. p.1

65. 4/6/68. News American. Baltimore, MD

66. 4/7/68. "Scramble Oscar" the Code to Order all 8,000 Maryland Guardsman to the Armories. The Sun. Baltimore, MD. p.10

67. Utilization of the National Guard In Coping with Civil Disturbances, Langsdale Library Special Collections Dept. 1420 Maryland Avenue. Baltimore, MD. 21201-5779

68. 4/8/68. 5 Dead, 350 Hurt as Few Make Use of Refugee Centers. Evening Sun. Baltimore, MD

69. Ibid

70. 4/6/68. News American. Baltimore, MD

71. Ibid

72. 4/7/68. City Curfew Imposed; Agnew Sends Troops as Unrest Spreads — One Killed. The Sun. Baltimore, MD. p.1

73. Mueller, Robert. 1/10. Interview

74. - 77. Ibid

Chapter 7 *Greenmount Avenue — Put Out and Get Out*

1. Greenmount Cemetery: http://en.wikipedia.org/wki/Greenmount_Cemetery 6/17/10

2. Mueller, Robert. 1/10. Interview

3. Ibid

4. 4/8/68. 5 Dead, 350 Hurt as Few Make Use of Refugee Centers. Evening Sun. Baltimore, MD

5. 4/7/68. City Curfew Imposed; Agnew Sends Troops as Unrest Spreads — One Killed. The Sun, Baltimore, MD. p.1

6. D'Alesandro III, Tommy. 3/9/11. Interview

7. 4/7/68. City Curfew Imposed; Agnew Sends Troops as Unrest Spreads — One Killed. The Sun, Baltimore, MD. p.1

8. Ibid

9. 4/8/68. 5 Dead, 350 Hurt as Few Make Use of Refugee Centers, Evening Sun, Baltimore, MD.

10. Ibid

11. City Curfew Imposed; Agnew Sends Troops as Unrest Spreads — One Killed. 4/7/68. The Sun. Baltimore, MD. p.1

12. Ibid

13. 4/6/68. News American. Baltimore, MD

14. 4/7/68. City Curfew Imposed; Agnew Sends Troops as Unrest Spreads — One Killed. The Sun. Baltimore, MD. p.1

15. Urban, Charles. 1/10. Interview

16. Ibid

17. Murray, William A. 1969. The Unheralded Heroes. E.John Schmitz & Sons, Inc. Baltimore, MD. p.180

18. Ibid

19. Urban, Charles. 1/10. Interview

20. Ibid

21. Ibid

22. 4/6/68. News American. Baltimore, MD

23. 4/7/68. City Curfew Imposed; Agnew Sends Troops as Unrest Spreads — One Killed. The Sun. Baltimore, MD. p.1

24. 4/7/68. "Scramble Oscar" the Code to Order all 8,000 Maryland Guardsman to the Armories. The Sun. Baltimore, MD. p.10

25 Ibid

26. Ibid

27. Peterson, John J. 1973. Into the Cauldron. Clavier House. Clinton, MD. p.40

28. 4/6/68. News American. Baltimore, MD

29. Mueller, Robert. 1/10. Interview

30. Ibid

31. Shanks, Doug. 12/23/08. Interview

32. Ibid

33. Lester Helfrich Interview - 2010

34. Ross, Joseph B. Jr. 2008. Arundel Burning, Chesapeake Publishing Company, Baltimore, MD

35. Helfrich, Lester. 1/10. Interview

36. Ibid

37. Ibid

38. Phelps, Burton. 2008. Interview

39. 4/6/68. News American. Baltimore, MD

40. Peterson, John J. 1973. Into the Cauldron. Clavier House. Clinton, MD. p.44

41. Ibid

42. Ibid p.45

43. Ibid p.47
44. 4/6/68. News American. Baltimore, MD
45. 4/9/68. Good God Gassed Again. News American. Baltimore, MD.
    p.2A
46. Ibid
47. Mueller, Robert. 1/10. Interview
48. 4/6/68. News American. Baltimore, MD

Chapter 8: Palm Sunday-A Hair's Breath

1. Baltimore '68: Riots and Rebirth. 4/08. University of Baltimore.
   Baltimore, MD. (Notes from seminar and website timeline)
2. Ibid
3. 4/8/68. 5 Dead, 350 Hurt as Few Make Use of Refugee Centers.
   Evening Sun. Baltimore, MD
4. 3/31/42. City is Emerging From Snow Pile. The Sun. Baltimore, MD.
   p.26
5. 4/7/68. Mayor Tours a Scarred City Seeking to Avert a Second Night
   of Violence. The Sun. Baltimore, MD.
6. Utilization of the National Guard In Coping with Civil Disturbances,
   Langsdale Library, Special Collections Dept, 1420 Maryland Avenue,
   Baltimore, MD. 21201-5779. http://archives.ubalt.edu.
7. Baltimore '68: Riots and Rebirth. 4/08. University of Baltimore.
   Baltimore, MD. (Notes from seminar and website timeline)
8. Helfrich, Lester. 1/10. Interview
9. 4/7/68. Mayor Tours a Scarred City Seeking to Avert a Second Night
   of Violence. The Sun. Baltimore, MD
10. 4/8/68. 5 Dead, 350 Hurt as Few Make Use of Refugee Centers.
    Evening Sun. Baltimore, MD
11. Imhoff, Ernest F. 4/3/98. A Palm Sunday of Contrast. The Sun.
    Baltimore, MD. p.27A
12. Riedel, Frederick. 11/09. Interview
13. Ibid
14. Murray, William A., 1969. The Unheralded Heroes. E. John Schmitz &
    Sons, Inc. Baltimore, MD. p.116
15. Riedel, Frederick. 11/09. Interview
16. - 19. Ibid
20. Spiegel, Adam. 4/8/68. Profiles of Rioters: Young bomber, Older
    Looter, Even a Mother of Six. Evening Sun. Baltimore, MD. p.A1
21. 4/8/68. 5 Dead, 350 Hurt as Few Make Use of Refugee Centers.
    Evening Sun. Baltimore, MD
22. Baltimore '68: Riots and Rebirth. 4/08. University of Baltimore.
    Baltimore, MD. (Notes from seminar and website timeline)
23. Ibid

24. 4/8/68. 5 Dead, 350 Hurt as Few Make Use of Refugee Centers. Evening Sun. Baltimore, MD
25. Peterson, John J. 1973. Into the Cauldron. Clavier House. Clinton, MD. p.68
26. Ibid p.70
27. Ibid
28. Kernan, Michael. 10/11. Interview
29. Ibid
30. 4/8/68. Shopping Areas Downtown Quiet. News American. Baltimore, MD. p.4b
31. Ashworth, George W. 4/10/68. Massive recovery efforts. The Christian Science Monitor. p.3
32. Peterson, John J. 1973. Into the Cauldron. Clavier House. Clinton, MD. p.86
33. 4/8/68. 5 Dead, 350 Hurt as Few Make Use of Refugee Centers. Evening Sun. Baltimore, MD
34. Imhoff, Ernest F. 4/3/98. Recalling Baltimore's 1968 Riots. The Sun. Baltimore, MD. p.27A
35. Baltimore '68: Riots and Rebirth. 4/08. University of Baltimore. Baltimore, MD. (Notes from seminar and website timeline)
36. Peterson, John J. 1973. Into the Cauldron. Clavier House. Clinton, MD. p.102
37. 4/12/68. Warehouse Fire Mars New-Found City Peace. The Sun. Baltimore, MD. p.C22
38. Spiegel, Adam. 4/8/68. Profiles of Rioters: Young bomber, Older Looter, Even a Mother of Six., Evening Sun. Baltimore, MD. p.A1
39. Ibid
40. 4/8/68. Evening Sun. Baltimore, MD
41. 4/6/68. News American. Baltimore, MD
42. Spiegel, Adam. 4/8/68. Profiles of Rioters: Young bomber, Older Looter, Even a Mother of Six., Evening Sun. Baltimore, MD. p.A1
43. Parshall, Gerald. 4/1/69. Happy to be out of the grocery business. The Sun, Baltimore, MD.
44. Ibid
45. 4/8/68. Evening Sun. Baltimore, MD
46. 4/8/68. 5 Dead, 350 Hurt as Few Make Use of Refugee Centers. Evening Sun. Baltimore, MD
47. Peterson, John J. 1973. Into the Cauldron. Clavier House. Clinton, MD. pp.88-89
48. Ibid
49. 4/8/68. 5 Dead, 350 Hurt as Few Make Use of Refugee Centers. Evening Sun. Baltimore, MD

50. Peterson, John J. 1973. Into the Cauldron. Clavier House. Clinton, MD. p.57
51. 4/6/68. News American. Baltimore, MD
52. Lemmon, Walter. 7/11. Interview
53. Ibid
54. Ibid
55. Haywood, Mary Ellen and Belfoure, Charles. 1999. The Baltimore Rowhouse. Princeton Architectural Press, NY. p.100
56. Ibid
57. Ibid p.125
58. Kelly, Jacques. 1982. Bygone Baltimore, Donning Company Publishers, Norfolk/Virginia Beach, VA. p.190
59. Kiehl, Stephen. 4/08. When Baltimore Burned — Sun Special Report. The Sun, Baltimore, MD
60. Ibid
61. Ibid
62. 4/8/68. Police, Guard Both Irked. News American. Baltimore, MD. p.2A.
63. Ibid
64. Ibid
65. 4/8/68. 5 Dead, 350 Hurt as Few Make Use of Refugee Centers. Evening Sun. Baltimore, MD
66. Peterson, William, E., Dr., Zumbrum, Alvin, T. A report of the Baltimore Civil Disturbance of April 1968. The Maryland Crime Investigating Commission, Baltimore, MD.
67. Baltimore '68: Riots and Rebirth. 4/08. University of Baltimore. Balt., MD. (Notes from seminar and website timeline)
68. Ibid
69. Ibid
70. 4/6/68. News American. Baltimore, MD
71. 109
72. 4/8/68. Police, Guard Both Irked. News American. Baltimore, MD. p.2A
73. Ibid
74. Ibid
75. 4/8/68. 5 Dead, 350 Hurt as Few Make Use of Refugee Centers. Evening Sun. Baltimore, MD
76. 4/8/68. Police, Guard Both Irked. News American. Baltimore, Maryland. p.2-A.
77. Jennings, John., Lally, James., Linsley, Louis. 4/8/68. First looter shot to death. News American. Baltimore, MD. p.1A
78. Ibid

79. 4/8/68. Lt. Gen York Commander Here of US Troops, Active in Three Wars. Evening Sun, Baltimore, MD. p.A4
80. Baltimore '68: Riots and Rebirth. 4/08. University of Baltimore. Baltimore, MD. (Notes from seminar and website timeline)
81. Ibid
82. 4/8/68. Police, Guard Both Irked. News American. Baltimore, MD. p.2A.
83. 4/8/68. 5 Dead, 350 Hurt as Few Make Use of Refugee Centers. Evening Sun. Baltimore, MD.
84. Baltimore '68: Riots and Rebirth. 4/08. University of Baltimore. Baltimore, MD. (Notes from seminar and website timeline)
85. Ibid
86. Ibid
87. Ibid
88. 4/8/68. 5 Dead, 350 Hurt as Few Make Use of Refugee Centers. Evening Sun. Baltimore, MD
89. Ibid
90. Jennings, John., Lally, James., Linsley, Louis. 4/8/68. First looter shot to death. News American. Baltimore, MD. p.1A
91. Ibid
92. Ibid
93. 4/8/68. Lt. Gen York Comannder Here of US Troops, Active in Three Wars. Evening Sun, Baltimore, MD. p.A4
94. Ibid
95. Jennings, John., Lally, James., Linsley, Louis. 4/8/68. First looter shot to death. News American. Baltimore, MD. p.1A
96. Baltimore '68: Riots and Rebirth. 4/08. University of Baltimore. Baltimore, MD. (Notes from seminar and website timeline)
97. Jennings, John., Lally, James., Linsley, Louis. 4/8/68. First looter shot to death. News American. Baltimore, MD. p.1A
98. Ibid
99. 4/6/68. News American. Baltimore, MD

Chapter 9 : North Avenue - A Match Waiting to be Struck

1. 4/8/68. One Hour's Log After Curfew: Calls Inundate Baltimore's CD Command Post. The Sun. Baltimore, MD. p.A9
2. 4/8/68. 5 Dead, 350 Hurt as Few Make Use of Refugee Centers. Evening Sun, Baltimore, MD
3. Jennings, John., Lally, James., Linsley, Louis. 4/8/68. First looter shot to death. News American. Baltimore, MD. p.1A
4. Olesker, Michael. 4/10/83. The Riots were 15 years ago and nothing has changed. The Sun. Baltimore, MD

5. Ibid
6. Ibid
7. 4/8/68. 5 Dead, 350 Hurt as Few Make Use of Refugee Centers. Evening Sun, Baltimore, MD
8. Ibid
9. Ibid
10. Murray, William A., 1969. The Unheralded Heroes. E. John Schmitz & Sons, Inc. Baltimore, MD. p.26
11. 4/8/68. 5 Dead, 350 Hurt as Few Make Use of Refugee Centers. Evening Sun, Baltimore, MD
12. - 14. Ibid
15. Pickett, Edward J. 4/8/68. Efficient, Weary Guardsmen Unable to Halt Looting. The Sun. Baltimore, MD. p.A1
16. D'Alesandro III, Tommy. 3/19/11. Interview
17. Peterson, John J. 1973. Into the Cauldron. Clavier House. Clinton, MD. p.76
18. Ibid
19. 1,900 U.S. Troops Patrolling City; Officials Plan Curfew Again Today, 4 Dead, 300 Hurt, 1350 Arrest ed. 4/8/68. The Sun. Baltimore, MD. p.A1
20. Peterson, John J. 1973. Into the Cauldron. Clavier House. Clinton, Maryland. p.138
21. Klasmeier, Kenneth. 2010. Interview
22. 4/8/68. The Fires are Better — The Looting is Worse. The Sun. Baltimore, MD
23. 4/6/68. News American. Baltimore, MD
24. Ibid
25. Baltimore '68: Riots and Rebirth. 4/08. University of Baltimore. Baltimore, MD. (Notes from seminar and website timeline)
26. Pickett, Edward J. 4/8/68. Efficient, Weary Guardsmen Unable to Halt Looting. The Sun. Baltimore, MD. p.A1
27. Lawall, Henry "Butch." 9/09. Interview
28. Ibid
29. Ibid
30. Glasgow, Jesse. 4/14/68. Riots to push store improvement. The Sun, Baltimore, MD. p.Sect. K
31. Baltimore '68: Riots and Rebirth. 4/08. University of Baltimore. Baltimore, MD. (Notes from seminar and website timeline)
32. McCartin, William. 2009. Interview at the Maryland Fire Museum, Lutherville, Maryland
33. Ibid
34. 1,900 U.S. Troops Patrolling City; Officials Plan Curfew Again Today, 4 Dead, 300 Hurt, 1350 Arrest ed. 4/8/68. The Sun. Baltimore, MD. p.A1

35. Baltimore '68: Riots and Rebirth. University of Baltimore. Baltimore, MD. (Notes from seminar and timeline)

36. Ibid

37. 1,900 U.S. Troops Patrolling City; Officials Plan Curfew Again Today, 4 Dead, 300 Hurt, 1350 Arrested. 4/8/68. The Sun. Baltimore, MD. p.A1

38. 4/8/68. Few Answers. Evening Sun. Baltimore, MD

39. Baltimore '68: Riots and Rebirth. University of Baltimore. Baltimore, MD. (Notes from seminar and timeline)

40. Ibid

41. Ibid

42. Glasgow, Jesse. 4/14/68. Riots to push store improvement. The Sun. Baltimore, MD   p.Sect K

43. Baltimore '68: Riots and Rebirth. University of Baltimore. Baltimore, MD. (Notes from seminar and website timeline)

44. 5 Dead, 350 Hurt as Few Make Use of Refugee Centers. 4/8/68. Evening Sun. Baltimore, MD

45. Spiegel, Adam. 4/8/68. Profiles of Rioters: Young bomber, Older Looter, Even a Mother of Six. Evening Sun, Baltimore, MD.

46. Ibid

47. Marcus, Lloyd. 11/09. Interview

48. Baltimore '68: Riots and Rebirth. 4/08. University of Baltimore. Baltimore, MD. (Notes from seminar and website timeline)

49. Ibid

50. 4/8/68. 1,900 U.S. Troops Patrolling City; Officials Plan Curfew Again Today, 4 Dead, 300 Hurt, 1350 Arrested. The Sun. Baltimore, MD. p.A1

51. Ibid

52. 4/6/68. News American. Baltimore, MD

53. Baltimore '68: Riots and Rebirth. 4/08. University of Baltimore. Baltimore, MD. (Notes from seminar and website timeline)

54. Gallagher, Joseph. 4/4/88. A week in Baltimore 1968. The Sun. Baltimore, MD.

55. Ibid

56. 4/8/68. Fires called worst since 04. Evening Sun, Baltimore, MD. p.C26

57. Milliken, Jr., M.K. 4/8/68. Most injuries incurred in riots are minor, Johns Hopkins says. Evening Sun. Baltimore, MD

58. Ibid

59. 4/8/68. 5 Dead, 350 Hurt as Few Make Use of Refugee Centers. Evening Sun, Baltimore, MD

60. Ibid

61. Marcus, Lloyd. 11/09. Interview

62. Samuel, Paul D. 4/11/68, Rumor Mills Kept Busy During Riot. Evening Sun, Baltimore, MD. p.F12
63. Baltimore Riot of 1968 www.answeers.com/topic/baltimore-riot-of-1968.
64. Baltimore Riot of 1968 — Wikipedia, the free encyclopedia. http://en.wikipedia.org/wiki/Baltimore_riot_of_1968

Chapter 10: West Baltimore — The Flames were on Their Own

1. Baltimore '68: Riots and Rebirth. 4/08. University of Baltimore. Baltimore, MD. (Notes from seminar and website timeline)
2. Ibid
3. Ibid
4. Ibid
5. Ibid
6. 4/8/68. Fires called worst since 04. Evening Sun, Baltimore, MD. p.C26
7. - 9. Ibid
10. Baltimore '68: Riots and Rebirth. 4/08. University of Baltimore. Baltimore, MD. (Notes from seminar and website timeline)
11. Ibid
12. 4/8/68. 5 Dead, 350 Hurt as Few Make Use of Refugee Centers. Evening Sun. Baltimore, MD
13. 4/6/68. News American. Baltimore, MD
14. Baltimore '68: Riots and Rebirth. 4/08. University of Baltimore. Baltimore, MD. (Notes from seminar and website timeline)
15. 4/8/68. 5 Dead, 350 Hurt as Few Make Use of Refugee Centers. Evening Sun, Baltimore, MD
16. Pomerleau, D.D. 4/13/68. Baltimore Police Department Report 1968 Riots. p.23
17. Ibid
18. Ibid p.24
19. Baltimore '68: Riots and Rebirth. University of Baltimore. Baltimore, MD. (Notes from seminar and website timeline)
20. Ibid
21. Bready, James H. 4/3/98 Editorial, The Sun, Baltimore, MD
22. Chaney, Bud. Interview. 2/2010
23. 4/9/68. Free Brown appeal falls. The Sun. Baltimore, MD. p.A11
24. Jennings, John., Lally, James., Linsley, Louis. 4/8/68. First looter shot to death. News American. Baltimore, MD. p.1A
25. 5/31/68. Trials under the gun. Time Magazine. New York, NY
26. Ibid
27. 9/1/67. Florida: two for monologue. Time Magazine. New York, NY

28. Orangeburg Massacre. Wikipedia, the free encyclopedia, http://en.wikipeida.org/wiki/orangeburg_massacre.
29. 3/2/68. "Ten Detroits for Every Orangeburg" Afro-American. Baltimore, MD. p.1
30. 4/9/68. Free Brown appeal falls. The Sun. Baltimore, Maryland. p.A11
31. Baltimore '68: Riots and Rebirth. University of Baltimore. Baltimore, MD. (Notes from seminar and website timeline)
32. 4/8/68. The Sun. Baltimore, MD
33. Baltimore '68: Riots and Rebirth. University of Baltimore. Baltimore, MD. (Notes from seminar and timeline)
34. Chapelle, Suzanne Ellery Greene. 2000. Baltimore — An Illustrated History. American History Press. Sun Valley, CA. p.192
35. Ibid
36. Ibid
37. Pennsylvania Avenue in Baltimore. http://www.soulofamerica.com/baltimore-pennsylvania-avenue.phtml
38. Chapelle, Suzanne Ellery Greene. 2000. Baltimore — An Illustrated History, American History Press. Sun Valley, CA. p.194
39. Miller, Floyd. 1968. How Baltimore Fends Off Riots. Readers Digest, 3/68. pp.109 Condensed from the Baltimore Sunday Sun, 2/11/68. Baltimore, MD
40. 4/8/68. The Sun. Baltimore, MD
41. Ibid
42. Peterson, John J. 1973. Into the Cauldron. Clavier House. Clinton, MD. p.142
43. Edmondson Village. http:www.livebaltimore.com/neighborhoods/list/Edmondsonvillage/
44. 4/9/10, Federal Forces Rises to 4,900 as Violence fans out from the Slums. The Sun. Baltimore, MD. p.A8
45. Ibid
46. 4/8/68. 5 Dead, 350 Hurt as Few Make Use of Refugee Centers. Evening Sun. Baltimore, Md.
47. Shanks, Doug. 12/23/08. Interview
48.- 50. Ibid
51. Ross, Joseph B. 2008. Arundel Burning. Chesapeake Publishing Company. Baltimore, MD. pp.110-111
52. Murray, William A., 1969. The Unheralded Heroes. E. John Schmitz & Sons, Inc. Baltimore, Maryland. p.21
53. German, Tom. 2009. Interview
54. - 59. Ibid
60. Donellan, Thomas, 4/08, Roman Catholic Priest. Passager, University of Baltimore, Baltimore, MD. p.32
61. German, Tom. 2009. Interview

62. 4/9/10, Federal Forces Rises to 4,900 as Violence fans out from the Slums. The Sun, Baltimore, MD. p.A8
63. Berryman, John. 12/10. Interview
64. - 70. Ibid
71. Basoco, Richard, 4/9/68. West Baltimore is an Ugly No Man's Land. The Sun. Baltimore, MD
72. Ibid
73. 4/9/10, Federal Forces Rises to 4,900 as Violence fans out from the Slums. The Sun, Baltimore, MD. p.A8
74. Ibid
75. Ibid
76. Chapelle, Suzanne Ellery Greene. 2000. Baltimore — an Illustrated History, American History Press. Sun Valley, California. p-42
77. Bean, Jonathan J.. Fall 2000. Burn Baby Burn: Small Business in the Urban Riots of the 1960s. The Independent Review. Volume V, Number 2. Southern Illinois University. Carbondale, IL. pp.165 — 182
78. Ibid
79. 4/9/68. Curfew is Given Credit for the Reduction in Fires. News American. Baltimore, MD. p.2A
80. Baltimore '68: Riots and Rebirth. University of Baltimore. Baltimore, MD. (Notes from seminar and website timeline)
81. Peterson, John J. 1973. Into the Cauldron. Clavier House. Clinton, MD. p.142

Chapter 11: Lombard Street-Snipers and Flag Court

1. Baltimore '68: Riots and Rebirth. University of Baltimore. Baltimore, MD. (Notes from seminar and website timeline)
2. McNally, Carol. 2011. Interview
3. Baltimore '68: Riots and Rebirth. University of Baltimore. Baltimore, MD. (Notes from seminar and website timeline)
4. Baltimore Civic Center. Wikipedia, the free encyclopedia http://en.wikipedia.org/wki/Baltimore_Arena
5. Ibid
6. Peterson, John J. 1973. Into the Cauldron. Clavier House. Clinton, MD. p.137
7. George, Deborah., Executive Producer. 3/31/08 - 4/2/08. The fire next time. A special WYPR Radio series. Producers Sunni Khalid, Mary Rose Madden and Fraser Smith, Baltimore, MD
8. 11/1/55. Baltimore Civic Center, Report #5781 to Greater Baltimore Committee. Maryland History, Enoch Pratt Library. Baltimore, MD
9. Peterson, John J. 1973. Into the Cauldron. Clavier House. Clinton, MD. p.187

10. Ibid p.14
11. George, Deborah., Executive Producer. 3/31/08 - 4/2/08. The fire next time. A special WYPR Radio series. Producers Sunni Khalid, Mary Rose Madden and Fraser Smith, Baltimore, MD.
12. Murray, William A., 1969. The Unheralded Heroes. E. John Schmitz & Sons, Inc. Baltimore, Maryland. p.127
13. Steadman, John. 4/8/10. Colt great calls for Peace in the city. News American. Baltimore, MD. p.5A
14. Ibid
15. Ibid
16. Jenning, John Roberts, Bryan. 4/9/68. New curfew 7: pm - 5:am, city is tense clam. News American. Baltimore, MD. p.5-A
17. Ibid
18. 4/9/68. Halt the Holocaust — Editorial. News American. Baltimore, MD. p.C8
19. 4/8/68. Editorial. The Sun. Baltimore, MD. p.A11
20. Anft, Michael. 12/22/99. Half Staff Facing the End at Flag House Courts — The Cities Last High Rise Project. Baltimore City Paper. Baltimore, MD
21. Star Spangled Banner Flag House. Wikipedia, the free encyclopedia http://wikipedia.org/wk/Flag-House
22. Anft, Michael. 12/22/99. Half Staff Facing the End at Flag House Courts — The Cities Last High Rise Project. Baltimore City Paper. Baltimore, MD
23. Ibid
24. Ibid
25. Olesker, Michael. 4/10/83. The Riots Were 15 Years Ago and Nothing Has Changed. The Sun. Baltimore, MD. pp.30-31
26. Chaney, Bud. 2010. Interview
27. Ibid
28. Ibid
29. Hartman, Christopher. 4/9/68. Lombard lullaby: Burn baby burn. News American. Baltimore, MD
30. Ibid
31. Mueller, Robert. 1/10. Interview
32. Peterson, John J. 1973. Into the Cauldron. Clavier House. Clinton, MD. pp.170 - 171
33. Chaney, Bud. 2010. Interview
34. - 38. Ibid
39. Helfrich, Lester. 2010. Interview
40. 4/9/68. City Streets Become Concrete Battlefield. News American. Baltimore, MD. p. A1
41. Peterson, John J. 1973. Into the Cauldron. Clavier House. Clinton, MD. p.172

42. Baltimore '68: Riots and Rebirth. University of Baltimore. Baltimore, MD. (Notes from seminar and website timeline)
43. Erlandson, Robert A. 4/8/68. War Room is Center of Fight on Disorder. The Sun. Baltimore, MD. p.A9
44. Ibid
45. German, Tom. 2009. Interview
46 Ibid
47. Ibid
48. Ibid
49. Ibid
50. Ibid
51. Ibid
52. Williams, Jr., Herman. 2002. Firefighter. Mountain Press., Carlsbad, CA. p.173
53. Ibid
54. Pickett, Edward J. 4/8/68. Efficient, Weary Guardsmen Unable to Halt Looting. The Sun. Baltimore, MD. p.A1
55. Interviews conducted during Baltimore City Fire Officers meeting — 1/2010
56. Baltimore '68: Riots and Rebirth. University of Baltimore. Baltimore, MD. (Notes from seminar and website timeline)
57. Peterson, John J. 1973. Into the Cauldron. Clavier House. Clinton, MD. p.143
58. Moltz, Jane, Report on Baltimore Civil Disorders April 1968. Middle Atlantic Region American Friends Service Committee, Baltimore, MD.
59. Peterson, John J. 1973. Into the Cauldron. Clavier House. Clinton, MD. p.188
60. 4/9/68. 1900 More GIs Join Riot Forces as Snipers Peril Police, Firemen. The Sun. Baltimore, MD. p.A1
61. Baltimore '68: Riots and Rebirth. University of Baltimore. Baltimore, MD. (Notes from seminar and website timeline)

Chapter 12: "That's Enough Baby"

1. Baltimore '68: Riots and Rebirth. University of Baltimore. Baltimore, MD. (Notes from seminar and website timeline)
2. Miller, Mark. 4/8/88. "They said it wouldn't happen here. Evening Sun, Baltimore, MD
3. 4/9/68. 55,000 Troops Apparently Most in U.S. History Are Deployed. The Sun. Baltimore,MD. p.A10
4. Ashworth, George W. 4/10/68. Massive Recovery Efforts. The Christian Science Monitor. p.3
5. 4/8/68. With in a Hairs Breath. The Sun. Baltimore, MD

6. Charles Carroll Barrister. Wikipedia, the free encyclopedia http://en.wikipedia.org/wiki/Charles_Carroll_(barrister)
7. Klasmeier, Kenneth. 2010. Interview
8. Ibid
9. Ibid
10. Ibid
11. Ibid
12. Ibid
13. Kenneth Klasmeier Interview - 2010
14. Ibid
15. Ibid
16. Alfinito, Jerry. 2010. Interview
17. Ibid
18. Ibid
19. Shofer, Henry. 2010. Interview
20. Ibid
21. Ibid
22. Klasmeier, Kenneth. 2010. Interview
23. Baltimore Riot of 1968 — Military Response. Wikipedia, the free encyclopedia http://en.wikipedia.org/wiki/Baltimore_riot_of_1968
24. Erlandson, Robert H. 4/9/68. War room is center of fight on disorder. The Sun, Baltimore, MD. p.10
25. Ibid
26. 4/8/68. With in a Hairs Breath. The Sun. Baltimore, MD
27. Erlandson, Robert A. 4/8/68. War Room is Center of Fight on Disorder. The Sun. Baltimore, MD. p.A9
28. Moltz, Jane, Report on Baltimore Civil Disorders April 1968. Middle Atlantic Region American Friends Service Committee, Baltimore, MD
29. Backbone of Riot Reported Broken-Return to Normal Could be Near. The Sun. Baltimore, MD. p.A1
30. 4/9/68. Police Halt Thousands of Morning Commuters. News American. Baltimore, MD
31. Ibid
32. Sunderland, Lowell F. 4/12/68. City Surveys Food Stores. The Sun, Baltimore, MD p.C6
33. Ever On the Watch — The History of the Baltimore City Police Department by Retired Officer W.M. Hackley http://mysite.verison.net/vzesdp09/baltimorepolicehistorybywmhackleyz/id76.html
34. Ibid
35. Roberts, Bryon. 4/10/68. Baltimore Quiet — troops still patrol the city. News American. Baltimore, MD. p.A4
36. 4/9/10. Weary firefighters Get Help From Two Counties. The Sun, Baltimore, MD. p.A8

37. Ibid
38. Ibid
39. 4/8/68. Police, Guard Both Irked. News American. Baltimore, MD. p.2A
40. Dilts, James D. 4/14/68. The Changing City — The Fire This Time. The Sun. Baltimore, MD. p.3
41. Ibid
42. Ibid
43. Jennings, John., Lally, James., Linsley, Louis. 4/8/68. First Looter Shot to Death. News American. Baltimore, MD. p.A1
44. Lemmon, Walter. 2010. Interview
45. Ibid
46. Casey, Jim. 5/68. The Crisis in Our Cities. Fire Engineering. New York, NY. p.52
47. Ibid
48. Ibid
49. Ibid
50. Ibid
51. Kneece, Jack. 4/9/68. Looters Mock General York. News American. Baltimore, MD
52. Peterson, John J. 1973. Into the Cauldron. Clavier House. Clinton, MD. p.185
53. Baltimore '68: Riots and Rebirth. University of Baltimore. Baltimore, MD. (Notes from seminar and website timeline)
54. Hartman, Chris. 4/8/68. County Fire Companies Used on Stand-by Basis. News American. Baltimore, MD. p.2A
55. Furgurson, Ernest B. 4/10/68. 150,000 March Final Time With Slain Leader. The Sun. Baltimore, MD. p.1
56. Basoco, Richard. 4/10/68. Riot Loss Put At $10 Million, The Sun, Baltimore, MD. p.1
57. 4/8/68. With in a Hairs Breath. The Sun. Baltimore, MD
58. Ever On the Watch — The History of the Baltimore City Police Department by Retired Officer W.M. Hackley http://mysite.verison.net/vzesdp09/baltimorepolicehistorybywmhackleyz/id76.html
59. Ibid
60. Backbone of Riot Reported Broken-Return to Normal Could be Near. The Sun. Baltimore, MD. p.A1
61. Ibid
62. Ibid
63. Garvin, Steve. 4/9/68. Man About Town — Daily Column. News American. Baltimore, MD
64. Moltz, Jane, Report on Baltimore Civil Disorders April 1968. Middle Atlantic Region American Friends Service Committee, Baltimore, MD

65. Basoco, Richard. 4/10/68. Riot Loss Put At $10 Million. The Sun. Baltimore, MD. p.1

66. Backbone of Riot Reported Broken-Return to Normal Could be Near. The Sun. Baltimore, MD. p.A1

67. Baltimore '68: Riots and Rebirth. University of Baltimore. Baltimore, MD. (Notes from seminar and website timeline)

68. Ibid

69. Ibid

70. Ibid

71. Backbone of Riot Reported Broken-Return to Normal Could be Near. The Sun. Baltimore, MD. p.A1

72. 4/9/10. Riots Delay Phone Strike. The Sun. Baltimore, MD. p.A10

73. Backbone of Riot Reported Broken-Return to Normal Could be Near. The Sun. Baltimore, MD. p.A1

74. Ibid

75. Lynton, Stephen J. 4/11/68 New Violence Fears Voiced. The Sun. Baltimore, MD. p.C-8

76. Ibid

77. Wharran, Forrest. 2009. Interview

78. Ibid

79. Ibid

80. Ibid

81. 4/11/68. New Calm Interrupted by Fires Shortly Before Curfew. The Sun, Baltimore, MD. p.C8

82. Ibid

83. 4/9/68. Curfew is Given Credit for the Reduction in Fires. News American. Baltimore, MD. p.2A

84. 4/11/68. Sightseers Tour City Areas Torn by Rioting. The Sun. Baltimore, MD

85. Roberts, Bryon. 4/10/68. Baltimore Quiet — troops still patrol the city. News American. Baltimore, MD. p.A4

86. 4/9/68. Public Phones Out in the Riot-Torn Areas. News American. Baltimore, MD. p.3b

87. Pomerleau, D.D. 4/13/68. Baltimore Police Department Report 1968 Riots. p.40

88. 4/11/68. Orioles Defeat Athletics in Opener. The Sun. Baltimore, MD.

89. Ibid

90. Hanneman, Jim. 4/7/68. Orioles Lose Pitcher to Guard Duty. News American. Baltimore, MD. p.B1

91. 4/11/68. New Calm Interrupted by Fires Shortly Before Curfew. The Sun, Baltimore, MD. p.C8

92. Ibid

93. Roberts, Bryon. 4/10/68. Baltimore Quiet — troops still patrol the city. News American. Baltimore, MD. p.4A

94. Peterson, John J. 1973. Into the Cauldron. Clavier House. Clinton, MD. p.190
95. Baltimore '68: Riots and Rebirth. University of Baltimore. Baltimore, MD. (Notes from seminar and website timeline)
96. 4/11/68. New Calm Interrupted by Fires Shortly Before Curfew. The Sun. Baltimore, MD. p.C8
97. 4/23/68. Agnew Seeks New Riot Aid. The Sun. Baltimore, MD. p.C24

Chapter 13: The Smoke Clears

1. Kraus, Kathy. 4/3/68. Union Aides Consider Strike Against the City. News American. Baltimore, MD. p.B2
2. Ibid
3. Sunderland, Lowell F. 4/12/10. City Surveys Food Stores. The Sun. p.C6
4. Ibid
5. Oishi, Gene. 4/12/68. Negroes Quit Conference with Agnew. The Sun. Baltimore, MD. p.C22
6. 4/12/68. Fire Mars New Found City Peace — 4 Alarms. The Sun. Baltimore, MD.
7. Kiehl, Stephen, April 2008, When Baltimore Burned — Sun Special Report. The Sun. Baltimore, MD.
8. Chaney, Bud. 2010. Interview
9. Ibid
10. Oishi, Gene. 4/12/68. Negroes Quit Conference with Agnew. The Sun. Baltimore, MD. p.C22
11. Ibid
12. Ibid
13. Cisack, Alex. Student Presentation. University of Baltimore. "Letters '68 Riots and Rebirth Seminar" April 2008.
14. Witcover, Jules. 1972. White Knight. Random House, New York. p.22
15. Streets of Fire: Governor Spiro Agnew and the Baltimore Riots, April 1968. Maryland State Archives, Annapolis, Maryland http:teachingamericanhistorymd.net
16. Oishi, Gene. 4/12/68. Negroes Quit Conference with Agnew. The Sun. Baltimore, MD. p.C22
17. Ibid
18. 9/20/68. The Counter Puncher. Time Magazine. New York, NY. p.37
19. Ibid
20. Oishi, Gene. 4/12/68. Negroes Quit Conference with Agnew. The Sun. Baltimore, MD. p.C22
21. Erlandson, Robert. 4/12/68. Mayor Reacting to Agnew's Remarks Ask For Restraint. The Sun. Baltimore, MD.
22. Oishi, Gene. 4/12/68. Negroes Quit Conference with Agnew. The Sun. Baltimore, MD. p.C22

23. Editorial, 4/12/68, The Sun, Baltimore, Maryland
24. 4/12/68. President told order restored. News American. Baltimore, MD
25. Oishi, Gene. 4/13/68. Agnew's Riot Stand Praised by Callers, Deplored by Critics. The Sun. Baltimore, MD. p.B16
26. Editorial, 4/12/68. The Sun. Baltimore, MD
27. Ibid
28. Sengstock, Mary C. 1968. The Corporation and the Ghetto: An Analysis of the Effects of the Corporate Retail Grocery Sales on Ghetto Life. In Riot in the Cities: An Analytical Symposium on the Causes and Effects, edited by Richard A. Chikota and Michael C. Moran. Rutherford, N.J.: Fairleigh Dickinson University Press. p.169
29. Peterson, John J. 1973. Into the Cauldron. Clavier House. Clinton, Maryland. p.160
30. Sengstock, Mary C. 1968. The Corporation and the Ghetto: An Analysis of the Effects of the Corporate Retail Grocery Sales on Ghetto Life. In Riot in the Cities: An Analytical Symposium on the Causes and Effects, edited by Richard A. Chikota and Michael C. Moran. Rutherford, N.J.: Fairleigh Dickinson University Press. p.168
31. Ibid. p.169
32. Ibid
33. Ibid. p.166
34. Peterson, John J. 1973. Into the Cauldron. Clavier House. Clinton, Maryland. p.168
35. Sengstock, Mary C. 1968. The Corporation and the Ghetto: An Analysis of the Effects of the Corporate Retail Grocery Sales on Ghetto Life. In Riot in the Cities: An Analytical Symposium on the Causes and Effects, edited by Richard A. Chikota and Michael C. Moran. Rutherford, N.J.: Fairleigh Dickinson University Press. p.166
36. Ibid. p.171
37. Ibid. p.166
38. Ibid
39. Ibid
40. Ibid
41. Utilization of the National Guard In Coping with Civil Disturbances, Langsdale Library, Special Collections Dept, 1420 Maryland Ave., Baltimore, Maryland. http://archives.ubalt.edu
42. 4/12/68. Riot Over, Out of a Job, Army General Says. News American. Baltimore, MD
43. 4/13/68. Three Agencies Seek Origin of the Riots. The Sun, Baltimore, MD. p.6
44. 4/12/68. Fatal Fire Mars Curfew End as Crime Picks Up. News American. Baltimore, MD. p.C1
45. 4/14/68. Arrest Lag Shows City Near Normal. The Sun. Baltimore, MD. p.22

46. Ibid
47. Macnees, James. 4/13/68. Police Hailed on Two Fronts. The Sun. Baltimore, MD. p.B6
48. Ibid
49. Rauf, Jr., Mohammed. 4/13/68. Ban Off, Breweries Busy. News American. Baltimore, MD. p.3A
50. 4/13/68. U.S. Air Force B-52 Bombers Bomb Mekong Delta. News American. Baltimore, MD. p.A1
51. 4/15/68. Riot Bans Are Lifted, Guard Free. News American. Baltimore, MD. p.C1
52. 4/15/68. Lumber Yard Engulfed by 5-Alarm Fire. The Sun. Baltimore, MD. p.C20

Chapter 14: A Divided Community

1. Miller, Mark. 4/8/88. "They Said It Wouldn't Happen Here. The Sun. Baltimore, MD
2. Olesker, Michael. 4/10/83. A Match Waiting to be Struck-The Riots were 15 years ago and nothing has changed. The Sun. Baltimore, MD
3. Defended Pomerleau. 4/17/68. The Sun. p.C2
4. Ibid
5. Ashworth, George W. 4/10/68. Massive recovery efforts. The Christian Science Monitor. Boston, MA. p.3
6. 4/13/68. Police Riot Controls Cut. News American. Baltimore, MD. p.3A
7. Ahearn, David. 4/11/68. Pressman Raps — Weak Kneed Riot Handling. News American. Baltimore, MD. p.1A
8. 4/12/68. Riot Over, Out of a Job, Army General Says. News American. Baltimore, MD
9. Connelly, Mary. 4/12/68. Merchant Victims, Police Bitter About Open Looting. News American. Baltimore, MD
10. Azrael, Louis. 4/14/68. Should looters have been shot? News American, Baltimore. MD. p.5B
11. 4/13/68. Three Agencies Seek Origin of the Riots. The Sun. Baltimore, MD. p.6
12. Utilization of the National Guard In Coping with Civil Disturbances, Langsdale Library, Special Collections Dept, 1420 Maryland Ave., Baltimore, MD. 21201-5779 http://archives.ubalt.edu
13. Samuel, Paul D., 4/11/68, Rumor Mills Kept Busy During Riot. Evening Sun, Baltimore, MD. p.F12
14. Ibid
15. Utilization of the National Guard In Coping with Civil Disturbances, Langsdale Library, Special Collections Dept, 1420 Maryland Ave., Baltimore, MD. 21201-5779 http://archives.ubalt.edu

16. Witcover, Jules. 1972. White Knight. Random House, New York. p.17
17. Samuel, Paul. 1969. One Year After the Riots — Inner City Small Business Find Crime More A Concern. The Sun. Baltimore, MD
18. Report of the National Advisory Commission on Civil Disorders, New York, E.P., Dutton   and Company Inc. NY. April 1968. p.392
19. Kearns, Doris. 1976. Lyndon Johnson and the American Dream. Harper & Row Publishers. New York, NY. p.305
20. Baltimore '68: Riots and rebirth. University of Baltimore. Baltimore, MD. (Notes from seminar and timeline)
22. Hammett, Corrin. 4/14/68. Leader Charges Rioting Planned. News American. Baltimore, MD. p.1A
23. Ibid
24. Ibid
25. Dilts, James D. 4/14/68. The Changing City — The Fire This Time. The Sun. Baltimore, MD. p.3
26. Ibid
27. D'Alesandro III, Tommy. 3/9/11. Interview
28. Ibid
29. Ibid
30. Ibid
31. Kiehl, Stephen, April 2008, When Baltimore Burned — Sun Special Report. The Sun. Baltimore, MD
32. Baltimore '68: Riots and Rebirth. University of Baltimore. Baltimore, MD. (Notes from seminar and timeline)
33. Kiehl, Stephen, April 2008, When Baltimore Burned — Sun Special Report. The Sun. Baltimore, MD
34. Ibid
35. Ibid
36. Ibid
37. Baltimore Riot 1968. http://www.answeers.com/topic/baltimore-riot-of-1968.
38. Lewis, Larry. 4/13/1969. Fighting Fires and Mobs. Maryland Living/ News American. Baltimore, MD. p.7
39. Ibid
40. Ibid
41. Ibid
42. Ibid
43. Marcus, Lloyd. 2009. Interview
44. Utilization of the National Guard In Coping with Civil Disturbances, Langsdale Library, Special Collections Dept, 1420 Maryland Ave., Baltimore, Md. http://archives.ubalt.edu
45. Baltimore '68: Riots and Rebirth. University of Baltimore. Baltimore, MD. (Notes from seminar and timeline)

46. Ibid
47. 4/9/68. Public Phones Out in the Riot-Torn Areas. News American. Baltimore, MD. p.3B
48. Samuel, Paul. 1969. One Year After the Riots — Inner City Small Business Find Crime More A Concern. The Sun. Baltimore, MD
49. 4/15/68. Agnew Declares Crisis Ended. The Sun. Baltimore, MD. p.C10
50. Baltimore '68: Riots and Rebirth. University of Baltimore. Baltimore, MD. (Notes from seminar and timeline)
51. Samuel, Paul. 1969. One Year After the Riots — Inner City Small Business Find Crime More A Concern. The Sun. Baltimore, MD
52. Ibid
53. Ibid
54. Ibid
55. Ibid
56. Glasgow, Jesse. 4/14/68. Riots To Push Store Improvement. The Sun. Baltimore, MD.   Sect. K
57. Ibid
58. Lisicky, 2009. Michael J. Hutzler's — Where Baltimore Shops. The History Press. Charleston, SC. p102
59. Ibid
60. Ibid. p93-94
61. Mock, William. 1969. One Year After the Riots — Inner City Small Business Find Crime More A Concern. The Sun. Baltimore, MD .
62. Ibid
63. Ibid
64. Ibid
65. Utilization of the National Guard In Coping with Civil Disturbances, Langsdale Library, Special Collections Dept, 1420 Maryland Ave., Baltimore, Md. http://archives.ubalt.edu
66. Ibid
67. Black's Law Dictionary. 1991. West Publishing Company. Saint Paul, MN. p.984
68. Utilization of the National Guard In Coping with Civil Disturbances, Langsdale Library, Special Collections Dept, 1420 Maryland Ave., Baltimore, Md. http://archives.ubalt.edu
69. Hanst, George. 1969. One Year After the Riots — Justice During the Riots Was Swift But Legal Ideals Were Blunted. The Sun. Baltimore, MD.
70. Ibid
71. Ibid
72. Samuel, Paul. 1969. One Year After the Riots — Inner City Small Business Find Crime More A Concern. The Sun. Baltimore, MD

73. Baltimore '68: Riots and Rebirth. University of Baltimore. Baltimore, MD. (Notes from seminar and timeline)
74. Randall, Louis L. Baltimore '68: Riots and Rebirth. University of Baltimore. Baltimore, MD. (Notes from seminar)
75. 7/3/74. City Granted Injunction in Trash Strike. The Sun. Baltimore, MD. p.A1
76. Cramer, Richard Ben. 7/15/74. Union Call Trash Strike Pact Closed. The Sun. Baltimore, MD. pA1.
77. Struek, Doug. 1974. City Agrees To Bargaining With a Police Union. The Sun. Baltimore, MD. p.C1
78. Ibid
79. Cramer, Richard Ben. 7/13/74. Situation Seems Calm. The Sun. Baltimore, MD. p.A1.
80. Cramer, Richard Ben. 7/12/74. Police Strike; West Side Hit Hard; Looting Erupts. The Sun. Baltimore, MD. p.A1
81. Rozhon, Tracie. 4/25/76. Gaiety Marks Gay Streets Oldtown. The Sun. Baltimore, MD. p.A1
82. Cramer, Richard Ben. 7/12/74. Police Strike; West Side Hit Hard; Looting Erupts. The Sun. Baltimore, MD. p.A1
83. 29 History of the Baltimore City Police Department. Wikipedia, the free encyclopedia
http://en.wilkipedia.org/wiki/Baltimore_city_police_department
84. Fraternal Order of Police. Wikipedia, the free encyclopedia
http://en.wikipedia.org/wiki/Fraternal_Order_of_Police
85. Pietila, Anero. 1974. Police Firing urged for Strike Leader. The Sun. Baltimore, MD.
86. Struek, Doug. 1974. City Agrees To Bargaining With a Police Union. The Sun. Baltimore, MD. p.C1.
87. 8/16/74. Pomerleau Fires Police Union's Hoyt for role in Strike. The Sun. Baltimore, MD. p. C20
88. 7/16/74. Trash Strike Ended With a 19% Raise; Police Union Urges Return to Work. The Sun. p.A1.
89. 3/18/79. Baltimore's Own People of the Abyss. The Sun. Baltimore, MD. p.K1
90. Ibid.
91. Warmkessel, Karen E. and Luxemberg, Steven M. 2/28/79. Storm-Tied Arrests Held Overestimated at 25%. The Sun. Baltimore, MD
92. Sandler, Gilbert. 3/15/94. Oh Give Us a Home Where the Pomerleau Roam. Baltimore Glimpses
93. Baltimore Demographics. Wikipedia, the free encyclopedia
http://en.wikeipedia.org/wiki/Baltimore
94. Baltimore Police. Wikipedia, the free encyclopedia.
http://en.wikeipedia.org/wiki/Baltimore

95. Rosenberg, Neil D. 3/10/69. Major Crime Rates in City Rise in 1968. The Sun, Baltimore, MD. p.C18.
96. Baltimore. Wikipedia, the free encyclopedia. http://en.wikeipedia.org/wiki/Baltimore
97. Ibid
98. Baltimore City F.D. website. http://www.baltimorecity.gov
99. Olesker, Michael. 4/10/83. The Riots were 15 Years Ago and Little Look of Change. The Sun. Baltimore, MD
100. Reston, James. 4/8/88. Editorial. Evening Sun. Baltimore, MD
101. Miller, Mark. 4/8/88. Four Nights and Three Days. Evening Sun, Baltimore, MD
102. Olesker, Michael. 4/3/88. Riots Spawned Few Changes. The Sun. Baltimore, MD
103. Azrael, Louis. 4/14/68. Should looters have been shot? News American. Baltimore, MD. p.5B

Bibliography

Newspaper Articles

Agnew Declares Crisis Ended. 4/15/12. *The Sun.* Baltimore, MD. p.C10

Agnew Seeks New Riot Aid. 4/23/68. *The Sun.* Baltimore, MD. p.C24

Ahearn, David. 4/11/68. Pressman Raps — Weak Kneed Riot Handling. *News American.* Baltimore, MD. p.1A

Anft, Michael. 12/22/99. Half Staff Facing the End at Flag House Courts — The Cities Last High Rise Project. *Baltimore City Paper.* Baltimore, MD

Arming Urged by Carmichael. 4/5/68. *Evening Sun.* Baltimore, MD.

Arrest Lag Shows City Near Normal. 4/14/68. *The Sun.* Baltimore, MD. p.22

Ashworth, George W. 4/10/68. Massive recovery efforts. *The Christian Science Monitor. p.3*

Assaults In The Streets. *News American.* 4/3/68. Baltimore, MD. p.2B

Azrael, Louis. 4/14/68. Should looters have been shot? *News American,* Baltimore. MD. p.5B

Backbone of Riot Reported Broken-Return to Normal Could be Near. *The Sun.* Baltimore, MD. p.A1

Backlash Victim — Editorial. *The Sun.* Baltimore, MD. 10/4/66. p.A16

Baltimore's Own People of the Abyss. 3/18/79. *The Sun.* Baltimore, MD. p.K1

Basoco, Richard, 4/9/68. West Baltimore is an Ugly No Man's Land. *The Sun.* Baltimore, MD

Basoco, Richard. 4/10/68. Riot Loss Put At $10 Million, *The Sun,* Baltimore, MD. p.1

Bready, James H. 4/3/98. Editorial. *The Sun*. Baltimore, MD

Carson, Larry. 4/6/68. When Baltimore erupted in rage. *News American*, Baltimore, MD

City Granted Injunction in Trash Strike. 7/3/74. *The Sun*. Baltimore, MD. p.A1

City is Emerging From Snow Pile.3/31/42. *The Sun*. Baltimore, MD. p.26

City Curfew Imposed; Agnew Sends Troops as Unrest Spreads — One Killed. 4/7/68. *The Sun*, Baltimore, MD. p.1

City Streets Become Concrete Battlefield. 4/9/68. *News American*. Baltimore, MD. p. A1

Connelly, Mary. 4/12/68. Merchant Victims, Police Bitter About Open Looting. *News American*. Baltimore, MD

CORE Demonstration Protest Wage Scales. 7/11/66. *Evening Sun*, Baltimore, MD. p. B24

Cramer, Richard Ben. 7/15/74. Union Call Trash Strike Pact Closed. *The Sun*. Baltimore, MD. pA1.
Cramer, Richard Ben. 7/13/74. Situation Seems Calm. *The Sun*. Baltimore, MD. p.A1.

Cramer, Richard Ben. 7/12/74. Police Strike; West Side Hit Hard; Looting Erupts. *The Sun*. Baltimore, MD. p.A1

Curfew is Given Credit for the Reduction in Fires. 4/9/68. *News American*. Baltimore, MD. p.2A

Defended Pomerleau. 4/17/68. *The Sun*. p.C2

D'Alesandro to Name Russell as Solicitor. 12/5/67. *The Sun*. Baltimore, MD. p.C24

Dilts, James D. 4/14/68. The Changing City — The Fire This Time. *The Sun*. Baltimore, MD. p.3

Erlandson, Robert A. 4/8/68. War Room is Center of Fight on Disorder. *The Sun*. Baltimore, MD. p.A9

Eight Alarm Fire at Maryland Penitentiary-blaze Destroys Print/tag Shop. 7/8/66. *Evening Sun.* Baltimore, MD. p.B28

End of a Myth-Editorial. *Evening Sun.* 4/8/68. Baltimore, MD. p.A16

Erlandson, Robert. 4/12/68. Mayor Reacting to Agnew's Remarks Ask For Restraint. *The Sun.* Baltimore, MD

Erlandson, Robert. 4/9/68. War room is center of fight on disorder. *The Sun,* Baltimore, MD. p.10

Erlandson, Robert. 3/11/68. D'Alesandro Take Stock of First 100 Days on the Job. *The Sun.* Baltimore, MD. p.C-22

False Alarm Total Soars. 12/6/67. *The Sun.* Baltimore, MD. p.C7

Fatal Fire Mars Curfew End as Crime Picks Up. 4/12/68. *News American.* Baltimore, MD. p.C1

Federal Forces Rises to 4,900 as Violence fans out from the Slums. 4/9/68 *The Sun.* Baltimore, MD. p.A8

Federalized Guard Took Pay Cut. 4/14/68. *The Sun,* Baltimore, Maryland. p.17

Few Answers. *Evening Sun.* 4/8/68. Baltimore, MD

Fires are Better, The — The Looting is Worse. 4/8/68. *The Sun.* Baltimore, MD

Fire Board Cool on Special Drive — Aid for Firemen's Widow Draws Opposition. 12/28/67. *The Sun.* Baltimore, MD. p.C-4

Fires called worst since 04. 4/8/68. *Evening Sun,* Baltimore, MD. p.C26

Fire Stations Request Hit — D'Alesandro Says Other Plans Merit Priority. 3/19/66. *The Sun.* Baltimore, MD. p.A7

Firefighter is overcome during blaze. *The Sun.* Baltimore, MD. 2/7/60. p.24

Flowers, Charles. 11/13/62. Council Fight is Shaping Up. *The Sun. Baltimore, MD. p.10*

Frames, Robin. 7/22/67. Rioting here is doubted by church civil rights leader. *Evening Sun*. Baltimore, MD. p.4

Free Brown appeal falls. 4/9/68. *The Sun*. Baltimore, MD. p.A11

Furgurson, Ernest B. 4/10/68. 150,000 March Final Time With Slain Leader. *The Sun*. Baltimore, MD. p.1
Garvin, Steve. 4/9/68. Man About Town — Daily Column. *News American*. Baltimore, MD

Gelston Appoints Harris Police Community Aide. 6/24/66. *Evening Sun*. Baltimore, MD. p. B-30

Get Tough Police — Editorial. 2/17/68. *Afro-American*. Baltimore, MD. p.4

Gallagher, Joseph. 4/4/88. A week in Baltimore 1968. *The Sun*. Baltimore, MD.

Glasgow, Jesse. 4/14/68. Riots to push store improvement. *The Sun,* Baltimore, MD. p.Sect. K

Good God Gassed Again. 4/9/68. *News American*. Baltimore, MD. p.2A

Grunts, Edward, 4/08. Short-term lease for old station. *The Sun*. Baltimore, MD

Guardsman, Police Throughout the State Stay on Alert. 4/6/68. Evening Sun. Baltimore, MD. p. 20

Halt the Holocaust — Editorial. 4/9/68. *News American*. Baltimore, MD. p.C8

Hammett, Corrin. 4/14/68. Leader Charges Rioting Planned. *News American*. Baltimore, MD. p.1A

Hanneman, Jim. 4/7/68. Orioles Lose Pitcher to Guard Duty. *News American*. Baltimore, MD. p.B1

Hanst, George. 1969. One Year After the Riots — Justice During the Riots Was Swift But Legal Ideals Were Blunted. *The Sun*. Baltimore, MD.
Hartman, Christopher. 4/9/68. Lombard lullaby: Burn baby burn. *News American*. Baltimore, MD

Hartman, Chris. 4/8/68. County Fire Companies Used on Stand-by Basis. *News American*. Baltimore, MD. p.2A

Hiltner, George J.. 11/23/68. Five Years Given in Riot Break In. *The Sun*. Baltimore, MD. p.B20

Hiltner, George J. 8/5/66. Court Asked to Lift Ban on Racist. *The Sun*. Baltimore, Maryland. p.C26.

Imhoff, Ernest F. 4/3/98. A Palm Sunday of Contrast. *The Sun*. Baltimore, MD. p.27A

Imhoff, Ernest F. 4/3/98. Recalling Baltimore's 1968 Riots. *The Sun*. Baltimore, MD. p.27A

Insurance estimates varied. 4/10/68. *New American*. Baltimore, MD. p.2-A

Jennings, John., Lally, James., Linsley, Louis. 4/8/68. First looter shot to death. *News American*. Baltimore, MD. p.1A

Jenning, John Roberts, Bryan. 4/9/68. New curfew 7: pm — 5:am, city is tense clam. *News American*. Baltimore, MD. p.5A

Kane, Gregory. 40 Years after the Kerner Commission, A Question Remains. *The Sun*. Baltimore, MD. 3/5/08

Khe Sanh Relief — Just One Mile Away. 4/4/68. *News American*. Baltimore, MD. p.1A

Kiehl, Stephen. 4/08. When Baltimore Burned — Sun Special Report. *The Sun*. Baltimore, MD

Kneece, Jack. 4/9/68. Looters Mock General York. *News American*. Baltimore, MD

Kraus, Kathy. 4/3/68. Union Aides Consider Strike Against the City. *News American*. Baltimore, MD. p.B2

Lewis, Larry. 4/13/1969. Fighting Fires and Mobs. Maryland Living. *News American*. Baltimore, MD. p.7

Lt. Gen York Commander Here of US Troops, Active in Three Wars. 4/8/68. Evening Sun. *Baltimore, MD. p.A4*

Lukas, Anthony. 4/24/62. Grady-Tawes Link Seen as Judge Deal. *The Sun.* Baltimore, MD. p.36

Lumber Yard Engulfed by 5-Alarm Fire.4/15/68. *The Sun.* Baltimore, MD. p.C20

Lupo, Alan. 7/13/66. Tommy III seeks his own identity. *Evening Sun.* Baltimore, MD. C-1.

Lupo, Alan. 6/24/66. Redistricting issue appears as key solving many racial problems. *Evening Sun.* Baltimore, MD. p. A8

Lynton, Stephen J. 4/11/68 New Violence Fears Voiced. *The Sun.* Baltimore, MD. p.C-8

Lynton, Stephen J. 4/6/68. Baltimore Sad But Peaceful as Negro and White Mourn. *The Sun.* Baltimore, MD. p.B22

Macnees, James. 4/13/68. Police Hailed on Two Fronts. *The Sun.* Baltimore, MD. p.B6

Maryland Society — The Baltimore Assembly. 1/7/67. *The Sun.* Baltimore, MD. p.A6

Mayor Chooses Lacy as President of Fire Board. 12/12/67. *The Sun.* Baltimore, MD. p.C24

Mayor Tours a Scarred City Seeking to Avert a Second Night of Violence. 4/7/68. *The Sun.* Baltimore, MD

Mayor Urges Calm — City Joins in Mourning. 4/5/68. *News American.* Baltimore, MD

Mayors - A Befogged History. 12/5/67. *The Sun.* Baltimore, Maryland. p.A16

Milliken, Jr., M.K. 4/8/68. Most injuries incurred in riots are minor, Johns Hopkins says. *Evening Sun.* Baltimore, MD

Miller, Floyd. 1968. How Baltimore Fends Off Riots. *Readers Digest.* 3/68. p.109 Condensed from the *Baltimore Sunday Sun,* 2/11/68. Baltimore, MD

Miller, Mark. 4/8/88. Four Nights and Three Days. *Evening Sun.* Baltimore, MD

318   Bibliography

Miller, Mark. 4/8/88. "They said it wouldn't happen here. *Evening Sun*. Baltimore, MD

Mock, William. 1969. One Year After the Riots — Inner City Small Business Find Crime More A Concern. *The Sun*. Baltimore, MD

Multi-Million Dollar Fire Destroys Pier and Ship Here. 1/17/51. *The Sun*. Baltimore, MD. p.1

News American. 4/6/68. Baltimore, MD. p.A1

New Calm Interrupted by Fires Shortly Before Curfew. 4/11/68. *The Sun*, Baltimore, MD. p.C8

Off Duty Policeman Rescues 5 In Fire. 4/5/68. *News American*. Baltimore, MD. p.2B.

Oishi, Gene. 4/12/68. Negroes Quit Conference with Agnew. *The Sun*. Baltimore, MD. p.C22

Olesker, Michael. 4/3/88. Riots Spawned Few Changes. *The Sun*. Baltimore, MD

Olesker, Michael. 4/10/83. A Match Waiting to be Struck-The Riots were 15 years ago and nothing has changed. *The Sun*. Baltimore, MD

One Hour's Log After Curfew: Calls Inundate Baltimore's CD Command Post. 4/8/68. *The Sun*. Baltimore, MD. p.A9

Orioles Defeat Athletics in Opener.4/11/68. *The Sun*. Baltimore, MD.

Fire Mars New Found City Peace — 4 Alarms.4/12/68. *The Sun*. Baltimore, MD.

Parks, Brad. How the good will in a city gave way to good byes. *The Star Ledger* — A Special Reprint. Newark, NJ. 4/08.

Parshall, Gerald. 4/1/69. Happy to be out of the grocery business. The Sun, Baltimore, MD.

Parks, Michael. A Year Later City Officials, Community Leaders Appraise the Impact of the Rioting. 4/7/69. *The Sun*. Baltimore, MD.

Pietila, Anero. 1974. Police Firing urged for Strike Leader. *The Sun.* Baltimore, MD.

Pickett, Edward J. 4/8/68. Efficient, Weary Guardsmen Unable to Halt Looting. *The Sun.* Baltimore, MD. p.A1

Police Action Taken After "Study-In" at State House. 4/5/68. *The Sun.* Baltimore, MD. p.C28.

Police Commissioner Interviews Start. 7/26/66. *Evening Sun.* Baltimore, MD. p.B28

Police, Guard Both Irked. 4/8/68. *News American.* Baltimore, MD. p.2A.

Police Halt Thousands of Morning Commuters.4/9/68. *News American.* Baltimore, MD

Police officers deny holding Lively warrants. 5/9/68. *Evening Sun.* Baltimore, MD. p.E-8

Police Riot Controls Cut. 4/13/68. *News American.* Baltimore, MD. p.3A

Police Throughout the State Stay on Alert. 4/6/68. *Evening Sun.* Baltimore, MD. p.20

Police Union Need Denied. 1/17/67. *The Sun.* Baltimore, MD. p.C7

Pomerleau Agrees with Riot Report. 3/2/68. *The Sun.* Baltimore, MD. p.B20

Pomerleau Fires Police Union's Hoyt for role in Strike. 8/16/74. *The Sun.* Baltimore, MD. p. C20

President told order restored. 4/12/68. *News American.* Baltimore, MD
Public Phones Out in the Riot-Torn Areas. 4/9/68. *News American.* Baltimore, MD. p.3B

Rauf, Jr., Mohammed. 4/13/68. Ban Off, Breweries Busy. *News American.* Baltimore, MD. p.3A

Reston, James. 4/8/88. Editorial. *Evening Sun.* Baltimore, MD
Riot Bans Are Lifted, Guard Free. 4/15/68. *News American.* Baltimore, MD. p.C1

Riot Control Gas Ok'd by Gelston. 8/8/67. *News American.* Baltimore, Maryland. p.2C

Riots Delay Phone Strike. 4/9/10. *The Sun.* Baltimore, MD. p.Al0

Riot Over, Out of a Job, Army General Says. 4/12/68. *News American.* Baltimore, MD

Roberts, Bryon. 4/10/68. Baltimore Quiet — troops still patrol the city. *News American.* Baltimore, MD. p.A4

Rosenberg, Neil D. 3/10/69. Major Crime Rates in City Rise in 1968. *The Sun.* Baltimore, MD. p.C18.

Rozhon, Tracie. 4/25/76. Gaiety Marks Gay Streets Oldtown. *The Sun.* Baltimore, MD. p.A1

Runkel, David. 3/1/68. City Developing Program to Soothe Racial Woe. *Evening Sun.* Baltimore, MD. p.C16

Samuel, Paul. 1969. One Year After the Riots — Inner City Small Business Find Crime More A Concern. *The Sun.* Baltimore, MD

Samuel, Paul D. 4/11/68, Rumor Mills Kept Busy During Riot. *Evening Sun*, Baltimore, MD. p.F12

Sandler, Gilbert. 3/15/94. Oh Give Us a Home Where the Pomerleau Roam. *Baltimore Glimpses*

"Scramble Oscar" the Code to Order all 8,000 Maryland Guardsman to the Armories. 4/7/68. *The Sun.* Baltimore, MD. p.10

Shopping Areas Downtown Quiet. *News American.* 4/8/68. Baltimore, MD. p.4b

Sightseers Tour City Areas Torn by Rioting. 4/11/68. *The Sun.* Baltimore, MD

Spiegel, Adam. 4/8/68. Profiles of Rioters: Young bomber, Older Looter, Even a Mother of Six. *Evening Sun.* Baltimore, MD. p.A1

Steadman, John. 4/8/10. Colt great calls for Peace in the city. News American. Baltimore, MD. p.5A

Struek, Doug. 1974. City Agrees To Bargaining With a Police Union. *The Sun*. Baltimore, MD. p.C1

Sunderland, Lowell F. 4/12/68. City Surveys Food Stores. *The Sun*. Baltimore, MD p.C6

Tawes Ends Police Post Interviews. 9/3/66. *The Sun*. Baltimore, MD. p.B20

"Ten Detroits for Every Orangeburg" *Afro-American*. 3/2/68. Baltimore, MD. p.1

Three Agencies Seek Origin of the Riots.4/13/68. *The Sun*. Baltimore, MD. p.6

Transit of Massachusetts Volunteers and Other Troops. *The Sun*. 4/20/61. p.1

Trash Strike Ended With a 19% Raise; Police Union Urges Return to Work. 7/16/74. *The Sun*. p.A1.

U.S. Air Force B-52 Bombers Bomb Mekong Delta. 4/13/12. *News American*. Baltimore, MD. p.A1

Warehouse Fire Mars New-Found City Peace. 4/12/68. *The Sun*. Baltimore, MD. p.C22

Warmkessel, Karen E. and Luxemberg, Steven M. 2/28/79. Storm-Tied Arrests Held Overestimated at 25%. *The Sun*. Baltimore, MD

Weary firefighters Get Help From Two Counties. *The Sun*. Baltimore, MD. p.A8

Williams, Juan. Marshalls Law. 1/7/90. *Washington Post*. Washington D.C.

Within a Hairs Breath. *The Sun*. 4/8/68. Baltimore, MD

Whiteford, Charles. 6/25/67. Official Mayoral Candidacy Announcing D'Alesandro. *The Sun*. Baltimore, MD. p.24

Woodruff, John E. 6/3/67. Police Fire Pension Shift is Proposed. *The Sun*. Baltimore, MD. p.B20.

5 Dead, 350 Hurt as Few Make Use of Refugee Centers. 4/8/68. *Evening Sun*. Baltimore, MD.

1900 More GIs Join Riot Forces as Snipers Peril Police, Firemen. 4/9/68. *The Sun*. Baltimore, MD. p.A1

1,900 U.S. Troops Patrolling City; Officials Plan Curfew Again Today, 4 Dead, 300 Hurt, 1350 Arrested. 4/8/68. *The Sun*. Baltimore, MD. p.A1 55,000 Troops Apparently Most in U.S. History Are Deployed. 4/9/68. *The Sun*. Baltimore, MD. p.A10

$10 Million in Budget Cut Sought. 5/14/67. *The Sun*. Baltimore, MD. p.F20.

Books

Black's Law Dictionary. 1991. West Publishing Company. Saint Paul, MN. p.984

Brugger, Robert J. 1988. *Maryland, A Middle Temperament 1634 — 1980*. Johns Hopkins University Press. Baltimore, MD.

Chapelle, Suzanne Ellery Greene. *Baltimore — An Illustrated History*, American History Press. Sun Valley, CA. 2000

Cohen, Art. *Passager*. University of Baltimore, Baltimore, MD. 4/08.

Gilbert, Ben W. 1968. *Ten Blocks From The White House — Anatomy of the Washington Riots of 1968*. Fredrick A. Praeger Publishers. New York, NY. p.16

Haywood, Mary Ellen and Belfoure, Charles, *The Baltimore Rowhouse*. Princeton Architectural Press, NY. 1999.

Kallen, Stuart A., 2001. *Life in American during the 1960s*. Lucent Books, San Diego, CA

Keating, Dennis. *The Suburban Racial Dilemma: Housing and Neighborhoods* . Temple University Press. ISBN 1566391474. 1994

Kearns, Doris. 1976. *Lyndon Johnson and the American Dream*. Harper & Row Publishers. New York, NY. p.305

Kelly, Jacques. 1982. *Bygone Baltimore*. Donning Company Publishers. Norfolk/Virginia Beach, VA. p.190

Lyons, Paul Robert. *Fire in America*. National Fire Protection Association (NFPA). Boston, MA. 1976

Melton, Tracy Matthew. *Hanging Henry Gambrill — The Violent Career of Baltimore's Plug Uglies, 1854-1860*. The Press at the Maryland Historical Society. Baltimore, MD. 2005

Murray, William A. *The Unheralded Heroes*. E. John Schmitz & Sons, Inc. Baltimore, MD. 1969

NFPA Handbook. 13th Edition. National Fire Protection Association Quincy, MA. 1969

Olesker, Michael. *Journeys to The Heart of Baltimore*. Johns Hopkins University Press. Baltimore, London. 2001

Peterson, John J. 1973. *Into the Cauldron*. Clavier House. Clinton, MD.

Ross, Joseph B. *Arundel Burning — Maryland's 1956 Oyster Roast Fire*. Chesapeake Publishing Company, Baltimore, MD. 2008

Sauter, Van Gordon and Hines, Burleigh. *Nightmare in Detroit*. Henry Regency Company. Chicago, IL. 1968

Simon, David. 1991. Homicide — *A Year on the Killing Streets*. Henry Holt and Company, New York, New York

Toomey, Daniel Carroll. *The Civil War in Maryland*. Toomey Press. Baltimore, MD. 1988

Welden, George R. *No Reason to Burn-The story of the Great Baltimore Fire*. Fire Museum of Maryland. Lutherville, MD. 2004

Williams, Jr., Herman. *Firefighter*. Mountain Press., Carlsbad, CA. 2002

Witcover, Jules. 1972. *White Night*. Random House, NY. p.10
World Book Encyclopedia, World Book Company, Chicago J-K Volume 11 2007

Lisicky, 2009. Michael J. *Hutzler's — Where Baltimore Shops*. The History Press. Charleston, SC. p102

Magazines

Casey, Jim, May 1968, *Fire Engineering*. The crisis in our cities. PennWell Corp. Fairlawn, NJ.p.39

Counter Puncher, The. *Time Magazine*. 9/20/68. New York, NY

Elizabeth Eisenhauer, 2/01. *GeoJournal*. Volume 53, Number 2

Fredrick, Gary. 7/09. Baltimore City Fire Department. *Firehouse*. Melville, NY. 7/09. pp.140 - 142

Florida: two for monologue. 9/1/67. Time Magazine. New York, NY

Heinl, R.D., Jr. July 1968. Washington's Three Days of Burning. *Fire Engineering*. PennWell Corp. Fairlawn, NJ. p.38.

March on Gwynn Oak Park. *Time Magazine*. New York, NY. 7/12/63

Miller, Floyd. 1968. How Baltimore Fends Off Riots. *Readers Digest*, 3/68. p.109. Condensed from the *Baltimore Sunday Sun*, 2/11/68. Baltimore, MD

Nation: The Unlikely Number Two. 8/16/68. *Time Magazine*. New York, NY

Trials under the gun. *Time Magazine*. 5/31/68. New York, NY

Risen, Clay. The Unmaking of the President. *Smithsonian Magazine*. New York, NY

White, Jack. 1968. *Time Magazine*

On Line Sites

Afro-American newspaper. Wikipedia, the Free Encyclopedia. On line at http://en.wikipedia.org/wiki/Afro-American_newspaper. 2011

Assassination of Martin Luther King — Lorraine Motel, Memphis, TN. 2010. Wikipedia, the Free Encyclopedia http://en.wikipedia.org/wiki/ Martin_Luther_King,_Jr.#Assassination_and_its_aftermath

Baltimore. Wikipedia, the Free Encyclopedia. On line at http://wn.wikipedia. org/wki/Baltimore_city. 2009

Baltimore City F.D. website. http://www.baltimorecity.gov

Baltimore City Police Department, History of. 2010. Wikipedia, the Free Encyclopedia http://en.wilkipedia.org/wiki/Baltimore_city_police_ department

Baltimore Police. Wikipedia, the free encyclopedia. http://en.wikeipedia. org/wiki/Baltimore

Baltimore City History of Mayors, Thomas J. D'Alesandro III, Mayor of Baltimore 1967-1971, http://mdarchives.us/megafile/msa/speccol)

Baltimore Civic Center. Wikipedia, the free encyclopedia http://en.wikipedia. org/wki/Baltimore_Arena

Baltimore Demographics. Wikipedia, the free encyclopedia http:// en.wikeipedia.org/wiki/Baltimore

Baltimore Riot of 1968 www.answeers.com/topic/baltimore-riot-of-1968.

Baltimore Riot of 1968 — Wikipedia, the free encyclopedia. http:// en.wikipedia.org/wiki/Baltimore_riot_of_1968

Baltimore Riot of 1968 — Military Response.   http://en.wikipedia. org/wiki/Baltimore_riot_of_1968

Bascom, Reverend Marion, http://www.thehistorymakers.com/biography

Brown vs. Board of Education. Wikipedia, The Free Encyclopedia. On line at http://en.wilkipedia.org/wki/Brown_v_Board_of_education. 2010

Cambridge - Governor Tawes sent in the National Guard. Wikipedia, the Free Encyclopedia. On line at   http://en.wikipedia.org/wiki/cambridge riot_1963. 2009

Charles Carroll Barrister. Wikipedia, the free encyclopedia http:// en.wikipedia.org/wiki/Charles_Carroll_(barrister)

Civil Rights Hoax Gone Bad, A — Baltimore, http://soulofamerica.com/ baltimore-civil-rights-hoax.phtml.

Detroit — The Twelfth Street Riot. Wikipedia, the Free Encyclopedia. On line at http://en.wikipedia.org/wiki/12th_Street_riot. 2009

Donald D. Pomerleau, Baltimore Police Commissioner (1966-1981) 6/29/09. Wikipedia, the Free Encyclopedia http://en.wilkipedia.org/wki/Donald_Pomerleau

Edmondson Village. http:www.livebaltimore.com/neighborhoods/list/Edmondsonvillage/)

Emancipation Proclamation. Wikipedia, the Free Encyclopedia. On line at http://en.wikipedia.org/wiki/Emancipation_Proclamation. 2010

Ever On the Watch — The History of the Baltimore City Police Department by Retired Officer W.M. Hackley   http://mysite.verison.net/vzesdp09/baltimorepolicehistorybywmhackleyz/id76.html

Fish, Pat. Gwynn Oak Park — Baltimore Civil Rights. On line at http://blogcritics.org/archives/2005/06/18/121501.php. 2005

Frederick Douglas (1818 — 1895). Wikipedia, the Free Encyclopedia. On line at http://en.Wilkipedia.org/wiki/Frederick_Douglass. 2010

Fraternal Order of Police. Wikipedia, the free encyclopedia http://en.wikipedia.org/wiki/Fraternal_Order_of_Police

Ghettos. Wikipedia, the Free Encyclopedia. On line at http://wn.wikipedia.org/wki/. 2009

Governor Tawes sent in the National Guard, http://en.wikipedia.org/wiki/cambridge _riot_1963.

Great Migration (African-American). Wikipedia, the Free Encyclopedia. On line at http://en.wilkipedia.org/wiki/chicken_bone_express. 2010

Greenmount Cemetery: http://en.wikipedia.org/wki/Greenmount_Cemetery 6/17/10

Gwynn Oak Amusement Park. Wikipedia, the Free Encyclopedia On line at http://en.wilkipedia.org/wki/Gwynn_Oak_Amusement Park. 2009

History of the Maryland National Guardhttp:llen.wikipedia.org/wiki/Maryland_Army_National_Guard

Jim Crow Laws. Wikipedia, the Free Encyclopedia. On line at http://en.wikipedia.org/wiki/Jim_Crow_laws. 2010

Kerner Commission. Wikipedia, the Free Encyclopedia. On line at http://en.wikipedia.org/wki/kerner_commission. 2009

Lawrence Shehan. 2012. Wikipedia, the Free Encyclopedia. On line at http://en.wikipedia.org/wiki/Lawrence_Shehan. 2012

Lyden, Jackie. Maryland Town Recalls Racial Unrest in 1967. On line at http://www.npr.org/templates/story/story-php?storyId=12420016 NPR. 4/9/08

Johns Hopkins Hospital. 2010. Wikipedia, the Free Encyclopedia http://en.wikipedia.org/wiki/Johns_Hopkins_Hospital

"Martin Luther King". The Nobel Foundation. 1964. http://nobelprize.org/nobel_prizes/peace/laureates/1964/king-bio.html. Retrieved 4/20/07
Maryland Army National Guard, History of. 2010. Wikipedia, the Free Encyclopedia http: llen.wikipedia.org/wiki/Maryland_Army_National_Guard

Maryland Civil Rights. On line at http://mdcivilrights.org/timeline.htlm. 2009

Martin Luther King. The Nobel Foundation. 1964. On line at http://nobelprize.org/nobel_prizes/peace/laureates/1964/king-bio.html. 4/20/07

Molotov Cocktail. Wikipedia, the Free Encyclopedia. On line athttp://en.wilkipedia.org/wiki/molotovcocktail. 2009

Old Baltimore City Police Stations, 12/8/09, http://www.kilduffs.com/policestations.html

Orangeburg Massacre. Wikipedia, the free encyclopedia, (http://en.wikipeida.org/wiki/orangeburg_massacre.

Pennsylvania Avenue in Baltimore. http://www.soulofamerica.com/baltimore-pennsylvania-avenue.phtml

Rap Brown. Wikipedia, the Free Encyclopedia. On line at http://en.wikipedia.org/wiki/H._Rap_Brown. 2009

Redlining. On line at http://www.encyclopedia.chicagohistory.org/pages/1050.html. 2010

SNCC 1960 — 1966, Six Years of the Student Non-violent Coordinating Committee http://www.ibiblio.org/sncc

Shot Tower. 12/7/09. Wikipedia, the Free Encyclopedia   http://en.wikipedia.org/wiki/Phoenix_Shot_Tower_

Small Businesses in the Urban Riots of the 1960s http://www.independent.org/pdf/tir/tir_05_2_bean.pdf p.168

Star Spangled Banner Flag House. Wikipedia, the free encyclopedia http://wikipedia.org/wk/Flag-House

Streets of Fire: Governor Spiro Agnew and the Baltimore Riots, April 1968. Maryland State Archives, Annapolis, Maryland http:teachingamericanhistorymd.net

U.S. Senate website http://www.senate.gov/artandhistory/history/common/generic/VP_Spiro_Agnew.htm

Utilization of the National Guard In Coping with Civil Disturbances, Langsdale Library, Special Collections Dept, 1420 Maryland Ave., Baltimore, MD.. 21201-5779 http://archives.ubalt.edu

Williams, Juan. Marshall's Law. Washington Post Magazine Article. Washington, D.C. On line at http://www.thurgoodmarshall.com/speeches/tmlaw_article.htm. 1/7/90

Watts Riots, Los Angeles, California 1965 — http://en.wilkiedia.org/wki/watts_riots 9/17/09

2nd Great Migration (African-American) Wikipedia, the Free Encyclopedia. On line at http://en.wikipedia.org/wki/second_Great_Migration_%28African_America%29. 2010

Government and Department Reports

African-American Mosaic — A Library of Congress Resource Guide for the story of black history and culture.

Baltimore Civic Center, Report #5781 to Greater Baltimore Committee, 11/1/55, Maryland History, Enoch Pratt Library.

African-American Mosaic — A Library of Congress Resource Guide for the story of black history and culture. 2010

Moltz, Jane, Report on Baltimore Civil Disorders April 1968. Middle Atlantic Region American Friends Service Committee, Baltimore, MD

Peterson, William, E., Dr., Zumbrum, Alvin, T. A Report of the Baltimore Civil Disturbance of April 1968. The Maryland Crime Investigating Commission. Baltimore, MD

Pomerleau, D.D. 4/13/68. Baltimore Police Department Report 1968 Riots. p.23

"Racial" Provisions of FHA Underwriting Manual 1938
Report of the National Advisory Commission on Civil Disorders, New York, E.P., Dutton and Company Inc. New York, NY. April 1968.

Report of the National Advisory Commission on Civil Disorders (Kerner Commission), New York, E.P., Dutton and Company Inc. NY. April 1968.

Interviews

Alfinito, Jerry. 1/10. Interview   (Retired BCFD Firefighter)

Baltimore City Retired Fire Officers meeting — 1/2010 (Various Officers gave their account of the riots)

Berryman, John. 12/10. Interview (Retired BCo.FD Lieutenant)

Chaney, Bud. Interview. 2/2010 (Retired BCFD Batt. Chief)

City Police Officer Interview (Retired — wanted to remain anonymous)

Cooke, Joseph. 1/10. Interview (Retired BCPD Colonel)

D'Alesandro III, Tommy. 3/9/11. Interview (Retired Balt. City Mayor)

German, Tom. 2009. Interview (Retired AACo.FD Firefighter)

Helfrich, Lester. 1/10. Interview (Retired BCFD Asst. Chief)

Kernan, Michael. 10/11. Interview (Retired BCFD Asst. Chief)

Klasmeier, Kenneth. 2010. Interview (Retired AACo.FD Lieutenant)

Lawall, Henry "Butch." 9/09. Interview (Retired BWI Airport Firefighter)

Lemmon, Walter. 7/11. Interview (Retired BCFD Lieutenant)

McCartin, William. 2009. Interview at the Maryland Fire Museum, Lutherville, Maryland

McNally, Carol. 2011. Interview (Brooklyn resident during the riots)

Marcus, Lloyd. 11/09. Interview (Retired BCFD Firefighter)

Mueller, Robert. 1/10. Interview (Retired BCFD Lieutenant)

Phelps, Burton. 12/08. Interview (Retired AACo.FD Dep Chief)

Riedel, Frederick. 11/09. Interview (Retired BCFD Captain)

Shanks, Doug. 12/23/08. Interview (Retired BCFD Firefighter)

Urban, Charles. 1/10. Interview (Retired BCFD Lieutenant)

Wharran, Forrest. 2009. Interview (Retired AACo.FD Firefighter)

Professional Works and Misc

April 1968. Passager. 4/08. University of Baltimore. Baltimore, MD. p.21

Baltimore '68: Riots and Rebirth. 4/08. University of Baltimore. Baltimore, MD. (Notes from seminar and website timeline)

Bean, Jonathan J.. Fall 2000. Burn Baby Burn: Small Business in the Urban Riots of the 1960s. The Independent Review. Volume V, Number 2. Southern Illinois University. Carbondale, IL. pp.165 — 182

Breihan, John R. 4/4/08. Why No Rioting in Cherry Hill? (notes from conference presentation) Baltimore '68: Riots and Rebirth. University of Baltimore. Baltimore, MD.

Cisack, Alex. Student Presentation. University of Baltimore. "Letters '68 Riots and Rebirth Seminar" April 2008.

Dennis, William. 1994. The Suburban Racial Dilemma: Housing and Neighborhoods. Temple University Press. 1994. ISBN 1566391474

Donellan, Thomas, 4/08, Roman Catholic Priest. Passager. University of Baltimore. Baltimore, MD. p.32

Flamm, Michael William. "Law and Order": Street Crime, Civil Disorder, and the Crisis of Liberalism. Ph.D. diss., Columbia University. 1998

Frey, William H. 6/79. Central City White Flight: Racial and Nonracial Causes. American Sociological Review, Vol. 44, No. 3. pp. 425-448

George, Deborah., Executive Producer. 3/31/08 — 4/2/08. The fire next time. A special WYPR Radio series. Producers Sunni Khalid, Mary Rose Madden and Fraser Smith, Baltimore, MD. 3/31/08-4/2/08

Levy, Peter. The Dream Deferred: The Assassination of Martin Luther King Jr. and the Holy Week Uprisings of 1968. (handout from conference presentation) Baltimore '68: Riots and Rebirth. University of Baltimore. Baltimore, MD.

Levy, Peter. Civil War on Race Street. 4/08 (Handout from Baltimore '68: Riots and Rebirth seminar. University of Baltimore. Baltimore, MD)

Randall, Louis L. Baltimore '68: Riots and Rebirth. University of Baltimore. Baltimore, MD. (Notes from seminar)

Sengstock, Mary C. 1968. The Corporation and the Ghetto: An Analysis of the Effects of the Corporate Retail Grocery Sales on Ghetto Life. In Riot in the Cities: An Analytical Symposium on the Causes and Effects, edited by Richard A. Chikota and Michael C. Moran. Rutherford, N.J.: Fairleigh Dickinson University Press. p.168

The Rise and Decline of the American Ghetto. David M. Cutler, Edward L. Glaeser, Jacob L. Vigdor The Journal of Political Economy, Vol. 107, No. 3 (Jun., 1999), pp. 455-506

Turner, Harry. 4/08. A City Wide Riot. Passager. University of Baltimore. Baltimore, MD. p.18

Index

Guardsmen, 1
militia, 54
summer mecca, Ocean
City, 24
"turn upside down", 77
wind, 115
Maryland Avenue, 134, 139
Maryland Bar, 58
Maryland Congressional
Delegation, 234
Maryland Fire and Rescue Institute
(MFRI), 116
Maryland Freedom Union, 50
Maryland General Hospital, 158
Maryland House of Delegates, 37,
57, 68
Maryland, Hurricane Agnes, 17
Maryland Legislature, 57
established police
department, 46
Maryland State Correctional
Facility, 56, 57
Maryland, State of, 58, 150, 259
Maryland State Police, 96, 119,
136, 139, 216, 237, 240,
247, 259, 260
Bowie State College crisis,
62
Davidson, Lt. Col. George,
65
trained and alert for
violence, 57
training chief, 50
Maryland State House, Annapolis,
62
Maryland Training Center, 158
Mason-Dixon Line, 59
Massachusetts Regiment, 6th 2, 3
Maude Avenue, 154, 166
McClellan, Major General George
B., 4
McCulloh Homes, 9
McCulloh Street, 93, 125, 130

McHenry Street, 187
McKeldin, Mayor, 25
McMechen Street, 124, 125, 161,
222
McNally, Carol, 190
Medal of Honor, 99
Mekong Delta, 244
Memorial Stadium, 135, 224, 232
Memphis, TN
Dr. M.L. King shot, 62
FDIC Instructor's
Conference, 220
National Police Executive
Conference, 51
Mencken, H.L., 177
Mercy Hospital, 140
Merchant Marine, 40
Merhige, Judge Robert, 171
Meuse-Argonne Action, France,
World War I, 54
Meyerhoff, Jacob and Joseph, 173
Miami, FL, 49, 52, 53
Middle Atlantic, 227
Middle East, tensions, 19
Middle River, 9
Midway Gas Station, 141
Mike's Cut Rate Liquor Store, 167
Mildred Monroe Elementary
School, 132, 142
Miller, Floyd, 50
Miller, Mark, 209, 245, 263
Millersville, MD, 116
Milton Avenue, 47, 96, 97, 100,
106, 121, 126, 137, 139,
149, 165, 174, 191
Milwaukee, WI, 5
1967, racial disorder, 21
Ministerial Alliance, Black, 67
Minneapolis, 5
1967, racial disorder, 21
1968, riot deaths, 252
Missouri, 4, 210
Mitchell, Parren J., 95, 96, 118,
248

At quarter past 6 o'clock on a cool Saturday evening on April 6, 1968, Baltimore's Oldtown Gay Street was in turmoil. As a fire engine tried to maneuver through the excited and unruly crowds to fight a blazing furniture store fire, firefighters were astonished as mobs of people heckled and shouted profanity at them. The streets were packed with people throwing objects through large glass store windows to shatter them into a million shards. Men, women and children ran from stores with armfuls of cigarette cartons, lamps, small televisions and radios. Cars were backed up to stores loading up looted goods. The police officers were overwhelmed and powerless. And, this was just the beginning of the rampage and devastation that lasted for the next four nights and days.

ABOUT THE AUTHOR - Joseph B. Ross Jr., CFPS, retired in 2000 as a division chief after 33 years with the Anne Arundel County, Maryland, fire department. He has served on the faculty of the University of Maryland, Maryland Fire and Rescue Institute, is currently a Fire Program Specialist with the federal government, and has written extensively for fire service journals. He also authored *Arundel Burning, The Maryland Oyster Roast Fire of 1956*. He resides with his wife Kathy in Linthicum, Maryland.